The Complete Guide to

Ethnic
New
York

The Complete Guide to

Ethnic
New
York

Zelda Stern

Library of Congress Cataloging in Publication Data

Stern, Zelda.
    The complete guide to ethnic New York.

    1. New York (City)—Description—1951–   —Guidebooks.
    2. Minorities—New York (City) I. Title.
F128.18.S68   917.47′10443   79-25603
ISBN 0-312-15735-5
ISBN 0-312-15736-3 pbk.

ACKNOWLEDGMENTS

There is not enough space to list all the people who were helpful to me in the course of preparing this book. I would like to give special thanks, however, to Robert Baron, Mike and Noni Connor, Lenny Davis, Ed Goodgold, Betsy Jaeger, Fred Koury, Bella Mirabella, Hideo Nakanishi, Elaine Rosner, Jorge Soto Sanchez, Jessica Stern, Wendy Stern and Jane Wong for their assistance in the research of a particular community, willingness to go to unknown restaurants at a moment's notice, and general support and encouragement. Culinary expert and food enthusiast Marjorie Greenberg gave me invaluable tips on ethnic foods, food stores and restaurants. Gil Konishi and Natalie Sonevytsky began the train of thought that led to the idea for this book. The Mighty Sparrow generously gave his permission for the use of his lyrics to "Labor Day in Brooklyn" in the chapter on West Indian New York. Donald T. Pitcher prepared the maps. I am also grateful to my first agent, Ruth Ann Waite, for her assistance and to Thomas Tracy for his editorial suggestions in the early stages of the book.

Finally, I owe special thanks to my editor, Rebecca Martin, for her unflagging enthusiasm and unerring judgment, and to my husband, Ralph Bradburd, who was always ready to go anywhere and eat anything, and whose countless suggestions improved every chapter.

LIST OF MAPS

CONTENTS

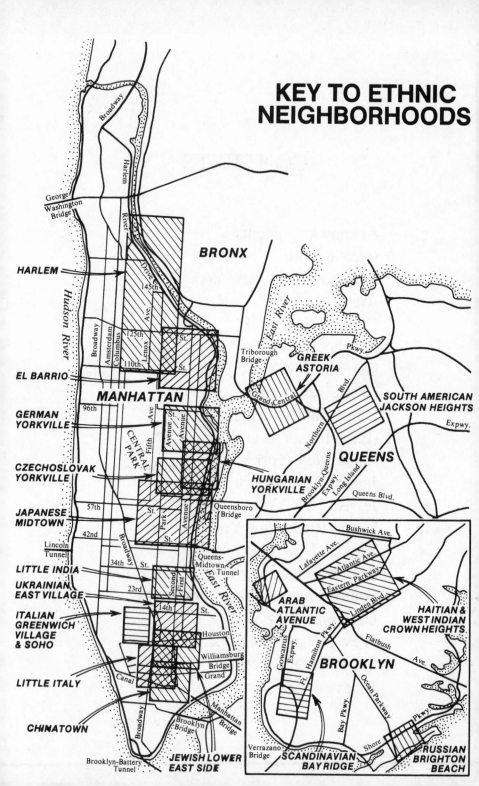

KEY TO ETHNIC NEIGHBORHOODS

INTRODUCTION

Look in any New York bookstore and you will find shelves of guidebooks
on the city: guides to the stores of New York, to the restaurants of New
York, to the buildings of New York, to the bars of New York. But until
now, there has never been a guide to what really makes New York New
York: its people and their extraordinary cultural diversity.

New York is home to more different kinds of people than any other
city in the world. And because all the immigrants who have settled in this
city have brought their own cultures and cuisines with them, you really
can travel around the world without ever leaving New York.

In what other city can you have breakfast at an Italian café, lunch at a
Japanese sushi bar, tea at a German *konditorei* and dinner at a Hungarian
restaurant—all in the same day? Where else in the world can you browse
in a Swedish or Russian or Chinese bookstore; shop in a Spanish market;
stroll down a street of Arab groceries and bakeries; listen to calypso in a
Caribbean record store; see a Chinese opera, a Yiddish musical or an
Indian movie; hear a concert of balalaikas, *banduras*, sitars or steel
drums; then go out dancing in a Greek, Brazilian or Latin *salsa* nightclub—all without leaving one city's limits, much less crossing a border?

This is the first guide completely devoted to ethnic New York. It
describes the neighborhoods, restaurants, groceries, gift shops, bookstores, bakeries, cultural centers, music and dance groups, theaters,
museums galleries, churches, nightclubs, festivals, food and history of
seventeen of New York's ethnic communities. Of course, there are
many, many more than seventeen ethnic groups in New York; it would be
impossible to cover every group in one book. In deciding which groups to
include, I gave priority to those communities that have identifiable
neighborhoods or concentrations of shops and restaurants that would be
of interest to the visitor. At the back of the book there is a Short Takes
section with brief notes on the smaller and more dispersed ethnic communities.

Each chapter is devoted to a different ethnic group and includes: a brief history of the community; a description of at least one neighborhood with a map and, in some cases, a suggested walking tour (for those larger neighborhoods where several routes are possible); an Around Town section with information about shops, cultural centers and restaurants outside the neighborhood; a description of holidays and festivals celebrated by the community; a brief introduction to its cuisine; and a menu glossary to help you when ordering in restaurants.

In selecting what to include in each chapter, I have used the broadest, most all-embracing definition of "ethnic." So you will find, for example, East Side Indian art galleries and a Fifth Avenue purveyor of expensive Russian antiques listed along with more typically ethnic neighborhood establishments.

Any visitor to the ethnic enclaves of New York may expect to find that some neighborhoods have retained a more distinct identity than others. A few neighborhoods—like Czechoslovakian, German and Hungarian Yorkville—are only remnants of what once were thriving ethnic communities. Others, like Greek Astoria or Chinatown, have such a strong ethnic flavor that you might easily imagine yourself in another country.

No city—least of all New York—stays the same. I have tried to give preference to those shops, restaurants and cultural centers that are well-established (without, however, neglecting promising newcomers), and all information was double-checked and updated immediately before this manuscript was handed to the publisher. It is always a good idea, however, to call ahead to make sure a place is still in business. In any case, although individual restaurants and shops come and go, neighborhoods don't change so quickly. If you make a trip to Queens only to find that the restaurant you had hoped to have lunch at has since moved to Brooklyn, don't give up: ask around. There's bound to be a new restaurant to replace the old, or another one just as good or better down the block, and perhaps you will make a discovery.

Users of this guide may wonder how I chose which restaurants to include. In general, my method was to ask knowledgeable members of the ethnic community. Surprisingly, in most communities, there was a clear consensus as to which were the top restaurants in each price category.

A guidebook is not useful unless it makes evaluations and comparisons; this I have tried to do whenever possible, indicating what I feel to be the best restaurant or shop in the area, and also giving my own impressions and reactions to the food, ambiance, service and specific dishes in restaurants.

Each chapter includes restaurants in various price categories from cheap to expensive. The price classifications are based on the following 1979 prices for a complete dinner for one, without wine, drinks or tip:

C $4 or less (Cheap)
I $5–$8 (Inexpensive)
M $9–$15 (Moderate)
E above $15 (Expensive)

If a restaurant is much more expensive than even the E classification would indicate, this fact is clearly noted.

In doing the research for this book, I found that the same rules that make for good traveling abroad make for good traveling in New York: you will learn more and have a better time if you stop to talk to people instead of just rushing through to see the sights; it pays to try new things instead of sticking to what you know; most people appreciate the effort to speak their language; and "when in Rome. . . ."

I hope this book will lead you, as it did me, to adventures and surprises: to meeting people you would not otherwise have met, eating foods you would not otherwise have tried, visiting neighborhoods you have never been to, taking part in festivals you never knew about—in short, seeing and celebrating a New York you may never have known was there.

Zelda Stern
New York City
January, 1980

AFRO-AMERICAN NEW YORK

Harlem: city within a city

A black city within the city, bounded by the Harlem and East rivers, Amsterdam Avenue and Morningside Park, 111th and 168th streets—a five-and-a-half-square-mile chunk of Manhattan where over 300,000 Americans of African descent live. A city of legends, alive with the ghosts of Marcus Garvey, W.E.B. DuBois, Bill "Bojangles" Robinson, Joe Louis, Bessie Smith, Duke Ellington, Ethel Waters, Malcolm X, Adam Clayton Powell and all the others who lived here, whose names, taken together, would form a Who's Who of Black America. New York's old playground, once the home of nightclubs famed throughout the world. A neighborhood of poor tenements and bleak projects; of luxury high-rises and elegant turn-of-the-century brownstones. A ghetto of no jobs and high crime. To some, a place to avoid, to drive through on the way to Queens with car doors locked and windows rolled tight. To the people who live here—home.... There are many Harlems.

Once a genteel suburb for the city's wealthiest families, Harlem to this day has an open, uncramped feeling uncharacteristic of most of Manhattan. Its main streets—125th, Adam Clayton Powell Jr. Boulevard (Seventh Avenue), Lenox Avenue (Sixth Avenue), Frederick Douglass Boulevard (Eighth Avenue), and St. Nicholas Avenue—are wide and spacious, and there are few high-rise buildings to crowd the airspace in this part of town.

Visitors to Harlem are usually prepared for the burned-out, boarded-up buildings, rubbled vacant lots and general shabbiness that are the legacy of years of ghetto poverty, but they are often taken by surprise at the pockets of grandeur and beauty: the stately old Hotel Theresa on 125th Street, the elegant houses built for nineteenth-century millionaires on Strivers' Row, the handsome facade of the Abyssinian Baptist Church of 138th Street, the charming old wooden homes on Sylvan Terrace.

Although blacks have lived in Harlem in substantial numbers only since the beginning of this century, they have been in New York City almost since its founding. In 1626, the Dutch West India Company brought over eleven Africans to New Amsterdam, the first of many slaves to be transported to the colony. These men built a wagon road from New Amsterdam to a northern part of the colony that the Dutch had named Niew Haarlem.

Most of the Africans who lived in New Amsterdam were slaves, but some, including the first eleven, managed to gain their freedom after long periods of service. Under the English, however, who conquered the Dutch in 1664 and gave New York its present name, freedom was rarely granted and chattel slavery became an institution. In 1709, the English set up open slave markets at the foot of Wall Street.

New York State abolished slavery in 1827, but the black people of New York City led an uncertain existence—neither slaves nor citizens—until national emancipation in 1863. At the end of the Civil War, there were fifteen thousand black freemen in New York City, most of whom lived in lower Manhattan.

By 1890, many of the city's black people were running small businesses—hotels, bars, stores and restaurants—that catered to both blacks and whites, and the center of black settlement had shifted to an area west of Sixth Avenue below 34th Street known as The Tenderloin. By 1900, it had moved farther north to West 53rd and the San Juan Hill area (West 61–63 Sts.). There was still no large black ghetto, however; small pockets of blacks were scattered throughout the city (including Harlem), and upper-class blacks formed a separate colony of their own in Brooklyn.

Harlem in the late 1800s was still an upper-class white community. From a rural area of farms and country estates, it had gradually become the city's first suburb, considered by most New Yorkers a bit remote (it took an hour to get to City Hall) but, with its magnificent river views, beautiful gardens and tree-lined boulevards, a fine place to live. When, in the late 1890s, construction began on new subway routes into the neighborhood, the future of Harlem—as a choice residential area within easy commuting distance of downtown—seemed assured. Speculators began feverishly buying up Harlem real estate, and whole new blocks of luxury apartment buildings began to appear almost overnight.

After the smoke had cleared, it became apparent that more housing had been built than demand warranted. Recognizing the possibilities, a black realtor named Philip A. Payton persuaded a few landlords to rent their empty buildings to black families, who, given the opportunity to move into decent housing, were only too happy to pay the high rents. White families in Harlem, fearing major changes in the neighborhood, began to move out, fulfilling their own prophecies, and over the years, more and more buildings in Harlem were occupied by black families.

During and after World War I, black Harlem expanded enormously with the arrival of over a million Afro-Americans from the rural South, who came to New York seeking higher wages and a better life. A large number of West Indians also settled in Harlem in this period; at one time, almost one quarter of Harlem's population came from the Caribbean.

By the 1920s, Harlem was well established as a black city within the city. This was Harlem's golden age, a period of extraordinary creative activity when black writers, artists and intellectuals from all over the country flocked to Harlem, the mecca of black America and "the black capital of the world." The writings of Harlem-based poets and novelists like Langston Hughes and Claude McKay began to receive national recognition; in every field of black endeavor, Harlem led the way. Harlem became a magnet for white café society as well; it was in the '20s that whites began going uptown to listen to jazz in Harlem's cabarets.

The Great Depression put an end to the era that was later dubbed the Harlem Renaissance. Harlem, which even during its renaissance had suffered from poverty and overcrowding, fell on yet worse times; by the '30s, it had replaced the Lower East Side as the city's largest slum. This was the era of Harlem's famous rent parties, when for a small entrance fee (which went to pay the rent), you could join the party at someone's apartment and, if you were lucky, hear the likes of young Fats Waller playing sweet and hot on the piano. Whites who had the money came uptown to hear Duke Ellington and his band at the Cotton Club.

Harlem never really recovered from the hard times of the Depression. By the '60s, those who could have moved out, and those who couldn't were demanding changes. This new militancy, and the much-publicized Harlem riots of '68, resulted in the funneling of city, state and federal funds to the problem-riddled community. Despite some gains, however, some things in Harlem haven't changed: most of the property in Harlem is still white-owned, and the unemployment rate in Harlem is still much higher than the national average. In some ways, the very opportunities that opened up for blacks in recent decades worked against Harlem: blacks could make it outside the ghetto; Harlem was no longer the mecca.

Recently, however, a countertrend has begun. Many middle-class and professional blacks are choosing to stay in Harlem, partly because the rents for large apartments are more reasonable in this part of town, but also because they feel their roots are here.

Today, Brooklyn's Bedford-Stuyvesant area has supplanted Harlem as the city's largest black ghetto; poor blacks live here or in sections of the Bronx. Middle-class blacks who don't live in Harlem live in middle-class black communities in Queens or are scattered around the city. Even though Harlem is no longer the city's largest black community, it remains the symbolic center of black New York.

So Harlem—the reality, the symbol, the soul of black New York—hangs on. For better or worse, there is nothing in the world quite like it; if you haven't seen Harlem, you haven't really seen New York.

HOW TO SEE HARLEM

A good way to introduce yourself to Harlem is to take the "In-Depth-As-It-Is" three-hour **bus tour** operated by the black-owned **Penny Sightseeing Company**. The bus, which is usually filled with European tourists, makes three stops: at the Schomburg Library, the Jumel Mansion and the Abyssinian Baptist Church. The bus departs from the company's office, 303 West 42nd Street (Eighth–Ninth aves.), at 10 A.M. every Monday and Thursday, and 11 A.M. every Saturday from March through November. For ticket information and reservations, call 247-2860. The Penny Sightseeing Company will also arrange special group tours.

The **Uptown Chamber of Commerce** (209 W. 125 St., 427-7200) also conducts individual and group tours of Harlem and publishes "The Greater Harlem Informational Map and Guide," available for a small fee.

If you have a **car**, you can easily take yourself on a tour of Harlem. A car has the added advantage of allowing you to stop where you like—to see the latest exhibit at the Studio Museum, to browse in a second-hand furniture store (as one of the oldest sections of Manhattan, Harlem is a good hunting ground for antique collectors) or to lunch in one of Harlem's restaurants.

Walking is of course the best way to explore any neighborhood, and, contrary to popular opinion, it is possible to walk around in Harlem and live to tell the tale. Harlemites will be the first to tell you, however, that this part of Manhattan is a high crime area. So, unless you know your way around and are pretty streetwise, it is probably best to make your first visit by car or guided tour.

(Note: in what follows, Adam Clayton Powell Jr. Blvd. is abbreviated to ACPJ Blvd.; Frederick Douglass Boulevard, to FD Blvd.)

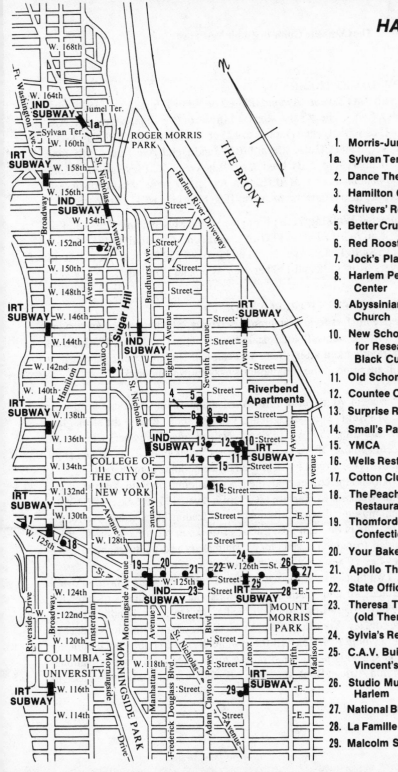

HARLEM

1. Morris-Jumel Mansion
1a. Sylvan Terrace
2. Dance Theater of Harlem
3. Hamilton Grange
4. Strivers' Row
5. Better Crust Bakery
6. Red Rooster
7. Jock's Place
8. Harlem Performance Center
9. Abyssinian Baptist Church
10. New Schomburg Center for Research in Black Culture
11. Old Schomburg Center
12. Countee Cullen Library
13. Surprise Rotisserie
14. Small's Paradise
15. YMCA
16. Wells Restaurant
17. Cotton Club
18. The Peach Tree Restaurant
19. Thomforde's Confectionary
20. Your Bakery
21. Apollo Theatre
22. State Office Building
23. Theresa Towers (old Theresa Hotel)
24. Sylvia's Restaurant
25. C.A.V. Building and Vincent's Place
26. Studio Museum in Harlem
27. National Black Theater
28. La Famille Restaurant
29. Malcolm Shabazz Masjid

HOW TO GET THERE

By subway: *Seventh Avenue IRT* #2 or #3 to 116, 125, or 135 St. (and Lenox Ave.). The #3 also stops at 148 St.; or *IND Eighth Avenue* A, AA, B, CC or *Sixth Avenue* D trains to 125 or 145 St. (and St. Nicholas Ave.). The AA, B and CC also stop at 116 St. (and Eighth Ave.) and 135 St. (and St. Nicholas Ave.). **By bus:** *M1* (Fifth Ave.); *M2* (Seventh Ave.); *M3* (St. Nicholas Ave.); *M10* (Eighth Ave.); *M7* or *M102* (Lenox Ave.). There are also *crosstown buses* on 125, 135, 145 and 155 Sts.

Suggested Walking Tour: From the Studio Museum on Fifth Ave. near 125 St. to ACPJ Blvd. or FD Blvd., north on ACPJ Blvd. to 135 St., east on 135 St. to Lenox Ave., north on Lenox to 138 St., west on 138 St. to Strivers' Row (138 and 139 between ACPJ and FD Blvds.).

WHAT TO SEE IN HARLEM: A TOUR
Lined with fast-food restaurants, bakeries, clothing stores and record shops whose sidewalk loudspeakers blast out the latest hits, **125th Street** is Harlem's main artery; here you can feel Harlem's pulse. On or near 125th are some of the community's best-known landmarks.

If you begin your tour at Fifth Avenue and 125th Street and head west (east of Fifth is Spanish Harlem), you will soon come to the sleek glass **CAV Building** (55 W. 125 St.). Named after its owner, Charles A. Vincent, whose office is on one of its upper floors, this fifteen-story structure is the largest black-owned office building in the nation.

Around the corner from the CAV Building, on Fifth Avenue, is the **Studio Museum in Harlem** (2033 Fifth Ave., 125–126 Sts., 427-5959), a small museum that exhibits the work of leading black artists. Above the gallery, the public can take a look at works in progress in studio space provided to painters, sculptors, printmakers and photographers. *Open Tues.–Fri. 10 A.M.–6P.M.; Sat.–Sun. 1P.M.–6 P.M.*

Two blocks west, on the northeast corner of Adam Clayton Powell Jr. Boulevard and 125th Street, towers Harlem's tallest structure, the **State Office Building** (163 W. 125 St.). Built to house the administrative offices of New York State (after much debate over whether its presence in Harlem would really benefit the community), the controversial building and its spacious plaza stand on the former site of Michaux's National Memorial African Bookstore. The sidewalk in front of Michaux's used to be Harlem's Hyde Park; many black nationalists, including Malcolm X, made speeches and held rallies in this square.

Diagonally opposite the Harlem State Office Building is a tall, dignified white building ornamented with terra-cotta tiles—the old **Theresa Hotel** (2090 ACPJ Blvd.). Fidel Castro and Nikita Khruschev stayed at the Theresa when they came to New York after the Cuban Revolution, and embraced each other on the hotel's balcony. The hotel has been converted into an office building, Theresa Towers.

If you continue west on 125th, you will soon see the marquee of the fabled **Apollo Theatre** (253 W. 125 St., ACPJ–FD Blvds., 749-1800). In its heyday, the Apollo was the launching pad to stardom for many black entertainers. Bessie Smith, Ella Fitzgerald, Nat King Cole, Bo Diddley, James Brown, Aretha Franklin, Ray Charles, Louis Armstrong and Cab Calloway all appeared on the Apollo stage early in their careers. Performers used to say that if they liked your act at the Apollo, you could take it anywhere. (On amateur night, if they didn't like the act, the audience would laugh and jeer, sirens would go off and a big hook would descend on stage to drag the performer off.) Closed for many years, the Apollo has now reopened (for the first time under black management) with a mixture of legitimate theater, rock groups, movies and jazz.

On the northwest corner of 125th Street and Frederick Douglass Boulevard is **Your Bakery** (301 W. 125 St., 666-7340), owned and operated by memebers of the black Muslim sect founded by Elijah Muhammad. The Shabazz bean pie is the thing to get here—a good crust filled with a creamy yellow custard of cooked navy beans, cream, eggs, sugar and spices. *Open daily, 11:30 A.M.–9 P.M.*

An old-fashioned ice cream parlor that looks just as it did when it was built in 1903, **Thomforde's Confectionary** (351 W. 125 St., at St. Nicholas Ave., UN5-0015) has a real marble soda fountain, magnificently carved and polished hardwood moldings and a tin ceiling from which hang the original ceiling fans; I doubt if there is another place like Thomforde's left in Manhattan. You can get sundaes and malteds and frappes here, or a full meal. (A sign behind the counter advertises Fresh Porgies and Collard Greens.) *Open Mon.–Sat. 8 A.M.–8:30 P.M. Cl. Sun.*

Leaving 125th Street, you can either head north or south. Nine blocks south is the **Malcolm Shabazz Masjid** (102 W. 116 St. at Lenox Ave.). This mosque, which is topped by a dome with a revolving star and crescent, was founded by Elijah Muhammad and is part of a Muslim complex that includes a health-food store, a restaurant and a self-service market. Malcolm X was the minister at the mosque before his break with Islam.

Ten blocks north of 125th is the **Schomburg Center for Research in Black Culture** (515 Lenox Ave., 135–136 Sts., 862-4000), a beautiful, modern block-long building that houses one of the most important collections in the world for the study of black people. Arthur A. Schomburg, a black Puerto Rican, said he began his collection of books by and about Africans and Afro-Americans because one of his elementary school teachers had once said, "The Negro has no history."

The Schomburg Collection, which is continually being expanded, includes records of African folk music and Afro-American jazz and blues, microfilm files of over four hundred black newspapers, sheet music, photographs, personal papers, and examples of African arms and art, in addition to such rare items from the original library as the first novel written by an American Negro and firsthand accounts of the ancient royal houses and dynasties of western Sudan. It is fascinating to browse at the Schomburg, and you can always be sure that everything listed in the catalogue is there, since no book is allowed to leave the premises. *Open Mon.–Wed. 12 noon–8 P.M.; Tues.–Sat. 10 A.M.–6 P.M. Cl. Sun.*

Around the corner from the large, modern Schomburg Center is the modest three-story building (103 W. 135 St.) that used to house the collection. There are plans to convert this building into a museum. Many black writers stayed at the **YMCA** across the street (180 W. 135 St.) when they first came to New York. Langston Hughes lived here for a time in the '20s, and Claude McKay stayed here when he returned from his travels abroad.

Behind the new Schomburg Center on 136th Street is the **Countee Cullen Branch of the New York Public Library** (104 W. 136 St.), named after a major poet of the Harlem Renaissance. Step inside and take a look at the powerful WPA murals by black artist Aaron Douglass.

Harlem's "Sutton Place" lies east of the Schomburg Center, on or near Fifth Avenue. This is where Harlem's middle- and upper-class live, in large, duplex, terraced apartment complexes like the handsome **Riverbend Houses** (Fifth Ave., 138–142 Sts.) with their views of the river.

By now, if you have been paying attention, you have probably noticed that there are a lot of churches in Harlem. (W.E.B. DuBois, cofounder of an organization that was later to become the NAACP, once remarked in cool understatement, "Harlem is perhaps overchurched.") No one knows exactly how many churches there are in Harlem these days (it's hard to count because so many of them are ephemeral one-room storefront affairs), but estimates range from five hundred to a thousand.

Of all these, the most famous—indeed, the most celebrated black church in the country—is the **Abyssinian Baptist Church** (132 W. 138 St., ACPJ Blvd.–Lenox Ave.). Under the pastorship of Adam Clayton Powell and, after him, of his son, Adam Clayton Powell, Jr., the Abyssinian became a great policial force in Harlem.

Designed by a black architect, Charles W. Bolton, and built of New York bluestone, the Abyssinian is an impressive Gothic-style edifice. The interior of the church is lovely: stained-glass windows from Europe ornament the pale peach-colored walls, rows of polished wooden pews stand before the large Italian marble baptismal font, and the pipes of a grand organ form a beautiful two-story "sculpture" against one wall. (As a young man, the jazz pianist and composer Fats Waller, who had no piano of his own, used to practice on this organ, aided by the junior Powell. After helping Fats sneak through a basement window, Powell would pump the pedals of the organ for him.) One room of the church is devoted to memorabilia of Adam Clayton Powell, Jr.,'s life as pastor of the Abyssinian and, later, as congressman in the House of Representatives.

Any tour of Harlem must include **Strivers' Row**, two blocks (138 and 139 Sts., ACPJ–FD Blvds.) of some of the most elegant row houses in New York City.These 158 four-story buildings were commissioned in 1891 by a builder named David H. King and designed by some of the leading architects of the day (including Stanford White's firm, McKim, Mead and White, which did the buildings on the north side of 139 St.). The first occupants of the King Model Houses, as they were called, were white millionaires like Randolph Hearst. But since the early 1920s, the houses have been inhabited by affluent blacks—doctors, lawyers, successful entertainers, educators—the strivers of the community; hence, the nickname. The occupants of these distinctive homes have always kept their hedges carefully clipped, their brass door knockers brightly polished and the row's air of genteel elegance intact. (A sign posted on the wrought-iron gate of one of the carriageways still reads Private Road—Walk Your Horse.)

Do not leave Strivers' Row without stopping in at the **Better Crust Bakery** (2380 ACPJ Blvd., cor. 139 St., 862-0291) for the best sweet-potato pie north of the Mason-Dixon. Better Crust also makes a fantastic bread pudding and great brownies. *Open daily 8 A.M.–midnight.*

After Strivers' Row, the section of Harlem traditionally preferred by the black bourgeoisie was **Sugar Hill**, an area of high ground that extends from St. Nicholas to Edgecombe avenues, 143rd to 155th streets. Given its nickname because, for those who lived here, the living was sweet, Sugar Hill boasts a number of well-built prewar, high-rise apartment buildings with good views out over the bluffs. Many well-known black literary figures, entertainers and athletes have lived on Sugar Hill, among them Thurgood Marshall, Duke Ellington, Count Basie and Sugar Ray Robinson.

Bordering the south edge of Sugar Hill is the **Hamilton Grange** (287 Convent Ave., 141–142 Sts., 283-5154), once the country home of Alexander Hamilton, who is said to have been part black. The handsome house was built in 1802. Call for the hours the Grange is open to the public. Lovely old ivy-covered row houses cluster near the Grange from 141st to 145th streets on Convent Avenue.

Further north, on Edgecombe Avenue and 160th Street, is the **Morris-Jumel Mansion.** Roger Morris had this house built around 1765 as a summer home, and George Washington made the mansion his headquarters for part of the revolution. The mansion is *open daily 10* A.M.–*4* P.M. *Cl. Mon.* Nearby, at 16 Jumel Terrace, is the home once occupied by the great singer and actor Paul Robeson.

In front of the Jumel Mansion is **Sylvan Terrace**, the only street in Manhattan completely lined with nineteenth-century wooden homes. The Sylvan Terrace houses and the other row houses on Jumel Terrace— all built between 1882 and 1909—afford a glimpse of old New York we usually only see in antique prints.

RESTAURANTS

It has been over fifty years since the great migration of blacks from the South to the Northern cities, but fortunately, Harlemites are still cooking the way they did down home. Southern black or "soul" cooking is what you'll find in most of Harlem's eating houses, almost all of which are modestly priced.

First: ribs. Meaning barbecued spareribs in a highly seasoned sauce. Everyone in Harlem has his or her favorite rib joint, but one that has been around for quite some time is the **Surprise Rotisserie** (2319 ACPJ Blvd. at 136 St., 368-4121, **C–I**), start here, then find your own favorite. *Open weekdays 11* A.M.–*8*P.M.*; weekends, 11* A.M.–*9* P.M. *Cl. Wed.*

If you want a good meal and don't care about fancy surroundings, try **Sylvia's** (328 Lenox Ave., 126–127 Sts., 534-9114, **C–I**), a plain neighborhood luncheonette where Sylvia ("The Queen of Soul Food") Woods serves up the Southern dishes she learned to cook in her hometown of Hemingway, South Carolina. The "marble" tabletops are Formica, the "wood" paneling is fake, but Sylvia's Southern warmth is genuine and her food is some of the best to be had in Harlem.

A plate of Sylvia's smothered chops, deliciously seasoned greens, hot black-eyed peas, rice, candied yams and homemade cornbread spread with butter is completely soul-satisfying; even if you have never eaten soul food before, I guarantee you'll clean your plate. On weekends, try a bowl of Sylvia's famous okra-and-tomato gumbo. For dessert, you have a choice of apple or peach cobbler or banana pudding. Sylvia, who makes everything from scratch, also offers a real country-style Southern breakfast of salmon croquettes, hominy grits, country slab bacon and hot biscuits. The prices here are good for the wallet as well as the soul. Sylvia's is a short walk from the IRT 125th Street-Lenox Avenue stop, on a somewhat dicey block. *Open Mon.–Sat. 7:30 A.M.–10:30 P.M. Cl. Sun.*

For straightforward Southern cooking and a bit more atmosphere, try **La Famille** (2017 Fifth Ave., 124–125 Sts. LE4-9909, **C–I**), a restaurant that has been feeding Harlemites for more than twenty years. The bar is downstairs; you walk upstairs to the dining room, which is like a family living room—homey and at the same time a little bit formal (red flocked wallpaper, chandeliers). Spareribs, sugar-cured baked Virginia ham, and milk-fed baby veal patties are regulars on the dinner menu; most entrees except for steaks are under $6, but the buffet lunch, served Monday to Friday from 11:30 to 2:30, is the real bargain. A typical spread might include a homemade vegetable soup, cornbread, green salad, coleslaw, potato salad, breaded pork chops seasoned with rosemary, beef brisket, fried chicken, baked fish, assorted cooked vegetables (be sure to try the cabbage with hot pepper), bread pudding and coffee or tea. Heap your plate and go back to the table as often as you like—all for $3.25! *Open Mon.–Fri, 11 A.M.–11:30 P.M.; Sat. 4 P.M.–11:30 P.M.; Sun. 2 P.M.–10 P.M.*

If you happen to be in Harlem at 3 A.M. and suddenly get a craving for fried chicken, just walk over to **Wells** (2249 ACPJ Blvd., 132–133 Sts., 283-8244, **I–M**), which is famous for its fried chicken and waffles (a Southen combination) and for staying open all night. (*Cl. every day 5 P.M.–7 P.M. for cleaning.*)

More elegant than Wells or Sylvia's, **The Peach Tree** (557 W. 125 St. nr. Broadway, 864-9310, **I–M**) still serves good down-home cooking, and this restaurant will deliver anywhere in the city. *Open daily, 11 A.M.–11 P.M.; Fri., Sat. until 1 A.M.*

At this time, only the cafeteria remains open at **Vincent's Place** (55 W. 125 St., CAV Bldg., 2nd flr., 722-9002, **I–M**), a huge, swanky restaurant/cafeteria/cocktail lounge that was for a while *the* place to see and be seen in Harlem. Cafeteria *open Mon.–Fri. for lunch only.* Call about possible reopening of restaurant and lounge.

THEATER AND DANCE
There are two places to see black theater in Harlem: the **Harlem Performance Center** (2349 ACPJ Blvd. at 137 St., 860-0709) and the **National Black Theater** (9 E. 125 St. off Fifth Ave., 427-5615). Call for performance schedules and ticket information.

Arthur Mitchell, former soloist with the New York City Ballet, founded the **Dance Theatre of Harlem School** (466 W. 152 St., Amsterdam–St. Nicholas Aves., 690-2800) to give kids from the streets of Harlem a chance to study classical ballet. Over a thousand students are currently enrolled in the school, which is also the home of a professional all-black ballet company that has toured Europe, the Caribbean and the United States with a repertoire of classical and modern ballet. The first Sunday of each month is open house at the school.

A LITTLE NIGHT MUSIC
Once upon a time, when you wanted to go out on the town, you went uptown to Harlem. All the great jazz musicians played in Harlem in the late '20s and '30s; the Cotton Club, on Lenox Avenue near 143rd Street, glittered with gorgeous floor shows and high society; and at the Savoy Ballroom, on Lenox and 141st, you could be sure of learning the very latest dance craze, because all of them were invented there. On Saturday nights rich and poor streamed into Harlem. Limousines cruised Lenox Avenue, bearing their occupants from club to club. And so many people used to take the underground to Harlem in those days, there was a popular song about it—"Take the A Train."

Nowadays, the night trains to Harlem carry only workers coming home. You can hear jazz everywhere in the city, and the famous old Harlem clubs like Connie's and Minton's are gone. There have been some attempts to revive the old days—notably the reopening of the **Cotton Club** in new, elegantly retro quarters (666 W. 125 St., just east of the river, MO3-7980), but the old nightclub–floor show formula didn't work in the revival, and after a few months, the club closed for renovation and reopened as a disco. Such are the times.

The sole continuing survivor of the old big-name clubs (it never closed for any length of time) is **Small's Paradise** (2294 ACPJ Blvd., 134–135 Sts., 234-6330). Count Basie and Ella Fitzgerald used to perform at Small's, but after most of the best jazz groups started to play downtown, Small's made do with rhythm and blues and didn't enjoy the spotlight again until the '60s, when its Tuesday Night Twist Contests drew fantastic crowds. Now Small's gets by on vestiges of its past glamour, small jazz groups, "easy listening," and disco nights.

Jock's Place (2350 ACPJ Blvd., 137–138 Sts., 283-9288) and the **Red Rooster** (2354 ACPJ Blvd. nr. 138 St., 283-9252) have never seen the kind of limelight Small's was used to, but they are dependable neighborhood taverns where you can hear jazz over a drink or a meal. Even Jock's, however, now mixes in some disco.

Around Town In Manhattan

SOUL FOOD DOWNTOWN

You don't have to go all the way to Harlem for ribs and cornbread and southern-fried chicken. Downtown—which Harlemites define as anyplace south of Harlem—there are a number of restaurants that cater to the soul.

The **Pink Teacup** (310 Bleeker St., Grove–Barrow Sts., 243-8117, C) is the kind of great little treasure everyone loves to discover in New York. Painted pink inside and out, the Teacup is a luncheonette with a long counter to one side and six small tables covered with oilcloths that have been printed with a strawberry-runner design. You go to the Pink Teacup when you want pecan pancakes at 2 A.M., Southern hash or fried chops and grits at 6 P.M. or a cup of coffee and homemade peach cobbler (or pecan cake, or sweet-potato pie or the superb banana pudding) at 3 (A.M. or P.M.). Anyone (Frank Sinatra, Stevie Wonder) is liable to drop in; nothing costs more than $5; and the place is *open twenty-four hours a day Wed.–Sat., Sun.–Tues. 7 A.M.–midnight; in the summer, open all night Fri. and Sat. only.*

At the **Farmhouse** (175 Second Ave. at 11 St., 677-8807, I–M), bare plank walls, old country chairs and a fireplace lend a rural feeling. Ham hocks, smothered pork chops, barbecued spareribs and country-fried chicken are the Southern specialties here, but you can also get filet mignon. *Open Tues.–Sun. 6 P.M.–2 A.M. Cl. Mon.*

Jack's Nest (310 Third Ave., 23–24 Sts., 260-7110, **I–M**), is an informal place where everyone who walks through the door is made to feel welcome. The menu is about as down home as you can get downtown, serving up soul with real panache (the most expensive item on the menu is "chit'lins 'n' champagne") *Open Mon.–Thurs. 11 A.M.–11:30 P.M.; Fri. 11 A.M.–2 A.M.; Sat. 12 noon–2 A.M.; Sun. 12 noon–11:30 P.M.*

ALL THAT JAZZ

Jazz, which grew out of the Afro-American experience, has become America's classical music, and in New York City it can be heard in clubs all over town.

For good jazz and rhythm and blues, many Harlemites particularly like **Mikell's** (760 Columbus Ave. at 97 St., 864-8832), just south of Harlem proper—a smoky supper club with a good neighborhood feeling. *Open every night until 4 A.M.* Not far away, the **West End** (2911 Broadway at 113 St., 666-8750) near Columbia University features many of the old Harlem jazz bands. *Open every night until 3 A.M.*

New York is a good place to be if you like **blues** and **gospel**, the roots of jazz. There are quite a few gospel choirs that give concerts in New York, there are several resident blue singers, and occasionally some of the old-time Southern blues singers pass through town and give a performance or two. For up-to-date information about gospel concerts and blues and jazz performances around town, check *Routes: A Guide to Black Entertainment*, available at major newsstands.

BLACK THEATER AND DANCE

New York City is the best place in the country to see black theater and dance. To find out what is happening and where, call the **Black Theater Alliance** (410 W. 42 St., 564-2266). About fifty black theater and dance companies in the city belong to the BTA. *Routes: A Guide to Black Entertainment* also has theater and dance listings.

Holidays and Festivals

A bus tour of Harlem's historical landmarks, basketball clinics taught by some of the sport's superstars, a championship disco contest, ethnic food tasting and parades with floats are just some of the activities that might take place in Harlem during **Harlem Week**, an annual festival usually held the last week of August that is organized by members of the New York Urban Coalition, the Harlem Better Business Bureau, and others who want to show the positive side of Harlem. The week's activities culminate on **Harlem Day** (usually the last Saturday in August) with a carnival celebration.

In some years, Harlem has hosted a **Jazz Festival**. The festival, which in the past has been celebrated in August in conjuction with Harlem Week, features special concerts saluting Harlem's great jazz composers. Events for both Harlem Week and the Harlem Jazz Festival are listed ahead of time in the *Amsterdam News*, Harlem's own newspaper.

For one month during the summer, the Black Theater Alliance sponsors a **festival of black theater, music and dance** in New York City with showcases of the work of its member companies. Call 564-2266 for information.

The largest black parade in America, the **African-American Day Parade**, takes place in Harlem in September. Marching bands, beauty queens and floats dramatizing the African heritage form the parade, which makes its way from 111th to 142nd streets on Adam Clayton Powell Jr. Boulevard. (See ads for the parade in the *Amsterdam News*.)

Around Christmastime, many Afro-Americans celebrate **Kwanza**. "Kwanza" is the Swahili name for a week-long festival that takes place in non-Muslim parts of Africa when the first crops are ready to be harvested. Food, drink and song mark the "karamu" feast that is the climax of the holiday.

Soul Food

Soul food comes from the South; its origins go back to the days when the best food went to the plantation owners and whatever was left went to the slaves, who learned how to season the most humble foods to make them not only palatable but tasty.

The basic ingredients of soul food are pork—in the form of chitterlings, ham hocks, pork chops and spareribs—and corn—in the form of cornbread and grits. But fried chicken, fried fish (usually porgie or whiting), collard greens, black-eyed peas and candied yams are typical soul-food dishes as well. Bread pudding, peach cobbler, and sweet potato pie are "soul" desserts.

MENU GLOSSARY

chit'lins, chitlings, or *chitterlings:*   intestines of young pigs, emptied, thoroughly cleaned and soaked, then boiled or fried with onions and seasonings.

collard greens or *greens:*   in the cabbage family, a green similar to kale; usually stewed with salt pork.

grits: hulled ground corn, cooked to a mushy consistency and served as a side dish.

ham hocks: hind leg joints of hogs, which have been smoked, then cooked.

ribs: spareribs, barbecued with a special sauce.

smothered: covered with brown gravy (usually pork chops or chicken).

 **ARAB NEW YORK**

Arab Atlantic Avenue

Just across the East River from Manhattan, a small Arab oasis flourishes on Atlantic Avenue between Court and Clinton streets, on the southern border of Brooklyn Heights. No date palms grow in this part of Brooklyn, no rose gardens perfume the evening air and the only caravan ever spotted on the horizon is the line of traffic on the Brooklyn–Queens Expressway.

But never mind. Inside the Lebanese and Syrian stores that form a block-long bazaar on both sides of the avenue, you will find huge mounds of sticky dates from the palm trees of Iraq, coils and coils of Turkish Delight redolent of attar of roses and lines of customers wending their way to the cash register, arms laden with exotic foodstuffs from every corner of the globe.

Strolling down this part of the avenue is an exercise in temptation. Shopfront windows are an irresistible jumble of gleaming brass narghiles, fringed Syrian lamps, Egyptian *durbek* drums, sequined belly-dancing costumes and large trays bearing innumerable little bowls of spices, nuts and dried fruits to suggest to the passerby the vast selection to be found within. Bakeries send forth aromas of desert bread and display trays of *baklawa* and other butter-laden, nut-filled, syrupy sweets just waiting to be enjoyed with a demitasse of thick, cardamom-scented Arab coffee or a cup of tea made fragrant with cinnamon and mint. Arab restaurants—there are about a dozen in the area—post menus in their windows that beckon with promises of baba ghanooj, hommos, kibbee and shish kebab. Why even try to resist such enticements, especially when prices are so low?

New York's Arab community goes back to the 1870s, to the "Syrian Columbus," Moses David, a trader thought to have been the first Arab settler in New York. Other Syrian and Lebanese traders soon followed Mr. David's example, but the 1890s brought the first real wave of Arab immigration, when many Syrians fled Ottoman rule. After World War I, the upheavals of war and economic problems in Lebanon brought a second wave of Syrians and Lebanese. Palestinians (refugees from Jordan and the West Bank after the Six-Day War in 1967) and Yemenis (who have been coming in a steady trickle since about 1970) are relative newcomers to the city's Arab community, which also includes a sprinkling of Egyptians, Iraqis, Jordanians and Arabic-speaking Armenians from Lebanon.

In Arab New York, the earliest immigrants—the Syrians and the Lebanese—are also the most numerous. Fred Koury, editor of the city's oldest Arabic newspaper, *Al Hoda*, estimates the Lebanese population at about fifty-thousand, of which about 95 percent are American-born. No figures are available for the Syrian community, but it is sizeable.

Although in the Middle East, Christians are a minority, in New York's Arab community, they are the majority and include Maronites, Melchites and Syrian Catholics. The city's Yemenis are largely Muslim. The bond of language unites all New York's Arabs no matter what their religion or nationality, but the Lebanese and Syrians have especially close ties over and above this common denominator.

The first Arab neighborhood in New York (Atlantic Avenue is the second) was established in Lower Manhattan in the 1880s, on Washington Street from Rector Street to Battery Place—a stone's throw from Castle Garden, where all immigrants to the city landed before 1890. Little Syria, as the colony was known, lasted over a half-century, and in its heyday—the 1920s—was a center for expatriate Arab intellectuals and writers (among them the poet Kahlil Gibran), who used to meet in the coffee houses on Washington Street.

Despite its location on the shoulder of Wall Street, Little Syria managed to stave off urban development until the 1940s, when, displaced by construction of the Brooklyn Battery Tunnel, many Arabs from Little Syria moved to Atlantic Avenue in Brooklyn. (In the days when ferries plied the East River, Atlantic Avenue was the first stop on the line after the boat left Battery Park—the park was just below the Arab quarter—, and many Arab families had already settled there.)

Most of the present shopkeepers and restaurant owners on Atlantic Avenue are the children and grandchildren of those who made the move from Little Syria. They grew up on Atlantic Avenue and have watched it change over the years—from Italian to Arab, from Arab to polyglot, from poor to prosperous. In recent years, Atlantic Avenue has benefited from the resurgence of Brooklyn Heights, which, with its blocks of handsome old brownstones and proximity to Manhattan, has become one of the most fashionable residential areas in the city.

Though many Arabs now live in Bay Ridge and Prospect Park, Atlantic Avenue remains the Arab shopping center of New York. Visitors to the avenue (it's ony a half-hour subway ride from Manhattan) can combine shopping for exotic foods and dining on shish kebab with a tour of the old buildings and churches of Brooklyn Heights or perhaps a stroll along the Promenade with its splendid views of the Manhattan skyline (only ten blocks from the Arab shopping area). Arab Atlantic Avenue is worth a trip anytime of the year, but it is especially lively on the third Sunday of September, when it becomes an outdoor Arab bazaar for the annual Atlantic Antic.

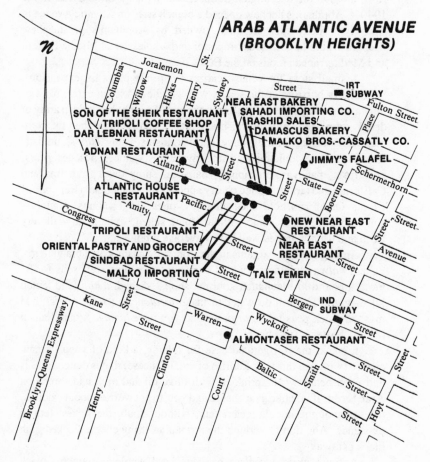

ARAB ATLANTIC AVENUE
(BROOKLYN HEIGHTS)

HOW TO GET THERE
By car from Manhattan: Brooklyn Bridge to Adams Street, Adams Street to Court, Court to Atlantic Avenue. **By subway** from Manhattan: *Seventh Avenue IRT* #2 or #3 to Borough Hall; or *Lexington Avenue IRT* #4 or #5 to Borough Hall; *IND* F train to Bergen St.

SAHADI
The undisputed sultan of Atlantic Avenue's food stores is **Sahadi** (nos. 187–189, Court–Clinton Sts., 624-4550).

A Lebanese trader, Abraham Sahadi, established the first Sahadi store in 1895 on Washington Street in Manhattan's Little Syria. In the 1940's, Abraham's nephew opened a branch store on Atlantic Avenue in Brooklyn; today this Sahadi's, owned by Abraham's greatnephew Richard, is the largest direct importer and wholesaler of Middle Eastern and Mediterranean foods on the East Coast.

A small store for what it carries (there are plans for expansion), Sahadi's is bursting at the seams with goodies. As you enter, rows of old-fashioned apothecary jars catch the eye. These hold a golden array of dried and glazed fruits: Turkish apricots (much plumper than the commercially packaged kind), huge Turkish raisins, white Turkish mulberries (use as you would raisins), fat Smyrna figs, quinces, peaches, pears, nectarines, papayas, pineapples, bananas, shiny dates from Iraq and California and tart little dried cherry apples from the People's Republic of China. Other jars hold nuts: almonds, pistachios, walnuts, pignoli— some with the shell, some without; some salted, some plain—all very fresh and usually priced well below average retail.

Among the best bargains in the store are Sahadi's own brand items: Sahadi *halwa*—plain or studded with nuts (the same stuff sells for $1 more a pound in Manhattan gourmet shops), Sahadi *tahini* (add lemon juice, garlic and a little water to make *taratour* sauce for *felafel*; add mashed chick peas to the *taratour* and you have *hommos*), and Sahadi Middle Eastern–style honey.

Look in the refrigerated case for *lebany*, a kind of yogurt cream cheese (with one third the calories of cream cheese) that is delicious as is and even better when sprinkled with olive oil and mint and spread on Arab bread. If you like goat cheese and you're not worried about calories, try some of the double-cream feta, without doubt the richest feta in existence. And don't overlook the Armenian string cheese flecked with black caraway.

Antique wood-and-glass cabinets hold whole cardamom, black

caraway, tart red sumak (mix with thyme and stir into lebany) and dried Syrian mint. Barrels on the floor hold California-grown bulgur wheat (*burghul* in Arabic) in medium and coarse cuts, couscous (semolina pasta), fragrant *basmatti* rice from Pakistan, and fifteen different kinds of olives from Greece, Syria, Peru and Morocco, as well as vine leaves packed in brine for stuffing with rice or ground lamb. Elsewhere in the store, you'll find little bundles of dried eggplant (when soaked, these expand to many times their size), frozen filo dough and frankincense and myrrh.

Amid the wonderful confusion of smells at Sahadi, the delicious aroma of raosted coffee beans draws one like a magnet to the coffee grinder in the middle section of the store. The coffee beans—100 percent South American—are ground to order, and one of the most frequent orders is for fine Turkish grind (in which the beans are almost pulverized) used to make Turkish—also known as Arab—coffee.

Sahadi's is always crowded, but the staff is always helpful, if rushed. *Open Mon.–Fri. 9 A.M.–7 P.M.; Sat. 8 A.M.–7 P.M. Cl. Sun.*

OTHER FOOD STORES
Although Sahadi's prices are very reasonable, if you enjoy bargain hunting, you can often find even lower prices in other stores on Atlantic Avenue. One shop where items are frequently cheaper is **Malko Brothers–Cassatly Co.** (no. 197, Clinton–Court Sts., 855-2455), a small store that nonetheless carries all the staples of Middle Eastern cuisine. Malko Brothers is also open on Sundays, when Sahadi's is closed. *Open daily 9 A.M.–9 P.M.*

Across the street from both Sahadi and Malko Brothers–Cassatly Co. is **Malko Importing** (no. 182, MA 4-2049), an old-fashioned, exceptionally tidy store, from its regimented lines of spice jars to its evenly laid out rows of fresh and very appetizing homemade pastries. Owner George Malko carries all the basics, along with a few specialties like Persian leaf tobacco from Iran (for water pipes), Syrian brass water pipes, belly dancers' *zills* (finger cymbals), Egyptian henna in three shades, vanilla and pistachio ice cream flavored with imported Syrian essences and rosewater-flavored apricot sherbet. You'll also find a large selection of sweet syrups here—almond, tamarind, pomegranate, rose-water—which can be mixed with water or soda for summer drinks or poured over shaved ice for Persian sherbet. *Open daily 9 A.M.–9 P.M.*

The tantalizing buttery smells of baking pastry at **Oriental Pastry and Grocery** (no. 170, Clinton–Court Sts., 875-7687) pull you in by the nose the minute you open the door. The pastries—*baklawa*, birds' nests, ladies' fingers and other many-layered, syrupy delights—are all made in the back of the store. If you would like to try your hand at making some of these yourself, you can also get homemade *filo* dough here—unbelievably thin dough which you can layer with nuts for *baklawa*, stuff with spinach for spinach pie or fill with sliced apples and roll into strudel.

True to its name, Oriental Pastry and Grocery also carries a full line of imported Middle Eastern foods. Among the foods carried here that I did not see elsewhere are Syrian pickled turnips in red beet juice (a favorite Arab appetizer) and cans of date jam, rose jam and fig jam.

Oriental Pastry and Grocery, is owned and run by a Syrian family, K. Moustapha and Sons. *Open daily, 10 A.M.–8:30 P.M.*

BAKERIES

"We're the Rolls-Royce of the Middle Eastern bakeries," says Eddie Alvarado of **Near East Bakery** (183 Atlantic Ave., Clinton–Court Sts., TR 5-0016), whose mother is Lebanese and whose father is Hispanic. "We bake our bread in the original brick ovens that were here over eighty years ago. Our products contain no preservatives, no additives. Everything is fresh."

The story of the Near East Bakery tells the story of Atlantic Avenue. The shop, which is in the basement of an old building, was originally an Italian bakery. When the Italian family moved out, an Armenian family took over. Eddie's uncle, Bob Kanatous, used to work for the Armenian family, and so when the Armenians left, the Kanatous family took over. Now two generations of the family work here—often for thirteen or fourteen hours at a stretch.

From the customer counter, you can see the machines used to mix and cut the dough as well as the eighty-year-old brick oven into which Bob Kanatous and his brother-in-law Arbeeny, using long-handled paddles, place the individual loaves. The *pita* bread that comes out is flat, round and hollow—a convenient pocket for *felafel* or *hommos*.

The Near East makes several varieties of *pita*: whole wheat, *zahter* (sprinkled with thyme, sumak, sesame seeds and oil), *simson* (large *pita* coated with sesame seeds) and *macook* or desert bread—the oldest bread in the world, according to Eddie Alvarado, who says that in biblical times, these very large, round, flat loaves were baked on top of hollowed-out rocks that held a fire.

The little triangular spinach pies here—made with fresh spinach—are hands down the best in town. (They can be frozen; just heat in the oven when you want to serve.) And the toothsome sweet *filo* pastries—*baklawa* and cashew-and-almond-filled *kul wa-shkur* (literally, "eat and

praise'')—stay fresh for three or four months without refrigeration because they are made with clarified butter, which doesn't spoil (just keep
away from extreme heat). *Open Tues.–Sat. 8* A.M.*–4:30* P.M., *6:30*
P.M.*–5:30* A.M.; *Sun. 8* A.M.*–1:30* P.M. *Cl. Mon.*

You will find the largest selection of Arab pastries on Atlantic
Avenue at **Damascus Bakery** (no. 195, Clinton–Court Sts., 855-1456),
a family-run business founded in 1930 by Henry Halaby from Damascus,
Syria. The tremendous variety of pastries at Damascus seems confusing
until you realize that most are variations on two themes: syrup-soaked filo
pastry layered or stuffed with nuts (*baklawa*, ladies' fingers, birds'
nests), and pastries made with semolina flour (honey-soaked cake or
hariset, sesame cookies or *barazet*, cupcakes impressed with a design
from a wooden mold called *mammoul* when filled with nuts, *ajweh* when
filled with dates). Triangles of *filo* filled with custard are *fatir bil ishta*;
shredded dough combined with syrup and nuts becomes *knafe*; plain
butter-cookie rings are *goraybe*.

All the pastries at Damascus are made downstairs, but the bread—
pita, macook, simson and *zatar*—comes from the Damascus plant in
another part of Brooklyn. *Open daily 8* A.M.*–10* P.M.

GIFTS, MUSIC, AND A COFFEE SHOP

Next door to Sahadi Food Imports is the **Sahadi Gift Shop** (no. 187,
624-4550), crammed with inlaid backgammon boards and tables from
Lebanon and Syria, clay or brass hand drums from Syria and Egypt,
enamel pots for making Arab coffee, porcelain demitasse coffee sets,
handleless Turkish tea glasses, leather hassocks from Istanbul, brass
trays from Syria (these make wonderful table tops when supported by
wooden stands, which are also sold here), Middle Eastern cookbooks,
wooden *mammoul* (cupcake) molds, and—one of the most popular items
in the store—belly-dancing costumes. A complete outfit—gold- or
silver-sequined bra, hip belt, and gauze skirt—is only about $30.

Sahadi's Gift Shop is officially *open only on Saturday, 8* A.M.*–7*
P.M. but if the salespeople in the grocery next door are not busy on other
days, they will open the gift store on request. *Cl. Sun.*

Brass lamps, brass trays and backgammon boards can also be found
in many of the Arab groceries on Atlantic Avenue.

Rashid Sales (no. 191, Court–Clinton Sts., 852-3298) specializes
in Middle Eastern music: tapes and recordings of popular Middle Eastern
singers, records to belly dance to and albums of instrumental music
featuring the *oud* (lute), *kannon* (zither), *durbek* (drum) and tambourine.
The store also carries some of these instruments. One section of Rashid's

serves as a small bookstore of Arabic publications. Also a distributor of Arab films made in Egypt and Lebanon, Rashid's sometimes presents Arab movies in local auditoriums. *Open Mon.–Sat. 9* A.M.*–7* P.M.*, Sun. 12 noon–5* P.M.

If, after an hour or two of shopping on Atlantic Avenue, you need a place to sit, head for the **Tripoli Coffee Shop** (no. 163, Clinton–Henry Sts., no phone). Here you can revive yourself with a cup of Turkish coffee and a piece of *baklawa*, homemade Lebanese ice cream (in flavors like cashew and apricot) or a bowl of refreshing, unsweetened milk pudding sprinkled with honey and nuts. Though it is a far cry from the coffeehouses of Manhattan's old Arab quarter, where men sat for hours sipping coffee and smoking narghiles, the Tripoli, with its minaret-shaped ''windows'' framing scenic murals and its tree-slab tables, is a pleasant place to while away some time. Tripoli (which is under the same management as the Tripoli Restaurant across the street) also sells dried fruits, glazed fruits, candied orange slivers, pumpkin seeds, pistachio nuts and homemade yogurt to go. *Open daily, noon–midnight.*

RESTAURANTS

Except for an Egyptian *felafel* stand called Jimmy's, all the Arab restaurants on or near Atlantic Avenue are owned by Lebanese or Yemenis. Most of the Lebanese restaurants specialize in Middle Eastern food, while the Yemeni restaurants (all owned by various members of the same enterprising Almontaser family) serve both Middle Eastern and Continental cuisine. Both the Lebanese and the Yemeni restaurants are modestly furnished and inexpensive. None have liquor licenses, but all allow you to bring your own beer and wine.

To start with the exception, **Jimmy's Felafel** (111 Court St., State–Schermerhorn Sts., 875-9137), owned by Tawfik and Jimmy Shehab from Cairo, specializes in the deep-fried balls of seasoned mashed chick peas and bulgur that are the hamburgers of the Arab world. You eat *felafel* sandwiched in *pita* bread, moistened with *taratour* sauce (sesame-seed paste, lemon juice and garlic) and, if you wish, further seasoned with a dab of fiery hot sauce.

You can get other things at Jimmy's besides *felafel*: *shawerma*, for instance. *Shawerma* (you can see it sizzling in the window) is meat—usually seasoned lamb—cooked on a vertical rotisserie. Jimmy uses breast of veal instead of lamb. Cooked slowly in this rotating manner, the veal acquires the flavor of meat that has been roasted on a spit over an open fire. For a *shawerma* sandwich, slices of meat are carved off the spit, placed on *pita* bread and served with a tasty sauce.

Other dishes always on hand at Jimmy's are *baba ghanooj* (seasoned eggplant-tahini puree), eggplant *munazali* (stew of eggplant, tomatoes, chick peas and onions), and *hommos* (mashed chick peas with *tahini* and lots of seasoning). All are served plain or on *pita* bread. To drink, there is soda, Arab coffee or Lebanese tea spiced with anise and cinnamon.

You can take your order out or eat it at one of the tables in the pleasant little dining area. *Open Mon.–Fri. 11* A.M.*–10*P.M.*; Sat.–Sun. 1* P.M.*–10*P.M. Free delivery.

The oldest Lebanese restaurant on Atlantic Avenue is **Son of the Sheik** (no. 165, Clinton–Henry Sts., 625-4023, **I**), a small, cozy place that serves delicious Middle Eastern food with a homemade touch. This Son is actually the second; the first, opened in 1932 by Tony Saidy, was on Washington Street, in Manhattan's old Little Syria. In that restaurant, a complete shish-kebab dinner cost 65¢. Prices have gone up since then (though not exorbitantly), and Tony has taken in his nephew Dave as a partner, but that's all that has changed. The food is prepared with the same care, and the beaded curtains, posters of Lebanon and old-fashioned air of the place seem to have been transported directly from Little Syria.

Meza—appetizers—are the special glory of an Arab dinner, and Son of the Sheik's menu (with Valentino in sheik's clothing on the cover) lists no less than fourteen different kinds. *Baba ghanooj, hommos* and *tabboule* (parsley-mint-bulgur salad) are the old standbys, but you can also get lamb-brains salad if you're in the mood.

The Lebanese national dish is *kibbee*—pounded or ground lamb mixed with bulgur—served in many different forms. At Son of the Sheik, you can get *kibbee nayah* (raw kibbee, an appetizer), baked *kibbee*, and *kibbee* meatballs. Another specialty of the house is shish kebab—not marinated, but simply charcoal-broiled plain, like a good steak. If you like stuffed vegetables, try the Lebanese Assorted Plate—grape leaves, squash, cabbage and eggplant stuffed with rice or lamb, each vegetable's insides delicately seasoned with a different combination of spices and herbs. Nine other combination dinners allow you to sample a variety of dishes in a single meal.

For dessert, there are Arab pastries, apricot sherbet and milk pudding. *Open Tues.–Sun. 11* A.M.*–10:30* P.M.*; Sat. until 12:30* A.M. *Cl. Mon.*

One of the most attractive restaurants on the street is **Sindbad** (no. 172, Clinton–Court, 624-9105, **I**). Owner Joe Hatoum, a young business-school graduate, has attempted to invest his place with a little more ambiance than most of the other Arab restaurants in the area, while still maintaining a completely authentic menu.

As you walk downstairs into Sindbad, you feel as if you are entering a sultan's harem. On one side of the room, cast-iron pillars form a small arcade, the ceiling of which is draped with a billowing canopy; on the other side, a cast-iron facade outlines minaret shapes on the patterned persimmon-colored wallpaper. Vases of cloth roses on each table and subdued Middle Eastern music add to the Arabian-nights effect.

Munch on the complimentary pickled turnips in red beet juice and hot pepperoncini while you contemplate the menu, and be sure to order the *filo* meat and spinach pie appetizers (the fillings are mixed with pine nuts). Other house specialties are the fresh *tabboule* salad, the shish kebab, the *kibbee* (baked and served with stuffed grape leaves or eggplant and a bowl of homemade yogurt) and the *couscous* (served with a bowl of cinnamon-fragrant chicken, carrots and squash).

The buttery-fresh pastries (everything is made on the premises except the pita bread) are worthy of a sultan's table; if Scheherazade had known how to make birds' nests like these, maybe she wouldn't have had to tell so many tales.

Arab coffee comes sweet (the sugar boiled with the grounds) or straight as you prefer, and the Lebanese tea is scented with mint and cinnamon. *Open Tues.–Sun. 12 noon–10 P.M.; Fri. and Sat. until 11:30 –P.M. Cl. Mon.*

The menu at **Dar Lebnan** (no. 151, Henry–Clinton Sts., 625-7998, I), one of the newest Lebanese restaurants on the street, boasts that all dishes are prepared by a European chef. Along with its kibbee and kebabs, it lists many Continental dishes. *Open Thurs.–Tues., Wed.; Cl. Mon.*

Across the street is another Lebanese restaurant, the **Tripoli** (no. 160, 596-0461, I), where you dine under an ancient-looking canopy (for some reason this one suggests desert tents rather than harems) and where the waiters wear embroidered vests. Tripoli's menu is completely traditional and includes a few unusual fish dishes (sautéed fish with *tahini* sauce, almonds and walnuts) and half-dozen interesting meatless entrees along with its standard lamb fare. *Open daily, noon–midnight.*

The grandfather of all the Yemeni restaurants on Atlantic Avenue is **Atlantic House** (no. 144, Clinton–Henry Sts., 858-7732, I), founded over a dozen years ago by Mohammad Almontaser. Since its establishment, Atlantic House has spawned six more Yemeni restaurants in the area all owned by the sons and nephews of the founder: the **Near East** (136–138 Court, Atlantic Ave.–Pacific St., 624-9257, I), the **New Near East** (139 Court, 625-9559, I), the two-floor **Almontaser** (218 Court, Warren–Baltic Sts., 624-9267, I), the **Adnan** (no. 129, Clinton–Henry

Sts., 625-8697, **I**), and the **Taiz Yemen** (172 Court St., Amity–Congress Sts., 625-3907, **I**).

The prototype for all the restaurants that followed, **Atlantic House** is a small, dark, paneled room furnished with two rows of cloth-covered tables under two rows of Japanese paper lanterns. Almost two thirds of the menu is Continental (Mohammad Almontaser studied at Restaurant Associates), but along with the frogs' legs provencale and the veal francaise Georgia (topped with peaches), there is the standard selection of Middle Eastern fare and two Yemeni dishes: a "ragu" of small pieces of lamb cooked with onions, green peppers and garlic in a spicy sauce and served with yellow rice, and Yemen *fata*—Arab bread in a spicy meat broth topped with lamb chunks in a garlic sauce.

Look hard among the crepes and cheesecakes listed on the menu and you will find two Arab desserts—*baklawa* and *kammer al-din*, the latter a sensational, creamy, translucent apricot pudding made with real apricots and topped with a dollop of whipped cream. The frothy Yemen coffee, spiced with cardamom and cinnamon, is delicious.

With minor variations ("Yemen ragu" becomes "*saba glaba*"), all the other Almontaser restaurants follow the patriarch's lead, down to the paneled walls and paper lanterns. Though it differs very little from the others, for some reason, **Adnan** seems the most attractive restaurant in the Almontaser chain.

All the Yemeni restaurants are *open 11 A.M.–11 P.M. seven days a week*.

Around Town In Manhattan

ISLAMIC CENTER
The main religious center of Greater New York's Muslim community, which includes many Arabs, is the **Islamic Center**, located, until a new mosque on the Upper East Side is completed, in a five-story town house at 1 Riverside Drive (362-6800). The center holds religious services, provides a Sunday school for Muslim children and Arabic classes for adults, and sponsors free lectures on Islam. *Open daily 9:30 A.M.–4 P.M. Cl. Sat.*

RESTAURANTS
New York's Lebanese community is unanimous in agreeing that the best Lebanese restaurant in New York is **Beirut** (43 W. 32 St., Fifth–Sixth Aves., 866-9642, **I–M**). Serving a largely Arab clientele, Beirut abstains from all Arabian-nights stage props. Instead, the formal color scheme

(deep red walls, black ceiling) old-fashioned button-leather chairs, chandeliers, Middle Eastern background music and above all the patrons, almost all of whom are expatriate Lebanese, make you feel as if you were dining in a restaurant in prewar Beirut, when that cosmopolitan city was still known as the Paris of the Middle East.

Beirut's extensive Arabic-English menu is completely Middle Eastern and completely authentic. While you look it over, order an *arak*. A strong, clear, licorice-flavored aperitif that becomes cloudy when added to water (the Egyptians call it lion's milk), *arak* is the customary drink with *meza*—the appetizers. To start you off, the waiter brings out a complimentary plate of hot peppers, radishes and raw carrots; from here on, the content of your *meza* is up to you. Whatever you order—fluffy *hommos*, smoky *baba ghanooj*, refreshing *tabboule*, creamy *lebany*—it will come with a basket of pita and it will be good.

As in any Middle Eastern restaurant, lamb dominates the menu here, but it comes in so many different forms that the fare actually is extraordinarily varied. The shish kebab (unmarinated, tender lamb chunks served with tiny whole mushrooms and a lovely pilaf) is excellent, as is the succulent breast of lamb stuffed with ground lamb and rice that has been seasoned with cinnamon. And the *kibbee* (ground lamb mixed with bulgur) comes in four or five delicious guises—raw (appetizer), baked, stuffed with pine nuts (*kibbee krass*) or lamb and rice, and topped with yogurt sauce.

For dessert, there are Arab pastries made on the premises (you can also get some at the front counter to take home), *halwah*, Turkish Delight and a cool, sweet (but not cloying) version of Arab pudding, or *mahalabia*. Strong, thick Turkish coffee is the only way to end a meal here.

Prices are amazingly low and service is smoothly professional. *Open daily, 11:30 A.M.–11 P.M.*

The dishes at **Andrée's** (354 E. 74 St., First–Second Aves., 249-6619, **E**), a restaurant specializing in Mediterranean cuisine, reflect the multicultural background of founder and chef Andrée Abramoff, an Egyptian Jew born and raised in Cairo who speaks English, Arabic, French and Italian, and whose family has branches in France and Greece.

Among the Egyptian dishes you can get at Andrée's, one—*meloukieh* soup, made with garlic and a green vegetable native of Egypt—dates back to the time of the Pharaohs. Andrée's *filo* pastries—cheese appetizers or pistachio *baklawa*—are extraordinarily delicate and buttery. Her main entrées take you on a tour of the Mediterranean, from Greek *moussaka* to Italian veal and prosciutto to Egyptian squab stuffed with pine nuts and bulgur. Everything is prepared with the finest ingredients and the utmost care and elegance. The perfect Arab coffee that ends the meal is made in a brass coffeepot handed down to Mrs. Abramoff by her grandmother in Cairo.

While Mrs. Abramoff cooks, other members of her family help with the serving, and you feel like an honored guest in the Abramoff home, which indeed you are: the restaurant is on the first floor of the family's town house. All meals are *prix fixe* ($18 for everything but squab and lamb at this writing); you must make reservations and choose you entrée in advance. Bring you own wine. Mrs. Abramoff also caters and teaches cooking classes. *Open Wed.–Sat. 7 P.M.–9:15 P.M. Wed., Thurs., one sitting; Fri. Sat., two sittings; at 7 and 9:15.*

ARABIAN NIGHTS

Long black hair flowing, belly rippling, eyes flashing and arms raised aloft with finger zills tapping in time to the music of the *oud* and *nai*, the dancer thrusts her hips from side to side, slowly gliding across the floor.

Such doings are a nightly occurrence at **El Sultan** (151 E. 50 St., Lexington–Third aves., 753-3429), a belly-dancing cabaret on the second floor of the Egyptian-owned discotheque Club Ibis. El Sultan's patrons, mostly well-to-do couples from the East side and the Middle East, come to the club to drink, to talk, to eat, to listen to Middle Eastern music, but most of all to watch the belly dancers—four different dancers on Friday and Saturday nights—practice a craft some say goes back to Eve.

Inches from the dancer, who works only a few feet from the tables, the blasé waiters walk back and forth bearing trays of drinks and food without so much as a glance in the direction of the performer. At the end of her act, the dancer circulates among the tables, stopping here and there for tips, which are customarily tucked into her costume.

El Sultan has a three-drink minimum, but no cover charge. *Open seven nights a week, 10:30 P.M.–3:30 A.M.*

Down in what used to be the "Belly Belt"—a strip of belly-dancing nightclubs on Eighth Avenue—a small, old-fashioned club called **Egyptian Gardens** (301 W. 29 St., 560-9535) hangs on. Don't be put off by the upstairs location and the crude painting of a belly dancer on the staircase. Once you get past these, you will find yourself not in a massage parlor as you had feared, but in a charmingly stagy backdrop for a grade-z production of *Casablanca*. Four palm-tree pillars hold up the old tin ceiling, the walls are painted with scenes of desert nomads and Eastern bazaars, and there is something in the still and stuffy air that makes it easy to imagine Sidney Greenstreet ensconced in a rattan armchair in

the corner, swatting a fly or two while perspiring under his fez.
The musicians at Egyptian Gardens are good—very good—and they
have been playing the same (blissfully unamplified) music for the past thirty
of forty years. The belly dancer comes on at 10:30 P.M. *Open Mon.–Sat.
nights 10:00 P.M.–4 A.M.* On weekends, there's a moderate minimum.
In Greenwich Village, a Turkish-owned nightclub, the **Darvish** (23
W. 8 St., Fifth–Sixth Aves., 475-1600) features Arab music and Middle
Eastern belly dancing. *Open Wed., Thurs., Sun., 9 P.M.– 2 A.M.; Fri.–
Sat. 9 P.M.–4 A.M.; Closed Mon.–Tues.*

SO YOU WANT TO BE A BELLY DANCER

Some say belly dancing originated with the exercises taught to young
Arab girls to prepare their muscles for childbirth; others say the dance
goes back to the first woman who wanted to show off her femaleness to
man. Whatever its origins, belly dancing in America has come out of the
shadows of the circus sideshow where it was relegated for many years and
into the sunlight of suburbia and the Y.W.C.A. New York, of course, is
the center—one might say the navel—of the belly-dancing fever that is
sweeping the country, and many professional dancers in the city now
offer instruction in their art. The following are some of the better known.

Cia Cirel Middle Eastern Dance School (317 Sixth Ave., 929-
2326) offers dance workshops limited to eight persons. Each month, Ms.
Cirel teaches a different dance—one month an Egyptian cane dance, the
next month a Turkish dance of welcome and so on—so that by the end of
a few months, the dancer has acquired a repertoire.

Serena Studios (138 W. 53 St., 354-9603) operates one of the
largest belly-dancing schools, offering two programs—one for fun and
exercise, one for professional dancers. Some of the graduates of Serena's
professional-level classes perform at El Sultan, and one of her star pupils
is now the main attraction at a Cairo nightclub.

Ibrahim Farah of the **Ibrahim Farah–Jerry Leroy Dance Studio**
(743 Eighth Ave., 595-1677), a second-generation Lebanese from Penn-
sylvania, did a lot of field research in the Middle East and discovered a
vast difference between Middle Eastern cabaret dancing and Middle
Eastern folk dancing. After studying both intensively, he organized his
own troupe, which now performs theatricalized versions of Middle
Eastern folk dance and has appeared at Carnegie Hall and Lincoln Center.
Mr. Farah, who also publishes a journal of Middle Eastern dance and
culture called *Arabesqué* (1 Sherman Sq., 595-1677), integrates Middle
Eastern cabaret style, folk dancing and his own techiniques in the classes
at his studio.

MUSIC

Belly-dancing nightclubs are by no means the only places in town where you can hear the rhythms and music of the Arab world. The **Alternative Center for International Arts** (28 E. 4 St., Lafayette–Bowery, 473-6072) and the **Society for Asian Music** at Asia House (112 E. 64 St., Park–Lexington, PL1-3210) occasionally present concerts of Arab classical and folk music.

EGYPTIAN ANTIQUITIES

Ancient amulets, scarabs, terra-cotta figures, faience beads and other trinkets from the tombs of the pharaohs are some of the items you will find at **The Secret Eye** (689 Madison Ave. nr. 62 St., 888-0788), dealers in Egyptian antiquities and Middle Eastern crafts. Prices start at $15 for a Greco-Roman coin and go up, up, up; objects date from the Eighteenth Dynasty to 30 B.C. *Open Mon.–Sat. 11 A.M.–6 P.M.*

New Egyptian restrictions bar the export of museum-quality art, but **L'Ibis Gallery** (667 Madison Ave. at 61 St., 935-0490) has a large collection of fine Egyptian pieces garnered in the '40s and '50s by the current director's French-Egyptian grandfather. *Open Tues.–Sat. 11 A.M.–6 P.M.*

Holidays and Festivals

An outdoor Arab bazaar, camel rides, belly dancing, shish kebab and baklawa are some of the attractions on Atlantic Avenue between Court and Clinton Streets at Brooklyn's annual **Atlantic Antic**, held on the third Sunday in September. For information call Sahadi, MA4-4550.

The biggest holiday of the year for New York's Arab Muslims is **Id al-Fitar**, the feast that marks the end of the month-long fast of **Ramadan**. During the entire month of Ramadan, which commemorates the time when the Koran was revealed to Muhammad, devout Muslims do not eat or drink till nightfall. The dates of Ramadan fall in different seasons because they are determined by the lunar calendar. The Islamic Center of New York (1 Riverside Drive, 362-6800) is the focus of religious activity at this time.

Arab Food

Lebanon's national dish may be *kibbee*, Egypt's may be *foul mudammas*, and Morocco's, *couscous*, but all Arabs share the same basic diet of lamb, rice, dried beans, bulgur, yogurt, vegetables, nuts and fruit. Olive oil and butter are the main cooking fats. Flat, round Arab bread is eaten with most meals. A special feature of Arab cuisine is *meza*—a course of appetizers that may range from a single dish of pickled turnips to a spread of dozens of dishes. *Meza* is washed down with *arak*, a strong, anise-flavored aperitif.

Arab sweets take the form of syrupy nut-*filo* pastries or milk pudding. A demitasse of thick Arab coffee or a cup of spiced tea ends the meal.

MENU GLOSSARY
(*Note*: Spellings vary wildly from one restaurant to another; use your imagination.)

ajweh   semolina cupcakes with date filling.

arak   anise-flavored aperitif distilled from grapes or dates.

baba ghanooj   eggplant-*tahini* dip.

baklawa   many-layered filo-dough pastry filled with nuts and soaked in sweet syrup.

bamia   okra; usually refers to a dish of lamb chunks cooked with fresh okra.

bird's nest   roll of filo pastry in circular nest filled with mound of pistachio nuts and soaked in syrup.

burghul   bulgur, or cracked wheat.

couscous   tiny semolina pasta served with meat-and-vegetable stew.

coussa   see *koussa*.

chawarma   see *shawarma*.

felafel or *falafel*   deep-fried balls of mashed chick peas and bulgur.

foul madammas or *medammas*   boiled, seasoned fava beans.

goraybe   butter cookies.

halwa   sweet sesame-paste confection, often studded with nuts.

hommos, hummus bi tahini   chick pea–tahini dip.

kafta kebab   chopped lamb mixed with onions and spices and cooked on a skewer.

kebab, kabob   skewered meat.

knafy, kanafi   shredded wheat pastry.

kibbee, kibbi, kibbeh   pounded or ground lamb combined with bulgur wheat, served raw or cooked, plain or with stuffing—the Lebanese national dish.

kibbee, ares   kibbee stuffed with lamb meat.

kibbee krass   kibbee stuffed with pine nuts.

kibbee nayah   raw *kibbee* (an appetizer).

koussa   stuffed squash.

kul wa-shkur   literally "eat and praise,"—a nut-filled pastry.

leban   yogurt.

lebany, labanee   yogurt-cheese spread.

loukoum   see *rahat loukoum*.

mahalabia   milk pudding.

malfouf   stuffed cabbage.

manazali, manazala   baked eggplant stew.

mammoul, ma-mul   semolina cupcakes with nut filling.

meloukieh   Middle Eastern vegetable similar to okra.

meza, mazza   course of appetizers.

rahat loukoum   Turkish Delight, a soft, chewy sweet, flavored with fruits, nuts or rose water.

shawerma   chunks of lamb or veal, rotisserie-cooked.

shish kebab   chunks of lamb charcoal-broiled on a skewer.

tabboule   salad of parsely, mint, bulgur, tomatoes, onions and lemon juice.

tahini   crushed sesame-seed paste.

taratour   sauce made with *tahini*, lemon juice and garlic.

yabrak   stuffed grape leaves.

CHINESE NEW YORK

Chinatown

Old women in loose cotton shirts and baggy trousers carry silk-clad baby grandsons in backslings as they shop for squid. Grocery stores sell dried sea urchins, shredded shark's fin, chrysanthemum tea. Fish-store tanks hold live carp and swimming turtles. In the bustling sidewalk markets, jade pyramids of bok choy and bitter melon alternate with wooden baskets of live blue crabs and pails of tea-soaked eggs.

Every other storefront is a tea parlor, a noodle shop, a restaurant; in one block, you can get dim sum and congee, Yunnan lamb and Peking duck, lion's head and chicken's feet. The strokes and daggers of Chinese characters cover movie-theater billboards and march across the fronts of banks, and everywhere you hear the shoots-and-ladder glides and glottal stops of spoken Cantonese. At a fourth-floor window, a woman fans herself and looks down at a never-ending source of entertainment—the street. . . . Chinatown. No other enclave in New York gives such a strong impression of being in another country.

In August, 1847, just before the exhibition junk *Kee Ying* (a huge eye painted on either side of its teakwood prow) left New York's harbor to return to China, a few sailors jumped ship; these men were probably the founding fathers of New York's Chinatown.

After the sailors, most Chinese who settled in New York came by way of California. The first of these was Lee Ah Bow, a tea merchant who, in the early 1850s, sailed from San Francisco as a cook aboard the New York–bound *Valencia*. The end of the gold rush and the completion of the transcontinental railroads brought more Chinese east in the ensuing decades. Many of these early arrivals worked as cigar makers, sandwich-sign carriers and laundrymen. By 1900, there were about thirteen thousand Chinese living in and around the city, and the triangular space bounded by Mott, Pell and Doyers Streets in Lower Manhattan had become firmly established as Chinatown.

Ninety-nine percent of New York's early Chinese community were male. Unlike other immigrant groups of the time, the Chinese who came to seek their fortunes in "Gold Mountain Land" did not plan to stay. Mostly married men, they had come to make money to buy land for their families who remained behind in China, and they regarded themselves as sojourners who would one day return. Some did go back—about half in the early years, fewer later—but many remained in America, "sojourners" all their lives.

In 1882, the United States passed the Exclusion Act prohibiting the entry of Chinese laborers into the country for ten years. Later there were more restrictions: the Chinese were not allowed to become citizens or to bring their wives over. The Chinese found ways to circumvent the act: becoming "paper sons" of already-established citizens or, after the San Francisco earthquake and fire of 1906 destroyed all birth records in that town, citizens born in San Francisco seeking "reentry." Nevertheless, the United States remained officially sealed to new Chinese immigrants until 1943, when the Exclusion Act was finally repealed. Even then, however, the annual quota for persons of Chinese ancestry was limited to 105.

When national-origins quotas were abolished in 1965, Chinese immigration to this country rose to fifteen to twenty thousand a year, and thousands continue to arrive each year. Almost all come from Hong Kong or Taiwan, and at least a third settle in New York's Chinatown.

Chinatown is workplace as well as home for many of these immigrants: the men often take jobs as waiters, chefs or dishwashers in the area's 150 restaurants and coffeeshops, and the women work in the 300 garment factories that supply Chinatown with its major source of jobs. They stay in Chinatown until they have saved enough to move to middle-class communities in Brooklyn or Queens. From there, if they become well-to-do, they move on to Long Island and New Jersey.

The great majority of Chinatown's residents speak the Cantonese dialect of southeast China and Hong Kong, but there are also groups who speak Mandarin, Shanghainese and Thai. Seven Chinese newspapers in Chinatown (5 pro-Taiwan, 2 pro-Peking) compete for over ninety thousand readers.

Mott, Pell and Doyers streets—the original boundaries of Chinatown—are now the center of a community that extends far north of Canal Street into the heart of Little Italy and what used to be the Jewish Lower East Side. Mott Street is still Chinatown's main street, just at it was in the 1860s.

Tourism is big business in Chinatown, and everything possible is done to attract visitors (even putting pagoda roofs on the phone booths).

Not that visitors need any arm-twisting. Chinatown's restaurants and tea parlors, which represent a variety of regional cuisines, offer a virtual playground for the palate, at prices almost everyone can afford. Although most visitors go to Chinatown solely to eat, the area offers other diversions, too: you can search for exotic ingredients in grocery stores and open-air markets; shop for silks, porcelain or Tientsin kites in shops that import from Hong Kong or the People's Republic (PRC); see a kung fu movie; or just stroll along the winding old streets to see what you can see. On summer weekends, the Chinatown Arts Council presents outdoor performances of Chinese music, dance and theater in Chinatown's Columbus Park. And in the winter—January or February, depending on the lunar calendar—Chinatown erupts in an earsplitting, lion-dancing, pyrotechnical celebration of Chinese New Year that is a welcome exclamation point in the long, dull paragraph between Western New Year and the arrival of spring.

HOW TO GET THERE

By subway: *BMT* RR, or EE, or N or QB to Canal and Broadway, or J or M to Canal or Centre St.; or *Lexington Avenue IRT* #6 to Canal and Lafayette or #4 to Brooklyn Bridge and Worth; or *IND* F to Canal and East Broadway. **By Bus:** *M101, M102* (from Lexington Ave. to the Bowery); or M15 (Second Ave. to Worth and East Broadway).

Suggested Walking Tour: Canal St. from Lafayette to Mulberry, down Mulberry to Park St., up Mott to Canal, down Elizabeth (with side trip through the arcade) to Bayard, down Bowery to Pell, turn onto Doyers, which curves back to the Bowery. Walk north on Bowery back to Canal.

FOOD: ONE-STOP SHOPS

It is only when you have wandered around a Chinese grocery store and come across something like dried conger maw suspended from the ceiling that you begin to fathom the vast uncharted, uneaten (by you, that is) expanses that lie beyond *moo shoo* pork with pancakes.

One of the best stores (because it has one of the largest selections) for such gastronomic contemplations is **Kam Man** (200 Canal, Mott–Mulberry, 571-0330), a two-level supermarket of Chinese food and utensils.

CHINATOWN

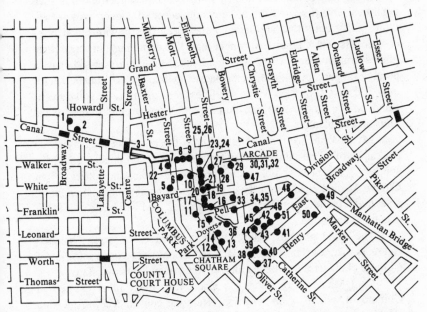

1. Orienhouse Enterprises
2. Canal Cinema
3. Sidewalk Market
4. Chinese American Trading
5. Hy Fund Fish
6. United Meat Market
7. No. 1 Chinese Restaurant
8. Kam Man Food Products
9. Chinese Merchants' Association
10. Big Wong
11. Wing Fat
12. Kam Kuo Food
13. Chinatown Fair Amusement Arcade and Museum
14. Peking Duck House
15. Fung Wong Bakery
16. Hong Gung Restaurant
17. Fon-On Inc.
18. Wing Woh Lung Co.
19. Mei Lai Wah Coffee Shop
20. Wah Sun Coffee Shop
21. Tai Heng Lee
22. Eastern States Buddhist Temple of America
23. Hong Kong Bookstore
24. Wonton King
25. Chinatown Books
26. Mayflower Tea Parlor
27. Pearl River Chinese Product Emporium
28. Mon Hueng Seafood House
29. Silver Palace Restaurant
30. Shui Hing Silk
31. Phoenix Garden Restaurant
32. H.S.F. Restaurant
33. Chan's Liquor Market
34. Vee's Fashions
35. Off Track Betting Office
36. Wonton Specialist
37. Mariner's Temple and Baptist Meeting House
38. Say Eng Look Restaurant
39. Pagoda
40. Chinese Native Products
41. New York Public Library, Chatham Square Branch
42. Szechuan Cuisine Restaurant
43. Jen Gen Im Fortune Cookie Mfg. Co.
44. Lam Kee Restaurant
45. Foo Joy Restaurant
46. Confucius Plaza
47. Sino American Tours
48. Canton Restaurant
49. Sun Sing Cinema
50. Sea and Land Church (First Chinese Presbyterian)
51. Hwa Yuan Szechuan Inn

Among the items you will find on the street level at Kam Man are: dried whole eel; fresh water chestnuts; snake soup (a reputed aphrodisiac); instant shark's fin soup; lychee honey; barbecued ducks; large apothecary jars filled with dried jellyfish, sea cucumber and other sea creatures; Ovaltine; and the aforementioned dried conger maw—great white puffy coils that are actually the (deep-fried) swim bladders of conger eels. The Chinese eat conger maw like dumplings, in soup. Huge glazed dragon crocks filled with mud-caked thousand-year-old eggs (a poetic exaggeration—the eggs are packed in lime-ash clay and buried for only 100 days, a process which solidifies them and turns the yolks green) stand on the floor. You can purchase the empty crocks; they make unusual tree planters.

My favorite section at Kam Man is the pharmaceutical, with its packages of chrysanthemum crystals ("an eye brightener and liver soother"), essence of chicken, tincture of deer antler, and bottles of Baji Chiew—a medicinal liquor the constant drinking of which "strengthens spleen and kidney, reinforces loins and knees, and will be helpful to the organ of generation."

The dried noodles, sauces, oils, canned fruits, woks, bamboo steamers, Chinese teas (green, black and oolong) and a large selection of Chinese china (rice bowls, teapots, covered mugs) are downstairs.

Kam Man is a bit more expensive than many other markets in Chinatown, but its wide selection offers the convenience of one-stop shopping. *Open daily 9 A.M.–9:30 P.M.; Fri. and Sat. until 10:30 P.M.*

On the other side of Chinatown, **Kam Kuo** (7 Mott St., Park–Worth Sts., 349-3097), under the same management as Kam Man, offers the same selection and prices in its spacious two-floor quarters. Same hours, too. The prices are lower at **Chinese American Trading** (91 Mulberry, Bayard–Canal, 267-5224), a very well stocked store which carries everything but fresh meats and produce. The employees are also less pressured here than at the big supermarkets, and so, more willing to help. The refrigerated case holds a wide selection of fresh dough products—black-bean buns, Peking steam bread, Mandarin scallion rolls, wonton skins and moo shoo pancakes—most which come with cooking directions in English. *Open 9 A.M.–8 P.M. daily.*

Unless you are looking for something really exotic, you will probably find all the ingredients for your Chinese cooking at **Wing Woh Lung Co.** (50 Mott cor. Bayard, WO2-3459), a small grocery. *Open daily 8 A.M.–7:30 P.M.*

SPECIALTY MARKETS
Wing Fat (35 Mott nr. Pell, WO2-0433) has an excellent selection of fresh produce. *Open daily, 8* A.M.–*10:30* P.M.

Many Chinatown residents shop for their fresh vegetables and fruits at the **sidewalk market** on the south side of **Canal Street** from Centre to Mulberry streets. Chinese vendors take care to make their displays eye appealing, and it is a pleasure to do your shopping amid geometrically stacked piles of bok choy (Chinese cabbage) or Chinese broccoli (leafier and more delicate in flavor than common broccoli), neat rows of mustard greens, Chinese okra and wrinkled bitter melon, pyramids of pink mangoes or purple plums and boxes mounded high with extralong green beans, bottle squash, Chinese parsley and basketball-sized creamy-skinned winter melon. In the spring, you can often get young ginger root (prized for its delicate, subtle pungency); in June or July, look for fresh, fragrant *litchis* with their haunting rose-grape flavor.

The Canal Street market is also an excellent source for cheap fresh fish, particularly blue crabs, fresh snails, conch, shrimp, whole sole and live lobsters.

An excellent *indoor* fish market, **Hy Fund** (75 Mulberry, Bayard–Canal, 233-8550) is a spacious store where four or five employees in white jackets spend much of the day with their backs to the customers, scraping, scaling and gutting fish at a long counter. Hy Fund carries all the fish that the Chinese favor: carp, sea bass, oysters, squid, conch, shrimp, snails, crab, sole, whitefish and shark. Also scallion and ginger and mustard greens to cook with the fish. *Open daily 8* A.M.–*7* P.M.

United Meat Market (84 Mulberry, Bayard–Canal, WO2-6440) seems to supply every Chinese cooking teacher in town. This tidy store sells Chinese-style duck liver, chicken wings and duck feet as well as the usual eye rounds and hams, and it also doubles as a Chinese sausage factory. Chinese sausage, made from pork or pork and duck liver can be steamed and eaten with rice or stir-fried with vegetables. *Open daily 8:30* A.M.–*7:30* P.M.

On those nights when it is too much bother to make dinner, many Chinese stop in at a Chinese barbecue shop (often the front end of a restaurant) and pick up a ready-cooked duck or two for supper. Barbecued, or Cantonese ducks—which you see hanging by their necks in windows all over Chinatown (and which are not to be confused with Peking ducks, prepared in a totally different manner)—have been filled with a savory bath of soy sauce and seasonings and then roasted to a deep golden brown. When you buy a ready-cooked roast duck, it is hacked up for you with a cleaver, and then put into a carton to be taken home and stir-fried with vegetables or eaten as is with spicy-sweet hoisin sauce.

The barbecue department on the first floor of the **No. 1 Chinese Restaurant** (202 Canal, Mulberry–Mott, 227-1080) makes some of the best roast ducks in Chinatown as well as excellent salt-baked chicken, barbecued spareribs and fantastic roast suckling pig. (The restaurant upstairs also serves a good dim sum lunch.) *Open daily 8* A.M.–*10* P.M.

FOOD FACTORIES

For absolutely fresh and very inexpensive bean curd and delicious home-made Chinese noodles, stop by **Fon-On Inc.** (46 Mott, Pell–Bayard Sts., 962-5196), a small-bean curd and noodle factory that caters to the wholesale trade but is not averse to selling retail if a salesperson is free (try around 4 P.M.). The rice noodles come in pound sheets, which can be cut thick or thin.

If you depend on fortune cookies rather than the *I Ching*, you might want to buy a large box (96 cookies) of these American inventions from **Jen Gen Im Fortune Cookie Mfg. Co.** (24 East Broadway, Catherine–Market Sts., WA5-2746).

MOON COOKIES AND MAO TAI

The Chinese eat their sweets not as desserts at the end of a meal but as a snack with tea or a separate course at banquets. The best source for fresh Chinese pastries in Chinatown is **Fung Wong** (30 Mott, Pell–Park Sts., CO7-4037), a festive bakery with beautiful window displays and towers of red and orange cake boxes stacked to the ceiling. All year long the Fung Wong bakery makes delicious almond, coconut, cashew and wal-nut cookies; little egg custard tarts; light-as-air steamed sponge cake; honey bows (fried noodles dipped in honey); and traditional Chinese wedding cakes—individual cookie-cakes baked in molds and stuffed with sweet paste. Around Chinese New Year, there are rice-flour cakes rolled in sesame seeds, and at the time of the Moon Festival in autumn, Fung Wong does a booming business in moon cakes filled with sweet melon seed, lotus seed preserves or sweet bean paste. *Open daily 8* A.M.–*9* P.M.

Traditionally, the Chinese drink soup with their meal, tea after. Liquor, like sweets, is reserved for banquets and special occasions or, in the case of medicinal wines, between-meal imbibing for the health. When they do drink, in fact, most Chinese prefer brandy, Scotch or good French cognac to their own rice wines. But if you are bent on trying some of the fiery, 106-proof *mao-tai* with which Nixon and Chou En-lai toasted Chinese-American rapprochement, you will find this potent brew at **Chan's Liquor Market** (24 Bowery, Pell–Bayard Sts., 962-0563),

along with Tsingtao vodka, a mild yellow rice wine called Shao Hsing
Hua Tiao Chiew, and Ng Ka Py, a popular five-herb medicinal wine that
can also be drunk with meals. *Open Mon.–Thurs. 9:30* A.M.*–10* P.M.*;
Fri., Sat. 9:30* A.M.*–11* P.M. *Cl. Sun.*

From the PRC

There was a time when **Chinese Native Products** (22 Catherine St.,
East Broadway–Henry, 732-0363) was the only store in Chinatown that
imported products from the People's Republic of China (PRC). Today,
many stores in the area carry China's sandalwood soap and pickled
vegetables, but none can match the selection of PRC goods at Chinese
Native Products. Except of course, its branch store, **Pearl River** (13–15
Elizabeth St., Bayard–Canal Sts., 966-1010).

Pearl River is at least twice the size of its parent store, and its
merchandise is more varied, ranging from inexpensive, gaily colored,
utilitarian enamel cooking pots to the ultimate in bourgeois decadence—
silk pajamas. Desperate gift hunters will find many imaginative solutions
here: china teapots, Tientsin kites, flowered rice bowls, lacquered paper
umbrellas (they really do keep out the rain). Tea connoisseurs will be
fascinated by the store's array of green, oolong, black and flower teas and
may anticipate exquisite pleasure if they purchase a tin of Dragon Well
(Lung Ching), a delicately captivating green tea grown and packed in
Hangchow.

No silk pajamas at Chinese Native Products—just blue workers'
caps and fabric shoes. But it's fun to browse here nonetheless and run
across such items as a tin box of Cheerful Biscuits blooming with red
roses, pink chrysanthemums and rosy-cheeked Chinese ballerinas. Both
Native Products and Pearl River carry the latest issues of *Renmin Ribao*
(the *People's Daily*), *China Pictorial*, and other PRC publications.
Chinese Native Products is open Mon.–Fri. 9 A.M.*–5:30* P.M. *Cl. Sat.
and Sun. Pearl River is open daily 10* A.M.*–7* P.M.

SILKS, PORCELAIN AND KUNG FU GEAR

No need to travel to Hong Kong for a figure-hugging, slit-up-the-side
Chinese silk dress. You can get one custom-made in Chinatown at **Vee's
Fashions** (5–7 Pell St., Bowery–Doyers St., 962-3063) or **Shui Hing
Silk** (#26 in the Arcade, Elizabeth St.–Bowery, 964-0548). At both
shops, bolts of shimmering silks and silk brocades in a rainbow of colors
line the walls and custom-made Chinese-style dresses start at $90 to
$100. Shui Hing also sells ready-made silk padded jackets and vests,
beaded silk evening bags and quilted velvet jackets. *Shui Hing is open
daily 11* A.M.*–7* P.M. *Vee's is open daily 10* A.M.*–6* P.M.

The aisles and cases of **Tai Heng Lee** (60A Mott St., Bayard–Canal Sts., WA5-2233) are so crowded with chinoiserie—porcelains, jade, carved ivory, chairs inlaid with mother-of-pearl, lacquered screens and curios old and new—there is barely space to walk around. Most of the old items come from old New York homes; the new ones are imported from Hong Kong. Be sure to look at the collection of jade, ivory, Peking glass, crystal, amethyst and lapis lazuli snuff bottles. *Open Tues.–Sun. 11* A.M.–*9* P.M.*, Mon. 1* P.M.–*9* P.M.

Rows and rows of new porcelain vases and bowls and shelves and shelves of neatly folded Chinese blouses take up half of **Orienhouse Enterprises** (424 Broadway, Canal–Howard Sts., 431-8060/61); the other half of this enormous store is filled with karate and kung fu outfits and equipment. Doting grandparents will want to stock up on the adorable Chinese silk brocade children's clothes and the tiny felt baby shoes embroidered with flowers also available here. *Open daily 9:30* A.M.–*7* P.M.*; Sun. 10* A.M.–*6* P.M.

BOOKS, MOVIES, TRAVEL

Chinatown has many bookstores, several of which are clustered on Mott Street. The **Hong Kong Bookstore** (#72, Canal–Bayard Sts.) and **Chinatown Books** (#78A) are typical.

Another way to learn about Chinese popular culture and familiarize yourself with the language is to see a Chinese movie. Almost all the movies shown in Chinatown are subtitled in both English and Chinese (the actors speak Mandarin, the audience Cantonese, but the written characters are the same). Kung fu and romance are the most popular movie themes. You can see Chinese movies at **Canal Cinema** (277 Canal St., Broadway–Lafayette St. 925-7954), **Sun Sing** (75 East Broadway cor. Forsyth St., 267-6356) and **Pagoda** (11 East Broadway, Oliver–Catherine Sts., 964-1825).

Of course, the best way to learn about Chinese culture is to visit the country, and **Sino American Tours** (37 Bowery, Confucius Plaza, 966-5866) can arrange a two- to three-week tour. Everyone on the staff has visited the PRC at least once. This travel agency also specializes in tours of the Orient. *Open 9:30* A.M.–*6* P.M.*; Mon.–Fri. Sat and Sun. 12 noon–4* P.M.

SIGHTS AND LANDMARKS

Chinatown's sights and landmarks are a motley collection of the old (predating Chinatown itself) and the new, the serious and the stagy.

Among the newest and most noticeable landmarks is **Confucius Plaza**, a large, modern complex of apartment towers rising above the tenements from a spacious plaza on the Bowery near Division Street. A statue of Confucius stands on the plaza.

Theatrical but endearing is the **Chinese Merchant's Association** (83 Mott, cor. Canal) with its gaudy pillared balconies and pagoda roof. At the **Eastern States Buddhist Temple of America** (64 Mott, Canal–Bayard Sts.), a small sanctuary perfumed with incense and illuminated with Christmas lights, you can see gilt statues of Kuan Yin and buy a fortune for a quarter.

The **Chinatown Fair Amusement Arcade** (8 Mott St., Park–Worth Sts.) gives you the chance to pit your wits against a live chicken or lose them at the pinball machines. Upstairs, in the **Chinese Museum** (964-1542), there's a Buddha statue, an eighteen-foot-long dragon with flashing electric eyes and moth-eaten exhibits on Chinese calligraphy, Chinese vegetables and China's contributions to the world (which, according to the display, include the wheelbarrow, mah-jongg, the abacus, gunpowder, paper money and the chafing dish).

The **Arcade** (46-48 Bowery) connecting the Bowery with Elizabeth Street is an enclosed bazaar of shops and restaurants that could be a street in Hong Kong.

Chinatown's red brick **Off-Track Betting Office** (18 Bowery, cor. Pell St.) is surely the most handsome and historical building used for betting purposes in New York. The pre-Revolutionary, Federal-style house was once owned by William Delancey, who lost it in 1775 when he put his money on the British.

The gray stone **Sea and Land Church**, which now doubles as the **First Chinese Presbyterian** (61 Henry St., cor. Market St.), was built in 1817. Chinese and Spanish services are held at the **Mariners' Temple and Baptist Meeting House** (12 Oliver St., cor. Henry St.), a Greek Revival sailors' church built in 1842.

The **Chatham Square Branch** of the New York Public Library (33 East Broadway, Catherine–Market Sts., 964-6598) was designed by the famous firm of McKim, Mead and White and contains the largest Chinese-language book collection in the city's library system: over 1000 hardbound and 2500 paperbacks. *Open Mon.–Wed. 10* A.M.–6 P.M.; *Thurs. 10* A.M.–8 P.M. *Cl. Fri.*

MUSIC, DANCE AND THEATER

Nourished by older residents' appreciation for tradition, the young people's interest in their cultural roots, and an occasional timely government grant, the ancient arts of China are flourishing in New York's Chinatown.

The **Yeh Yu Chinese Opera Association** is one of the most venerable of several Chinese opera companies that frequently perform in Chinatown and around town. Even if you don't understand Chinese and know nothing about Chinese music, you can enjoy Chinese opera as a theatrical spectacle, for mime, acrobatics and lavish costumes are as important to the art as the strenuous, high-pitched singing. (For information, call Alan Chow, 931-7630.)

The **Chinese Music Ensemble** (149 Canal St., 925-6110), a group of about thirty amateur musicians, has given concerts in traditional Chinese folk and classical music at Lincoln Center and Town Hall as well as in Chinatown. The melon lute (*p'i p'a*), the bamboo flute (*ti tzu*) and the four-stringed moon guitar (*yueh ch'in*) are some of the instruments the ensemble members play.

Several dance companies in Chinatown give performances and instruction in traditional Chinese folk dances and court dances. For information, call the Chinese American Arts Council (931-7630).

Chinatown even has its own community theater company. The **Four Seas Players** (Arts Inc., 32 Market St., 962-8231) puts on three productions a year at the Schimmel Center of Pace University. Past performances have included an English adaptation of China's greatest novel, *Dream of the Red Chamber*, and a Chinese version of *Macbeth*.

The **Chinese American Arts Council** (45 Canal St., 931-7630), a service association working with twenty-seven different Chinese arts organizations in New York, publishes a newsletter and calendar of events with information about what is happening in the Chinese arts. Alan Chow, a former actor (he played the lead in over thirty Hong Kong movies) is the current director of the the the Arts Council, as well as director of the Yeh Yu Opera Company. The council sponsors several Chinese Arts Festivals during the year (see Festivals), but Mr. Chow says that any individual or organization can arrange for a Chinese arts program by contacting him.

CHINATOWN'S RESTAURANTS

In these inflationary times, Chinatown's restaurants are among the last great bargains. Virtually all the restaurants in Chinatown are inexpensive when compared to restaurants in other parts of town, and the concentration of truly excellent eating houses in such a small area is astonishing.

If you must have soft lights, upholstered seats and quiet, spacious surroundings, however, go to one of the uptown East Side Chinese restaurants (where you will pay for such luxuries). The emphasis in Chinatown is on good food at low prices, not on elegance or atmosphere. The emphasis is also on vegetables, rice, noodles, meat and fish. Fortunately for those who take their desserts seriously, Little Italy borders Chinatown: five minutes after polishing off a Peking duck, you can be sitting at Café Roma, consuming a cannoli.

Because of the competition, Chinese restaurants are subject to shorter cycles of decline and fall than other kinds of restaurants. The only way to protect yourself against such fluctuations is to get plugged into a Chinese grapevine, for there are people who follow the movements of chefs from kitchen to kitchen and who can tell you which restaurant's star is rising, which is falling. Sooner or later, the newest discovery ends up in a restaurant review, the hordes descend, the lines grow long, the chef is bribed away to greener pastures or the management grows smug, and the brilliance of the kitchen begins to tarnish. The following restaurants, listed by regional cuisine, were chosen for their continued excellence in the face of success. All are open for lunch and dinner; at some, you may have to bring your own beer or wine. Keep in mind that Monday is often the chef's day off.

Cantonese   Cantonese cuisine, the first type of Chinese cooking introduced to America, was for a long time the only kind you could get in a Chinese restaurant. When other regional cuisines began to enter the scene, more sophisticated palates became enamored of hot and fiery Szechuan cooking. Now there seems to be a movement back to Cantonese, (which the Chinese themselves consider their finest cuisine), and a deeper appreciation of its variety, play of textures, and emphasis on natural flavors.

You will eat well if you stick to the menu at the **Canton** (45 Division St., Catherine–Forsyth Sts., 226-9173, **I–M**), and even better—though more expensively because the ingredients may be more rare—if you ask host Eileen Leong for recommendations. If you want, you can even make up your own dish; the kitchen is most obliging. At Mrs. Leong's suggestion, we had a marvelous herbed chicken flavored with ginger and cilantro, delicious beef with asparagus in brown bean sauce, and extraordinary squid cut with razor-sharp precision to resemble long flowers (the slicing quickens the cooking time) and accented with bits of sweet red and hot green pepper. On another occasion, the kitchen sent out a memorable conch dish—the conch resilient to the teeth but not chewy—in a garlic-ginger sauce and a black mushroom–bean curd *lo mein*. Canton's devotees also recommend the baked clams and the lettuce rolls. *Open Tues.–Sun., noon–9:30 P.M.; weekends until 10 P.M.*

The **Phoenix Garden** (#15 in the Arcade, Bowery–Elizabeth Sts., 233-6017, **I–M**) is a restaurant of spartan decor and wonderful food. Large crisp-skinned salt-and-pepper shrimp sautéed with garlic, small crisp-skinned roast squab (you dip morsels of it in salt), and bland smooth stir-fried milk with crabmeat (a custardlike but slightly crunchy dish that tastes faintly like fried hamburger) are a few of the special dishes that draw crowds here nightly, but even such ordinary dishes as mustard greens with oyster sauce—simple, sweet and tender—or vegetables with noodles are special here. Without your even requesting it, the dishes are served one or two at a time in harmonious procession instead of plunked down all at once. *Open Tues.–Sun., noon–10:30* P.M. *Cl. Mon.*

The best poached sea bass in town is at **Mon Hueng Seafood House** (18 Elizabeth St., Bayard–Canal Sts., 732-0974-75 **I–M**). Served in a light sauce flecked with scallions and slender matchsticks of ginger, its texture is puddinglike and its flavor incredibly delicate. Also recommended: the snails in a robust garlic black-bean sauce, shrimp lo mein, the sautéed watercress, Mon Hueng noodles, Peking chicken served with anise salt and lemon and the Jean Jeah dishes—chicken or beef casseroles with black beans and vegetables that come in black iron pots. *Open daily 11* A.M.*–midnight.*

Northern (Peking, "Mandarin") For Peking duck, that most festive of Chinese dishes, which is eaten on a special occasion, most restaurants require twenty-four hours' notice. But at the **Peking Duck House** (22 Mott, Pell–Worth Sts., 227-1810, **I–M**), you can walk in off the street and sit down to a Peking duck dinner.

The glory of Peking duck is its skin, which is a miracle of crispness attained through a process that includes pumping air under the skin to loosen it, scalding the bird repeatedly with boiling water and then brushing the skin with malt sugar before roasting. Traditionally, the skin is eaten first—pieces of it rolled up in a thin pancake with scallion and hoisin sauce—and the duck meat itself consumed later in the meal.

Purists might object to the serving of slices of the velvety duck meat with the skin at the Peking Duck House, but the diners here—Chinese and Occidental—don't seem to mind. They are too busy licking their fingers. The waiters make a great show of carving the duck beside your table. For a little extra, you can have three-way duck: first the skin and the best meat with the pancakes, then the duck meat that remains stir-fried with bean sprouts and finally, duck soup from the carcass. (One duck prepared this way is ample for four, though you might want to get a dish of the homemade noodles as well.) Other northern specialties of the house include mutton with green scallion, fried spring chicken Peking style and, on weekends, a fantastic Northern dim sum lunch (see Dim Sum). *Open daily 11:30* A.M.–*10:30* P.M.; *Fri., Sat. until 12:30* A.M.

Szechuan   Many lovers of Szechuan food stoke the fires of their admiration for this hot and peppery cuisine of China's western province at **Hwa Yuan** (40 East Broadway, Catherine–Forsyth Sts., 966-5534, **I–M**), a large, bustling restaurant where, even on weekday nights, you often have to stand in line. The outstanding dishes here are the cold appetizers (shredded chicken with pepper sauce, wonderful-taste chicken, cold noodles in sesame sauce) and the casseroles of pork- or fish-balls served in large ceramic pots. Also excellent are the sliced ginger shrimp, the pork-and-radish soup, the steamed carp in hot sauce and the chicken with pine nuts. *Open daily noon–10* P.M.; *on weekends until 11* P.M.

A few doors down, **Szechuan Cuisine** (30 East Broadway, 966-2326, **I–M**) packs them in every day—Caucasians at dinnertime, Chinese for weekend lunch. Solicitous service and superb Szechuan food are the drawing cards. Try the small steamed buns (ten of them stuffed with spicy pork and ginger served in a steamer) wontons in hot oil, whole carp with anything (the hot bean sauce made with yellow beans and preserved vegetables is outstanding), the eggplant with garlic sauce and the delicious apple or banana fritters, with caramelized honey coating (worth passing up Little Italy's *cannolis* for these). *Open 11:30* A.M.–*10* P.M. *Cl. Tues.*

Shanghainese   **Say Eng Look** (1 East Broadway at Chatham Sq., 732-0796, **I–M**), one of Chinatown's most venerable institutions, is also its leading representative of Shanghai cuisine, (though Peking and Cantonese dishes are also on the menu). Not to be missed here are the fried fish rolls—white fish wrapped in thin sheets of bean curd and lightly deep-fried until golden. The ho sai sea casserole of pork meatballs, fish balls, eggs, chicken, noodles and vegetables in a flavorful broth served in a large clay pot is warming, nourishing fare—just the thing for a cold night. Double-cooked pork and bean curd in hot sauce are extremely well prepared.

Many of the best dishes at Say Eng Look are not listed on the menu; look around to see what others are eating, then ask your waiter. Traditional Peking duck can be ordered here on fifteen minutes' notice. Aromatic duck—skin and duck meat eaten in steamed bread buns with fresh coriander—must be ordered twenty-four hours ahead. *Open daily 11 A.M.–10:30 P.M.; Fri.–Sat., until 11 P.M.* (Note: Say Eng Look's namesake "4-5-6" across the square on the Bowery is under the same management, but caters more to its Caucasian clientele; the food is good, but not as good as it is at Say Eng Look.)

Lam Kee (3 Catherine St., East Broadway–Chatham Sq., 966-4343, **I**) is a tiny six-table restaurant that, in the tradition of the cosmopolitan Shanghai school of cooking, offers a variety of Chinese regional dishes. The kitchen is erratic, and at peak hours, it's impossible to get a good, unhurried meal here. But come very late on a weekday night or at an off hour on the weekend and your chances of getting some brilliantly prepared dishes are greatly improved. Ask for the double-cooked pork with green peppers and bean curd (even without the pork, this would be an excellent dish) and the Chinese cabbage cooked in chicken fat (the cabbage wilts in a rich, golden broth). If you are feeling adventurous, ask the waiter to recommend something off the beaten path, but whatever you do, don't back off (even if he suggests something like fatty pork with sea slugs) or you'll be bullied into a bland chicken dish with snow peas. *Open Thurs.–Tues. 11:30 A.M.–9:45 P.M. Cl. Wed.*

Fukienese There is only one Fukienese restaurant in New York: **Foo Joy** (13 Division St. nr. Catherine St., 431-4931, **I–M**). Foo Joy's kitchen no longer shines with the same luster it once did, but if you order carefully, you will not be disappointed. Try the pork cutlets with scallions (brilliant red from food coloring), the crispy fish rolls fried in caul fat, crab Fukienese with egg stuffing, spiced beef Fukienese and lemon chicken. *Open daily 11 A.M.–11:30 P.M.*

NOTES ON ORDERING IN A CHINESE RESTAURANT
There is no main course in a Chinese dinner. The Chinese prefer a variety of shared dishes chosen for their contrasting tastes, ingredients, textures and methods of preparation. Unless you request that your dishes come one or two at a time banquet-style, most restaurants will serve them family style, all at once.

If you see a few slips of paper with Chinese characters on the walls, you might ask the waiter to translate; these are often the specials of the day and not listed on the menu. An invaluable aid to adventurous eating in Chinatown is Dorothy Farris Lapidus's *The Scrutable Feast*, which gives Chinese characters with detailed English descriptions for many authentic Chinese dishes.

If you would like to arrange a Chinese-style **banquet**, visit one of your favorite restaurants in Chinatown a few days before the feast to decide on a menu and make a deposit (at least 20% is usually required). Most restaurants have several banquet menus from which to choose. A banquet includes from ten to thirty-two dishes beginning, traditionally, with fruit and nuts and ending with soup!

CHINESE SNACKS: BAO TZU, DIM SUM, AND WONTON LUST
All restaurants in Chinatown are incredible bargains, but for even cheaper good eating, Chinatown offers a world of little fast food shops and dim sum parlors to explore.

Noodle, Rice and Coffee Shops   **Big Wong** (67 Mott St., Canal–Bayard Sts., 964-0540, **C**), a combination noodle shop and rice shop with a takeout Chinese barbecue counter, is a real find. Order the beef *nom mai fun* in soup—tasty chunks of beef belly with thin rice noodles served in broth. Sop up the broth with *You tiao*—nonsweet Chinese crullers that are also good with congee. And if you are two, get a platter of the fresh pork chow mein (light-years removed from canned supermarket chow mein)—a lovely, soft, gooey mess of pork, ginger and vegetables served over thin, hot, crispy noodles. If these choices don't appeal, try a *lo mein* (soft egg noodle) dish, or just look around to see what everyone else is having (the place is mobbed with Chinese families at lunchtime) and point to something that looks interesting. *Open 10* A.M.*–10* P.M. *Cl. Mon.*

For even cheaper eating, try a Chinese coffee shop. Yes, the Chinese drink tea, but not always: in coffee shops, they drink coffee— and eat snacks like roast pork buns (*cha shew bao*) wontonlike dumplings (*gow* or *kow*), or sweet little custard tarts. Chinatown's coffee shops make excellent coffee and, following a custom that has become all but extinct in the rest of the city, they serve it with pitchers of *real cream.*

Mei Lai Wah (64 Bayard St., Elizabeth–Mott St., 226-9186, **C**) is a typical Chinese coffee shop: you'll find a counter, two or three counter men, a few Formica tables, a glass case of Chinese pastries (stick to the cha shew bao and dumplings) and great coffee with cream (good iced coffee too). Mei Lai Wah is supercheap, and at lunchtime, the place rocks with the sounds of Cantonese. *Open daily 6:30* A.M.*–midnight.*

The below-street-level **Mayflower Tea Parlor** (76 Mott, Canal– Bayard, 226-3553, **C**), offers fresh Chinese pastries and excellent *cha shew bao* (which can be bought by the dozen here, frozen and reheated). *Open daily 7* A.M.*–11:30* P.M. At **Wah Sun** (56 Mott, Canal–Bayard,

226-9549, **C**), after you have stuffed yourself with little snacks, you can pick up a container of *tao fu fa*—translucent sweet white almond gelatin—for home consumption. *Open daily 8* A.M.*–8:30* P.M.

Wonton Lust   When consumed with wonton lust, there's only one solution: consume wontons. Where? At the **Wonton Specialist** (3 Doyers St. nr. the Bowery, 233-3282, **C**), or the **Wonton King** (72A Mott St., Canal–Bayard Sts., 226-4290, **C**), fast-food eateries offering numerous combinations of these delectable little dumplings with soup, meat, noodles and fish. Both also serve congee, the bland rice porridge eaten with strong-tasting tidbits (salty fish, pickled ginger, hardboiled eggs in soy sauce) and *youtiao* (nonsweet crullers) or sesame buns—that is the traditional Chinese breakfast. The Specialist is *open daily 10* A.M.*–10* P.M.; The King is *open daily 10* A.M.*–2* A.M.

Dim Sum   It is time to add another item to the long list of inventions for which we have the Chinese to thank: *dim sum*. Meaning literally "to dot the heart," *dim sum* is a generic term for an infinite array of dumplings and little appetite tempters that the Chinese eat for lunch or a light snack. Variety and surprise are what *dim sum* are all about.

You do not order from a menu at a dim sum parlor. A cart laden with little plates or steamers of goodies stops at your table and you take a dish if it appeals. Two rules for enjoying dim sum: sit close to the kitchen (the food will be hotter and you'll have first pick), and don't be afraid to try something that looks completely unfamiliar (one of the best dim sum I've ever had was spicy chicken feet in a dark soy gravy, but I might never have tried it if I had been able to recognize it).

H.S.F. (Hee Seung Fung, 46 Bowery cor. Arcade, 374-1319, **C–I**) serves a consistently delicious dim sum lunch. Paper shrimp (shrimp-balls encased in a rice-dough skin), stuffed crab claws, vegetarian egg rolls and sesame shrimp toast are some of the most tempting *dim sum* here. The decor is subdued for Chinatown—mostly white walls. It's crowded on weekends so if you can, come on a weekday. *Dim sum served 7* A.M.*–5* P.M. (Regular dinner menu, **I–M**, after.)

The dim sum can be disappointing at the **Silver Palace** (50 Bowery nr. Canal St., 964-1204, **C–I**), which is a shame, because this dinosaur of a restaurant (the dining room can seat 1000), with its eye-flashing dragon pillars and gaudy peacock murals, is an experience straight from Hong Kong. Come for Saturday or Sunday lunch, and the escalator that takes you up to the dining room is an ascending stream of Chinese families. Once inside the dining room, you won't believe that you are in New

York. The pork-and-shrimp dumplings and steamed packets of minced vegetables and peanuts are quite tasty; the shrimp balls encased in slices of bitter melon, exotic; the cubes of coconut gelatin refreshing. But the spicy squid can be tough, the chicken bundle greasy. And the peanut "Jell-o" not even George Washington Carver could have loved. *Open for dim sum daily 8* A.M.*–4* P.M. (Regular dinner menu, **I–M**, also available.)

A superb **Northern-style** tea lunch is served at the **Peking Duck House Restaurant** (22 Mott St., Worth–Pell Sts., 227-1810, **C–I**) on *weekends only, 11:30* A.M.*–3* P.M. Here you order by menu; there are no tea carts. Be sure to try the scallion pancakes—small, crispy fried flour cakes—and the juicy regular dumplings served in bamboo steamers. The fried egg rolls are crispy and light, and all the homemade noodle dishes are superior.

Hong Gung (30 Pell St., Bowery–Mott Sts., 571-0545, **C–I**) serves Cantonese dim sum *daily 8* A.M.*–3:30*P.M.

Around Town In Manhattan

INTRODUCING CHINESE CULTURE
In a small town house on a quiet street just north of midtown, **The China Institute** (125 E. 65 St., Park–Lexington Aves., 744-8181) is devoted to introducing Americans to Chinese culture. Twice a year a small but exquisite show of Chinese art is mounted in the institute's intimate gallery, and throughout the school year, courses and lectures are offered in Chinese history, art, calligraphy, language and cooking. When there is an exhibit, gallery hours are *Mon.–Fri. 1* P.M.*–5* P.M.*; Sat. 11* A.M.*–5* P.M.; Sun. 2 P.M.*–5* P.M. Around the corner, the **Asia Society** (112 E. 64 St., Park–Lexington Aves., PL1-3210) occasionally offers lectures or programs on Chinese culture as well.

Travelers to China, armchair and otherwise, can spend a happy hour browsing in **China Books and Periodicals** (125 Fifth Ave., 19–20 Sts., 677-2650), the East Coast outlet for publications from the People's Republic. To the sound of Chinese music, you can leaf through picture albums of the Yellow River and the Gobi Desert, inspect the latest rash of travel guides and Chinese phrase books, consult acupuncture charts and cookbooks, read snatches of Chinese poetry in Chinese or in translation, dip into the Little Red Book or peruse such manuals as "Take the Road of the Shanghai Machine Tools Plant in Training Technicians from Among the Workers." Besides books and the latest periodicals from China, the shop carries records and tapes of Chinese music, intricate Chinese paper-cut decorations and peasant poster art. *Open Mon.–Sat. 10* A.M.*–6* P.M.*; Fri. until 7* P.M.

"Old China in New Hands" is how one reviewer described a production of Peking opera staged by the **Pan Asian Repertory Theater**, an Asian-American company that performs at La Mama (74A E. 4 St.). Tisa Chen, actress and artistic director of the repertory, explains that the purposes of the group are to explore the traditional dramatic forms of Asia, to present Eastern and Western classics in a new way and to provide opportunities for Asian-Americans to perform under the highest professional standards. Past performances have included a bilingual adaptation of a Chinese opera, an English production of *Thunderstorm* (a 1920s domestic drama by the playwright Tsao Yü) and a version of *Midsummer Night's Dream* set in Chou-dynasty China. For information, call Ms. Chen, 749-7908.

IMPERIAL EMPORIUM
If you can't live any longer without a pair of silver chopsticks or a couple of antique jade bowls ($2200 the pair), it is time for a shopping trip to **King Fook** (675 Fifth Ave., 53–54 Sts., 838-6078). Pass through the automatic sliding glass doors of the red-and-gold pagoda palace facade and step into the jewelry room, full of jade, gold and pearls fit for an emperor's favorite concubine. Ivory carvings are on the second floor; fragile antique porcelains, silk embroidery and old coral and jade jewelry on the third; and Chinese carpets, lacquer screens and furniture on the fourth.

C. W. Young, founder of Hong Kong's King Fook (the name means "good fortune" in Cantonese and that's what most of the items will cost you), keeps his personal collection of Chinese antiques in the gallery below street level. *Open Mon.–Sat. 10* A.M.*–5:30* P.M.

RESTAURANTS
There are about seven hundred Chinese restaurants in New York. Chinatown has the largest number but the Upper East Side boasts the most elegant and—some say—the city's finest Chinese food.

It is certainly true that the East Side restaurants serve rare dishes you can't get downtown, like frogs' legs with gingko nuts, and pheasant. And it is probably true that, at its best, uptown Chinese food reaches gastronomic heights beyond anything you'll find in Chinatown.

But too often these heights are above the reach of ordinary mortals (i.e., anyone who walks in the door). You must know the owner, come with a friend who knows the manager or, through repeated visits and cajoling, convince the management that you are serious about Chinese food. And after all this, whether or not you end up getting a good meal, you pay for the luxurious surroundings and solicitous service. Though still moderate when compared to prices at French or Italian restaurants of comparable quality, dinner pirces in East Side Chinese restaurants are three times what they are in Chinatown.

The **Shun Lee Palace** (155 E. 55 St., Lexington–Third Aves., 371-8844, **E**) is generally considered to be the best uptown Chinese restaurant. Chef-owner T.T. Wang was the first to introduce the hotter-than-Szechuan cuisine of Hunan to New York, and some of the best dishes on the menu—the whole crisp fried sea bass in an impassioned hot sauce, cold chicken in fiery sesame paste, and smoke-flavored duck-ling—are Hunanese. Other specialties of the house are the vegetable duck pie, the mild velvet shrimp puffs with water chestnuts, and the three-way combination platter of appetizers (spicy shrimp, vegetable duck pie and spicy cucumbers). The secret at Shun Lee Palace is to convince the manager, Michael Tong, that you are someone who knows what's what; otherwise you'll get a decent meal but nothing extraordi-nary, and the Hunanese hot sauces, which should be wild and ferocious as a tiger, will come to your table mild and meek as a lamb. *Open daily noon–10:30* P.M.; *Fri.–Sat. until 11:30* P.M.

Rosenthal china, fresh flowers, comfort and elegance abound at **David K's** (1115 Third Ave. at 65 St., 371-9090, **E**), probably the most tastefully decorated Chinese restaurant in New York. The food, made with the best ingredients, is correctly prepared and consistently good but rarely makes you want to jump for joy. One of the most exciting dishes here is the Mongolian hot pot—platters of sliced meat, seafood, vege-tables and bean curd which you cook in a simmering broth at your table. Other good choices: minced squab soup, served in bamboo containers, and tangerine beef. *Open Sun.–Thurs. 12–12; Fri.–Sat. 12 noon–1:30* A.M.

David Keh of David K's, who started out as a waiter on Wall Street, is also the owner of **Uncle Tai's Hunan Yuan** (1059 Third Ave. nr. 62 St., 838-0850, **E**). The celebrated chef, Uncle Tai, who made this restaurant famous, has moved to Houston; though it is not the same without him, this is still one of the best restaurants of the uptown colony and the only Chinese restaurant in town that really specializes in prepar-ing game. You can get rabbit a number of different ways here, as well as venison and pheasant. Recommended: orange duck, diced squab in lettuce rolls, Uncle Tai's beef. *Open daily noon–11* P.M.; *Fri.–Sat. until 11:30* P.M.

Fortune Garden (1160 Third Ave. nr. 67 St., 744-1212, **E**) is a relative newcomer to the East Side Chinese restaurant scene but its menu and dishes show imagination and promise. Try the drunken crab (raw crab marinated in rice wine and soy), the fried flounder scented with anise, the lamb in hot pepper sauce, the snow white soup, black mushrooms marinated and cooked in oyster sauce with hearts of Chinese cabbage. *Open Sun.–Tues., noon–11 P.M.; Wed.–Sun., noon–midnight.*

Holidays and Festivals

The most important Chinese holiday of the year, **Chinese New Year**, celebrates the first day of the lunar year, which usually falls between the third week of January and the end of February on the Western calendar. On the last day of the old year, families smear malt syrup on the lips of a rice-paper image of the kitchen god so that when he flies up to heaven to make his annual report on the household to the Jade Emperor, no bad words—or at least only sweet ones—will issue from his lips.

The big lion dance that is the high point of the holiday begins around noon of New Year's Day, when dozens of young men, holding aloft long paper images of lions, zigzag down Mott Street accompanied by a crescendo of fireworks. Before long, the street is carpeted with the red paper casings of firecrackers, pungent smoke hangs in the air and people who haven't ducked into a restaurant for a little respite are walking around with fingers pressed to their ears.

In the late afternoon, the drum-and-bugle band of the New York Chinese School marches down Mott to East Broadway and the Bowery, followed by ribbon dancers and more fireworks. All afternoon there are martial-arts demonstrations, and in the evening, the Chinese Consolidated Benevolent Association usually sponsers a concert of traditional music and dance at its headquarters at 62 Mott Street.

Many restaurants in Chinatown serve twelve-course banquets on New Year's Day, and some of the bigger restaurants also offer special shows of Chinese opera or sword and ribbon dances. The Chinatown Planning Council usually arranges for a big banquet at the huge Silver Palace Restaurant. If you would like to join, call ahead (227-2630) to reserve a place.

Feasting and fireworks continue for another two weeks after New Year's Day, though in a much less frenzied fashion, and culminate on **Lantern Day,** observed in New York with a Chinese variety show at the

Fashion Institute of Technology (call the Chinese American Arts Council, 931-7630, for information).

The Chinese believe the moon is at its brightest on the fifteenth day of the eighth lunar month—the day of the **Autumn Harvest Festival.** On this day, the earth god is thanked for the harvest and round moon cakes are exchanged.

Every summer since 1970, the Chinese-American Arts Council has sponsored a two-month (mid-July to mid-September) **Summer Festival** of Chinese music and dance. During the festival, performances are given every weekend in Chinatown's Columbus Park. During the Council's **Spring Festival,** performances are given at Pace College, Chinatown's school auditoriums and Confucius Plaza. In mid-September, Columbus Park is the site of an **Asian-American Festival** featuring continuous performances by various of the city's Asian groups. For information, call the council, 931-7630.

Chinese Food

One of the great cuisines of the world, Chinese cooking is healthy, esthetically pleasing and infinitely varied.

Chinese cuisine embraces many regional styles of cooking. Most Chinese restaurants in New York serve **Cantonese** cuisine, considered the finest and most varied of all China's regional styles of cooking. Thickened sauces characterize many Cantonese dishes; the Cantonese are also known for their seafood dishes.

The cuisine of **Northeast** China—Peking and Shantung—sometimes called Mandarin, includes many elegant dishes, for Peking was the Imperial Capital. Many Northern dishes are flavored with brown bean paste, garlic and scallions. Northern cuisine is also known for its wheat-flour noodles and dumplings, Peking duck and Mongolian lamb dishes.

The food of **Szechuan** is highly spiced, peppery and oily. **Hunanese** cuisine is even hotter than that of Szechuan. The cuisine of the cosmopolitan city of **Shanghai** includes dishes from many regional styles and is known especially for its red-cooked dishes (stewed in soy sauce). **Fukienese** cuisine is famous for its light soups and many fish dishes.

A typical Chinese dinner consists of a variety of dishes (there is no main dish) shared by all. Traditionally, soup is drunk with the meal, tea after, but most New York Chinese restaurants keep your teapot filled throughout the meal. Wine can be drunk with Chinese food, but cold beer is a better choice. Dessert is sometimes served in New York's Chinese restaurants, but it is not customarily part of an ordinary Chinese meal.

MENU GLOSSARY
Although the Chinese language is written the same all over China, the same characters are pronounced differently in each dialect. The English transliteration of the Chinese character for "chicken," is "gai" in Cantonese, "ji" in Mandarin. The spellings below are the ones most commonly found on Chinese restaurant menus in New York. If you are in a Cantonese restaurant, look in the first column; in a Northern, Szechuan or Hunan restaurant, use the second. (Some items or terms may be found only in one column because they are unique to a particular regional cuisine.) If you are in a noodle or dumpling shop, look under Noodles and Dumplings.

Cantonese	*Northern, Szechuan, Hunan*

Cooking method
chow: stir-fried.	*cha*: deep-fried.
hung shu, *hung siew*: red-cooked, in soy sauce.	*ch'ao*: stir-fried.
jow: deep-fried.	*hung shao*: red-cooked.
shew, *shu*, *siew*: roasted, barbecued.	*hui kuo*, *hwei gwoh*: twice-cooked; first simmered whole, then sliced and sautéed.
ting: steamed.	*ja*: same as *cha*.
	shao: roasted, barbecued.

Ingredients
doufu: bean curd.	*chi*: chicken.
fun, *fon*: rice, or rice noodle.	*fan*: rice.
gai, *gee*, *guy*: chicken.	*hsia jen*, *hsia ren*: shrimp.
jyu yuk: pork.	*ji*: same as *chi*.
har, *ha*: shrimp.	*jou*: pork.
lung ha, *lung har*: lobster.	*lung hsia*: lobster.
mein: noodles.	
ngow yuk, *ngau yuk*: beef.	*niu jou*, *niu rou*: beef.
opp: duck.	*rou*: same as *jou*.
tang, *tong*: soup.	*t'ang*: soup.
yü, *yee*: fish.	*tofu*: bean curd.
	ya: duck.
	yang: lamb.
	yü: fish.

Food peice sizes

ding: cubed.
kow, kau: chunks.
luk: small pieces.
pin: sliced.
see: shredded.
soong: minced.

ch'iu: chunks.
ding: cubed
lu: small pieces.
p'ien: sliced.
ssu: shredded.
sung: minced.
ting: same as *ding*.

Noodles, dumplings, snacks *(Cantonese)*

bao, bau: a bun.

cha(r) shew (siew) bao: roast pork bun (yeast bun filled at the center with sweetened cubes of roast pork).

chow fun: fried wide rice noodles.

chow mai fun: fried thin rice noodles (rice vermicelli).

chow mein: fried noodles; may be crisp-fried or soft-fried.

dim sum (dien hsin in Mandarin): tea pastries, little snacks.

har kow: dumplings filled with ground shrimp.

jook: congee, or rice gruel.

kow, gow: dumpling.

lo mein: "tossed" or "mixed" noodles; noodles that have been parboiled and added to cooked meat and vegetable mixture.

mai fun: very thin rice-flour noodles.

tang mein: soup noodles.

wonton: dumpling; thin dough skin filled with meat or seafood mixture and cooked.

CZECHOSLOVAK NEW YORK

Czechoslovak Yorkville

In the days when a six-story tenement was the tallest building on First Avenue and a cold-water flat rented for $12 a month, Yorkville from about 65th to 77th Street was a Little Czechoslovakia, and First Avenue, with its Czechoslovak butcher shops and bakeries, was known as Czech Broadway. Old-timers in Yorkville remember when even the cops spoke Czech, and on holidays, the whole neighborhood smelled of roast goose.

Now most of the old brick tenements bedecked with elaborate wrought-iron fire escapes have given way to towers of smooth concrete. The luxury high-rises have attracted new residents—the well-to-do and those with aspirations—and Czech Broadway has become a chic address. The old Czech quarter? "I give it five to ten years, then it will all be gone," says Josef Sereda, who owns a Czechoslovak gift store in the area. "It's a shame," he adds. "It used to have character, this neighborhood."

Yorkville was not the first Little Czechoslovakia in New York. In the second half of the nineteenth century, when Czechs and Slovaks began coming to the United States in large numbers, they joined the international stew of immigrants who lived on the Lower East Side. As the Czechs became more prosperous, they began moving uptown. The Slovaks formed their own colony on the Lower East Side, east of Avenue A from 4th to 7th streets, but gradually they too began to move uptown.

Yorkville's Czech and Slovak populations continued to grow with the influx of new immigrants from Czechoslovakia in the 1920s and the late 1940s. But by the time the last wave of immigrants rolled in after the Russian invasion of Czechoslovakia in 1968, Czechoslovak Yorkville had already changed. Most of the second-generation Czechs and Slovaks had moved away, and with more and more high-rises replacing the old tenements, many older residents who couldn't afford the new rents had been forced to leave.

Present-day Czechoslovak Yorkville may be only a shadow of its former self, but there is more than enough left for the interested visitor to capture some flavor of the past. You can still get Czech sausages and sauerkraut in Yorkville. You can still buy Czech and Slovak newspapers, and Bohemian crystal. And at three Czechoslovak restaurants, you can still gorge yourself on dumplings and duckling cooked as only the Czechoslovakians know how.

CZECHOSLOVAK YORKVILLE

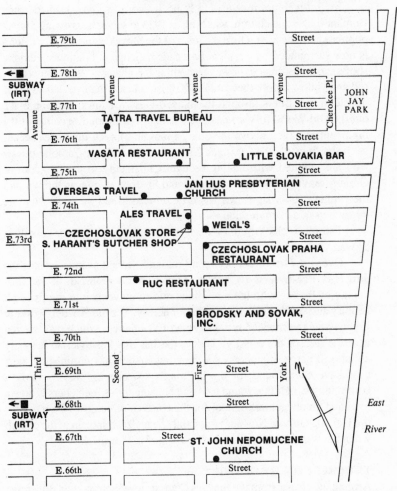

HOW TO GET THERE
By subway: *Lexington Avenue IRT* #6 to 68 or 77 Sts. Walk east to Second Ave. **By bus:** *M15* (northbound on First Ave., southbound on Second Ave.).

CHURCHES

The most enduring reminders of the old Czechoslovak community are the Czech and Slovak churches in Yorkville.

St. John Nepomucene (411 E. 66 St., cor. First Ave.), a handsome Romanesque-style church, was built in 1925 to serve the growing Slovak population in the area. Once the heart of the Slovak community, St. John is now surrounded by a typical East Side mélange of boutiques, antique shops and cafés. Inside, however, nothing has changed. Vigil lights glow red and yellow before the statues of Christ, and as your eyes adjust to the dim light that filters through the stained-glass windows, you can make out the Old World folk-art designs that adorn the turquoise celing of the high central nave. Above the altar, a mosaic triptych illustrates scenes from the lives of SS. Cyril and Methodius (two Greek Catholic priests who are credited with having brought Christianity to the kingdom of Great Moravia in the ninth century) and St. John, who was thrown into the Moldau River to drown when he refused to tell the king what the queen had said at confession.

The ten o'clock Sunday mass at St. John Nepomucene is still in Slovak.

Over on 74th Street between First and Second avenues stands the **Jan Hus Presbyterian Church**, named after a professor at the University of Prague who led a religious reform movement in the fifteenth century and was burned at the stake for heresy. The old Powder Tower in Prague was the model for the steeple of the church, which was erected near the turn of the century. Today, the Jan Hus Presbyterian has only about 150 active members. As the congregation has diminished, new uses have been found for the building's space; what was formerly a community center that found jobs and housing for its memebers is now a gym and an elementary school for the children of parents who work for the United Nations. Nowadays you only hear Czech spoken in the church when the senior citizens' luncheons are held in Pisek Hall.

THE CZECHOSLOVAK STORE

Around the corner from the Jan Hus Church, Josef Sereda sells Bohemian cut crystal, Czech books and newspapers and tapes and records of Czech music in the **Czechoslovak Store** (1363 First Ave., 73–74 Sts., 249-7414).

"Bohemian crystal is the best in the world," says Mr. Sereda. "It should be; they have been making it for over six hundred years." Cut crystal wineglasses, vases, pitchers, bowls and knickknacks of all kinds sparkle on the shelves of Sereda's little shop. Most of the neighborhood's Czech-speaking residents stop by the store at least once a week to buy newspapers and to chat with Sereda, who always has time to reminisce about the old days over a glass of wine and "vichy." Sereda came to the United States via France, but he was born in Czechoslovakia; as he tells it, he was the second most famous man to have been born in the town of Vseborice. And who was the first? "Zdenek Fibich," answers Sereda serenely, "the famous composer." If his listener still looks blank, Sereda obligingly hums a few bars of Fibich's most famous composition to jog the memory. *Open daily 5:30 A.M.–8 P.M.*

SAUSAGES, SAUERKRAUT AND BEER
The Czechoslovak Store shares its address with **S. Harant's Butcher Shop** (744-4497), whose owner, Stephen Harant, has sold sausages and meats on First Avenue for over twenty-five years. One whole wall of Harant's small shop is decorated with pictures of the Tatra Mountains, castles in the Czechoslovak countryside and other reminders of home.

Mr. Harant can usually be found at work at his butcher blocks, carving up huge sides of beef, his wide, genial face and huge hands as ruddy as the sausages that hang in his window. His specialty is *jaternicky,* a boiled Czech sausage made from ground pork, pork liver and bread crumbs seasoned with garlic, pepper and marjoram. But he also sells Czech *kobasa* (made with hot paprika) and Czech salami ("It's more garlicky than a garlic salami"). And since no sausage supper is complete without pickled cabbage, Harant sells sauerkraut—a special Czech kind that is more sour than the German. If you like goat's-milk cheese, try some of Harant's Bryndza, a pure sheep's-milk cheese made in Slovakia that is strong and salty, like Greek feta.

If all this salted and preserved food works up a thirst, Harant has just the solution: Carlsbad Mattoni Water, a pure, natural alkaline spring water from Czechoslovakia that is excellent and costs less than Perrier. *Open Mon., Tues., Thurs.–Sat. 7 A.M.–7 P.M. Cl. Wed. and Sun.*

Weigl's (1372 First Ave., RH4-8344), across the street from Harant's, is another butcher shop that has been around for a quarter-century. Weigl's makes *jelitka,* a blood-rice-liver sausage, as well as *jaternicky. Mon–Tues., Thurs.–Fri. 7 A.M.–6 P.M. Cl. Sun. and Wed.*

If even the sight of so many sausages at Weigl's and Harant's awakens a thirst, and mineral water is not exactly what you had in mind, you can get cold beer at the **Little Slovakia Bar** (423 E.75 St., First–

York Aves., 650-1313), a dark little watering hole that is one of the few places left in Yorkville where you can hear Slovak spoken regularly. The jukebox here plays Slovak tunes. *Open daily 8* A.M.–*4* P.M.

TRAVEL AND TUZEX

If you are planning a trip to Czechoslovakia or if you want to send a gift to someone in that country, stop in at one of the Czechoslovak travel agencies in Yorkville. Other travel agents may be able to make your plane reservations, but no one is as likely to know the best Tatra Mountain ski resort or the most charming old hotel in Prague. Most Czechoslovak travel agents are also authorized to run a gift service to Czechoslovakia; the service is called Tuzex. Whether you want to send your uncle in Bratislava a bottle of French cognac or a refrigerator made in Bratislava, you must arrange for the gift tranfer through a Tuzex agent.

Tatra Travel Bureau (1465 Second Ave., 76–77 Sts. RE7-5972) and **Overseas** (315 E. 74 St. First–Second Aves., TR9-4230) are two of the busiest travel/Tuzex agencies in Yorkville. The oldest is **Brodsky and Sovak, Inc.** (1319 First Ave. 70–71 Sts., BU8-5294), established in 1867 as a steamship agency primarily serving Czechs and Slovaks. **Ales** (1371 First Ave. 73–74 Sts., LE5-4944) is another old agency; it has been at the same location for over thirty years.

RESTAURANTS

The greatest attractions to the visitor in Czechoslovak Yorkville are the old neighborhood restaurants: the Czechoslovak Praha, Ruc, and Vasata. Lovers of roast duck from all over the city flock here for duck roasted in the special Czechoslovak way. Although techniques vary slightly from restaurant to restaurant, the basic method of cooking is the same: the chef places the ducks (Long Island ducklings) on a bed of giblets (and sometimes veal bones) in the oven and rubs the skins with caraway seed and salt. As the birds roast, they are turned often and their skins are pierced to let the fat run out. The result: duck that is golden, crisp-skinned, nongreasy, and wonderfully flavorful.

The usual portion served is half a duck, always accompanied by a pitcher of the natural juices (with the fat strained out), caraway-flavored hot sauerkraut or red cabbage and light round bread dumplings that are perfect for sopping up the natural juices and sauerkraut.

All three restaurants are moderately priced and serve excellent roast duck, but if a contest were held, the duck at the **Czechoslovak Praha** (1358 First Ave. at 73 St., 650-9787,**M**) might win by a nose (bill?). At the Praha, the duck is partially roasted and returned to the oven for its final cooking only when ordered.

Jennie Holecek opened the Czechoslovak Praha in 1938, her son Frank has been running it since 1943, and his son, Frank W., is the present maitre d'. A family restaurant in every sense, the Praha is where New Yorkers of Middle European descent hold many of their wedding and anniversary parties and general celebrations.

There is no mistaking the Praha for anything but a Czechoslovak restaurant. Above the bar as you enter are the heraldic crests of the four main provinces of Czechoslovakia: Bohemia, Moravia, Silesia and Slovakia. And the main dining room is dominated by a large mural of the lovely city of Prague as it looked in the early seventeenth century.

If duck is not your game, the Praha offers a rich roast goose, a lean loin of pork, rabbit in dill-flavored cream sauce, a variety of veal dishes, Serbian goulash (goulash over which the chef ladles a dollop of *lecho*—a sauce made from sautéed green peppers, onions and tomatoes), a sausage platter and beef with cream sauce among many other choices and a different special each day. With the possible exception of the somewhat bland consommé, the homemade soups are delicious and well worth ordering.

The liquor list includes *slivovitz* (plum brandy) and Czech Pilsner as well as Hungarian, French, German and Italian wines. And for dessert, there is *palacinky*—crepes—filled with apricot jam or *lekvar* (prune jam), or delectable plum dumplings served with a sweet butter sauce flavored with poppyseed. (You can also order the plum dumplings alone as a lunch or light supper.)

Open daily, noon–11 P.M.

Vasata (339 E. 75 St., First–Second Aves., 650-1422, **M**) is a cozy, charming restaurant whose wooden beams and white walls decorated with hand-painted Czech pottery suggest an old country inn. The owner, Jaroslav Vasata, once owned a restaurant in Prague that sat four thousand people. (A watercolor of the beautiful old building in which that restaurant was housed hangs on a back wall of Vasata.) After the Communist coup in Czechoslovakia, Jaroslav Vasata emigrated to New York, where friends encouraged him to buy an old Czech restaurant called the Beseda that had been in business since 1890. After remodeling the restaurant, he reopened it as the Vasata.

Vasata's menu includes roast duck, roast pork, roast chicken, a number of veal dishes, breaded calf's brains and duck livers in wine sauce as well as a daily special such as beef with dill sauce, lamb stew or veal paprika. In season, there is a fresh, crispy, sour-sweet cucumber salad, which is often made from cucumbers grown in the Vasatas' upstate garden. Among the desserts are *palacinky* (with apricot jam, chocolate sauce, or flambé with cognac) and a selection of incredibly rich Middle European pastries made on the premises.

Mrs. Linda Vasata supervises the kitchen, and daughter Linda Petlan is the hostess. *Open Mon.–Sat., 5–11* P.M., *Sun. noon–9:45* P.M.

Ruc (312 E. 72 St., First–Second Aves., 650-1611, **M**), the third Czechoslovak restaurant in Yorkville, is warm, inviting and cheerful and has the added attraction of a garden where you can dine outside in the summer. The specialties here are the usual roast duck, roast pork, boiled beef with dill sauce and veal dishes, but there is also an outstanding dish of apricot dumplings served with cheese, cinnamon, poppyseed or breadcrumbs that makes a spectacular dessert or light supper. *Open Mon–Fri., 5–11* P.M.*; Sat. and Sun. noon–11* P.M.

Around Town In Manhattan

Unquestionably the most beautiful Czech restaurant in the city is the striking **Czech Pavilion** (313 E. 58 St. nr. Second Ave., 752-9199, **E**). The pavilion, which sits demurely behind a little white picket fence (in midtown!), is a landmark town house that has been converted to a restaurant specializing in Czech castle cooking.

The Czech pavilion has two dining rooms, one on each floor of the house; both are handsomely wainscoted and richly colored in sophisticated tones of beige, deep rust and brown. Antique Czech folk costumes hang on the walls of the first-floor dining room. On the second, glass doors open onto a mirrored garden terrace, and an enormous skylight allows a view of the stars. Throughout, there are Oriental rugs, comfortable cane-backed chairs and sofas and fresh flowers and chandeliers.

A native of Czechoslovakia, Paul Steindler is the chef, and, with his wife Aja, the owner of the Czech Pavilion. His cuisine, like the castle kitchens of prewar Czechoslovakia, emphasizes fish and game, goose and duck. A few typical items from the menu: mousse of salmon in wine aspic, smoked eel with creamed horseradish (both appetizers); fresh trout baked with caraway seed and butter, preserved boneless goose served with red cabbage dumplings (an excellent dish), boiled topside of beef with wild mushroom sauce. Desserts include *palacinky* and a selection of lavish pastries made by the pavilion's own pastry chef. (If there is a dark chocolate–covered chocolate cake on the tray, grab it; it is a velvety pastry, rich yet light, and nothing short of incredible.) There is an interesting wine list—also Pilsner Urquell—and for after dinner, *slivovitz*, *borovicka* (juniper-berry brandy) and *visnovka* (cherry liqueur).

Unless the place is very crowded, the waiters at the Czech Pavilion are attentive, hovering near your table anxious to please. Periodically they circulate among the diners shushing the crowd so that conversation can return to normal decibel levels, at which point the cycle begins anew. *Open Mon.–Sat., 6* P.M.*–11:30* P.M. *Sun. 6* P.M.*–10* P.M. (Call about lunch; it varies with the season.) Tuesday through Saturday, a pianist plays Viennese waltzes, Czech songs and other pleasant dining music on the second floor.

Around Town In Queens

For over forty years, a small Czechoslovak community has thrived in Astoria, Queens. The social center of the community is **Bohemian Hall** (29–19 24 Ave., Astoria, 274-4925), an old brick building with a big, tree-lined backyard for picnics, a hall for dancing and a bar. SOKOL ("Falcon"), a Czechoslovak athletic club, holds gymnastic events at this hall.

Czechoslovak Food

Czechoslovakian cookery is varied and robust and reflects borrowings from Austria *(schnitzel)*, Hungary (goulash) and Germany (sauerkraut). Plump roast goose and duckling are Czechoslovak favorites, but the Czechs and Slovaks also enjoy veal, boiled beef (in a cream sauce), calves' brains and liver and a variety of pork sausages. Dumplings, both plain bread and sweet fruit, are a mainstay in the cooking. Cabbage is the most important vegetable, butter and lard the main cooking fats, caraway seed the most popular flavoring. The cuisine is also known for its hearty soups.

Pilsner—invented in old Bohemia—is an excellent light lager that goes well with Czechoslovak food. *Slivovitz* (plum brandy) is taken after dinner.

MENU GLOSSARY
The menus of all New York's Czechoslovak restaurants are completely in English, except for the menu at the Czech Pavilion, which gives both the Czech and English names for all dishes. Following are the only terms that might puzzle the diner.

jiternicky or *jatrnice*:   sausage of pork, liver and breadcrumbs.
lekvar: prune jam.
mak: poppyseed.
palacinky: dessert crepes filled with sweet fruit preserves or chocolate sauce.

GERMAN NEW YORK

German Yorkville

Germans have lived in Yorkville ever since this east Manhattan neighborhood of high-rises and trendy shops was a rural hamlet of country estates. In the early 1800s, prominent New York German families like the Rhinelanders and the Schermerhorns kept country homes in Yorkville by the East River, as did John Jacob Astor, a German immigrant who was to become the richest man in the country. After the New York and Harlem Railroad opened service to Yorkville in 1834, the aristocratic rural retreat became a booming middle-class suburb, attracting families like the Ehrets and the Rupperts, who had prospered in the brewing business.

In the nineteenth century, well-to-do Germans lived in Yorkville and in then-fashionable Harlem, but the majority of the city's German population lived downtown on the Lower East Side. Fleeing Bismarck's wars, crop failures and low wages at home, German immigrants had been coming to America in a steady stream throughout the nineteenth century, and though most went on to settle in the Midwest, many also stayed in their port of entry, New York. In this period, Germans outnumbered all other ethnic groups in the city, and the German colony on Manhattan's Lower East Side was New York's largest foreign community. Tompkins Square Park, known as *der Weisse Garten* ("the White Garden"), was the center of this *"Kleindeutschland."*

Around the turn of the century, Little Germany began to lose some of its Teutonic character as new waves of immigrants streamed into the city and Italian coffeehouses and Slavic establishments began to appear among the German beer halls and sausage shops on the already crowded Lower East Side. The movement of Germans to less crowded areas of the city had already begun when, in 1904, a terrible catastrophe hastened the demise of the Lower East Side as "Little Germany." On June 15 of that year, the excursion steamer *General Slocum* caught fire and sank, carrying with it almost a thousand people from the Tompkins Square area. Now painful memories were added to crowded conditions, and many German families sought escape from both by moving uptown to Yorkville or away from Manhattan. By the 1920s, Germans were spread throughout the five boroughs, with the largest number in Queens. But Manhattan's Yorkville, with its tightly concentrated German population, its *rathskellars* and *konditorei*, had become the new Little Germany of New York.

In the last few decades, the old brownstones in Yorkville that once housed German immigrants have given way to towering luxury apartment buildings. Only a small core of German-speaking residents, most of them elderly, remains. But, although the German community has shrunk to a shadow of its former self, and despite the fact that Hungarian and Czechoslovakian colonies have also flourished in the neighborhood, most older native New Yorkers automatically associate the name "Yorkville" with foaming beer steins, wiener schnitzel, Black Forest cake, delicatessens festooned with sausages, and pastry cafés overflowing with *gemutlichkeit* and *schlag*—all of which you can still find in this part of town, especially on 86th Street between Second and Third avenues.

How to Get There
By subway: *Lex Av IRT* #4, #5, or #6 to 86 St. **By bus:** Crosstown *M18* on 86 St.

BREMEN HOUSE
For anything German in New York, the place to go is **Bremen House** (218–220 E. 86 St., Second–Third Aves., 288-5500, 734-2500), a German supermarket, delicatessen, gift shop and record store all rolled into one. The deli section alone offers over sixty items, including sugar and salt-cured Black Forest bacon (made without preservatives), *saitenwurst* (a very fine quality wiener), and homemade German potato salad.

Imported foods take up most of the space in this huge store: dense, weighty, crustless Westphalian pumpernickel; spicy Düsseldorf mustard; German rosehip and strawberry preserves and fruit syrups; Austrian fruit cakes; Scandinavian herring fillets packed in every conceivable sauce (mustard, shrimp, beer, sour cream, lemon and burgundy, to name a few); dried Bavarian mushrooms; and organic German juices extracted from vegetables grown without insecticides. In the domestic line, Bremen House carries fresh farm butter and huge quarters of rye bread cut from loaves three feet in diameter.

The gift section in the front contains a mixture of sleekly designed modern items like slender Jena glass teapots (handmade in Germany) and old-fashioned knickknacks like china Hummel figures and porcelain shepherdesses. Bremen House claims to be the only store in New York that regularly carries cuckoo clocks carved in the Black Forest; these and its music boxes are big sellers, with fine Bavarian crystal, stainless-steel serving trays and German-made cutlery not far behind.

Bremen House always stocks a large selection of beer steins, ranging in height from six inches to well over two feet, and in decoration, from jousting knights to soccer players. The pewter covers on some of the steins are a throwback to the days when men drank their brew in outdoor beer gardens; the covers protected the beer from dust and flies between swallows.

The collection of records and cassettes at Bremen House ranges from Bach and Brahms recorded by German symphony orchestras to "Club Dancing in Der Bar Mit Friedrich Schröder."

Many European women visit Bremen House regularly to stock up on German hand creams and beauty lotions, and a large number of German-speaking New Yorkers stop in weekly for a copy of the *Staats-Zeitung and Herold* (which, established in New York in 1834, is the oldest German-American newspaper in the country), the latest issue of the *Aufbau* (a New York German-Jewish newspaper) or current issues of magazines published in Germany. *Open Mon.–Sat. 9 A.M.–8 P.M.; Sun. 10 A.M.–7 P.M.*

THE BEST WURSTS

Some of the busiest stores in Yorkville are the German butcher shops—Karl Ehmer's Pork Store and Schaller and Weber—big franchise operations that nonetheless offer Old World products and service.

Karl Ehmer's Pork Store (230 E. 86, Second–Third Aves., LE5-2129) is a wurst-lover's idea of heaven. For over twenty-five years, neighborhood residents have been coming here for *knackwurst* (fat frankfurters), *bratwurst* (spicy, coarsely textured sausages), *weisswurst* (a white pork-and-veal sausage for pan frying), *gelbwurst* (a mild veal bologna), *teawurst* (a sausage spread) and *bloodwurst* (a blood sausage). Customers also like Ehmer's *kassler rippchen* (a loin of pork that has been smoked and cooked) and hickory-smoked Westphalian ham, which resembles prosciutto in flavor, and which, like prosciutto, should be sliced very, very thin. Ehmer's *lachs-schinken*—a center cut of boneless loin of pork rolled in a thin layer of fat and cured and smoked like salmon—is well worth trying; its flavor is similar to that of lox.

GERMAN YORKVILLE

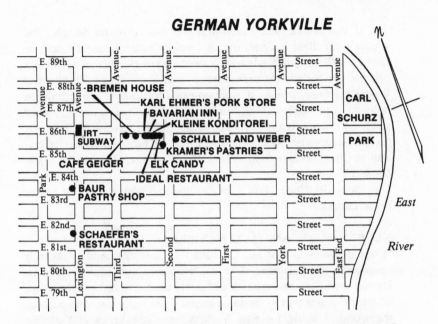

If you are partial to headcheese, try Ehmer's *suelze*, a gelatin loaf made from broth of pig's knuckles and pig's snout cooked in water and vinegar, flavored with spices and mixed with pickles and cubed pork meat.

Prices are somewhat lower at Ehmer's than at other meat stores in the neighborhood. *Open Mon., Tues. 8 A.M.–6 P.M.; Wed., Thurs., Sat. 8 A.M.–6:30 P.M.; Fri. 8 A.M.–7 P.M. Cl. Sun.*

Schaller and Weber (1654 Second Ave., 85–86 Sts., TR9-3047) is an elegant showcase of meats, a Tiffany's of butcher shops from its gorgeous red, finely marbled prime roasts to its gold-and-silver-foil-wrapped wursts and tender pale pink shells of Vienna *schnitzel*. The magnificent headcheeses—huge loaves of shimmering gelatin embedded with abstract terrazzo designs of tiny tiles of pork, whole Spanish olives and hard-boiled egg halves—are true works of art.

You can get beef specially cut for rouladen at Schaller and Weber; also smoked goose breast, rollmops (herring rolls stuffed with pickles), and *ochsenmaul salat* (sliced, cured and cooked muzzle-of-the-ox, a favorite German appetizer). You can get Westphalian ham and *nuss-schinken* (a smaller-size Westphalian ham), double-smoked bacon slow-cured over hickory embers, and *schinkenspeck* (the smoked and cured top round portion of the ham.) And of course you can get *wursts*.

If you are beyond *knackwurst* and *bratwurst*, try Schaller and Weber's excellent *bauernwurst*, a coarsely textured farmer's sausage flecked with mustard seeds and flavored with marjoram that is delicious pan-fried or boiled, and even better cooked in sauerkraut. Schaller and Weber's robust *tiroler*—a ready-to-eat Tirolian-style garlic-flavored bologna, and *jagdwurst*—a hearty Hunter's bologna—are very good sandwich *wursts*, but if your taste runs to milder flavors, try the finely textured liverwurst, which won a gold medal at the International Exposition at Utrecht. *Open Mon.–Thurs. 9 A.M.–6 P.M.; Fri., Sat. 8 A.M.–6 P.M. Cl. Sun.*

(See AROUND TOWN for Schaller and Weber and Karl Ehmer branch stores.)

KUCHEN, TORTE AND MARZIPAN PIGS

When it comes to pastries, Germans take the cake. And so do their neighbors, the Austrians. The delicious cake-and-topping creations known as *kuchen* and the rich and richly decorated *torte* of these two countries—once part of the same empire—are justly famed throughout the world. Luckily for New Yorkers, several bakeries in Yorkville produce the cakes that are the crowning glories of German-Austrian cuisine.

Some of the most seductive cakes in the city can be found at the **Baur Pastry Shop** (1232 Lexington Ave., 83–84 Sts., 988-3990), where, along with appealing apple *kuchen*, latticework *linzer tortes* (nut pastry filled with raspberry preserves), superb *sacher tortes* (an inspired combination of chocolate-iced chocolate cake filled with apricot preserves) and the chocolate–brandied cherries-and-whipped-cream extravaganzas known as Black Forest cakes, cake connoisseurs will find such rareties as *rehrücken* and Bodo Specials.

Rehrücken—literally "deerback"—is a rounded loaf of white pound cake iced with chocolate and decorated with two rows of almonds to resemble the mottled back of a young deer. A former Baur *konditier* (in the finest German and Austrian bakeries, the cakes are baked by a baker and decorated by a *konditier*) invented the Bodo Special that is named for him—a chocolate cake iced with chocolate butter-cream frosting and decorated with triangles of solid chocolate candy arranged in an overlapping pinwheel design.

Baur's also offers the thin chocolate-iced almond cookies known as chocolate leaves, light and airy cross-shaped "butterflies" with tangy lemon icing, Vienna marzipan layer cakes filled with raspberry and apricot preserves, and Dresden *stollen*—a very rich sugar-covered nut-

and-raisin-studded Christmas cake that this bakery carries all year round. And if even the Bodo Special fails to satisfy your chocolate lust, you can always take home a box of Baur's delicious homemade chocolates. *Open daily, 8 A.M.–7 P.M.*

Kramer's Pastries (1643 Second Ave., 85–86 Sts., LE5-5955), across from Schaller and Weber, offers fewer decadent chocolate-and-whipped-cream fantasies and more plain cookies and honest fruit *kuchen* topped with glazed peaches and strawberries. *Open Mon.–Sat. 8 A.M.– 7:30 P.M.* Call about Sunday; it varies with the season.

For sweets of a different sort, Yorkville has **Elk Candy, The Marzipan Store** (240 E. 86, Second–Third Aves., 650-1177), where you can get the following, all perfectly reproduced in marzipan: carrots, potatoes, oranges, pigs, bananas, ladybugs, frankfurters, strawberries and Westphalian hams. The marzipan strawberries are about life-size; fortunately the hams and pigs are not, though the ladybugs are veritable Amazons of the species.

Gingerbread houses and gingerbread men, chocolate-covered marzipan logs, and, in the fall and winter, *spitz kuchen* (chocolate-covered cookie filled with prune lekvar) and *domino steine* (chocolate-covered cookie filled with marzipan) are some of the other delights for sale in this store. Elk also sells its own homemade chocolates as well as imported European candies. *Open Mon–Sat. 9 A.M.–6:45 P.M.; Sun. 11 A.M.–6:45 P.M.*

KONDITOREIS-CAFÉS-RESTAURANTS

Part pastry shop, part café and part restaurant, the *konditorei kaffeehaus* is altogether a delightful institution, the invention of a people who see no reason why the pleasure of good eating should be confined to only three meals a day. In Germany and Austria, where such "coffee houses" thrive, people are as likely to drop into a *konditorei* for a mid-morning snack as for breakfast (It is not healthy to sit down to lunch on an empty stomach, warn the Austrians); a mid-afternoon refreshment as for a midday meal; a late-night pick-me-up of sandwiches and beer as for a complete soup-to-torte dinner. And few diners leave without tucking a box of the *konditorei*'s pastries under the arm to forestall faintness or hunger pains until the next meal.

New York boasts two traditional *konditorei*-cafés where you can get anything from a piece of cake to a sauerbraten-and-dumpling dinner.

For many years now, **Café Geiger** (206 E. 86 St., Second–Third Aves., RE4-4428,**M**) has held the position of number-one konditorei-café in New York. The pastries are what most people come for at Geiger;

the minute you walk through the door you are confronted by a row of elaborate cakes and pastries and a line of people in the throes of blissful, agonizing indecision. Should they get the fresh gooseberry or the fresh strawberry *kuchen*? One of the flaky pastry coils laden with whipped cream known as *Schillerlocken* (after the German poet's curls), or a slice of the luscious-looking Black Forest cake *mit schlag*? It is impossible to choose; the only solution is to order two or three to eat on the premises and a half-dozen more to take home.

Though it is famous for its pastries, Café Geiger also happens to be an excellent German restaurant offering an extensive and reasonably priced menu of authentic German dishes. Good choices for dinner here are the sauerbraten in a rich brown sweet-and-tart gravy; the beef rouladen (beef rolled around pickles, onions and bacon); the steak tartare garnished with capers, anchovy fillets and egg yolks; any of the *schnitzels* or *wursts*; and the *Schinkenhaeger Platte*, a wooden platter heaped with thick slices of smoked country ham and served with a shot of ice-cold *Steinhager* (German gin). The red cabbage here is pungent with juniper berries and the good bottled beers are imported from the best breweries in Germany. Try a Munich Spaten or a Stuttgart Dinkel Acker—both light beers—or ask the waitress to recite all the brands (a two-minute tongue-twister) and make your own choice. The menu also offers imported rhine wine or moselle, German fruit juices, Viennese iced coffee and tea in a glass. When you are ready, walk over to the pastry counter to decide on dessert.

The service, by older, experienced waitresses, is pleasant and efficient; the diners are mostly Germans, Austrians, Middle Europeans and neighborhood residents. Red walls alternating with wood paneling, red-brown carpeting, modern chandeliers that resemble miniature Guggenheim Museums and white napery provide a simple but warming ambiance. *Open daily 9 A.M.–midnight; Fri, Sat. until 1 A.M.*

Huge marzipan cream tortes fill the display cases at **Kleine Konditorei** (234 E. 86 St., Second–Third Aves., RE7-7130, **M**), a *konditorei-café* that has been in Yorkville for over forty years. The marzipan creations are wonderful, but the plain cherry *linzer torte*—a rich brown nut crust lavished with a sweet-tart cherry filling—is exceptional here, *mit* or *mit*out a dollop of *schlag*. In season, you'll also find excellent fresh fruit *kuchen*—strawberry, blueberry, peach and plum.

The lunch and dinner menus at Kleine Konditorei are short but interesting, with such dishes as veal goulash and homemade *spaetzle, koenigsberger klopse* (veal meatballs with caper sauce) and (only at dinner) roast duck. On cold winter days, diners warm themselves here with *gluehwein* (hot red wine) or grog (hot rum toddy) and in any weather the *Rudesheimer Kaffee*—superstrong coffee made with Asbach Uralt Brandy, whipped cream and chocolate sprinkles—is a treat.

The dining room, which is upstairs, is charmingly decorated with patterned wallpaper, wood paneling, graceful brass light fixtures and carpeting. *Open daily 11* A.M.*–midnight; Fri.–Sat. until 1* A.M.

RESTAURANTS

Yorkville has its restaurants as well as its *konditorei*-cafés, and one of the liveliest of these is the **Bavarian Inn** (232 E. 86 St., Second–Third Aves., 650-1056, **I–M**). Oompah music is piped out onto the street in front of the inn to attract passersby, who upon entering, find themselves in a Bavarian Alpine lodge: there are painted scenes of Bavaria behind the massive wooden bar, and in the dining area, plenty of dark wood paneling, red-and-white-checked tablecloths, roses or daffodils on every table, a stuffed deer head or two and an enormous cuckoo clock that actually keeps good time. The waiters wear *lederhosen*; the waitresses, barmaid costumes. And evenings, there's often a zither player.

The menu offers *hasen pfeffer* in season and a nice parsley-flecked liver-dumpling soup as well as a wide selection of *schnitzels, wursts* and Bavarian beer on draft. *Open daily noon–1:00* A.M.*; Sun. 10* A.M.*– 4* A.M.

For lunch or breakfast, many Germans in Yorkville like **Schaefer's** (1202 Lexington Ave., 81–82 Sts., 650-9492, **C–I**), an old-fashioned German luncheonette where you can get hearty homemade soups, good *knackwurst* and *bratwurst* (served with sauerkraut and home fries or a mound of potato salad), homemade headcheese and golden apple pancakes chunky with apple slices and so large they hang over the edges of the very big plates on which they are served. High, pressed-tin ceilings, walls adorned with German beer barrel covers and a deer head, and polka-dotted red tablecloths under glass give the place a period look that is genuine; Schaefer's has been around for about a half-century. The service is cheerful and brisk and the lunch crowd is a pleasant neighborhood mixture of older German couples and young mothers taking their children out for a treat. *Open Tues.–Sun. 11:30* A.M.*–10* P.M. *Cl. Mon.*

A small luncheonette much favored by older gentlemen in the area is the **Ideal** (238 E. 82, Second–Third Aves., 650-1632, **C**), a rather gloomy place featuring a long counter, a long menu of straightforward everyday German fare (pig's knuckles, kidney stew, potato pancakes), a few tables, generous portions and low prices. *Open daily, 7* A.M.*– 11:30* P.M.

CARL SCHURZ PARK

You have dined on *ochsenmaul salat*, liver-dumpling soup, *bauern-wurst*, sauerkraut and Black Forest cake *mit schlag*, and now it is time for a stroll before afternoon tea. Proceed east along 86th Street and in two or three blocks you'll come to **Carl Schurz Park**, a peaceful green respite overlooking the East River that is named after the German immigrant who became a friend of Abe Lincoln, served as secretary of the interior and was once an editor of the *New York Evening Post*.

Around Town in Manhattan

GOETHE HOUSE AND DEUTCHES HAUS

A series of Fritz Lang films, an exhibit of German circus posters from 1885 to the 1930s and a lecture by a Harvard scholar on the Weimar Republic are just a few examples of the kinds of activities sponsored by **Goethe House** (1014 Fifth Ave., 82–83 Sts., 744-8310), a German-government-funded cultural organization and branch of the Goethe Institute in Munich. In addition to its film programs, lectures and exhibits, Goethe House maintains a library of fifteen thousand books in German and English on German culture, and current issues of all the leading German newspapers and periodicals on the first floor of its town-house quarters. To be informed of upcoming events at Goethe House, ask to have your name added to the mailing list. *Open Tues. and Thurs. 11* A.M.*–7* P.M.*; Wed., Fri., Sat., 12 noon–5* P.M. *Cl. Sun., Mon.*

Deutsches Haus (42 Washington Mews, off Washington Sq., 598-2217), a branch of Goethe Institute at New York University, occasionally sponsors German film series. German language classes are held in this gracious old building, which is located on one of Greenwich Village's most charming streets.

GERMAN BOOKSTORES

The two leading German bookstores in New York City are **Rosenberg** (17 W. 60 St. nr. Columbus Circle, EN2-4873), and **Fuchs** (1841 Broadway cor. 60 St., 724-0833). Both stores deal mainly in scholarly German-language texts, though Fuchs also carries new novels and popular literature in German. *Rosenberg is open Mon.–Fri. 9* A.M.*–5:30* P.M.*; Sat. 9* A.M.*–3:30* P.M. *Fuchs is open Mon.–Fri. 10* A.M.*–5:30* P.M.

WURST STORES

Both Karl Ehmer and Schaller and Weber are large franchise manufacturers of sausages and sausage products. Outside of Yorkville, there are **Karl Ehmer** stores at 246 Third Avenue (673-8480), 730 West 181st Street (929-7770), 63–35 Fresh Pond Road, Ridgewood, Queens (456-8100); and **Schaller and Weber** stores at 1654 Second Avenue (TR9-3047), 28–28 Steinway, Astoria, Queens (AS4-3210), and 56–54 Myrtle Avenue, Ridgewood, Queens (VA1-7068).

BLACK FOREST PASTRY SHOP

"I don't want an ordinary bakery," says Peter Fuss, whose family has been in the business of making fine pastries since 1904, and whose father had a *konditorei* in Vienna. "I want to introduce Americans to new things, to special items they can't get anywhere else."

Some of the very special things you can get at Fuss's tiny **Black Forest Pastry Shop** (342 E. 11 St., cor. First Ave., 254-8181) that you can't get anywhere else include: Swiss twists (chocolate-covered nut brittle made with heavy French chocolate cream), rum-truffle cake (heavy chocolate sponge filled with raspberry jam and the same chocolate cream), chocolate banana (half a banana filled with chocolate cream), and an extraordinary, extra-moist poppyseed strudel. Around Christmas, Mr. Fuss has gingerbread houses and *gateau cardinale* (a dome cake filled with raspberry or Grand Marnier mousse). Come on a Saturday, and you'll find small individual meatloaves baked in puff rolls. *Open Mon. 3 P.M.–7 P.M.; Tues.–Fri. 12 noon–7 P.M.; Sat. 9 A.M.–7 P.M. Cl. Sun.*

LUCHOW'S

One of the few landmarks that remain from when the Lower East Side was New York's Little Germany, **Luchow's Restaurant** (110 E. 14 St. at Irving Place, GR7-4860, **M–E**) is a bit of turn-of-the-century New York preserved under glass (etched skylights, that is). Antique mahogany interiors, oompah bands, string trios that play the waltzes of Strauss and German draft beer almost make up for the mostly less-than-spectacular food that is dished out here in bounteous portions. Stick to the *wursts. Open daily noon–11 P.M.*

Holidays and Festivals

One would think that an *Oktoberfest* would take place in October, but New York's is in July. The Queens Botanical Garden sponsors the annual Big Apple **Oktoberfest**, which comes complete with oompah bands, polka music, Alpine bell ringers, crafts, sausages, sauerkraut and barrels and barrels of beer. For information, call 886-3800.

In September, usually Saturday or Sunday of the third weekend, New York's German Americans hold a **Steuben Day Parade** to pay tribute to the Prussian general, Baron Friedrich Wilhelm von Steuben, who served with Washington at Valley Forge and trained the American troops in the Revolution. High school bands, floats and costumed folk dancers are part of the parade, which wends its way from 61st Street up Fifth Avenue to 86th and then over to Third Avenue in Yorkville. For information, call the Steuben Society, TN7-1646.

German Food

As solid and ample as an old-fashioned German *hausfrau*, German cuisine is famous for its smoked pork and sausages, its marvelous hams, its sweet-and-sour dishes like *sauerbraten* and red cabbage and its rich, lyrical pastries that make inspired use of chocolate, fruit and whipped cream.

Though pork is the most important meat in German cooking, the Germans also eat a lot of fish (mostly in the form of pickled herring) as well as beef and veal, the latter pounded into *schnitzels* which are then fried or sautéed.

German beers and white wines are among the finest in the world.

MENU GLOSSARY

bauernschinken: smoked country ham.
baurnwurst: farmer's sausage.
bienenstich: coffee cake.
bratwurst: frying sausage.
eisbein: pig's knuckles.
gluehwein: hot red wine.
hackbraten: meatloaf.
hasen pfeffer: highly seasoned, marinated rabbit stew.
Johannesbeer saft: red current juice.
kalbs haxe: veal shank.
kassler rippchen: smoked loin of pork.
knackwurst: fat frankfurter sausage.
koenigsberger klopse: veal meatballs with caper sauce.
kuchen: cake topped with fruit or streusel (a crumbly topping made with flour, butter, sugar and cinnamon).
leber kase: loaf made of pork liver.
linzer torte: nut pastry cake filled with raspberry jam.

makronen torte: macaroon cake.

mandel torte: almond cake.

mohn strudel: poppyseed strudel.

mohrenkopf: Moor's head—small chocolate cake with cream.

nuss torte: nut cake.

ochsenmaul salat: appetizer salad made from sliced pickled meat from the muzzle (cheek, tongue, lips) of the ox.

rollmops: herring fillets rolled around pickles and onions.

roulade: beef slices rolled around bacon, pickles and onions.

sacher torte: Chocolate-iced chocolate cake filled with apricot jam.

sauerkraut: salted fermented cabbage.

sauerbraten: sweet and sour marinated pot roast.

schillerlocken: pastry coils filled with whipped cream, named after the curly locks of the German poet Schiller.

schlag: whipped cream.

schnitzel: veal escalope.

schnitzel a la Holstein: sautéed schnitzel garnished with fried egg, capers and anchovies.

spaetzle: tiny dumplings.

suelze: sour headcheese.

schwartzwalder Kirsch torte: Black Forest cake—a chocolate cake layered with brandied cherries and whipped cream.

weisswurst: white sausage.

wurst: sausage.

A NOTE ON GERMAN WINES

Although the Germans produce red wines, it is on their white wines that they stake their reputation. Most German white wines exported to this country come from three regions: the Mosel-Saar-Ruwer, the Rhine and the Franken or Franconian.

Wines from the *Mosel-Saar-Ruwer* region come in green bottles. They are light, dry and fruity. Made predominantly from riesling grapes (which produce some of the most elegant German wines) they are very good with fish. *Rhine (Rhein)* wines come in brown bottles. Made largely from riesling or sylvaner grapes, the Rhine wines are heavier and rounder than the Mosels and generally go nicely with ham or the more complex chicken dishes.

The *Franken* or *Franconian* wines, which are also made from sylvaner grapes, come in flagon-shaped green bottles and are robust, dry, earthy—the best all-round dinner wines of the German white wines.

Official German government panels taste and grade German wines to be exported. A wine labeled Qualitatswein is a "quality wine." One labeled Qualitatswein Mit Pradikat is the highest quality wine, specially graded and made from specific grape varieties.

 **GREEK NEW YORK**

Greek Astoria

Few New Yorkers are aware of it, but only fifteen minutes by subway from Times Square, a Greek city flourishes in the borough of Queens. The city has everything a town of its size in Greece would have: tavernas, Greek bakeries, Greek churches, Greek record stores, even a Greek movie theater. Restaurants in this part of Queens serve *moussaka* and roast lamb, coffee houses offer thick Greek coffee and sweet *baklava* and, at night, nightclubs throb with the music of the *bouzouki*. Walk down the main thoroughfares—Ditmars Boulevard, 31st Street under the El, Broadway—and you will hear more Greek than English. Many of the signs over the shops are in Greek, and even the English signs—Akropolis Meat Market, Homeric Tours, Knossos Home Improvement Center—are redolent of Greece and Greek mythology.

This Greek City is Astoria, a small section of northwest Queens that is home to almost eighty thousand persons of Greek descent. Residents of Astoria (many of whom are immigrants) are only half-joking when they say that you can live all your life in New York's Little Athens without ever having to speak a word of English.

When the Greeks began coming to New York in large numbers in the 1890s, they settled first on Madison Street between Catherine and Pearl streets on the Lower East Side. Over the years, they gradually moved to the West Side—to Eighth and Ninth avenues from 25th to 50th streets. Today, nothing but a few restaurants, shops and nightclubs remains of that colony, and although large numbers of Hellenic-Americans now live in Washington Heights and in the Sunset Park area of Bay Ridge in Brooklyn, the biggest Greek enclave—far surpassing others in size and "Greekness"—is in Astoria.

Only a few decades ago, the families who lived in the neat red-brick two-family homes that line the quiet side streets of Astoria were mostly first- and second-generation Italian. The Italians began moving out of Astoria and into the suburbs just as immigrants from the old Greek neighborhoods in Manhattan were becoming prosperous enough to buy their own homes. As one group moved out, the other moved in, and Astoria's Greek community took root. With the relaxation of immigration laws in the 1950s and the passage of the immigration act of 1965, which allowed more immigrants from southern Europe into the country, New York's Greek population nearly doubled (by most estimates it is now over 300,000) and Greek Astoria mushroomed. A Greek telephone directory to Greater New York, published by the city's Greek-speaking community, is over four hundred pages thick; more than half its listings are in Astoria.

Today, while many of the older ethnic neighborhoods in New York are dying, Greek Astoria is young and thriving. New immigrants settle down in Astoria on their arrival in New York; older residents, who like being near their families, friends and the church, don't want to leave. Some of the young people—the sons and daughters of immigrants— eventually move out when they marry and are ready to set up their own homes, but not necessarily because they no longer want to live in Astoria: there are simply not enough houses and apartments for all who want to stay.

Close to Manhattan yet still "undiscovered," Astoria offers the opportunity not just to eat a Greek meal or listen to bouzouki music, but to witness an ethnic neighborhood in its prime.

HOW TO GET THERE:
By subway: *BMT* QB or RR (which run along 31 St. in Queens) to Broadway or Ditmars Blvd. **By car** from Manhattan: 59 St. Bridge to Northern Blvd. to 31 St., *or* the Triborough Bridge and the Triborough Plaza to 31 St.

Suggested Walking Tour: Ditmars Ave. from 31 to 38 Sts., 31 St. below Ditmars. Greek businesses are also clustered along 23 Ave. and Broadway. (To get to Broadway from Ditmars, take the BMT subway that runs along 31 St.) Astoria is a safe neighborhood to walk in, day or night.

COFFEE HOUSES
The best vantage point from which to contemplate a tour of Greek Astoria (or any venture, for that matter) is from behind a table at a Greek coffee house, or *kaffenion*. Traditionally, the *kaffenion* is where the Greek male

does his hanging out: here he meets his acquaintances, drinks Greek coffee, eats baklava, and ponders his own problems and the world's— sometimes silently and alone, but more often aloud and at great length in the company of a few good friends. Years ago, in New York, the *kaffenion* was employment office, gambling room, community center, nightclub and coffee house all rolled into one, but today, other institutions have taken over most of these functions and the coffee house is mainly a place to socialize. Except for Saturday nights, when young men bring their dates or families come here for a sweet and coffee after dinner, the *kaffenion* is still largely a male preserve.

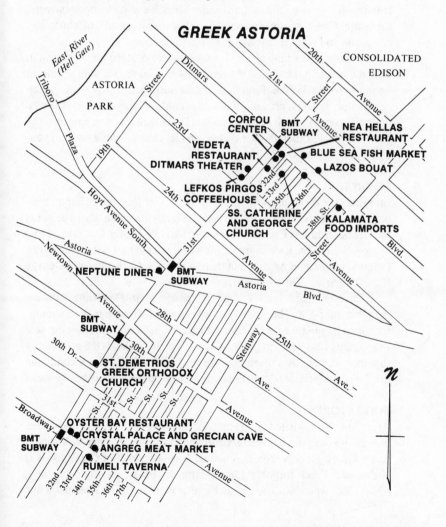

GREEK ASTORIA

Lefkos Pirgos (22-85 31 St., cor. 23 Ave., 932-4423) is a coffee house at the intersection of two of the busier streets in Astoria. The large windows allow a good view of passersby, the atmosphere is warm and congenial and the pastry counter displays every combination of honey, nuts and flour ever invented by a Greek baker. (For the uninitiated, the purpose of most Greek pastry seems to be to squeeze the greatest amount of honey and nuts into the smallest possible volume, resulting in what may be the sweetest, densest confections in the world.) Along with *baklava* (honey and nuts between thin layers of filo dough), *kataifi* (rolls of honey, nuts and shredded wheat), *galactombouriko* (flaky *filo* rolls filled with honeyed milk custard) and other rich and sticky honey sweets, there are Greek cream pastries like *chocolatina* (made of chocolate, chocolate and whipped cream) in refrigerated cases.

A word of warning about Greek coffee houses: the longer you sit in one, the harder it is to think of a good reason to leave. So, after a pleasant hour or two at Lefkos Pirgos, don't be surprised if you come to the conclusion that it is, after all, too hot (or cold, or rainy or sunny) to make your odyssey of Greek Astoria and that it really makes much more sense just to sit back, order another coffee, and let Greek Astoria come to you. *Open daily 8 A.M.–midnight.*

CHURCH
Important as they are to Greek Astorian social life, the coffee house–bakeries are only on the periphery of a community circle whose center is the Greek Orthodox Church. **St. Demitrios,** (30-11 30th Dr., cor. 31 St.) a large, yellow brick structure with a wavy, red tile roof is the main Greek Orthodox church in Astoria, but there is also **SS. Catherine and George** (22-30 33 St. nr. Ditmars Blvd.).

Reverend John Poulos, the busy pastor of St. Demitrios, calls his church a mini–City Hall because it takes care of so much in the community, from helping senior citizens who are ill find a doctor to helping new immigrants find jobs and places to live. The church holds the community together, serving as a meeting place for young and old, for second- and third-generation Greek Americans as well as newly arrived immigrants.

FOOD STORES
After you have visited St. Demitrios, or between visits to the coffee houses, you can stock up on feta cheese and filo dough at one of Astoria's many Greek grocery stores. A veritable supermarket of Greek foods is **Kalamata Food Imports** (38-01 Ditmars Blvd., 31–Steinway Sts., 626-1250), where you can get such exotic items as *orzo* (Greek pasta that

looks like rice grains), rose water, Greek figs, Turkish raisins, honey from Athens (Greek honey is rated among the finest in the world), Greek (in other neighborhoods it's known as Turkish) Delight and large tins of imported octopus pieces. In the refrigerated case, there are Greek cheeses: *feta,* a crumbly goat's-milk cheese for salads and omelets; *kasseri,* a sheep's-milk cheese used in casseroles; and *kefalotiri,* a harder sheep's-milk cheese which, when baked, becomes a savory appetizer called *saganaki.*

One entire section of Kalamata Food Imports is devoted to Greek spoon preserves—jars of sweet jam made from pears, cherries, lemons, eggplants or rose petals that every traditional Greek housewife keeps on hand to serve to guests with a small glass of liqueur. *Open Mon.–Sat. 9 A.M.–10 P.M.; Sun. 10 A.M.–3 P.M.*

A few blocks down from Kalamata on Ditmars Boulevard is one of the best fish stores in Astoria, the **Blue Sea Fish Market** (no. 33-14, 33–34 Sts., RA8-3387), a spacious, clean and very attractive store that carries the red mullets *(barbunia)* and white snappers favored by Greek cooks as well as live crabs ("You can tell the females because they wear lipstick," says the affable owner of the Blue Sea), squid and spiny sea urchins. *Open Mon.–Sat. 7 A.M.–6 P.M. Cl. Sun.*

Everywhere you go in Greek Astoria, you will pass butcher shops advertising lamb, which, along with fish, is a staple of the Greek diet. A typical Greek butcher shop is **Angreg Meat Market** (33-15 Broadway, 33–34 Sts., 728-1626), where the window display usually consists of neat rows of sheep's heads staring out at the street. (The Greeks use every part of the sheep or lamb in their cooking, including liver, intestines, head and brain. Baked or roasted sheep's head in particular is considered a real old-country delicacy.) Just before Greek Easter, Angreg does a brisk business in milk-fed baby lambs, kid goats and suckling pigs, which are traditionally roasted whole on a spit over coals. *Open Mon.-Sat. 8 A.M.–7 P.M. Cl. Sun.*

ICONS, KOBOLOI AND GREEK MOVIES
Scattered throughout Greek Astoria are stores that display a fascinating hodgepodge of religious and secular items ranging from plastic dash-board statues of Jesus to the latest record albums of Greek singing idols. One of the busiest of these "gift shops" in Astoria is the **Corfou Center** (22-13 31 St., Ditmars–23 Ave., 728-7212). A great many Astoria residents stop by the center's outdoor newsstand every day just to pick up one of the papers flown in from Greece or to get that day's issue of the *Greek National Herald,* a Greek-language daily published in New York

since 1915. Inside, the Corfou Center is a jumble of icons, Greek music tapes, Greek books and *lambathes*, the large candles decorated with tulle, embroidered cloth and artificial flowers that are used in Greek marriage and baptism ceremonies. If you bite your nails, smoke too much or pluck out the hairs of your mustache when you are tense, you might consider buying a string of *koboloi*—worry beads—at Corfou. *Open daily 6 A.M.–1 A.M.*

Not far from the Corfou Center is the **Ditmars Theater** (22-68 31 St., 932-1222) which shows only Greek movies.

RESTAURANTS

In many ethnic enclaves, if you ask someone what the best restaurant in the neighborhood is, he or she will laugh and say, "My kitchen at home. I don't know—I hardly ever eat out." This never happens in Greek Astoria. The Greeks love to go out to eat, and what's more they do so at all hours of the day and night. A *few* restaurants in Astoria may close before 4 A.M., but only on weekdays. Many stay open twenty-four hours every day.

Almost all the Greek restaurants in Astoria cater exclusively to Greeks. Most are *tavernas* or *psistarias,* where the food is filling and inexpensive, and where you "read" the menu by scanning the contents of the steam table. Menus vary little from restaurant to restaurant, and even the decor seems to follow an unspoken law that walls be painted with murals of Greece and tables be covered with red-and-white-checked tablecloths.

Despite this uniformity, a few restaurants do stand out. One of these is the **Rumeli Taverna** (33-04 Broadway, 33–34 Sts., 278-7533, **C–I**). A short walk from the Broadway–31st Street BMT station, Rumeli is the closest thing New York has to an authentic Greek taverna. There aren't any English menus here—you point to what you want at the steam table in front. A specialty of the house is the giant shish kebab—chunks of pork the size of Zorba's fists (in Astoria, most shish kebab is made with pork, which is cheaper than lamb). But there is also a full assortment of the usual Greek fare: lamb stews, spinach pie (very flaky and good), *moussaka,* baked lamb's head, warm bean salad (the version here, made with fava beans and artichokes and seasoned with fresh dill, is excellent), Greek salad and so on. The portions are huge, and nothing is priced over $5.

On a typical night at Rumeli's, two men with mustaches and dark eyes sit at the counter, arguing in Greek. Their hands slice the air and pound the counter as they talk, and as the argument grows more heated, they forget to eat. The sound of Greek conversation mingles with the plaintive strains of the Greek love songs floating up from the juke box and the loud sizzling of the giant shish kebab turning on a spit. Waitresses bustle back and forth between the steam table and the dining tables, bearing dishes of *spanakopita* and roast lamb, while on the walls, painted shepherds gaze over their flocks in the peaceful Greek countryside. A plate of *pastitsio,* a bottle of *retsyna* and it is easy to forget that you are in New York. Only the rumble of the subway outside reminds you that this taverna is in Astoria, not Athens. *Open daily 11 A.M.–3 A.M.*

Quieter than Rumeli's, but still typically Greek is the **Vedeta** (22-55 31 St., nr. 41 Ave., 728-9107, **C–I**), one of the older eating establishments in Greek Astoria (it has been here for over ten years) and a real restaurant as opposed to a taverna (no steam table). At the front of the long, narrow dining room, there is a rotisserie by the window, where from the street, you can see whole shoulders of lamb roasting invitingly. Partly because it is under the shadow of the El, the Vedeta is dark inside, and this, coupled with the cutout wall murals that are dramatically lit from behind, lends a certain formality to the atmosphere. Although the Vedeta gives the appearance of being more expensive than a taverna, its prices are actually about the same. *Open twenty-four hours a day.*

A good restaurant on Ditmars Boulevard is **Nea Hellas** (no. 31-15, 32–33 Sts.—the sign is in Greek—278-9728, **C–I**). Nea Hellas has one of the longest menus in the neighborhood and a good selection of Greek wines. The pleasant decor consists of the obligatory wall murals and ubiquitous checked tablecloths. Most entrees are between $3 and $4.50. The front of Nea Hellas is a souvlaki stand that opens out onto the street: here you can get *souvlaki* (shish kebab) or *gyro* (ground meat) on pita bread. *Open Sun.–Thurs. 8 A.M.–1 A.M.; Fri.–Sat. twenty-four hours a day.*

If it is now your fourth trip to Greek Astoria, and you are getting a bit tired of the wall murals, you can get Greek food in entirely different surroundings at the **Neptune Diner and Cocktail Lounge** (corner 31-05 Astoria Blvd., 31 St., 278-4853, **I–M**), which is barely an olive's throw from the Astoria Boulevard stop on the BMT RR line.

The Neptune might well be called a king among diners: it is large as diners go, its facade is splendid (lots of glass and a zigzag roof) and it is furnished in the height of diner opulence—huge booths with individual juke boxes, plush black leatherette banquettes and counter stools with comfortable padded backs. For more formal dining, just off the booths-and-counter area, there is a large room with tables and chairs, mirrored walls and chandeliers!

About a dozen authentic Greek dishes are listed among the myriad burger, bagel and seafood combinations on the Neptune's oversize menu. All the waiters and waitresses and at least half the patrons here speak Greek. *Open daily twenty-four hours.*

ASTORIA BY NIGHT
On Friday and Saturday nights, Greek Astoria never sleeps. The streets are full of people at two A.M., the restaurants are hopping all night and at the **Oyster Bay Restaurant** and the **Crystal Palace** (31-01 and 31-11 Broadway, 31–32 Sts., LH5-8402)—the biggest, most splendid catering and dance halls in Astoria—wedding parties and family groups often dance till dawn. The Crystal Palace, a lavishly chandeliered building, is where most of the dancing takes place. Here, as long chains of dancers coil and uncoil around the hall, you can hear their laughter and the music from the street. Every once in a while, one of the male dancers gives a shout that signals he is about to perform a solo, and while he leaps and twirls, everyone looks on and cheers. For a nominal (and sometimes no) fee at the door, the visitor can watch the dancing. Wedding parties are of course very joyous, but the most spirited dancing takes place on nights when a Greek fraternal organization has sponsored the party. Such affairs are fairly frequent: just about every region, town and village in Greece is represented by a society in New York.

If you want to be a participant and not just an observer, there are several Greek nightclubs in Astoria where, if the spirit moves you, you can dance in the aisles. And if the spirit doesn't move you, you can sit back and gorge your senses on food, drink, music and belly dancing.

One of the most popular Greek nightclubs in Astoria is the **Grecian Cave**, located in the Crystal Palace (31-11 Broadway, 545-7373). The Grecian Cave started out as a modest club in Manhattan's old Belly Belt—the cluster of Greek and Middle Eastern belly-dancing nightclubs in the 20s near Eighth Avenue, almost all of which, in recent years, have gone out of business or moved to Astoria. Now the Grecian Cave is in splendid new quarters and can seat four hundred, and just as it did in Manhattan, the club brings over big-name singers from Greece with a new act every seventeen days. The singers perform nightly; four or five nights a week including weekends, there's a belly dancer, too. The music begins around 10:30 P.M. and lasts until 4 A.M. *Open 7 nights a week.*

Over at **Lazos Bouat** (35-06 Ditmars Blvd., 721-0159), owner Serafin Lazos plays the guitar and sings popular Greek songs to a mostly college-age crowd. The shows start at 10:30 P.M. and 1 A.M. *Open nightly except Mon.*

Manhattan's Old Greek Quarter

Thirty or forty years ago, the area west of Seventh Avenue from 20th Street to 50th Street housed the city's biggest colony of Greeks. The Greeks have long since moved to Queens, Washington Heights and New Jersey, but sandwiched in between the Italian and Filipino stores that line Ninth Avenue and rubbing shoulders with the massage parlors and adult movie houses that overflow from Times Square onto Eighth, a few of the Old Greek shops and restaurants are doing a thriving business.

STORES

For Greek groceries, your first stop should be **Kassos Brothers** (570 Ninth Ave., 41–42 Sts., PE6-7473), a neat and orderly store with the largest selection of Greek foods in Manhattan. Brothers John and James Kassos, natives of Macedonia, started their business in 1935; now James owns a supermarket in Astoria.

John Kassos cures his own olives, which he keeps in circular bins sunk into a table in the back of his shop. Try his small, yellow-green *nafplious*, or the blackish-purple *calamatas*. If these are too strong for you, you might like the tender green, mildly sour pickled baby eggplants.

Closer to the front of the shop, a wooden pasta cabinet holds macaroni for *pastitsio*; long, twisted coils of fine soup noodles; and rice flour for making creamy Greek rice pudding. Kassos keeps two kinds of fresh *feta* cheese in wooden barrels: pure white goat's-milk *feta*, and slightly cream-colored cow's-milk *feta* (which many stores try to pass off as the goat's-milk kind; it's less expensive, but not as good). In other corners of the store, you will find jars of the pink caviar spread called *taramasalata*, sheets of tangy dried-apricot paste, figs from Izmir, bottles of orange-flower water and thick slabs of real old-fashioned *halvah* that is heavy and moist with sesame oil and incomparably better than the dry, foil-wrapped commercial kind. *Open Mon.–Sat. 8:30 A.M.–7:30 P.M. Cl. Sun.*

Two blocks down from Kassos Brothers is the **International Groceries and Meat Market** (529 Ninth Ave., 39–40 Sts., BR9-5514), where the Karamouzis Brothers carry foods from over twenty countries as well as Greece. Open sacks of spices and bins of dried beans and lentils crowd the store, and over twenty different brands of olive oil fight for space on the shelves. You may have to hunt around in this international jumble to find the Greek foods, but the search is bound to turn up what you need, as well as a few surprises—perhaps a bowl of freshly made *trusi* (a Greek salad of cauliflower, olives, peppers and carrots) or bunches of Greek mountain sage tea.

One section of International Groceries is a meat market where Sotirios Karamouzis prepares baby lamb or goat for grilling and sells marinated lamb chunks for shish kebab. Mr. Karamouzis also makes *lukanikia*, a wonderful lamb-and-veal sausage flavored with lemon, white wine, allspice and herbs. *Open Mon.–Sat. 8 A.M.–6 P.M. Cl. Sun.*

At the **Poseidon Confectionery** (629 Ninth Ave., 44–45 Sts., PL7-6173), a family of master bakers excels at the old and difficult art of making *filo* dough by hand. *Filo* (literally, "leaf") is the many-layered strudel dough the Greeks wrap around honey and nuts to make *baklava* and around spinach and cheese to make *spanakopitas*. The thinner each layer or leaf of the filo is stretched, the flakier and finer the pastry will be. At Poseidon, Michael and Menina Anagnostou and their sons Anthony and John all work on the dough, rolling it out and stretching it by hand until it is as thin as onion skin.

You can buy a variety of delicious homemade *filo* pastries at Poseidon, as well as homemade *filo* dough to make your own pastries. Poseidon will also send its *baklava* anywhere in the country. *Open Tues.–Sat., 9 A.M.–7 P.M.; Sun. 10 A.M.–4 P.M. Cl. Mon.*

Over on Eighth Avenue, oblivious to the adult-movie theaters that are creeping up from Times Square, **Kentrikon** (703 Eighth Ave., 44–45 Sts., 246-5945) continues to display statues of Grecian goddesses and blue-and-gold ceramic reproductions of ancient Grecian urns in its windows. Kentrikon's owner, Constantine Nicolis, has been selling Greek novelty goods in this area for over thirty-five years.

There are hundreds of Greek-music tapes and records at Kentrikon, and a rackful of Greek newspapers and magazines, but some of the biggest-selling items here are the little *martyriko* ribbons given out at Greek christenings. Each ribbon—pink for girls, blue for boys—is printed with the name of the baby, the date of birth and the names of the child's godparents, or *martyriko*. *Open daily 9 A.M.–5 P.M. Cl. Sun.*

RESTAURANTS

Of all the Greek businesses that remain on Eighth and Ninth avenues, the restaurants have fared the best. Being close to the theater district has helped, as has the lack of good Greek restaurants elsewhere in the city.

The best of the steam-table Greek restaurants in Manhattan is **Molfetas** (307 West 47 St., Eighth–Ninth Aves., 840-9537, **I–M**). Molfetas has been in business for over a quarter-century, and for ten of those years, the present owner, Nick Triantaphilon, worked as a cook for the previous owners. Nick, a native of Rhodes, still keeps a close watch on the kitchen, and he continues to do much of the cooking himself. Check the steam table in back for the day's specials. Often there is *kefalaki*, or lamb's head, and every day there is shish kebab (marinated for two or three days), fresh fish, roast lamb and *moussaka*. Both the yogurt and the excellent Greek pastries are made on the premises, and the well-stocked bar carries a complete selection of Greek wines. Although the restaurant is large, it is almost always crowded. *Open daily 11 A.M.– 1 A.M.*

The venerable grandfather of New York's Greek restaurants, **Pantheon** (689 Eighth Ave., 43–44 Sts., 840-9391, **I–M**), is more sedate than Molfetas (no steam table and the tables are covered with white tablecloths), but the prices are still very reasonable and the food is consistently well prepared. Pantheon's reputation among both Greeks and non-Greeks is such that, even at lunchtime, there is often a line of people waiting to get in. *Open daily 11:30 A.M.–11:45 P.M.*

Across the street from Pantheon is **Syntagma Square** (680 Eighth Ave., 43–44 Sts., 730-9520, **C**), a restaurant that specializes in the Greek equivalent of the American hamburger: *souvlaki*. Nowhere in New York is the souvlaki made better than at Syntagma Square, where the chunks of lamb are grilled to a mouth-watering sizzle, the chopped onions and tomatoes are plentiful, the *pita* has been grilled and anointed with the proper amount of oil and the "Greek sauce" or *tzatziki* that is poured over the *souvlaki* into the cone of folded *pita* bread adds just the right combination of moistness and seasoning. *Open daily 9 A.M.–4 P.M.*

Around Town In Manhattan

GREEK ISLAND LTD.

Since the gift shops in the city's Greek neighborhoods seem to carry mostly religious items and mass-produced plastic and ceramic urns, you have to go elsewhere to find Greek clothing and handicrafts. If you can't afford a trip to Greece, elsewhere is **Greek Island Ltd.** (215 E. 49 St., Second–Third Aves., EL5-7547), a beautiful shop that opens onto a lovely old courtyard in a very chic part of town. Greek Island specializes in clothing made from natural fabrics produced in Greece, and the shop is filled with items like kaftans and sun dresses made of the light striped cotton called *sendoni*, shirts and jackets of sturdy Greek workers' cotton and hooded capes made from the same rough boiled wool Greek shepherds wear to stave off the mountain cold. A few of the many gift possibilities here include colorful village head scarves (each village has its own print), warm Mykonos fishermen's hats and Greek cookbooks. There are no bargains at Greek Island (that "shepherd's" cape is over $275), but everything is well made and of the highest quality. *Open Mon.–Sat. 10 A.M.–6 P.M. Cl. Sun.*

EAST SIDE GREEK NIGHTCLUBS

Astoria is not the only place in New York where you can hear Greek music and dance the *syrtaki*. On Manhattan's East Side, two fancy supper clubs offer Greek entertainment and dancing in the aisles.

The chief attraction at **Sirocco** (29 E. 29 St., Madison–Park Aves., 683-9409), a spacious club done in white stucco and Mediterranean blue, is owner-singer Aris San and his band. San sings fluently in Greek and Hebrew (he is an Israeli who was born in Greece), and his energetic delivery and the pulsating rhythms of his music invariably cause waves of toe-tapping to wash over the club. The dance music that follows brings the crowd to its feet, where it stays for the rest of the evening. (When you begin to tire, the shish kebab will give you strength to carry on.) The music begins at 8:30, the show at 10, except on Saturdays, when there are two shows, at 9 and 12. *Cl. Mon.*

Named for the god of wine and fertility, **Dionysus** (304 E. 48 St., First–Second Aves., 935-6480) is the poshest Greek night spot in town. There are singers at Dionysus, but it is the dancing waiters who set the pace, with dazzling footwork and the wild abandon of villagers at harvest time. The cocktail hour begins at 4, dinner at 6, live music at 9, floor show at 10. Dinner runs about $15 a person, and there is a $3.50 music charge. Open on Sundays? *Never*

FOLK MUSIC AND DANCE

The **Balkan Arts Center** (514 West 110 St., 222-0550) is a nonprofit organization that sponsors many Greek dance workshops and music festivals during the year. If you are interested, have your name added to their mailing list.

A group called **Paleoparea** often performs at the Balkan Arts festivals. Founded by Thanassis Galanoupoulos, a singer and guitarist from Greece, Paleoparea seeks to promote appreciation of authentic Greek folk music and *rebetika* (a form of *bouzouki* music that developed in the 1920s). Paleoparea also performs at the **Alternative Center for International Arts** (28 East 4 St., Lafayette–Bowery, 473-6072).

Holidays and Festivals

For New York's Greek-American community, January 1 is **St. Basil's Day,** a day to exchange gifts, see relatives and friends and feast on **gourounaki** (roast pig). The climax of the day comes with the cutting of the *vasilopeta,* a large cake in which a coin is hidden. Whoever gets the coin is bound to have good luck for the year.

In the Eastern church, **Epiphany,** on January 6, is a day for blessing the waters. On this day in New York, the city's Greek Orthodox arch-bishop casts a cross into the Hudson River, and eager young men dive to retrieve it (often under ice floes). It is considered lucky to be the one to bring it up. The biggest Epiphany ceremony in New York takes place at St. George's in Asbury Park, Queens.

The most important religious holiday of the year for Greeks is **Easter,** which, for the Greek Orthodox who follow the Julian calendar, usually comes anywhere from one to five weeks after Roman Catholic Easter. (Some Greek Catholics, however, celebrate Easter at the same time as the Roman Catholics.) One of the most beautiful religious rituals in the city takes place on Holy Saturday before Greek Easter Sunday at the Cathedral of the Holy Trinity (319 E. 74 St., BU8-3215), where, in an outdoor ceremony, the Greek Orthodox archbishop of New York raises a lighted candle and at the stroke of midnight, ushers in the Orthodox Easter celebration with the joyous singing of "Christ is Risen" in Greek. A crowd of worshippers holding candles of their own joins in the music, and a flame passes from candle to candle, bathing the scene in a blaze of light. All over New York on Holy Saturday, Greeks exchange red-dyed Easter eggs, symbolizing the renewal of life.

On Sunday morning, Greek families traditionally break the Lenten fast with *mageritsa,* an Easter soup made with the entrails of baby lamb and seasoned with spring onions and egg-lemon sauce. The traditional main course at Easter dinner is a whole baby lamb or baby kid roasted on a spit over coals. After dinner, everyone partakes of the *koulloria,* a sweet bread ring decorated with a red Easter egg.

Greek Independence Day on March 25 usually falls during Lent, and so the **Greek Independence Day Parade** usually comes after Easter, in April or May. School bands, floats of young women in Grecian robes and representatives of every Greek organization in the city take part in the parade, which follows Fifth Avenue up to the 70s. (For information, call RE7-0012 or WA9-4200.)

A few years ago, the Federation of Greek Students held a three-day **Greek Festival** in Astoria, Queens, and the event was such a hit that it has been repeated every year since. In various years, the festival has included a live reenactment of a traditional Cypriot marriage, traditional folk dancing by members of the community, displays of handicrafts and photographs and a student production of a modern Greek play. The outdoor festival is held in the back yard of Bohemian Hall (29-19 24 Ave., Astoria, Queens) on a weekend in late April or early May. Call the federation (274-3804; evenings are best) for information.

In early October, the **St. Nicholas Greek Orthodox Church of Flushing** (196-10 Northern Blvd.) holds a three-day **festival** with folk dancing, *bouzouki* music and a tour of the relics of St. Nicholas. The biggest attraction at this festival is the food—*souvlaki,* roast lamb on a spit and an incredible array of Greek pastries baked by the women of the parish. Call 357-4200 for information.

Throughout the year, the **Balkan Arts Center** (514 West 110 Street, 222-0550) holds Greek folk-music concerts and festivals.

GREEK FOOD

Greek food is hearty and filling. Lamb, fish and goat- or sheep's-milk cheese are the staple forms of protein in the Greek diet. Eggplant, artichokes, spinach, green beans, tomatoes and onions are the most common vegetables. Olive oil is the principal cooking fat. Greek desserts are very sweet combinations of honey, nuts and the flaky, many-layered strudel dough called *filo.* Greek coffee, served in a demitasse cup, is sweet, black and thick with coffee grounds.

MENU GLOSSARY

avgolemono: egg-lemon sauce or soup.
baklava: sweet, flaky pastry made with *filo,* honey and nuts.
dolmas or *dolmades*:   stuffed grape leaves.
doner kebab: molded cone of minced lamb cooked on a vertical rotisserie, slices of which are cut off and eaten with *pita* bread.
feta: strong, crumbly cheese usually made from goat's milk.
filo: strudel dough.
galactomboureko: flaky filo pastry filled with sweet milk custard.
guvetsi: lamb *guvetsi* is lamb baked with *orzo.*
gyro: same as *doner kebab.*
horta: dandelion greens, or just greens.
kasseri: sheep's-milk cheese.

kataifi: sweet shredded-wheat pastry.

kefalaki psito: baked lamb's head.

kefalotiri: sheep's-milk cheese.

kokoretsi: sweetbread, lamb liver and lamb heart wrapped in lamb intestines and grilled.

moussaka: baked eggplant casserole.

orzo: pasta in the shape of rice grains.

pastitsio: macaroni casserole made with ground lamb, cheese and bechamel sauce.

pita: flat, round Greek bread.

saganaki: baked cheese appetizer.

shish kebab: grilled, skewered chunks of lamb.

souvlaki: small shish kebab served on *pita* bread.

spanakopita: spinach-filo pie with feta cheese.

taramasalata: caviar spread made from fish roe, olive oil, lemon juice and bread crumbs.

tiropetes: *filo*-cheese pie.

tzatziki: cold soup or sauce of yogurt, olive oil, garlic and herbs.

SOME GREEK WINES AND SPIRITS

When it comes to the temperature at which wine should be served, Greek taste differs from most of the rest of the world's. The Greeks consider red wine too heavy to drink at room temperature: chilling lightens it. By the same logic, white wine is light enough to be served warm. In Manhattan, however, most Greek restaurants have adapted to non-Greek preferences.

mavrodaphne: sweet, strong after-dinner wine.

metaxa: *Greek cognac (7* is the best).*

ouzo: anise-flavored aperitif.

retsina: light, aromatic wine flavored with resin; goes well with all Greek food.

roditys: light rosé.

# HUNGARIAN NEW YORK

Little Hungary

Many of the old Hungarian residents have moved to the suburbs; luxury high-rises have replaced the old brownstones; and young singles of all ethnic backgrounds have moved into the neighborhood in droves. Despite all these changes, Little Hungary—Yorkville from the mid-70s to the mid-80s—retains an Old World flavor. Food shops crammed with European delicacies still stock *lekvar* by the barrel and sell paprika by the pound. Immaculate meat stores festooned with sausages continue to cater to a mostly European clientele. And cozy restaurants and patisseries still serve hearty goulashes and rich pastries guaranteed to uplift the spirit as they expand the waistline.

Although there have been Hungarians in this country since the days of the American Revolution, there was no Hungarian community in New York until the ill-fated Hungarian Revolution of 1848 started a wave of immigration to the United States. During the peak years—1880 to 1914—nearly half of the thousands who left Hungary for the "land of opportunity" settled in their port of entry, New York. The abortive Hungarian Revolution of 1956 added new members to the community, and since then, there has been a steady trickle of refugees. Today, including first, second, and third generations, there are an estimated 100,000 Hungarian-Americans in Greater New York.

New York's first Hungarian neighborhood was on the Lower East Side, near Houston Street and Avenues A and B. As new immigrants arrived, the Hungarians began to move uptown, and since 1905, Little Hungary has been a section of Yorkville below the German neighborhood and above the Czechoslovak. Second Avenue is the Broadway of Little Hungary.

HOW TO GET THERE
By subway: *Lexington Avenue IRT* #4 or #5 to 86 St. or #6 to 77 St. or 86 St. Walk east to Second Ave. **By bus:** *M15* (Second Ave. southbound, First Ave. northbound); or *M101 or M102* (Third Ave. northbound).

PAPRIKA AND LEKVAR
One day in New York before the turn of the century, a woman complained to her husband that she missed the kind of paprika she was used to in her native Hungary. Isidor Weiss took his wife's complaint seriously and sent to the town of Szeged, where the finest Hungarian paprika comes

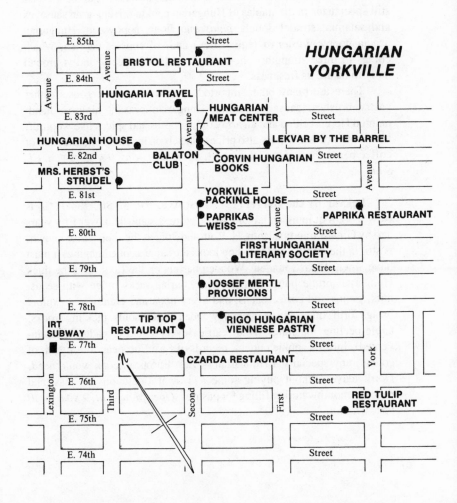

from, for two hundred pounds of the pungent red spice. When the shipment arrived, it wasn't long before neighbors began knocking at the door to beg or buy some. Mr. Weiss ordered more, and soon he began to peddle paprika in the neighborhood streets. Children cried out when they saw him coming, "Here comes Paprikas Weiss." Not long after, Mr. Weiss opened a little shop.

Two generations later, **Paprikas Weiss** (1546 Second Ave., 80–81 Sts., 288-6903) is one of the best-known gourmet stores in the city. The proprietor, Isidor's grandson Edward, keeps the shelves of this shop overflowing with items like Polish venison, Swiss chestnut puree, French truffles, Beluga caviar, Viennese raspberry drops, English cheeses and German spaetzle machines. True to its roots, however, Paprikas Weiss still specializes in the staples of Hungarian cooking: Hungarian sausages and salamis, strudel dough, *palascinta* flour, poppyseed, Hungarian acacia honey, *tarhonya* (egg barley) and, of course, paprika, which comes in three strengths—hot, sweet, and half-sweet—and is ground daily to insure its freshness.

There are many other imported items in this store: goose-feather pastry brushes, sausage stuffers, Hungarian peasant blouses, hand-painted Herend china and an array of rare herbs and spices like woodruff and mugwort. Mr. Weiss also prides himself on his excellent selection of coffee beans from around the world. *Open Mon.–Sat. 9* A.M.–*6* P.M. *Cl. Sun.*

Lekvar by the Barrel (1577 First Ave. cor. 82 St., 734-1110) is New York's quintessential Old World store. Established over fifty years ago by Great-Grandma Roth, H. Roth and Son, as the shop is also known, is still in the family, and the shop looks the same as one imagines it must have when it was founded. Wooden barrels on the floor hold the thick Hungarian prune butter called *lekvar*; burlap sacks bulge with seeds, nuts, grains and coffee beans; and every nook and cranny you explore brings forth something of interest: wooden butter molds, pickling crocks, apple-peeling machines (Roth carries every cooking gadget ever invented), bins of cookie cutters, records of East European music and, of course, any specialty a Hungarian or East European cook would need. Don't leave without buying some *lekvar*: it's delicious on toast and makes a mouthwatering filling for pastries. *Open Mon.–Sat. 9* A.M.–*6:30* P.M. *Cl. Sun.*

SALAMIS AND SAUSAGES

For Hungarian sausages, prime meats and the prized Hungarian Herz salami (some say it is the best dry salami ever made), head back to Second Avenue, where, within a few blocks of each other, three of the most appetizing meat shops in the city cater to a loyal following of European customers and gourmet cooks from all over New York.

At the spacious **Yorkville Packing House** (1560 Second Ave. cor. 81 St., 628-5147), you will find no less than thirty-six different kinds of salami, along with rice and goose liverwurst, old-country-style deep-fried belly pork, fried bacon chips (called *manna*), Hungarian potato bread and a wide selection of European preserves. *Open Mon.–Sat. 7 A.M.–7 P.M.*

Two blocks north, the tiny **Hungarian Meat Center** (1592 Second Ave., 82–83 Sts., 650-1015) is generally filled with Hungarian-speaking customers ordering paprika salami, liver sausage or perhaps some of the center's fine homemade bologna. *Open Mon.–Sat. 7 A.M.–7 P.M. Cl. Sun.*

Mertl's (1508 Second Ave., 78–79 Sts., RH4-8292) specializes in pork products: home-cured ham, fried pork cracklings (heat them for snacks or hors d'oeuvres), pig's feet and paprikas bacon—delicious paprika-coated Hungarian-style bacon that can be eaten hot or cold. Mertl's also makes the little bacon biscuits called *pogasca*. (Take warning: *pogasca* can become habit-forming, especially when warmed in the oven.) *Open Mon.–Sat. 7 A.M.–6 P.M. Cl. Sun.*

TRAVEL AND BOOKS

If you are planning a trip to Budapest, be sure to inquire at **Hungaria Travel** (1603 Second Ave. cor. 83 St., 249-9342) about this agency's very reasonable charter flights. Hungaria also offers one-, two-, and three-week tours of Hungary; the latter takes you to Budapest, Lake Balaton and throughout the Hungarian countryside. *Open Mon.–Sat. 9 A.M.–6 P.M. Cl. Sun.*

Armchair travelers will find Hungarian newspapers, magazines and books at **Corvin Hungarian Books** (1590 Second Ave., 82–83 Sts., 879-8893). If you don't read Hungarian, you will probably be more interested in the embroidered children's blouses and pillow cases. Hungarians come here for a service known is *ikka*—the transfer of money and gifts to friends and relatives in Hungary. *Open Mon.–Sat. 9 A.M.–7 P.M. Cl. Sun.*

CHURCHES AND CLUBS

Less conspicuous than the commercial establishments in Little Hungary are the churches and social clubs that dot the neighborhood and form its social underpinning. **St. Stephen's** (414 E. 82, First–Second Aves.), a large Roman Catholic Church, is the major neighborhood landmark of this sort. On the same street, farther west, are the much smaller Byzantine Rites Catholic Church, the Hungarian Reformed Church and a small Hungarian synagogue.

About six hundred senior residents of the neighborhood are members of **The First Hungarian Literary Society** (323 E. 79 St., First–Second Aves., 650-9435). When the society was first founded, its members used to discuss literature; now, almost any night of the week, visitors to the society's headquarters will find at least ten lively pinochle games in progress. Members of the **Balaton Club** (1586 Second Ave., cor. 82 St., 650-9097), named after Hungary's largest lake, prefer nursing an espresso for hours or playing a round of pool in the back of the club. Both clubs are open only to members and their guests.

Hungarian House (213 E. 82 St., Second–Third Aves., 249-9360), a red brick building, is used only for meetings or social events.

PASTRY SHOPS

For true devotees of Hungarian pastry (a fat but fanatic sect), there are only two reasons for coming to Little Hungary: Rigo Bakery and Mrs. Herbst's.

Rigo Bakery (318 E. 78, First–Second Aves., 988-0052) makes the best *rigo jansci* in town. Named after a famous Hungarian gypsy, this rich chocolate-cream confection falls somewhere between a cake and a mousse: Rigo's *rigo* is like a chocolate cloud. But don't overlook the poppyseed strudel, the *linzer* tarts filled with jam, or the *Dobos torte,* a splendid six-layer cake filled with chocolate frosting and crowned with a golden sheet of caramelized sugar. *Open Mon.– Sat. 8 A.M.–6:30 P.M.; Sun. 9 A.M.–5:30 P.M.*

Warm and cozy, its walls painted with pictures of happy Hungarian peasants, its kitchen bursting with good smells and good things to eat, **Mrs. Herbst's Strudel Shop** (1437 Third Ave., 81–82 Sts., 535-8484) looks like it just popped out of a children's storybook. Stop in one morning, sit down at one of the little blue formica tables in the back, order a coffee and croissant and—through the glass partition that divides the shop from the bakery—watch the sorcerers at work. Every once in a while, someone will come out bearing a tray of freshly baked temptations: a seductive *sacher torte* (apricot jam between chocolate layers), newly iced, meltingly lovely *petits fours* or perhaps some of the flaky strudels for which the place is justly famous. Regular patrons of Mrs. Herbst's may not be svelte, but they are generally too happy to care. *Open Mon.–Sat. 8:30* A.M.–*6* P.M. *Cl. Sun.*

RESTAURANTS

If it is mealtime and you had something more substantial than chocolate clouds in mind, you don't have to go far for a bowl of goulash soup or a plate of chicken paprikas. There is a restaurant nearby just about everywhere in this neighborhood that will suit every taste, whether you want a simple, unpretentious luncheonette that serves food with a homemade touch or a restaurant with the ambiance of a country inn; whether you like your goulash with gypsy violins or merely with a smile and sour cream.

With its dark beams and whitewashed walls hung with colorful hand-woven rugs and strings of dried red peppers, **Czarda** (1477 Second Ave., cor. 77 St., 472-2892, **M**) looks like an inn in the Hungarian countryside, and indeed, "country inn" is what *czarda* means in Hungarian. Start out with the excellent stuffed peppers in a sweet-sour tomato sauce, or the *lecsos kolbasa*, a stew of old Slavic origin made with garlic sausages, onions, green peppers, tomato and paprika. The paprikas dishes—chicken, veal or chicken livers smothered in a rosy paprika–sour cream gravy—are all deliciously prepared, as are the home-fried potatoes and delicate fried onion rings. Thin slices of cucumber in a sweet vinegar dressing accompany all dishes.

What to order for dessert? *Palascinta*, of course. Here these Hungarian dessert crepes are rolled around apricot jam and sprinkled with ground walnuts. Portions are generous. The waitresses are warm and efficient. Only wine and beer are served. *Open Mon.–Fri. 5* P.M.–*11* P.M.*; Sat. noon–11* P.M.*; Sun. noon–10* P.M.

Furnished with bare wooden tables, Hansel-and-Gretel chairs and colorful Hungarian folk art, the **Red Tulip** (439 E. 75 St., First–York Aves., 734-4893, **M–E**) is the most charmingly decorated restaurant in Little Hungary. The food is excellent (try the tart and creamy sour-cherry soup and the roast chicken prepared according to a secret family recipe). And since Hungarians feel that a meal in a restaurant should feed all the senses, a gypsy ensemble plays every night. (And rather loudly: this is no place to come for a quiet talk.) No reservations are accepted, so be prepared for long lines waiting to get in. *Open Tues.–Sun. 6* P.M.–*midnight. Cl. Mon.*

The winning formula at **Paprika** (1529 York Ave. cor. 81 St., 650-9819, **M**), a neighborhood institution for more than twenty years, is dependably good food, courtly Old World service and, perhaps, the warm red wallpaper. In recent years, Paprika has also added a gypsy band and a singer who performs in twelve languages. *Open Tues.–Sun. 11:30* A.M.*–3* P.M.*, 5* P.M.*–11:30* P.M. *Cl. Mon.*

Restaurants like **Tip-Top** (1489 Second Ave., 77–78 Sts., 650-0723, **C–I**), a nondescript-looking luncheonette, are rare in New York. The food here is just like the food mother used to make—if mom was Hungarian and a fantastic cook. The menu is extensive (you can get anything from a bowl of soup to a three-course roast-duck dinner or a Hungarian mixed grill) and the prices low. If you are willing to forego atmosphere in return for inexpensive, top-quality food, this is your Hungarian restaurant. It's worth a trip just for Mrs. Keszely's *palascinta*.

Do get the day's special soup, especially if it is cream of cauliflower. The homemade *nokkedly* (noodle dumplings) served with paprika gravy or, as a dessert, with walnuts or jam, are as comforting as mother's love. And the stuffed cabbage is just what it should be.

Tip-Top's juke box plays Hungarian melodies. Bring your own wine; the liquor store across the street imports Hungarian varieties. *Open daily 1* P.M.*–10:30* P.M. *Cl. Tues.*

For variety, you might try the **Bristol** (1636 Second Ave., 84–85 Sts., 988-1424, **I–M**), an unpretentious neighborhood restaurant. The Transylvanian goulash—veal cooked with sauerkraut, onions and paprika and topped with sour cream—is one of the best dishes in the house. *Open daily noon–11* P.M.*; Fri., Sat. until midnight.*

Around Town in Manhattan

PASTRY SHOPS

A sister to the Rigo Bakery in Yorkville is the just-as-wonderful **Rigo Bakery** a bit downtown (841 Madison Ave. cor. 70 St., 535-0158). *Open Tues.–Sun. 10* A.M.*–6* P.M. *Cl. Mon.*

On the Upper West Side, the **Hungarian Pastry Shop** (1030 Amsterdam Ave., 110–111 Sts., 866-4230) is a favorite meeting place for Columbia students, who flock here to linger over a cup of espresso and a piece of strudel. The pastries are not what they once were (the shop is no longer under Hungarian management), but Yorkville is far away, and for the residents of Morningside Heights, this patisserie is an oasis of warmth and good cheer. *Open Mon.–Thurs. 8* A.M.*–11:30* P.M.*; Fri, Sat. 9* A.M.*–9:30* P.M.

RESTAURANTS

Conceived by the creative Hungarian-born genius George Lang (whose corporation came up with the organizing concept for Citycorp Market), **Hungaria** (The Market at Citycorp Center, Lexington Ave. at 53–54 Sts., 755-6088, **E**) boldly breaks away from the flowered folk art approach of all the other Hungarian restaurants in the city, taking its inspiration instead from the traditional bourgeois Hungarian home. The restaurant is cleverly divided into several different dining spaces to give an illusion of intimacy and privacy while making maximum use of space. Curtained, semiprivate alcoves are hidden behind the wide, polished bar; in another section, three curtained, semiprivate dining rooms with painted "wallpaper" make you feel as if you are dining in a well-to-do Magyar home. The rest of the space is filled with banquettes and tables (here, however, the tables are too close together for true comfort). In the daytime, the focus of the room is a sausage "tree" hung with the Hungaria's own homemade salamis and *wursts*; at night, a panel in one corner of the room revolves to reveal a small stage for musicians who play under the stars that shine through a skylight.

Of course, no matter how cleverly it is designed, a restaurant's first obligation is to serve good food. And this Hungaria does, with chefs trained in Hungary who turn out a marvelous *gulyas* soup (you can get it here in a kettle, the way it was traditionally served, with warm *pita* bread, which you rub with a clove of garlic), delicious Hungarian sausages, perfectly poached blue trout and such unusual dishes as a fisherman's broth made with live carp (stored in tanks in the kitchen) and a "bridal soup" (chicken) garnished with quails' eggs. Not all the entrees live up to the fanfare of the menu (the Spiced Beef Tokony is a rather humdrum beef stew), but the desserts surpass all expectations. The *somlo* square cake—rich chocolate, chestnut puree, rum and whipped cream—is worth skipping the entree for, and the Deer Tongue—oval biscuits filled with a light custard—should not be missed—unless of course you have set your heart on the puree of chestnuts with vanilla whipped cream and chocolate liqueur. Hungarian wines and brandies are served.

When Hungaria opened, George Lang negotiated with the Hungarian government to bring one of the leading gypsy bands of Budapest over for a six-month stint at Hungaria. Since then, he has continued to feature Hungarian musicians of the highest caliber.

Hungaria is a stimulating rather than restful place to dine; it is always crowded and noisy. The waiters are efficient but rushed. Reservations are a must. *Open daily noon–3 P.M.; Mon.–Thurs. 5:30 P.M.–10:30 P.M.; Fri., Sat. 5:30 P.M.–11:30 P.M.; Sun. 5:30 P.M.–9 P.M.*

If you just want to sample Hungaria's pastries, you can eat at Hungaria's patisserie-café **Small Pleasures,** also in the Citycorp Market. In addition to pastries, Small Pleasures serves sandwiches, espresso and ice cream.

Jacques' Tik Tak (210 E. 58 St., Second–Third Aves., 753-5513, **M–E**) avoids ethnic reference altogether in its decor, but the menu is typically Hungarian and a gypsy band plays nightly. (There's also a pianist.) Try the scrambled eggs and brains with hot paprika, and whatever you order as an entree, ask for a side order of the fried onion rings: they are dipped in batter and sweet, and a specialty of the house. Reservations necessary. *Open daily noon–3* P.M.*, 5* P.M.*–midnight.*

Holidays and Festivals

On May 15, the Hungarian-American community commemorates Louis **Kossuth** and the struggle he led for independence in the Hungarian Revolution of 1848 with a parade from Yorkville to the statue of Kossuth which stands on Riverside Drive and 113th Street.

The first king of Hungary is honored with a parade sponsored by the Hungarian Catholic League on **St. Stephen's Day,** August 20.

Hungarian Food

The sophisticated cuisine of Hungary is both hearty and subtle. Soups and stews seasoned with paprika (Hungary's national spice) are a mainstay, and these are often accompanied by noodles or dumplings that soak up the rich goulash gravies or sour cream–paprika sauces. Stuffed peppers, stuffed cabbage and *fatanyeros* (a mixed grill of Transylvanian origin) are other well-known dishes of this cuisine.

Palascinta (crepes filled with apricot jam) is probably the most traditional Hungarian dessert; Hungarian cakes and pastries are among the richest and most seductive in the world.

MENU GLOSSARY

csipetke: tiny dumplings added to soups.

fatanyeros: mixed grill of breaded pork chops, veal cutlets, small steaks and sausages served on a wooden platter.

gulyas, goulash: soup or stew traditionally cooked in a kettle and made with cubed beef, veal or pork, onions and potatoes.

lesco: sausage-onion-pepper-tomato stew, often thickened with eggs.

nockeddli, nockerl: egg noodle-dumplings.

palascinta: thin dessert crepes filled with apricot preserves, nuts or sweetened cottage cheese.

paprikas: stew seasoned with paprika in which sour cream is blended into the gravy.

porkolt: thick stew of meat, onions and paprika.

Szekely gulyas: stew of cubed pork, cabbage, sour cream and paprika.

tarhonya: barley-sized grains of egg pasta.

Transylvanian gulyas: veal-sauerkraut stew topped with sour cream.

HUNGARIAN WINES

Most of New York's Hungarian restaurants stock at least a half-dozen imported Hungarian wines. *Egri-bikaver* (literally, "Bull's Blood of Eger") is a full-bodied burgundy. *Badacsonyi keknyelu* and *Badacsonyi Szurkebarat*, both from the vineyards on the slopes of the extinct volcano near Hungary's Lake Balaton, are two very good white wines. *Tokaji aszu* (Tokay) is Hungary's famous sweet dessert wine.

(EAST) INDIAN NEW YORK

Little India: The Spice Route

Columbus sailed halfway around the world to find a new route to the precious spices of India. But in New York, you need only take the Lexington Avenue subway to 28th Street to discover all the spices of the East. Here, in the cluster of little shops from 27th to 29th Streets on Lexington, you'll find pepper and poppyseed, fennel and fenugreek, cumin, coriander, caraway, cardamom and cloves. Green or dried, whole or freshly ground, heaped loose in wooden barrels or tightly packed in plastic bags, spices fill the air of every shop—and sometimes the street itself—with the pungent aromas of an Indian spice bazaar.

Sweet shops, sari shops and several Indian restaurants dot The Spice Route and 29th and 30th Streets between Lexington and Fifth Avenues. Although most Indians in New York live in Queens, Little India—the small enclave of Indian stores on and near Lexington Avenue in Manhattan—is *the* marketplace for Indian goods in New York. On Saturdays and Sundays, the shops are filled with sari-clad women, turbaned Sikh men and Indian families from all over the city and New Jersey who have come to do their weekly shopping.

As late as the mid-1960s, there was no Indian community in the city: only a handful of students, consulate officials and yogis. It was not until immigration laws were liberalized in 1968 that Indians began coming over in great numbers. Today New York's Indian population is well over 100,000 and growing fast.

In its variety of peoples and cultures, India is comparable to Europe, and New York's Indian community—which speaks thirteen Indian languages, represents every state in India and includes Hindus, Muslims, Christians, Sikhs, Jains, Zoroastrians and Jews—mirrors this diversity.

Whatever their ethnic or religious backgrounds, most Indian immigrants in New York are professionals—doctors, engineers, architects—or business people. And the great majority live in Flushing, Jackson Heights, Rego Park and Elmhurst, Queens. So large is the Indian community in this borough that Queens now boasts an authentic Hindu Temple, the only one of its kind in all of North America.

The temple is perhaps the most exotic sign of the growing Indian presence in New York, but there are many other signs: two full-time Indian movie theaters (one in Queens, one in Manhattan), over fifty Indian restaurants (ranging from tiny eat-and-run diners to lavishly appointed palaces), frequent performances of Indian music and dance and—Little India.

HOW TO GET THERE

By subway: *Lexington Avenue IRT* #6 to 28th St. and Park Ave. So. Walk one block east to Lexington Ave.; or *BMT* RR to 28 St. and Broadway. **By bus:** *M1* along Park Ave. So.; or *M101, M102* (northbound on Third Ave., southbound on Lexington Ave.).

LITTLE INDIA

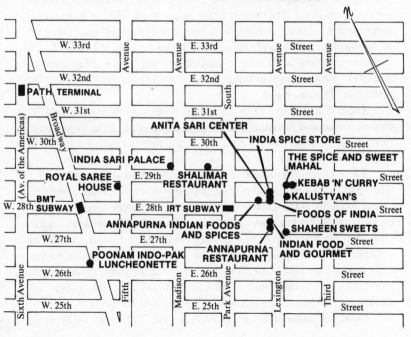

THE SPICE ROUTE

The spices in the shops of Little India are not only fresher and more flavorful than the bottled kind at your supermarket, they are generally far cheaper as well. While you are shopping for spices, you can stock up on the other staples of Indian cuisine—rice, nuts, dried lentils, wheat flours, pickles and chutneys, dried chilies, cooking oils and jars of golden *ghee* (clarified butter, which never needs refrigeration). If there is an exotic ingredient you have been omitting from your recipes because you can't find it at your local supermarket, chances are you will find it in one of these stores, whether it is asafetida or tamarind, dried pomegranate seeds or *jaggery*, rose water or Bombay duck (which is not a duck at all but a kind of fish).

Competing for space on the shelves of every store are also many nonfood items: massage oils, sandalwood soaps, incense, herbal medicines, tapes of Indian music and the stainless-steel trays and tumblers used for serving Indian food.

It is worth visiting at least two or three of the shops: prices differ slightly from one to another, and each has a character all its own.

Kalustyan's (123 Lexington Ave., 28–29 St., 685-3416), the oldest food and spice store in the neighborhood, was founded over forty years ago as a supplier of Turkish and Middle Eastern foodstuffs, and was the first shop in the area to cater to the Indian trade. Most of Kalustyan's business is wholesale, so the spices, nuts, dried fruits and grains here are stored loose in barrels and sold in bulk. There's a good selection of oils, including almond- and jasmine-scented coconut hair oil. Try some of Kalustyan's own mango or lime chutney. *Open Mon.–Sat. 10 A.M.–7:30 P.M.; Sun. 11 A.M.–6 P.M.*

India Spice Store (126 Lexington Ave., 28–29 Sts., 679-1151) carries Indian and Pakistani groceries, Bangladesh and Darjeeling teas, fresh coconuts in season, coconut graters and several kinds of *pappadum*. *Open daily 9 A.M.–8 P.M.*

The owners of **Annapurna** (127 E. 28 St., Park–Lexington Aves., 889-7540) are from the palm-fringed state of Kerala on India's Malabar coast. Aside from the usual Indian groceries, they carry special superhot pickles and Nilgiri tea from south India, instant *chappati*-makers, Indian tapes and records, Indian newspapers published in New York, jars of water from the holy River Ganges and a large selection of colorful posters depicting Hindu deities like the handsome, dusky blue (color-of-rain-clouds) Krishna, the monkey-god Hanuman and Lakshmi, goddess of wealth. *Open Mon.–Sat. 10 A.M.–7:30 P.M.; Sun. 12–5 P.M.*

Foods of India (120 Lexington Ave. cor. 28 St., 683-4419) is an exceptionally tidy shop with neatly stacked shelves of orange, yellow and green *dals* (dried lentils) and packages of spices. You can get all the ingredients to make Indian snacks here, including *bikanari sev* (chick-pea noodles) and *dalmoth* (a mixture of *sev*, lentils and spices). The shop also stocks snuff from Madras. *Open Mon.–Sat. 10* A.M.*–8* P.M.*; Sun. 11* A.M.*–5* P.M.

Indian Food and Gourmet (110 Lexington Ave., 27–28 Sts., 686-8955) carries a variety of ready-made Indian snacks (packaged without preservatives) and several varieties of loose Darjeeling tea in bulk, including inexpensive (but very good) Green Label Lipton and expensive (but worth it) top-grade Lop Chu. *Open Mon.–Sat. 10:30* A.M.*–7:30* P.M.*; Sun. 11:30* A.M.*–6* P.M.

The **Spice and Sweet Mahal** (135 Lexington Ave., cor. 29 St., 683-0900) has the usual spices and Indian staples, but the main attraction here is the counter of freshly made Indian sweets: milk-fudge *barfi*, little cakes of *ras malai* swimming in sweetened milk, spongy balls of fried *gulab jamun* dipped in rose water, chick pea–flour *laddoo* and sticky pretzels of orange *jalebi* oozing with syrup. You can also get fresh *kulcha* (a type of Indian bread made from white flour) here. *Open Mon.–Sat. 10* A.M.*–8* P.M.*; Sun. 11* A.M.*–6* P.M.

SARI STORES

The woman who wears saris never has to worry about the rise and fall of hemlines—or the dimensions of her waist. The sari's graceful floor-length design hasn't changed for centuries, and it fits all sizes.

There are several shops in Little India where you can purchase sari lengths of fabric, the long half-slips worn underneath and the tight-fitting *choli* blouses worn with the sari, which leave the midriff bare. Shop attendants will show you how to tuck one end of the sari into the waistband of the slip and then how to drape it around. An everyday sari of Japanese nylon fabric may cost as little as $15, one of elaborate gold-embroidered Benares silk (in richly saturated shades of peacock blue, magenta, red, green or purple) may run $100 or more and red silk wedding saris encrusted with gold thread cost several hundred dollars.

Anita Sari Center (124 Lexington Ave., 28–29 Sts., 683-4518) is a small shop with a large selection of silk, silk chiffon, silk brocade, nylon and cotton sari fabrics, ready-made *cholis* (Anita will also arrange to have *cholis* custom-made), sari slips and accessories such as handmade leather sandals, Indian perfume, jewelry and embroidered woolen shawls from Kashmir. *Open Mon.–Sat. 10* A.M.*–7* P.M.*; Sun. 12 noon–6* P.M.

India Sari Palace (102 Madison Ave., cor. 29 St., 725-5630) is the largest sari store in the area, with space enough for mannequins and counters of American cosmetics. All the salespeople are male. *Open Mon.–Sat. 10 A.M.–7 P.M.* **Uma** (30 E. 30 St., Park–Madison Aves., 532-1382) carries an especially good selection of Indian cottons and silks. *Open Mon. –Sat. 10 A.M.–7 P.M.; Sun. 12 noon–5 P.M.* **Royal Saree House** (262 Fifth Ave., 28–29 Sts., 889-3456) stocks mostly Japanese synthetics. *Open daily 10 A.M.–7 P.M.*

CURRY ON THE RUN
Strolling along the Spice Route with its tantalizing curry smells is bound to make you hungry. Luckily, there are several places en route or nearby to stop for lunch, including three fast-food eateries.

Kebab 'n' Curry (130 E. 29 St. nr. Lexington Ave., 683-0900, **C**) is an Indian cafeteria, with paper plates, self-service and lots of orange Formica. You can get a good, filling curry lunch here for $2.50 and up. The excellent Indian sweets come from the Spice and Sweet Mahal (same owners) next door. This is one of the few places in town where you can get *bhelpuri*—the spicy, savory Bombay snack of puffed rice and lentils. *Open Mon.–Sat. 11:30 A.M.–9 P.M.; Sun. 11:30 A.M.–7 P.M.*

Shaheen Sweets (99 Lexington Ave. cor. 27 St., 683-2139,**C**) is an Indian sweet shop and self-service curry luncheonette. The food and prices are on a par with Kebab 'n' Curry, so if one is crowded, try the other. *Open daily noon–9 P.M.*

A bit west of Little India proper, in the heart of an enclave of Indian import firms, is **Poonam Indo-Pak Luncheonette** (1141 Broadway, cor. 26 St., 689-4716, **C**), a tiny (eight-stool) diner where you can watch your *parathas* being grilled two feet from the counter. The daily special here, of chick-pea (*chana*) curry served with deep-fried puffs of Indian bread called *batura*, is fantastic and very cheap, but there are also other curries, and, on Thursday and Friday, *tandoori* chicken. Forget your fork here and scoop up your curry with bread, the way all the other diners do. And if you like it hot, spoon on the blazing chili-soaked raw-onion chutney. Free delivery. *Open Mon.–Sat. 7 A.M.–6:30 P.M. Cl. Sun.*

RESTAURANTS
For more leisurely dining, there are two reasonably priced Indian restaurants in Little India.

At **Annapurna** (108 Lexington Ave., 27–28 St., 684-8564, **I–M**), a mural of a sunset over a palm-fringed Kerala beach reminds you of the south Indian origins of the owners (who also own the Annapurna grocery around the corner). At lunchtime, you can get the south Indian paper-thin crepes called *dosa* here (filled with curried vegetables and eaten with spicy *sambar* and coconut chutney), but the dinner menu features north Indian cuisine. Annapurna's lamb *shahjahani* (lamb cooked in a sauce thickened with almond paste, according to a recipe that goes back to Emperor Shahjahan) and mildly-spiced shrimp *saag* (shrimp cooked with puree of spinach, onions and fresh mint) are outstanding, and the vegetarian thali—a large round tray bearing small dishes of vegetable curry, soupy *dal* and *rayta* as well as *pappadum*, rice and creamy, cardamom-scented *khir*—is uncommonly good. The Indian *masala* tea is spiced with cardamom. The waiters are very helpful in explaining and recommending dishes. *Open daily 11:30–3 P.M., 5 P.M.–11 P.M.*

The oldest Indian restaurant in the area is **Shalimar** (39 E. 29 St., Park–Madison Aves., 889-1977, **I–M**). Once considered one of the better moderately priced Indian restaurants in New York, Shalimar is not what it used to be. But it is one of the few, if not the only restaurant in the city, to offer such unusual (for restaurants in this country) regional Indian dishes as *Dhan Shak* (a Parsi dish from Bombay, of lamb cooked with lentils and vegetables), *Simla mirch* (vegetarian stuffed pepper as it is made in the Himalayan hill station, Simla), and Cochin crab meat (curried crab meat on the shell); each day, the menu features a different regional specialty. Shalimar is long, narrow and dimly lit; its white stucco walls are randomly embedded with bits of mirror and colored glass. *Open daily, noon–midnight.*

Around Town in Manhattan

MOVIES
Indians are avid moviegoers, supporting one of the world's largest motion picture industries. This enthusiasm for the cinema flourishes in New York's Indian community, which patronizes one full-time Indian movie theater in midtown Manhattan, another one in Queens, and a half-dozen movie clubs that screen Tamil, Telugu, and other regional-language films at school auditoriums every weekend. One Indian New Yorker who lives on the Upper West Side says he now has a better choice of Indian movies within walking distance than he did when he was living in Bombay!

Bombay Cinema (225 W. 57 St., Broadway-Seventh Ave., 581-4740) regularly features Hindi blockbusters, which, like many of our old Hollywood musicals, tend to be fluffy mixtures of melodrama, music, lavish sets and happy endings. Occasionally, the Bombay shows the more serious films of internationally acclaimed directors Satyajit Ray or Shyam Benegal.

MUSIC AND DANCE
Ever since the Beatles began using Indian instruments in their own music, Indian music has achieved a strong foothold in America, influencing both jazz and rock. New York offers many opportunities for hearing Indian music: musicians on tour from India always stop in New York, and the city has its own resident Indian musicians.

Vasant Rai, director of the **Alam School of Indian Classical Music** (220 W. 21 St., Seventh–Eighth Aves., 255-5066) and professional performer of the sarod (a lutelike, many-stringed instrument), studied with the late Alauddin Khan, father of Ali Akbar Khan and teacher of Ravi Shankar. His school offers instruction in the sarod, sitar, flute and voice. Mr. Rai, who has toured the United States and Europe, frequently performs in New York and, when time permits, he and his staff give demonstrations at schools in the New York area.

At the **Kirana Center for Indian Classical Music** (275 Church St., Franklin–White, 966-4089), Pren Nath teaches the intricate art of raga singing to advanced students. His disciples, La Monte Young and Marian Zazuela, teach beginners and Pren Nath's classes when he is away. Pren Nath occasionally gives a recital at the center, and since a raga, or melody, is always associated with a particular time of day, the center attempts to present him in morning, afternoon and evening concerts.

Concerts of Indian music are also frequently given at the **Alternative Center for International Arts** (28 E. 4 St., Lafayette St.–Bowery, 473-6072), as well as major concert halls in midtown.

Indian **classical dance**, with its symbolic hand gestures and expressive eye movements, intricate stamping rhythms and sumptuous costumes, is very exciting to watch even if you are unfamiliar with the subtleties of its tradition. New York boasts several resident Indian dancers, and visiting dancers from India always perform in New York. New York is also the home of a Punjabi men's folk dance club called **Young Living Hearts of the Punjab,** which frequently performs the vigorous North Indian dance known as *bhangra* at Indian festival celebrations during the year. To find out about upcoming performances, check the calendar of events in *India Abroad* or *News and Ciné India*, available at Annapurna, Foods of India, Anita Sari Center, and other shops in Little India.

ART

About a half-dozen galleries on Madison Avenue from 72nd to 76th Street specialize in Indian art or include Indian art in their collections. One of the best known in this cluster is **William H. Wolff** (22 E. 76 St. nr. Fifth Ave., 988-7411). Mr. Wolff deals in Far Eastern antiquities ("Seventeenth century is modern to me," he says), particularly in sculpture. His prices range from several hundred dollars to figures in six digits. *Open Mon.–Sat. 10 A.M.–5 P.M.*

Doris Wiener (41 E. 57 near Madison Ave., 593-1270) deals in Indian miniatures and bronze statues from India and Southeast Asia. *Open Tues.–Sat. 10:30 A.M.–6 P.M. Cl. weekends in July and Aug.*

Ed Waldman (231 E. 58 St., Second–Third Aves., 838-2140) has a fascinating collection of Indian folk art, including temple hangings, erotic Tantric art and rare paintings by the Warlis, an isolated tribal people who live several hundred miles from Bombay. *Open Mon.–Sat. 9 A.M.–5:30 P.M.*

The nonprofit **Asia Society** (112 E. 64, Park–Lexington Aves., PL1-3210) occasionally mounts an exhibit of Indian art in its gallery. The Society also sponsors lectures and programs on Indian art and culture.

RESTAURANTS

If you ask an Indian New Yorker to recommend a good place to get Indian food, he or she will invariably mention **Tandoor** (40 E. 49 St. off Madison Ave., 752-3334, **M–E**), a large, plush restaurant that specializes in *tandoori* cooking.

Tandoori refers to chicken, meat or fish that has been marinated in a blend of yogurt and spices and then grilled over charcoal in a jar-shaped clay oven called a *tandoor*. Chicken *tandoori*—roasted red-brown on the outside and succulent and moist within—would score high in any contest of the world's great chicken dishes, and the *tandoor*-baked *nan* that is always served with *tandoori* grill is one of the world's most delicious breads. As you would hope in a restaurant of this name, Tandoor's *tandoori* is superb.

While you are enjoying your *tandoori*, you can watch the cooking process through the glass walls of a tandoor kitchen. Don't feel obligated to get tandoori, however: everything on the menu is well prepared. The fly in the ointment: when it's crowded, service sometimes grinds to a near-halt. *Open Mon.–Sat. 11:30 A.M.–2:30 P.M.; daily 5:30 P.M.–10:30 P.M.*

· **Raga** (57 W. 49 St., Rockefeller Ctr., 757-3450, **E**) is New York's most opulent Indian Restaurant. All the furnishings in the high-ceilinged, palatial dining room—carved wooden pillars, striped rugs, the green silk that covers the banquettes and pillows at the bar—were brought from India. Antique Indian musical instruments hang on the walls.

The menu features north Indian Mughal cuisine, with some unusual dishes such as Murg Ki Chat—chicken and potatoes in a tamarind sauce—and oyster appetizers with fresh ginger. Raga's chefs and managers were trained at the world-famous Taj Mahal Hotel in Bombay, and though there were some rough edges when the restaurant first opened, the food and service seem to have smoothed out to consistently first-class. Live Indian music. *Open Mon.–Fri. noon–2:45 P.M., 5 P.M.–10:45 P.M. Sat., Sun. 5 P.M.–10:45 P.M.*

Gaylord (50 E. 58 St., Madison–Park Aves., 759-1710, **M–E**), a branch of a famous restaurant chain in India, was once considered the best Indian restaurant in New York. Gaylord has since slipped from its pedestal, partly because its success as the first "high-class" Indian restaurant in the city paved the way for the opening of other restaurants of this type. Many members of New York's Indian community still think highly of Gaylord, however, and many of the dishes served here, including the lamb *vindaloo*, lamb *pasanda* and chicken *do piaza*, are beyond reproach. (The "Quick Lunch," however, may take up to forty minutes to show up at your table.) Indian folk art adorns the walls, seating is comfortable, lighting dim. A palmist circulates predicting futures (for a contribution), and on Sunday, there's a special brunch and entertainment in the form of Indian music, films and guest speakers. *Open Mon.–Fri. 11:30 A.M.–3 P.M., 5:30 P.M.–11 P.M.; Sat., 5:30 P.M.–11 P.M.; Sun. brunch noon–3 P.M., dinner 5:30 P.M.–11 P.M.*

The chic, sleek, spacious **Shazan** (8 W. 58 St. off Fifth Ave., 371-1414, **E**) specializes in the Muslim cuisine of Pakistan and north India. "What we serve here is the food we ate in our own home," says owner-manager Maisie Krikliwy, who comes from Lahore, and who maintains that authentic Pakistani Muslim cuisine need not be highly spiced nor swimming in sauces. If you dine here, be sure to order the superb *seekh kabab Mughlai* (ground beef mixed with spices and herbs and cooked in a *tandoor*). Shazan's rice *pulao* made with fragrant Pakistani *basmatti* rice cooked in chicken stock, is one of the best *pulaos* in the city. The delicious halwa, made with carrots, dates, nuts and milk, is served warm.

Judging from the decor—neutral gray carpeting on the walls,

travertine floors, shiny reflecting ceiling and Bauhaus-style chairs—one would never know this is an Indian restaurant. Candle-lamps and brass plates glow on every table. The service is smoothly professional. *Open Mon.–Fri. noon–3* P.M., *6* P.M.*–11* P.M.*; Sat. 6* P.M.*–11* P.M. *Cl. Sun.*

Madras Woodlands (310 E. 44 St., First–Second Aves., 986-0620, **M**) is the only exclusively south Indian restaurant in New York and probably the only purely vegetarian (no meat, no fish, no eggs) one. Happily, it is also very good.

The cuisine of Hindu south India which is served here remained uninfluenced by the tastes of the meat-eating Moghuls who ruled north India for centuries. Besides being vegetarian, it is spicier, starchier and often hotter than north Indian cuisine.

Try Woodlands' *masala dosa* (huge, paper-thin rice-lentil crepes wrapped around a filling of spiced potatoes, onions and nuts), which you eat with *sambar* (spicy lentil puree) and fresh coconut chutney. The *iddly* (steamed lentil patties, served as an appetizer here) have a slightly sour, pleasantly bland flavor and a very satisfying texture. The *gobhi masala* (a rich cauliflower curry) is a knockout when eaten with balloons of *batura* (huge puffs of deep-fried Indian bread). The special *uppuma* (cereal mixed with tomatoes, vegetables and cashews) is worth ordering on the side. If you like *hot* chutney, order the special mixture of coriander and green chilies.

If it is your first visit to Madras Woodlands, the waiter will do his best to talk you into getting the New York Special—a sampler of south Indian foods. Let him persuade you, but if there are two of you, one of you order something else (perhaps the *gobhi masala* or a vegetarian *thali*) and share, or you will end up with a very starchy meal. The frothy Mysore coffee, served with milk, is deliciously strong and sweet.

There are two dining areas: a red-and-black one where the bar is, and another larger room furnished with Indian-style chairs and tables. Service is solicitous; Indian music plays softly in the background. On weekends, the place is filled with Indian families. *Open Mon.–Fri. noon–2:30* P.M., *5:10* P.M.*–10:30* P.M.*; Sat., Sun. 1* P.M.*–10:30* P.M.

Tucked away up a long flight of stairs, **Nataraj** (807 Lexington Ave., 62–63 Sts., 832-9438, **I–M**) is extraordinary only in that it is a good, modestly priced Indian restaurant in a very expensive part of midtown—a place to remember if you're shopping or seeing a movie in the area. *Open daily noon–3* P.M., *5* P.M.*–10* P.M.

Established in 1913 by a former Ceylonese stick dancer who had traveled with the Ringling Brothers Circus, **Ceylon India Inn** (149 W. 49 St. nr. Seventh Ave., 730-9293, **M**) is the oldest Indian restaurant in

New York, which also makes it the oldest Indian restaurant in America. The inn has been at its present upstairs location (now over a topless bar) in the theater district since 1924. The main attraction at Ceylon India Inn is not the food, which is only passable, but the present owner, Rustam Wadia, who is a Parsi (Zoroastrian) from Bombay and a born storyteller. Ask Mr. Wadia to join you, and he will regale you with delightful tales about his life and the characters (including Sabu!) whom he has known. *Open Mon.–Fri. noon–11 P.M.; Sat. noon–11:30 P.M.; Sun. 5 P.M.–10 P.M.*

Around Town in Queens

Its sculptured white tower rises high above the telephone wires on a quiet street in Flushing; inside, black granite sculptures of Hindu gods stand like gigantic chess pieces on a white marble floor. Built in 1977 by workers and stonecarvers sent for from Andhra Pradesh, the **Hindu Temple** (45–57 Bowne St. between Holly Ave. and 45 Ave., Flushing, 539-5262) is modeled after the temples built in south India over two thousand years ago: it is the only genuine Hindu temple in all of North America.

The Hindu Temple welcomes visitors. *Puja* (the presentation of offerings to the gods) is conducted daily, but most visitors come on weekend mornings, when there are special ceremonies as well. Be prepared to leave your shoes at the door (a Hindu gesture of respect for a holy place).

On Saturday and Sunday mornings, before the chanting begins, worshippers walk around the central room of the temple, stopping before the god standing in each corner: Siva (represented by a stone phallus); the six-faced Shanmuga; Lord Vishnu; and Lakshmi (goddess of wealth). In the center of the room is a statue of the elephant deity, Ganesh—god of wisdom and remover of obstacles. Offerings of coconuts, oil and flowers are placed before the gods by the temple priest.

When the chanting begins, you may join the worshippers seated crosslegged on a rug facing the elephant god. Afterward, the priest pours a libation of milk over Ganesh and then showers this cheerful-looking deity with handfuls of rose petals.

To get to the Hindu Temple by *subway*, take the *Flushing IRT #*7 to Main St. Change to *Q27* bus; get off at Holly Ave. By *car*, take Main St. exit on Long Island Expressway, go north on Main, turn right onto Franklin Ave., cross Kissena Blvd. and Union St., turn right on Bowne.

A short walk from the Hindu Temple, **Kalpana** (42-75 Main St., Franklin–Cherry Aves., 961-4111) offers one-stop shopping for Indian groceries, supplies and records. The Kalpana Bookstore in this row of shops carries English-language comic books based on the Hindu epics and Indian history—a nice way to introduce Indian culture to a child. The **Kalpana Indian Restaurant** (42-87 Main St., 939-0500, **M**) is quite good. The Kalpana shops are *open Tues.–Sun. 10* A.M.–*7:30* P.M. *Cl. Mon.*

Bombay Cinema (99 St. at Long Island Expressway, Rego Park, 271-6464) is the Indian movie theater in Queens.

Festivals and Holidays

Central Park Mall (entrance 72 St.) is the site of the annual **India Festival** held in June or July. The festival features performances of Indian music and dance, sari fashion shows and food stalls selling Indian snacks and sweets. (Check Indian newspapers in Little India for information.)

Divali, the Hindu Festival of Lights, is usually celebrated in November (the date is decided by the lunar calendar). On Divali (also called Deepavali), the darkest night of the year, every family lights lamps to show returning souls the way back to earth. Divali marks the beginning of the Hindu New Year, and Indian stores in New York always advertise special sales in this season.

All Hindu holidays, including Divali, **Dussehra** (which comes in September or October and commemorates the triumph of Prince Rama over the evil demon Ravana) and **Holi** (the spring Festival of Love) are celebrated in New York with social get-togethers, traditional foods and cultural programs. For information about programs on these days, or on **Indian Independence Day** (August 15) or **Republic Day** (January 26), check *India Abroad*, available in shops in Little India.

The most important festival of the year for Indian and Pakistani Muslims is **Ramadan**, a month of general prayer and fasting culminating in a great feast and celebration. Ramadan generally comes in late August or September. (For details, call the Islamic Center, 362-6800).

Indian Food

Indian food is highly seasoned, though not necessarily hot. While some dishes set the mouth afire, others are quite bland or only mildly tingling to the tongue. Usually restaurants indicate their hottest dishes on the menu.

Because of the Hindu proscription against meat, India—especially south India—has developed a varied and delicious vegetarian cuisine. In north India, however, meat—especially lamb and chicken—is very important. Rice is a staple in both cuisines. North Indian cuisine is famous for its kebabs, wheat-flour unleavened breads and *tandoori* dishes, which are baked in a clay oven. *Masala dosa* and *iddli* are the best-known south Indian dishes. Almost all of New York's Indian restaurants serve north Indian cuisine, and all include a selection of vegetarian dishes on their menus.

Carrot *halwa*, rice pudding, spiced ice cream and condensed-milk or syrup-soaked fritter sweets are the most typical Indian desserts and are usually accompanied by good Indian tea, often spiced with cardamom (though south Indians prefer their own delicious coffee). Ice-cold beer goes better than wine with spicy Indian curries. A refreshing nonalcoholic Indian yogurt drink is *lassi*.

MENU GLOSSARY

achar: hot pickle.

alu, aloo: potato.

bhelpuri: Bombay snack of puffed rice, lentils, onions, herbs.

bhindi: okra.

bhujia, bujia: vegetable fritters (chick-pea flour batter).

bhuna: cooked dry, with little or no sauce.

biriani: Moghul dish of lamb, beef or chicken cooked with rice, spices and nuts.

chat, chaat: sauce made with potatoes, onions, tomatoes, radishes and mint.

chawal: plain boiled rice.

curry: English approximation of south Indian Tamil word *kari*, meaning "sauce." On most Indian menus, it means any dish cooked with a sauce.

dal, dhal: mild lentil puree.

do peaza, do piaza: cooked with onions.

dosa, dosai: paper-thin rice-and-lentil crepes (so. India).

firni: rice pudding.

ghee: clarified butter.

gobhi: cauliflower.

gosht: lamb.

halwa: confection made from condensed milk, grated carrots or fruit and sugar and nuts.

iddly: steamed lentil patties (so. India).

kababs: small pieces of meat or fish or vegetables broiled on a skewer.

katchumber: mixed salad of cucumber, tomatoes, onions.

keema: ground meat.

khir, kheer: special rice cooked with milk and sugar, served with nuts.

kofta: ground meatballs.

korma;   cooked with yogurt or cream.

kulfi: Indian ice cream flavored with cardamom and saffron.

lassi, lhassi: spiced yogurt drink, may be sweet or salted.

makhani, makhanwala: usually chicken *makhani—tandoori* chicken cooked in tomato-butter sauce.

masala: blend of spices.

mattar paneer: pressed cubes of homemade cottage cheese cooked with green peas, yogurt and spices.

mulligatawny: spicy soup, often with a chicken broth base.

murg, murgh: chicken.

nargisi kofta: spiced ground lamb packed around hard-boiled eggs.

pakora: fritter appetizers.

pillaw, pillao, pullao: rice cooked with spices, herbs, often mixed with meat, seafood or vegetables, nuts and dried fruits.

raita, rayta: salad of yogurt mixed with raw vegetables or fruits and herbs.

rasam: thin, very hot lentil soup (so. India).

rava dosa: lacy, crispy rice-lentil crepe (so. India).

sag, saag: spinach.

sambar, sambhar: spicy, thin lentil puree (so. India).

samosa: deep-fried turnover stuffed with spiced ground meat or potatoes and peas.

seekh kabob: minced or ground lamb mixed with spices, herbs and onions and cooked on skewers over charcoal.

shorba: soup.

tandoor: north Indian clay oven shaped like a huge jar; uses a charcoal fire.

tandoori: cooked in a *tandoor*, usually marinated in yogurt and spices first.

thali: large, round, shallow tray. A vegetarian thali holds small bowls of vegetable curries, a mound of rice, dal, yogurt or raita, pickles and pappadum.

uppuma: cereal cooked with spices and vegetables (so. India).

vindaloo: curry made with vinegar base, usually searing hot.

Indian breads

batura, bhatura: large, puffy, white-flour bread, deep-fried in oil.

chappati: thin wheat-flour bread cooked on a griddle without butter.

kulcha: fine, soft, white-flour bread, often stuffed with onions.

nan, naan: teardrop-shaped, soft, white-flour bread baked against the inside wall of the *tandoor* oven.

papad, pappadum: paper-thin, crispy lentil-flour wafer, spiced with pepper and cooked in oil.

paratha: multilayered whole-wheat-flour bread grilled with butter.

puri: small puffy breads deep-fried in oil.

ITALIAN NEW YORK

Little Italy

Italians have played an important role in the history of New York City ever since 1524, when Giovanni de Verrazano, a Florentine navigator, sailed into the harbor of what was to become New York and became the first European to set eyes on Manhattan.

A number of Italians were among the residents of Dutch New Amsterdam, and a small group of Waldensians (Italian Protestants) are thought to have settled in Stony Brook, Staten Island, in 1657. In the first half of the nineteenth century, many Italian revolutionaries found refuge in New York after a series of unsuccessful uprisings in Italy against Austrian rule. By 1880, there were about twelve thousand Italians living in New York City, most of them from northern Italy.

The great floodtide of Italian immigrants rolled in between 1880 and 1910, when severe poverty, overpopulation and cholera and malaria epidemics in southern Italy drove over three million Italians to leave their birthplace and settle in America (which, at the time, was in the midst of rapid industrial expansion and in need of masses of unskilled labor). Millions of immigrants were streaming into the country from all over Europe during these decades, but no group of newcomers was as numerous as the Italians.

Most of these Italian immigrants came from the southern part of the country—from Sicily, Abruzzia, Calabria, Apulia. Almost 80 percent were men who sent the money they made in their adopted land back home to their families in Italy, or got seasonal work and returned to their homeland every year.

The most heavily populated Italian area of the city in this period was Mulberry Bend (the lower portion of Mulberry Street, which curves between Park and Bayard Streets). The Italian colony stretched north from there to Houston Street and east and west from Broadway to the

Bowery. Mulberry Bend became notorious for its squalid tenements and extreme overcrowding and was eventually torn down to be replaced by Columbus Park. Today, Columbus Park is in the heart of Chinatown, and the southern border of Little Italy has receded to Canal Street.

World War I and the quota system severely restricted Italian immigration after 1910. And today, although the quota system is no longer in effect, only about twenty thousand Italians enter the United States every year. Of these, thousands remain in New York City.

The Italian-American population in New York today is estimated to be over 1.5 million. The great majority are of southern Italian ancestry, but within the broad division of north and south, there are many smaller subgroups based on regional or town affiliations. Even today, there are still sections of the city populated by immigrants or descendants of immigrants all of whom come from the same village in Italy. A neighborhood in Carroll Gardens, Brooklyn, for example, still maintains close ties with its "hometown"—Pozzallo, Sicily.

The oldest Italian quarter in New York, Little Italy today is also one of the city's biggest tourist attractions. At night, neon signs illuminate the main street—Mulberry—advertising cafés and restaurants, and on weekends, these "neighborhood" establishments overflow with visitors from other parts of town. Behind its plastic pizza parlors and carnival air, however, there does exist a true neighborhood in Little Italy—a community of families who have lived here so long and know each other so well that in the summer, they often leave the doors to their apartments wide open to catch any passing breeze, without fear of burglars.

In recent years, the neighborhood has undergone a face-lift. The old six-story tenements bristling with fire escapes are still there, looking much the same as they did over a half-century ago, but many of the storefronts and restaurants have been renovated by Morello and Savoie, two young architects who have added the clean, sleek lines of modern Italian design to the old-fashioned, ornate Italianate that used to prevail.

Despite such signs of new life, Little Italy is shrinking. Of the fourteen thousand people who live in the neighborhood, only 60 percent are still Italian-American. The young people do not stay, and as immigrants from Hong Kong pour into bordering Chinatown, more and more signs like Tai Wai Sportswear are turning up next to the Caffee Napolis in the old Italian neighborhood. Still, the visitor will find Italian restaurants, bakeries and cafés galore, and there is no mistaking Mulberry above Canal for anything but an Italian street.

Many New Yorkers make an annual pilgrimage to Little Italy for the

San Gennaro Festival in September, when a statue of the saint is paraded up and down Mulberry Street, which becomes a fairground of food and game booths. The festival is a spectacle worth seeing, but to explore the neighborhood itself, go on a summer evening, when the sidewalks are filled with women sitting in folding chairs, men wandering in and out of "members only" clubs, children playing and tourists strolling—the latter two usually with *gelati* in hand. Off in the distance, the Empire State Building rises high above the tenements of Mulberry, a reminder that this Italian "village" exists in one of the biggest cities in the world.

HOW TO GET THERE
By subway: *Lexington Ave. IRT* #6 to Canal St. or Spring St.; or *IND* D, B, or F to Broadway-Lafayette-Houston; or *BMT* N or RR to Canal St.–Broadway. **By bus**: *M15* (First Ave. northbound, Second Ave. southbound); or M102 (Third Ave.–Bowery).

Suggested Walking Tour: Mulberry Street from Canal to Prince streets, with side trips down Grand St. to Elizabeth St., Broome St. to Mott St. and Spring St. to Lafayette St.

CHEESE, MEAT, PASTA AND BREAD
No one who lives in or near Little Italy shops in a supermarket. People go to one store for their cheese, another for their bread, a third for their pasta, a fourth for their meat. The Italian food stores carry specialties that attract customers from all over, including, on occasion, tourists from Italy who crave the taste of home. Prices for domestic and imported Italian food products are substantially cheaper here than at uptown gourmet shops.

Alleva Dairy (188 Mulberry St. cor. Grand St., 226-7990), a cheerful, old-fashioned *latticini freschi* with molded tin ceiling and sawdust on its tiled floor, has been supplying the residents of Little Italy with fresh homemade ricotta and mozzarella cheese since 1892. Alleva's mozzarella, made fresh daily (as is the ricotta), comes plain, smoked, unsalted, rolled up with *prosciutto* (slice in spirals as an appetizer) or as *manteche* (rolled around a ball of butter, an old Italian way of preserving butter). Alleva also carries a few imported cheeses, including *taleggio* (made from dry, salted curds) and *stracchino* (a lightly sharp Gorgonzola). Huge logs of imported provolone hang from the ceiling, sharpening in flavor as they age. *Open Mon.–Sat., 8:30 A.M.–6 P.M.; Sun. 8:30 A.M.–2 P.M.*

Di Palo's Dairy (206 Grand St. cor. Mott St., 226-1033) also makes fresh ricotta and mozzarella daily (some of the mozzarella is fashioned into small giraffes and horses). But Di Palo's is best known for its wide selection of imported cheeses and salamis. Around 6 P.M., the small store is crammed with people on their way home from work, all clamoring for gorgonzola, Sicilian pepper cheese, olives or prosciutto ham. Get some of the creamy basil *mascarpone*, a natural cream cheese from northern Italy layered with gorgonzola and flavored with basil. When melted, *mascarpone* becomes a sauce for pasta, but it can also be eaten unmelted, with crackers or fruit. *Open Mon.–Sat. 8:30 A.M.–7 P.M.; Sun. 8:30 A.M.–2 P.M.*

Across the street from Alleva's on Mulberry, is the **Italian Food Center** (186 Grand St., 925-2954), where you can get wonderful hero sandwiches and *pizza rustica* (a deep-dish cheese-pork-onion pie) as well as imported olive oils, canned tomatoes, pasta of all kinds, Italian-cured ham, salamis, bread sticks, pignoli nuts, grated parmesan, dried red pepper and just about any staple you can think of for Italian cooking. At the antipasto counter, there are marinated artichokes and seafood salad. *Open daily 8 A.M.–8 P.M.*

For fresh pasta, everyone in Little Italy goes to **Piemonte's Ravioli** (190 Grand St. next to Alleva's, 226-0475). Once you have tasted the fresh ravioli, fettucini or *gnocchi* made here, it is impossible to go back to supermarket-packaged macaroni. Fresh pasta, by the way, needs to be cooked only four or five minutes. If you're not going to use it within a day or two, freeze the pasta and cook without thawing (frozen, it takes a little longer). *Open Mon.–Sat. 8 A.M.–6 P.M.; Sun. 8 A.M.–3 P.M.*

For the finest imported pasta from Italy, stop in at **D. Lampariello and Son** (210 Grand St., Elizabeth–Mott Sts., 226-3441), a U.S. distributor for DeCecco pasta, which is made in the town of Faro St. Martino in the Abruzzi region. DeCecco pasta is famous among gourmet cooks for its ability to absorb a sauce. Along with fettucini or spaghetti, try a pasta you have never had before, like whole wheat thin spaghetti or *lingue de passero* ("sparrow's tongues"). *Open Mon.–Fri. 8 A.M.–5 P.M.; Sat. 8 A.M.–1 P.M. Cl. Sun.*

Esposito Meats (120 Mulberry, Canal–Hester Sts., 226-0050) is the place to go for thin shells of pounded veal or fresh Italian sausages. *Open Mon.–Sat. 7 A.M.–6 P.M. Cl. Sun.*

For good Italian bread, without which no Italian dinner is complete, walk up to **Parisi Bakery** (98 Mott St., Spring– Kenmare Sts., CA6-6378), a shop that has been in the business of bread making for over seventy-five years. In addition to its crusty loaves of four-corner bread

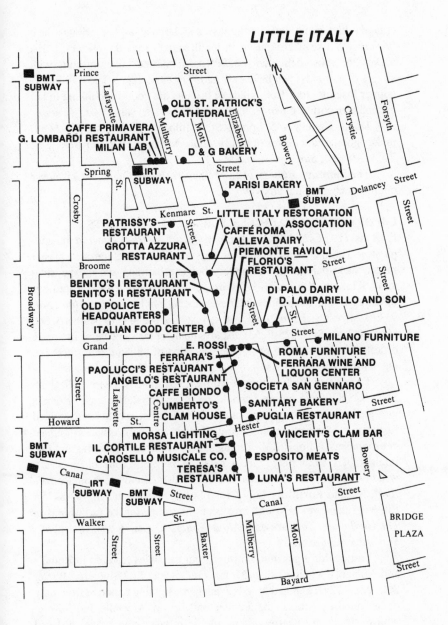

LITTLE ITALY

BMT SUBWAY

Prince Street

Lafayette

Mulberry

Mott

Elizabeth

Bowery

Chrystie

Forsyth

OLD ST. PATRICK'S CATHEDRAL

CAFFE PRIMAVERA
G. LOMBARDI RESTAURANT
MILAN LAB

D & G BAKERY

Spring Street
St.

IRT SUBWAY

PARISI BAKERY

BMT SUBWAY

Delancey Street

Street

Crosby

Kenmare St.

LITTLE ITALY RESTORATION ASSOCIATION

PATRISSY'S RESTAURANT

CAFFÉ ROMA
ALLEVA DAIRY

GROTTA AZZURA RESTAURANT

PIEMONTE RAVIOLI
FLORIO'S RESTAURANT

Broome

Street

BENITO'S I RESTAURANT
BENITO'S II RESTAURANT

DI PALO DAIRY
D. LAMPARIELLO AND SON

OLD POLICE HEADQUARTERS

Broadway

ITALIAN FOOD CENTER

St.

Street

Grand

MILANO FURNITURE

E. ROSSI

ROMA FURNITURE

FERRARA'S

FERRARA WINE AND LIQUOR CENTER

PAOLUCCI'S RESTAURANT
ANGELO'S RESTAURANT

Street

SOCIETA SAN GENNARO

Lafayette

CAFFE BIONDO

SANITARY BAKERY

Centre

UMBERTO'S CLAM HOUSE

PUGLIA RESTAURANT

Street

Howard

St.

Hester

MORSA LIGHTING

VINCENT'S CLAM BAR

BMT SUBWAY

IL CORTILE RESTAURANT
CAROSELLO MUSICALE CO.

ESPOSITO MEATS

Bowery

Canal

TERESA'S RESTAURANT

LUNA'S RESTAURANT

IRT SUBWAY

BMT SUBWAY

Street

Street

Walker

St.

Baxter

Mulberry

Mott

Canal Street

Street

BRIDGE PLAZA

Bayard

Street

(shaped like squat Ionic columns) and large-as-a-plate whole-wheat *biscotti* ("I like it broken up in lentil soup," says the owner), Parisi makes the most delicious *friselle* (hard, toasted butter biscuits with slivers of almonds) you have ever had. Try the *darelles* (lard-and-black-pepper biscuits) too. Both kinds of biscuits are good for dunking in hot chocolate or coffee. *Open Mon.–Sat. 8 A.M.–6 P.M.; Sun. 8 A.M.–12 noon.*

D&G Bakery (45 Spring St., Mulberry–Mott Sts., 226-6688) makes good round loaves of hearty whole-wheat bread. *Open Mon.–Sat. 7 A.M.–6 P.M.; Sun. 8 A.M.–noon.*

The **Sanitary Bakery** (132 Mulberry, Hester–Grand Sts.) is never open, but check it out anyway.

IMPORTS: PASTA MACHINES, FURNITURE AND LIGHTS

E. Rossi (191 Grand St. cor. Mulberry St., 226-9254) is an old ma-and-pa store jammed with all sorts of treasures: pasta machines and plaster saints, hand-painted Italian pottery bowls (charming and inexpensive) and "Kiss me, I'm Italian" T-shirts, espresso machines and recordings of Caruso. Also magazines and newspapers from Italy. *Open Mon.–Sat. 9:30 A.M.–8 P.M.; Sun. 9:30 A.M.–5 P.M.* **Carosello** (119 Mulberry St., Hester–Canal Sts., 925-7253) displays many of the same items in a more orderly fashion and carries a larger selection of Italian *dischi* (records). *Open Mon.–Fri. 9:30 A.M.–10 P.M.; Sat., Sun. 10 A.M.–midnight.*

To say that the furniture at **Roma** (215 Grand St., Mott–Elizabeth Sts., 925-8200) is baroque would be to understate the case. Roma's jam-packed showrooms contain some of the most lavishly ornamented furnishings in the city: elaborate revolving chandeliers, ornate gilt-edged bedroom sets, "Louis XV" dining suites, crushed velvet sofas and fine inlaid tables from Italy. Get a *gelati* at Ferrara's (one block west), window shop here, then walk one block further east to check out Roma's rival, **Milano Furniture** (227 Grand St. cor. Elizabeth St., 431-8475). Either of these stores could have been the source for the furnishings in *The Godfather. Both are open Mon.–Thurs. 10 A.M.–9 P.M.; Fri., Sat., Sun. 10 A.M.–6 P.M.*

You couldn't get much further from the styles featured in Roma's and Milano's windows than **Morsa** (182 Hester St., Mulberry–Baxter Sts., 226-4324), a shop that sells avant garde lighting imported from Italy or designed by Morsa (the architectural firm of Morsello and Savoie, whose offices are nearby). If no one is in when you arrive, just call 226-4324 (the number of the design firm) and someone will be there in two minutes. *Open Mon.–Fri. 9:30 A.M.–5 P.M. Call for app't. on Sat. Cl. Sun.*

NEIGHBORHOOD LANDMARKS
A moving force behind much of the renovation in Little Italy is the **Little Italy Restoration Association** (LIRA, 334 Broome St., 431-3500), whose aim it is to preserve the Italian flavor of the neighborhood. LIRA has plans to convert the ornate old Renaissance-Revival style **Police Headquarters** building (240 Centre St., Grand–Broome Sts.) into an Italian cultural center.

St. Patrick's (236 Mulberry St., Mott–Prince Sts.) was New York's first cathedral and the first Catholic church attended by Italians in New York. The Fifth Avenue St. Patrick's was built when a fire damaged this one.

The **Societá San Gennaro** (140 Mulberry St.) is the headquarters for the annual festa held in honor of the saint, whose jeweled miter is displayed in the society's storefront.

WINES AND LIQUORS
Next door to Ferrara's, Little Italy's most famous café, is **Ferrara's Wine and Liquor Center** (203 Grand St., Mott–Mulberry Sts., 226-1714), a beautiful glass-and-brick Morsa-designed store, which stocks over three hundred wines from Italy. *Open Mon.–Thurs. 9 A.M.–10 P.M.; Fri., Sat. 9 A.M.–midnight. Cl. Sun.*

There are still a lot of Italians in New York who make their own wine, and to supply them, as well as anyone else who wants to attempt the art, **Milan Lab** (57 Spring St., Lafayette–Mulberry Sts., CA6-4780) sells grape presses, oak kegs, wine-making kits and manuals, bottle corkers, siphons—in short, everything but the grapes. A basic wine kit that makes a chablis you can drink in three weeks costs about $30; beer-making kits start at $60 (but your second batch will cost you only $6). You can also get extracts for baking or making liqueur (just mix with vodka and sugar syrup) in flavors like blackberry, cinnamon and tangerine and rare herbs and spices like woodruff, sandalwood powder, frankincense and myrrh. Be sure to look at the old apothecary bottles on display; these contain rare oils and essences collected by the founder of Milan Lab, Anthony Miccio. His grandson and namesake, who runs the store now, freely dispenses advice and, for a fee, will analyze spoiled wine and recommend remedies. (Anthony Miccio's brother has opened a health food–wine supply store next door, but this shop—#57—is the original.) *Open Mon.–Fri. 8:30 A.M.–5:30 P.M.; Sat. 9 A.M.–4:30 P.M.; Sept.–Apr., Sun. 9 A.M.–1 P.M.; May–Aug., cl. Sun.*

CAFFÉS

Lots of people come to Little Italy just to sit and talk over an espresso and a *cannoli* in one of its many caffés. The two *grandes dames* of the neighborhood are Ferrara's and Caffé Roma.

Ferrara's (195-201 Grand St., Mott–Mulberry Sts., 226-6150), a neighborhood landmark (not to be confused with La Bella Ferrara, a caffé on Mulberry Street), has been around since 1892, and is the splashiest as well as the most traditional place to go in Little Italy for coffee and dessert. The caffé has been redesigned so that it is less of a contrast to its sleek new liquor store next door, but the long striped awning outside is still there (in summer, you can sit under it, sip your *cappucino* and pretend you are in Italy), and at Easter, the windows still display giant chocolate bunnies. Inside, all is bright and festive.

Ferrara's pastry counter is a long glass wall of tempting delights: *cannoli* (hard pastry tubes filled with sweetened ricotta studded with tiny chocolate bits or citron), *sfogliatelli* (flaky, layered ricotta-pastry triangles), *baba au rhum* (rum cake), airy *bigné* (cream puffs) and *pasticiotto* (small cupcakes made with cream or ricotta). All are made fresh daily in Ferrara's own bakery. (Some restaurants in Little Italy don't even bother to serve dessert; it's just assumed you'll go to Ferrara's.) It goes without saying that Ferrara's espresso, *cappucino* and hot chocolate (with whipped cream) are marvelous, and there are also Italian soft drinks like orzata (almond), tamarind and grenadine. *Open daily 8 A.M.–midnight.*

Caffé Roma (385 Broome St., Mulberry–Mott Sts., CA6-8413) is not shiny, bright and new like Ferrara's; Roma glows rather than shines, and its chairs and long tables show comfortable signs of wear. The floor is old white tile; one wall is painted with a scene of Venice. The place is smaller than Ferrara's and perhaps a bit cheaper. The pastries, espresso and ices are all just as good. (Get a rich ricotta cream-filled concoction to eat here, and then take a box of the delicious pignoli-nut cookies home.) On weekends, Roma's bakers make miniature pastries so you can sample one of everything to find your favorites. *Open daily 8 A.M.–midnight.*

Summer isn't summer in New York without at least one trip to Ferrara's or Roma for *granite*—Italian ices. There are only three flavors, but each is a knockout: the *limone* is like biting into an iced sweet lemon; the chocolate has more than a hint of cinnamon; and the espresso is just that—frozen coffee.

Caffé Biondo (141 Mulberry St., Grand–Hester Sts., 226-9285) and **Caffé Primavera** (51 Spring St. cor. Mulberry St., 226-8421) are the most attractive of the new glass/exposed-brick/hanging-plant caffés in Little Italy. Both serve good espresso and pastries.

RESTAURANTS

Little Italy has the greatest concentration of restaurants of any ethnic neighborhood in the city except Chinatown. Restaurants in Little Italy range in price from cheap to expensive, but almost all serve the robust cuisine of southern Italy and almost all are mobbed on Friday and Saturday nights. To avoid crowds and lines, try to come instead on a weekday night or weekend afternoon.

A tip: if you order selectively, almost any Italian restaurant is affordable—just get a plate of mixed appetizers and a pasta. (Conversely, even an inexpensive restaurant becomes expensive if you order antipasto, pasta, soup, entree, vegetable, salad, espresso and dessert.)

Benito's (II at 163 Mulberry St., I at 174½, Broome–Grand Sts., 226-9007 and 226-9012, **M**), of all the restaurants in Little Italy, probably gives you the best value for your money, especially if you stick to the Sicilian dishes. The appetizers are some of the best things here: order any of the stuffed vegetables or the mussels in tomato broth. On Fridays only, there's a good seafood salad. Except for the *gnocchi*, which are heavy and pasty, the pastas are all good, and the spaghetti Meitro di Otel, in a special tomato-onion-mushroom-parsley sauce flavored with bits of ham, is wonderful. The escarole sautéed in oil with garlic is properly limp, oily and garlicky; the fried zucchini, crisp and light. For dessert, get either the homemade Sicilian *cannoli* filled with light clouds of anisette-flavored cream or the warm and frothy *zabaglione*.

It's always daytime at Benito's II, a brightly lit restaurant with cheerful yellow walls hung with a couple of still lifes. Owners and cooks Benito and Gina Giacalone both run Benito's II during the week; on weekends, Mrs. Giacalone goes across the street to the tiny Benito's I. *Benito's II open Mon.–Sat. 1 P.M.–3 P.M., 5 P.M.–11 P.M. Cl. Sun. Benito's I open Fri., Sat. 5 P.M.–11 P.M.. Cl. Sun.*

In the expensive category, one of the best of the old-style restaurants in Little Italy is **Patrissy's** (98 Kenmare St., Mulberry–Lafayette Sts., 226-8509, **E**), a solid, dignified, formal restaurant where landscape paintings hang on red walls above dark wood paneling; the food here is Neapolitan.

Start off with the *fritto misto*—zucchini, artichokes, broccoli, mozzarella and hard-boiled eggs dipped in batter and deep-fried (a little greasy, but good all the same). The special *contadina* (for two) is an enormous platter piled high with strips of steak, chunks of chicken, sausage, fried potatoes, mushrooms, green pepper, garlic and herbs. The lobster *fra diavolo* (grilled) in a garlicky marinara sauce is a specialty of the house. For dessert, get the rich, rum-soaked homemade Italian cheesecake. Your cup of espresso comes with a bottle of anisette on the side. The waiters are as experienced and professional as they come, but even they can't quite cope with Patrissy's on a Saturday night. Bar. *Open daily noon–midnight.*

Among the chic new restaurants that have sprung up in Little Italy in the past few years, probably the best and certainly the most beautiful is **Il Cortile** (125 Mulberry St., Canal–Hester Sts., 226-6060, **E**). Outside, a gleaming dark hardwood facade frames huge glass windows and gives the restaurant a turn-of-the-century look, which is continued inside with bentwood chairs, tile floor, old pressed tin ceiling and brick pillars. Yet the design, inside and out, is contemporary, clean and uncluttered.

Though the chef is from southern Italy, the ambitious menu (completely in Italian) includes many northern dishes and such elegant preparations as *pollo allo champagne* (chicken in champagne-grape sauce). We tried and found delicious the hot mixed appetizers (stuffed clam, eggplant, mushroom and fried zucchini wrapped in mozzarella, all in a light tomato sauce garnished with fresh basil leaves) and the *pollo scapariello* (chicken shoemaker's style—pieces of chicken on the bone, sautéed in oil and garlic with sausage and mushrooms—a hearty, earthy dish). The pasta is cooked *al dente*, and much of it comes in the same light tomato sauce as the appetizers. A big basket of good breads, *friselle* and breadsticks accompanies every meal.

Il Cortile's waiters are very helpful and not at all hesitant about making recommendations. *Open Mon.–Thurs. noon–midnight; Fri.–Sat. noon–1 A.M.; Sun. 1 P.M.–midnight.*

Young people who visit Little Italy regularly eat at Luna's or Puglia's, which are fairly cheap restaurants that give you a lot of food.

Luna's (112 Mulberry St., Canal–Hester Sts., 226-8657, **I–M**) is a loud and lively place serving loud and lively Neapolitan cuisine. The stuffed vegetable appetizers here are worth ordering, and the *saltimbocca* (lit. "jump in the mouth")—a huge platter of layers of veal, prosciutto, egg and mozzarella in wine sauce on a bed of escarole—is one of the best things in the house. The *zuppa de pesce*—piles of mussels, fish and clams in an undistinguished tomato broth—comes in a bowl the size of a small dinghy. "What's the best thing here?" I ask the waiter. "The food," he replies. *Open daily noon–1 A.M.*

All kinds of things go on at **Puglia's** (189 Hester St., Mulberry–Mott Sts., 966-6006, **I**), a raucous, old restaurant (founded in 1919) decorated with murals of old Little Italy. The waiters at Puglia's banter with the customers (at no extra cost), and sometimes they dance. A guitarist plays and sings on Friday and Saturday nights. Occasionally local street characters drop in for a visit. The food is strong Sicilian fare (you can even get sheep's head if you so desire), and you eat at long communal tables. *Open daily noon–1* A.M. *Cl. Mon.*

Vincent's Clam Bar (119 Mott St. cor. Hester St., 226-8133, **I**) offers a limited menu of clams, mussels, *scungilli* (squid), shrimp, oysters, soft-shell crab and shrimp balls. Everything is served with a medium or hot tomato sauce. *Open daily noon–3* A.M. **Umberto's Clam House** (129 Mulberry St. cor. Hester, 431-7545, **I**) is where Joey Gallo met his end, "in the heart of Little Italy." Good clams with linguine and hot sauce here. *Open daily 11* A.M.*–6* A.M.

The best pizza in Little Italy is made at **Florio's** (192 Grand St., Mulberry–Mott Sts., 226-7610, **I**), a small sit-down restaurant that is a lot more than a pizza bar. Be sure to order the fried zucchini on the side. *Open Tues.–Sun., 11:30* A.M.*–11:30* P.M.*; Mon. 4* P.M.*–11:30* P.M.

At **Theresa's** (117 Mulberry St., Canal–Hester Sts., 226-6950, **I–M**), you can listen to Italian opera singers while you dine. **Grotta Azzura** (387 Broome St. cor. Mulberry St., 226-9283, **E**) is a blue-lit underground den serving hearty, garlicky Sicilian food. **Paolucci's** (149 Mulberry St., Grand–Hester Sts., 925-2288, **M–E**), a traditional old Italian restaurant, is housed in the original Stephen van Renssalaer House, a Federal-style two-story brick house built in 1816. **G. Lombardi** (53 Spring St., Mulberry–Lafayette Sts., 226-9866, **E**), in renovated Art Deco quarters, is a very attractive restaurant, but the food can be disappointing. **Angelo's** (146 Mulberry St., 226-8527, **M–E**) is a good old Neapolitan standby.

Italian Greenwich Village and Soho

Northern Italians began to settle in Greenwich Village as early as the 1880s, and after 1900, large numbers of southern Italians moved into the area, both from the Mulberry Bend area and directly from the ships. By the end of World War I, the entire eastern half of the Village was Italian. Over the years, many Italian Village residents moved to the outlying boroughs or the suburbs of New Jersey, and the Italian community dwindled. All that remains today of the old Italian Village is a tiny colony around Sullivan and Thompson streets south of Houston in a section of the city now known as Soho, a cluster of Italian food stores on Bleecker Street between Sixth and Seventh avenues near the Church of Our Lady of Pompeii, and a score or so of old Italian cafés and restaurants that are sprinkled throughout the area.

HOW TO GET THERE

By subway: To Soho: *IND* AA or E to Spring St.–Sixth Ave., walk east to Sullivan St. To Bleecker St. between Sixth and Seventh avenues: *Seventh Avenue IRT* #1 to Christopher St.–Sheridan Sq., walk across W. 4 St. to Sixth Ave., then to Bleecker St.; or *Seventh Avenue IRT* #1 to W. Houston, walk east one block to Sixth Ave., north to Bleecker St., then west on Bleecker; or *IND* A, AA, B, CC, D, E, or F to W. 4 St.–Washington Sq., walk south on Sixth to Bleecker St., then west on Bleecker St.

To other parts of Greenwich Village, see map.

LITTLE LITTLE ITALY IN SOHO

Sullivan and Thompson streets below Houston Street have been Italian for so long that this area is sometimes known as Little Little Italy. Of all the Italian enclaves in the city, this one gives the impression of having changed the least. Long rows of old six-story tenements line the streets. There are no restaurants to attract tourists here, and the shops do not seek customers outside the neighborhood. It is not unusual to hear Italian spoken on the streets.

Standing guard over the neighborhood is **St. Anthony's Shrine Church** (153 Sullivan St. cor. W. Houston). Built in 1866, St. Anthony's is the second oldest church attended by Italians in the city (the first was the Old St. Patrick's Cathedral in Little Italy). Every year for two weeks in June, Little Little Italy holds a street *festa* in honor of St. Anthony.

Joe's Dairy (156 Sullivan St., Houston–Prince Sts., 677-8780) is a small shop which makes its own ricotta, basket cheese and mozzarella. It's been in the neighborhood for over eighty years. *Open Tues.–Sat. 7 A.M.–6:30 P.M. Cl. Sun., Mon.*

Porcelli Brothers (179 Prince St., Sullivan–Thompson Sts., 673-2756) is known for its fine baby veal. *Open Mon.–Sat. 8 A.M.–6 P.M. Cl. Sun.*

Raffeto Ravioli (144 W. Houston, Sullivan-MacDougal Sts., 777-1261) is on the Village side of the border with Soho, but people from both neighborhoods have been coming here since 1906 for the fine homemade pastas. (The spinach pastas are the biggest sellers.) You can also get fresh-grated Parmesan cheese here as well as imported rice (*risotto*), olive oils and semolina flour. *Open Tues.–Sat. 7:30 A.M.–6 P.M. Call for hrs. on Sun.*

BLEECKER STREET

On Bleecker Street between Sixth and Seventh avenues, there used to be an Italian pushcart market where peddlers sold zucchini, *finochio*, pomegranates and other vegetables and fruits considered exotic by the non-Italian inhabitants of the city. A man named Fortunio, who owned a restaurant on Bleecker in this era, is said to have been the first to import broccoli to this country.

THE ITALIAN GREENWICH VILLAGE AND SOHO

Today there are about a half-dozen Italian stores on this stretch of Bleecker, several of which have acquired a city-wide following.

Ottomanelli's Meat Market (#281, 675-4217) is famed throughout the city for its fine meats and Italian-style specialties like seasoned veal roast wrapped with bacon; pork *braciole* stuffed with parsley, garlic and cheese; veal shank for *osso buco* and fresh game. Around Christmas, Ottomanelli's makes a special sausage from venison or wild boar. *Open Mon.–Fri., 6:30 A.M.–6:30 P.M.; Sat. 6 A.M.–6 P.M. Cl. Sun.*

Mario Bosco (#263, 242-6790) has been selling imported pastas, cheese and homemade *cotechini* (pork sausage) for over eighty years (the store still has its original fixtures). Depending on the season, you'll find dried wild mushrooms from Italy, chestnut flour (for Christmas *gnocchi* and lasagne), marinated eels, imported Italian fruit mustard (a sweet, spicy relish served with meats) and black and white truffles. Arthur Capelli, the present owner, also carries *risotto* and *polenta* (Italian corn meal), and his selection of cold cuts includes cured (not smoked) Italian bacon, prosciutto, prosciuttino (a delicious pepper ham) and hot Sicilian Genoa salami. At lunchtime, he makes mouth-watering hot roast pork or salami sandwiches to go. *Open Mon.–Sat. 9 A.M.–6 P.M. Cl. Sun.*

Eduardo Faicco, an immigrant from Naples, founded **Faicco's Pork Store** (#260, 989-6234) in 1900. Brother and sister Edward and Ann Faicco—grandchildren of Eduardo—run the shop now, and the pride they take in their store is apparent in each lovingly made salami and sausage they sell. Some of their specialties are sweet sausage, hot sausage, *sopressata* (a salami made with whole peppercorns or hot pepper and paprika) and *panceta* (Italian bacon that has been cured in brine for four days and is used in the sauce for spaghetti *alla carbonara*). Ann volunteers recipes if you're interested. For her *cotechini*, she suggests boiling an hour to a pound with peppercorns, onion, salt and thyme and serving with lentils. Try some of her homemade pizza rustica. *Open Tues.–Thurs. 8 A.M.–6 P.M.; Fri. 8 A.M.–7 P.M.; Sun. 9 A.M.–2 P.M.*

When Frank Sinatra stays in town, he has his breakfast bread delivered fresh every morning from **Zito Bakery** (#259, 929-6139). Zito's breads—whole wheat or Sicilian white—are baked in old brick ovens, just as they were fifty years ago; this is very likely the best Italian bread in town. Charlie Zito runs the place now. *Open Mon.–Fri. 5 A.M.–6:30 P.M., Sat. 5 A.M.–6 P.M., Sun. 5 A.M.–2 P.M.*

For Italian pastries on Bleecker Street, you have a choice: **Dellarovere and Musa** (#245, 242-4959) or **Rocco's** (#243, 242-6031). At both, you can get homemade coffee cake or *panettone*—the light, high Milanese kind made with raisins and citron, or the heavier Genovese kind, flavored with anisette and fennel and studded with pignoli nuts, raisins and citron. Either is wonderful with morning coffee.

Of course, there are cannoli and other typical Italian pastries, and Rocco's also makes *pasticciotto sanguinacci*—cupcakes filled with a mixture of beef blood and dried fruit that looks and tastes like chocolate. Rocco's, which has tables, serves espresso, and in the summer, frozen mocha or cappucino ice. *Dellorovere and Musa is open Mon.–Thurs. 7:30 A.M.–7 P.M.; Fri., Sat., 7:30A.M.–7:30 P.M. Rocco's is open daily 8 A.M.–11 P.M. Cl. Mon.*

Across the street from Rocco's, on the corner of Bleecker and Carmine streets, is the imposing **Church of Our Lady of Pompeii** (25 Carmine St.) founded by the Scalabrini Fathers and erected in 1925.

ITALIAN BOOKSELLER
S. F. Vanni (30 W. 12 St., Fifth–Sixth Aves., OR5-6336) has been in the business of selling Italian books ever since 1884 (when it opened on Bleecker Street). Vanni's carries Italian-language classics, current Italian literature, philosophy, history, Italian-language journals and children's books as well as popular paperbacks and Italian translations of Shakespeare. *Open Mon.–Fri., 9 A.M.–6 P.M.; Sat. 9 A.M.–4 P.M. Cl. Sun.*

CAFFÉS
What would Greenwich Village be without its Italian caffés? Where would lovers meet, students sit, intellectuals intellectualize? **Caffé Reggio** (119 MacDougal, Third–Bleecker Sts., 475-9557) is old, smoky, dark and crowded, with marble-topped tables and an old brass espresso *machina*; this is *the* classic Village coffee house. *Open daily 11 A.M.–2 A.M.*

Northwest of Washington Square Park is the **Peacock Caffé** (24 Greenwich Ave. cor. 10 St., 242-9395), an Old World coffee house that serves great hot chocolate and cappucino. The caffé is named for the painting depicting the birth of a peacock that has hung on its walls for over thirty years. *Open Sun., Tues.–Thurs. 1 P.M.–1 A.M.; Fri., Sat. 1 P.M.–2A.M. Cl. Mon.*

RESTAURANTS
Dozens of Italian restaurants dot Greenwich Village in a holdover from the days when this area was completely Italian (long before the Village was associated with beatniks or with unaffordable charm as it is today).

The best *north* Italian restaurant in the Village—many say in the

entire city—is **Trattoria da Alfredo** (90 Bank St. at Hudson, 929-4400,
E), an informal restaurant done up in white and sea blues that has become
so extraordinarily popular that you must make your reservations at least a
week in advance.

Pastas are the thing to order here; all are perfectly prepared, and you
have a choice of imaginative sauces. The *penne all'Arrabbiata* are short,
straight tubes of pasta "rabid" with hot sausages, tomatoes and artichokes. The *tortelline della nonna* are little meat-filled circlets tossed in
a light cream and cheese sauce. The spaghetti *puttanesca* (spaghetti
"whore's style") comes in a shamelessly colorful tomato sauce enlivened with tuna fish, black olives, capers and anchovies.

The same panache characterizes the appetizers, all of which are
wonderful. (Two examples: vegetables stuffed with a mixture of tuna,
anchovies, capers, pimentoes, cheese and bread; zucchini filled with
ground beef, cheese and sausage.) The antipastos and pastas are hard acts
to follow and the entrées suffer by comparison. But your meal will end on
a high note if you order Gino's special chocolate cake. Bring your own
wine. Reservations are a must. *Open Mon., Wed., Sat. noon–2* P.M.;
Mon., Wed., Sun. 6 P.M.*–11:30* P.M. *Cl. Tues.*

Da Silvano (260 Sixth Ave. nr. Bleecker, 982-0090, E) is the only
restaurant in New York that serves Florentine cuisine. Small, brightly lit,
with one exposed brick wall and as many tables as can be squeezed in (too
many), this restaurant is typical of a new breed in the Village—intimate
eateries that place the emphasis on food and favor simplicity and clarity
of design over lots of decoration.

Start off with the *panzanella*, or bread salad, a house specialty. The
salad is a mixture of roasted peppers, tomatoes, cucumbers, onions and
herbs with cubes of bread that have been soaked in the delicious, vinegary
dressing. The *crostini*—chicken liver paté flavored with anchovies,
capers and onions—served on Italian bread is also good. But then all the
appetizers are.

Except for the leaden *gnocchi* (only occasionally available anyway),
all the pastas are excellent, especially the *tortellina alla panna*—tortellini in a cheese and cream sauce seasoned with nutmeg. Along with the
regular menu, there are different specials every day; these sometimes
include game (the hare is well cooked but there is so little meat it hardly
seems worth the trouble). *Open Mon.–Sat., 6* P.M.*–11:30* P.M.*; Sun. 5*
P.M.*–11* P.M.

Joe's (79 MacDougal St. nr. Bleecker St., 471-8834, E), a classy,
very New York restaurant, has been around for a long time. Joe's is long
and narrow and brightly lit, with shiny black-and-white checkerboard

floors and a clientele that includes gentlemen of certain connections who may be seen searching through a thick wad of hundred-dollar bills to find a $20 tip for the waiter. Order the fried zucchini and the delicious and unusual stuffed mushrooms (filled with cheese). The hot antipasto is good, too. Also recommended: the spaghetti *puttanesca*, the homemade egg noodles in carbonara sauce, the extraordinary cheese cake and the zabaglione. *Open Wed.–Mon. 11 A.M.–11:30 P.M. Cl. Tues.*

As you leave Joe's, notice the **Tiro a Segno Club** next door (77 MacDougal St.), which started out over ninety years ago as a shooting and hunting club. Over the years, the meals that followed the hunt became more important than the shooting, and now the members of the club—gourmets and gourmands all—claim they have the best Italian food in the city. (Sorry, you have to be nominated by a member to join.)

Mary's (42 Bedford St., Leroy St.–Seventh Ave., 243-9755, **E**), an old, tiny, intimate restaurant tucked away on a quiet side street, looks like a secret hideaway, like the old Prohibition restaurants that used to flourish in the Village. Though it looks like a real find, everyone knows about Mary's, and the owners exploit the place's charm for all it's worth: *everything* is à la carte.

The owners are from Abruzzi, and the dishes have the boldness characteristic of that region's cuisine. Mary's spaghetti *alla carbonara* is justly famous. The eggplant *imperiale*—lightly breaded eggplant rolled around muenster cheese with a tomato-mushroom sauce—is superb. Another interesting dish is the "wild pork"—pork chops in hot sauce. *Open daily noon–11:30 P.M.; weekends until 12:30 A.M.*

Rocco's (181 Thompson St., Bleecker–Houston Sts., 677-0590, **M**) is a spirited neighborhood restaurant. Order the fresh fish of the day in *brodetto* (a wine-stock broth) and you won't be sorry; get the stuffed vegetable appetizers overflowing with soggy breadcrumbs, and you will. Excellent service. *Open daily noon–11:30 P.M.*

Italian Bensonhurst

"You've gotta' be Italian just to walk down this street," jokes one storekeeper on the avenue—Eighteenth Avenue, that is—in Bensonhurst, Brooklyn, the main shopping street of one of the city's most solidly Italian neighborhoods. The shopkeeper might almost have said Sicilian instead of Italian since almost 90 percent of the people who live here are of Sicilian ancestry.

Except perhaps for the restaurants, Bensonhurst's Eighteenth Avenue from 60th to 86th streets has everything Manhattan's Mulberry Street does, without the carnival atmosphere. And unlike Little Italy, this is a neighborhood where the young people stay: every other store on the avenue sells wedding gowns, wedding catering services or baby clothes.

Two- and three-story connected houses, each with its own driveway, garage and postage-stamp lawn, line the quiet side streets off Eighteenth Avenue. At a window here and there, you might see an old woman dressed in black staring out at the street through lace curtains.

If you go to Eighteenth Avenue, be sure to visit the **Alba Pastry Shop** (#7001, 70–71 Sts., 232-2122). Alba's Sicilian *cassata, cannoli*, and Italian cheese cake have been famous among Brooklyn's Italians for four generations. *Open Tues.–Sat. 9 A.M.–9 P.M.; Sun. 8:30 A.M.–6 P.M. Cl. Mon.*

The **Bari Pork Store** (7117 Eighteenth Ave., 71–72 Sts., 837-1257)—you can tell it by the gigantic pig wearing a crown in the window—is the neighborhood's biggest *salumeria. Open daily, Mon.–Sat. 8 A.M.–6 P.M.; Sun. 8 A.M.–2 P.M.* **Queen Ann Ravioli** (72–05 Eighteenth Ave., 72–73 Sts., 256-1061) is one of the most popular pasta stores in Bensonhurst. *Open Tues.–Sat. 8 A.M.–6 P.M.; Sun. 8 A.M.–2 P.M. Cl. Mon.*

Local men like to sit and talk over an espresso at the **Gran Caffé Italia** (6917 Eighteenth Ave. near 70 St.). The **Walker Theater** (6401 Eighteenth Ave., 64–65 Sts., 232-4500) shows Italian films on Sunday, Monday and Tuesday. All up and down the street gift shops sell hand-painted Italian china, espresso sets and Italian records.

HOW TO GET THERE
By subway from Manhattan: *IND* D train to 50 St. or W. 4 St., change to B train to Eighteenth Ave. Get off at 71 St. and Sixteenth Ave. and walk two blocks east; or at 79 St. and Seventeenth Ave. and walk one block east; or at Eighteenth Avenue and 85 St. The ride takes about an hour.

Around Town in Manhattan

NINTH AVENUE ITALIAN GOURMET SHOPS
Ethnic food stores of all nationalities abound on Ninth Avenue (from 37 to 52 streets), and some of the oldest and finest Italian gourmet stores in the city are located here.

Founded in 1893 and still at its original location, **Manganaro's Grosseria** (#488, 37–38 Sts., 563-5331) is now being run by the third generation of Manganaros, who call their store America's Foremost Italian Grocery. When you walk in, you can see why. Dozens of huge provolone cheeses shaped like a giant's salamis hang from the rafters; gigantic drums of romano repose on a marble counter; hundreds of sausages ranging from dark red and very lean to pale, chubby and mottled with fat are strung on a rack overhead; one table is a pyramid of imported *panettone*; on the shelves are regiments of olive oil tins and canned tomatoes. One entire section of the store is devoted to Italian breads; another to freshly made *cannolis, cassatas* and ricotta cheese cakes. Manganaro's stocks more than five-hundred different sizes, shapes and brands of pasta, as well as its own fresh pasta, which is made on the premises and cut to order. A *partial* list of the Italian cheeses carried here would include: ricotta, mozzarella, manteche, parmesan, provolone, gorgonzola, taleggio, pecorino romano (a tangy grating cheese), ricotto Siciliano (an aged spicy cheese for grating or the table), bel paese (a mellow table cheese) and incannestratata (a sharp, afterdinner cheese). Gourmets shop here for delicacies like fresh truffles in season, pickled scungilli, smoked oysters and baked stuffed figs with almonds. This is also one of the few stores in town where you can get a *gnocchi* and *cavatelli* machine or a *cannoli* tube. In short, if you can't go to Italy to do your Italian grocery shopping, Manganaro's is your next best bet.

After you have inspected the store to your heart's content and purchased all the fixings for a Roman feast, sit down to an inexpensive home-style lunch in the restaurant at the back of the store (there's another room upstairs, too). You can get wonderful hero sandwiches here as well as hot pasta dishes. The stove is right out in plain sight, so you can see what's cooking.

Manganaro's handles mail and phone orders and will deliver anywhere in Manhattan, the Bronx, Brooklyn or Queens. *Open Mon.–Sat. 8* A.M.*–7* P.M. *Cl. Sun.*

Not to be confused with Manganaro's Grosseria and Restaurant is **Manganaro's Hero-Boy** next door (#492, 942-7325). Heroes are Made, Not Born at this no-nonsense fast-food emporium, where at lunchtime, the smell of roast peppers is strong and the lines waiting for prosciutto, provolone and pepper heroes, long. Manganaro's Hero-Boy will also prepare a six-foot hero for delivery on twenty-four hours' notice. *Open Mon.–Sat. 6:30* A.M.*–7:30* P.M. *Cl. Sun.*

In addition to its fine Italian sausages, veal and prime meats, **Luigi's Meat Store**, also known as **Jimmy's Meat Market** (494 Ninth Ave., 37–38 Sts., 279-8273) often carries rabbit, pheasant, goat meat and suckling pig. And with enough notice, this shop will get you just about any kind of meat or fowl you want, including—as one customer requested and received—peacock. *Open Mon.–Sat. 7:30* A.M.–*7:30* P.M. *Cl. Sun.*

Farther uptown on the same block is the **Giovanni Esposito and Son Pork Shop** (500 Ninth Ave., 37–38 Sts., 279-3298), where a fascinating variety of pork products are on display: long coils of sausage flavored with cheese and parsley, pig snouts, tripe, tongue, hot and sweet sausages. All the sausages are prepared in the back. If you would like to try your hand at making your own, you can get the ground pork and casings here. *Open Mon.-Sat. 8*A.M.–*7:30* P.M. *Cl. Sun.*

Molinari Brothers (776 Ninth Ave., 51–52 Sts., 582-5048) is a fine meat market, where aside from the usual beef, poultry, pork and lamb, you can get squab, rabbit, duck, sweetbreads, tripe and calf's head. The *cotechine* and delicious patés are made on the premises. *Open Mon.–Sat. 8:30*A.M.–*5:30* P.M. *Cl. Sun.*

For fresh, snaky Sicilian breads and really good *biscotti*, head for *Casa Italia Bakery* (#545, 40–41 Sts. 563-4153). *Open daily 6* A.M.–*8* P.M. *D'Auito's* (494 Ninth Ave., nr. 38 St.) and *Pozzo Pastries* (688 Ninth Ave., 47–48 Sts.) carry a full line of Italian pastries. Pozzo is *open Mon.–Sat. 7* A.M.–*6* P.M. *Cl. Sun.* D'Auito's is *open Mon.–Sat. 8* A.M.–*6:30* P.M. *Cl. Sun.*

For fresh ravioli, *tortellini, manicotti* and *gnocchi,* **Bruno Ravioli** (#653, 45–46 Sts., 246-8456) is king. Buy a jar of Bruno's good homemade tomato sauce and a supply of your favorite pasta, freeze the pasta, and the next time you don't have time to make dinner, just boil the pasta (no need to thaw), heat the sauce and thank Bruno. *Open Mon.–Sat. 5*A.M.–*5* P.M. *Cl. Sun. (Before 9* A.M. *when the retail shop officially opens, you have to knock.)*

P. Carnevale and Sons (#631, 44–45 Sts., 765-0640) is a gourmet shop that has been in the neighborhood for over forty years. The store is medium-sized and carries a little bit of everything: sausage, cheese, bread, imported pasta. Gourmets come here for the paté campagne, made with wine, pork livers, salt and spices. Also for the pork liver paté. A good place to shop for special dinners, or if Manganaro's overwhelms you. *Open 9:30* A.M.–*5:30* P.M. *Cl. Sun.*

ITALIAN CULTURAL CENTERS

Not even counting the marvelous collections of Italian art in the city's museums, New York offers a wide range of opportunities for learning about Italian culture, from lessons in Italian language and cuisine to lectures on the Italian Renaissance.

The **Istituto Italiano di Cultura of New York** (686 Park Ave., 68–69 Sts., TR9-4242) is the Italian government's cultural agency in the United States. The *istituto* houses a library with some 25,000 books of Italian interest, a periodical room with over 400 Italian and American publications and files of clippings on Italy and Italian-Americans. Videotaped interviews with leading Italian film directors are among the educational materials the institute loans out to schools and cultural institutions on request. If you are thinking of studying or teaching in Italy, ask for the institute's yearly listing of summer courses and academic programs in that country.

Casa Italiana of Columbia University (1161 Amsterdam Ave. at 117 St., 280-2306) is a center for the study and appreciation of Italian culture. Funds for the building were raised by New York's Italian-American community as a result of a campaign (in 1914) by students in the Romance Languages Department, and the Italian Renaissance piazza was built with volunteer work by Italian-American skilled laborers. The *casa*—home of Columbia's Italian Department—sponsors many performances of Italian music and theater, Italian art exhibits and Italian film series.

The **America-Italy Society** (667 Madison Ave., 60-61 Sts., 838-1561) is a nonprofit institution that runs an Italian-language school for its members and offers Italian cooking classes.

NANNI'S AND RAO'S

Outside of Little Italy and Greenwich Village, the largest concentration of Italian restaurants and some of the best Italian food in the city is in midtown. It would take an entire book just to review all the fine Italian restaurants in this part of the city. Here is one, singled out because it is one of the oldest, one of the best-known, and one of the most beloved.

As far as decor goes, **Nanni's** (146 E. 46 St., Lexington–Park Aves., 697-4161, **E**) is really nothing very special: there's a bar, and beyond the bar, a room with tables and dark wood walls covered with travel posters. That's all; but somehow, it all manages to be very chic, very exclusive. And the food, though geared to an expense-account budget (it's hard to eat here for less that $25 a person), is wonderful.

Begin with the refreshing seafood salad (not on the menu) in a lemon-oil dressing. Don't skip the pasta—much of it comes in an extraordinary sauce that is pink instead of tomato red because it includes large quantities of cheese. Chicken *scarpariello* here is chicken cooked in the manner of the most aristocratic of shoemakers—large chunks of tender meat on the bone sautéed in oil, wine, a little garlic and herbs—hardly a peasant dish. Only the salad is disappointing—mostly iceberg lettuce (though the dressing is nice), but the dessert—a big bowl of warm *zabaglione* lathered over strawberries—makes up for it. The waiter is all attention and charm. *Open Mon–Sat. noon–3 P.M., 5:30 P.M.–11P.M. Cl. Sun.*

Uptown, Nanni has opened a very elegant (chandeliers, pink linen tablecloths, wall murals) restaurant called **Il Valletto** (133 E. 61 St., Lexington-Park Aves., 697-4161, **E**). The menu is not the same as at Nanni's, but here too, the food is wonderful. *Open Mon.–Sat. 5:30 P.M.–midnight. Cl. Sun.*

Far uptown, in Spanish Harlem, where few would think to look for an Italian restaurant, is **Rao's** (455 E. 114 St., cor. Pleasant Ave., 534-9625, **E**), not only a good Italian restaurant, but probably the city's best for southern Italian cuisine. Rao's, on a block that is practically all that remains of old Italian Harlem—a small Italian island in a Spanish sea—is what most of us have always dreamed of finding—the ultimate restaurant: perfect food, perfect service, and prices that, while above this book's moderate range, are very reasonable for a restaurant of this calibre.

Rao's is old—over eighty years old. Dark varnished wood panels the walls halfway up; above that, it's all white marble. The place is small, dimly lit, with hardly more than a half-dozen tables. You walk past the immaculate kitchen as you enter. There's a bar, some Christmas lights and a tropical-fish tank. The crowd is surprisingly toney—many Madison Avenue types (Rao's is no secret)—yet withal, Rao's has the feeling of a neighborhood restaurant outside New York, one in New Jersey, perhaps.

Everything on the menu is worth ordering. The pasta is perfection; just al dente. The sautéed escarole in garlic and oil is just oily and garlicky enough. The chicken *scarpariello* here comes with sweet or hot peppers (with hot, it's a lusty, extraordinary dish). The *calamari* is utterly fresh and incredibly tender; the veal—with whatever sauce—melts in your mouth. The lemon chicken comes with crisp charcoal skin and tart lemon-wine sauce. Everything is carefully prepared; the chef seems to have calculated exactly how many meals he can handle in good conscience, and that is exactly the number of seats in the house. A larger restaurant just couldn't do as good a job. There are no desserts; only espresso with a bottle of anisette on the side. Service is purposely leisurely; each course arrives at just the right moment. Prices, though moderate for a restaurant with this kind of food and service, can add up if you don't watch it.

This part of East Harlem is considered so tough by many cabbies that you may have trouble convincing one to take you here. If you arrive by taxi, tell your host at Rao's immediately that you will need a cab back, and one will be called for you. If you have a car, by all means drive here: parking is available right outside the restaurant, and this block is safe. *Open Mon.–Fri. 6* P.M.*–11* P.M. *Cl. Sat. and Sun.* Reservations are essential. Rao's does not accept credit cards.

Around Town in the Boroughs

RESTAURANTS IN BROOKLYN AND QUEENS
Some of the best Italian restaurants in New York are not in Manhattan at all, but in Brooklyn, Queens, or the Bronx.

The best pizza in the city, for example, is in Bay Ridge, Brooklyn, at **Lento's** (7003 Third Ave., 70–71 Sts., 745-9197, **I**). What makes Lento's pizza unique is the crust, which is very, very thin, thus leaving more room for the marvelous sauce (the meat sauce is the best) and the cheese, both of which are mounded on with a lavish hand. You eat this pizza in old-fashioned dark wood booths; each booth is a semiprivate alcove, with its own coat rack and a buzzer (nonworking) for service. The service—by a waiter with an uncanny knack for avoiding your eye—is *lento*. But it's all part of the ambiance. There's a bar up front. *Open daily noon–midnight.*

Over in Coney Island, there's **Gargiulo's** (2911 W. 15 St., Surf–Mermaid Aves., 266-0906, **E**), a gigantic (the place seats 500) high-ceilinged palace of a restaurant that may have been great once, but seems to have fallen back on its reputation ever since it got a four-star review in the *New York Times* a couple of years ago. At least when we visited, the stuffed mushrooms were rubbery and soggy, the escarole in garlic and oil was overcooked and too oily, the entrées disappointing and the cheesecake, so-so. The *mozzarella en carozza* was excellent, however. You may need reservations on weekends. *Open daily noon–midnight.*

The foremost representative of Italian cuisine in Queens is **Buonavia** (101-19 Queens Blvd., 67 Ave.–67 Dr., 275-6743, **E**) in Forest Hills, a three-room restaurant decorated principally with still-life oils and one or two paintings of nudes. The owners are from Trieste, and their specialty is pasta. Ignore the printed menu and concentrate on the mimeographed sheet of daily specials: these are what make this restaurant unique.

The *gnocchi* here are the best I have tasted anywhere—so light they melt on the tongue. The *montanara* soup—a blend of vegetables, herbs and pasta in broth—is utterly delicious and well worth ordering, as is the red snapper in *brodetto*. Buonavia is a family restaurant—noisy, crowded. Reservations recommended. *Open Tues., Thurs., Sun., 1* P.M.*–11* P.M.*; Fri. 1* P.M.*–12:30* A.M.*; Sat. 4* P.M.*–12:30* A.M. *Cl. Mon.*

THE ITALIAN BRONX
Arthur Avenue in the Bronx is the center of an old, old Italian neighborhood that figured largely in *The Godfather*—both in the book and in the movie. The place to eat here is **Mario's** (2342 Arthur Ave., 184–186 Sts., 548-1188, **E**) *Open Tues.–Sun. noon–11* P.M. *Cl. Mon.*

There are *bocce* (game played with small, heavy balls that are rolled) courts in Central Park and elsewhere in Manhattan, but the biggest *bocce* club in the city is at the **Van Nest Recreation Center** in the Bronx (475 Van Nest Ave., TA2-9895). Ninety members compete regularly every weekend; the courts are indoors, so they can play year round.

Festivals and Holidays

All Italian festivals in New York are celebrations of the feast days of specific saints. A procession in which an image of the saint is carried through the streets is the highlight of these *festas*, which almost always include street fairs with food and game booths, rides and music.

The biggest, most popular Italian festa in New York is the **Festival of San Gennaro** (San Gennaro is the patron saint of Naples), celebrated on Mulberry Street in Little Italy for ten days during the week of September 19. On the Feast Day itself, a special high mass is held at the Most Precious Blood Church (113 Baxter St.), and throughout the festival, Mulberry Street, decorated with colored lights and tinsel arches, is a paradise for *cannoli-*, pizza-, *zeppole-*, and sausage-lovers of every ethnic background from all over the city. There's a procession, of course, in which a statue of the saint is paraded through the streets of Little Italy, after which San Gennaro, his robes pinned with hundreds of dollar bills (donations from the crowd), spends the rest of the festival surveying the whole scene on Mulberry from a high pedestal. The Festival of San Gennaro has become such a New York tradition that if, for some reason, it were to cease, September in the city just wouldn't be the same. As with all Italian *festas*, weekends are the liveliest. For information, call the San Gennaro Society, CA6-9546.

Early June brings the two-week **Festival of St. Anthony**, honoring the patron saint of lost property, and celebrated on Sullivan Street from Spring to West Houston streets near the Shrine Church of St. Anthony (cor. W. Houston and Sullivan Sts.) in Little Little Italy. The procession includes an Italian band and little girls in folk costumes as well as a life-size statue of St. Anthony borne on the shoulders of four men. There's a ferris wheel and other rides, and booths selling food from around the world. Not as crowded as the San Gennaro Festival, but just as spirited. For information, call SP7-2755.

In the latter part of July, you can test your spaghetti-eating ability by seeing how long it takes you to eat one hundred feet of this pasta at the ten-day **Festa Italiana** held in front of Our Lady of Pompeii Church (25 Carmine St. cor. Bleecker St.). The *festa* kicks off with an opening concert by the Mother Cabrini Band. For information, call TE8-1324.

A nighttime candlelight procession down Second Avenue and through the streets around Mt. Carmel Church (448 E. 115 St.) is the climax of the week-long **Feast of Mt. Carmel** in old Italian Harlem around the second week of July. Puerto Ricans and Italians march together in this procession, which many people view from the top of parked cars—makeshift grandstands—that line the procession route. Call LE4-0681 for information.

Also in July, Italian-Americans in Williamsburg, Brooklyn, honor **St. Paulinius of Nola** with dancing in the streets and the carrying—by 150 men—of a five-story monument or *giglio* through the neighborhood to the Our Lady of Mt. Carmel Church (275 No. 8 St.). Call 384-0223.

Italian Food

Italian cuisine is divided into two main schools: northern and southern. The food of northern Italy is characterized by more delicate seasoning, the use of butter as the principal cooking fat, rice as a stapel and pastas that are flat and enriched with eggs. Northern Italian cooking is ranked next to French and Chinese as one of the world's great cuisines. The earthy, robust cuisine of southern Italy uses bold seasonings (lots of garlic), olive oil, and pastas that are tubular and eggless. Within these two broad divisions, there are many regional variations. Most of New York's Italian restaurants serve southern (especially Neapolitan and Sicilian) cuisine.

Italian cuisine is famous for its pastries and ricotta cheese cake, ice creams and ices and delicious ways of preparing coffee.

MENU GLOSSARY
affogato: poached.
aglio: garlic.
Alfredo: tossed with cream, butter and cheese (as in fettucini Alfredo).

Amartriciana, all':   in the Amartrice chef's way: often, this means with a sauce of tomatoes, onions and bacon cooked in pork fat and served with
  sharp, grated pecorino cheese.

antipasto: "before the meal": hors d'oeuvre.

Arrabiata, all':   "rabid style": usually a sauce that includes hot pepper or a very spicy ingredient.

arreganato: with oregano.

arugola: sharp-tasting green similar to watercress.

braciola: cutlet or steak.

brodo: broth.

brodetto: soup, usually containing fish: fish broth.

cacciatora: "hunter's style": cooked with tomatoes, wine, mushrooms and herbs.

cacciucco: fish stew.

calamari: squid.

campagnola: "in the country way": with tomatoes, onions and vegetables.

cannoli: hard pastry tubes filled with sweetened ricotta cheese mixed with chocolate bits or citron.

cappricciosa, alla: in a capricious way: often, garnished colorfully.

cappuccino: coffee with hot milk.

carbonara, alla: "in the charcoal burner's way"; black; a sauce made with black pepper, bacon or salt pork and egg (spaghetti alla carbonara).

casalinga: homemade.

contadina: rustic dish: platter of mixed small steaks, pieces of chicken sausages, green pepper, garlic.

costata: rib chop.

cotechino: spicy pork sausage.

cozze: mussels.

crostino: crouton, or piece of toasted bread.

espresso: strong black coffee made by forcing steam through ground beans.

fagioli: dried kidney beans.

fegato: liver.

filetto di pomodoro: "fillet of tomatoes"—a light tomato sauce.

Fiorentina, alla: in the Florentine way. Bistecca alla Fiorentina is steak charcoal-broiled with olive oil, salt and pepper.

formaggio: cheese.

forno, al: in the oven: baked.

fra diavolo: in the devil's way: grilled.

francese, alla: in the French way: usually, with a light wine sauce.

frittura: fried food.

fresco: fresh, uncooked.

fritelle: fritter.

frittata: omelet.

fritto: fried.

fritto misto: mixed fry.

frutti di mare: "fruit of the sea": variety of shellfish.

funghi: mushrooms.

insalata di pesce: cold seafood salad.

gelato: ice cream.

granite: flavored ices.

marinara, alla: "in the sailor's way": sauce of tomatoes, oil, garlic and oregano.

matriciana, alla: same as *Amatriciana*.

melanzana: eggplant.

Milanese, alla: "in the Milan way"—often means a dish contains rice, but veal Milanese is veal fried in egg and breadcrumbs.

minestrone: vegetable soup with rice or pasta.

mozzarella in carozza: mozzarella "in a carriage": sandwich of bread and mozzarella dipped in flour and egg and fried.

Napolitana, alla: "in the Neapolitan way."

oreganata: with oregano.

osso buco: veal shank stewed with tomatoes, onions, wine and stock.

panna: cream.

pastina: tiny pasta, served in soup.

pesto: paste of fresh basil, parmesan cheese, garlic, and oil.

piccata: small, flattened slice of veal in sauce.

piccante: highly seasoned.

pizzaiuola: spicy tomato sauce.

pollo: chicken.

posillipo: light tomato sauce flavored with garlic; named after a town near Naples.

puttanesca: "whore style": with chunks of tomato, garlic, black olives, capers and anchovies.

rapa: bitter broccoli.

ripieno: stuffed.

risotto: rice.

rollatine: stuffed, filled rolls, usually of beef.

Romana, alla: in the Roman way.

saltimbocca: "jump in the mouth": slices of veal layered with slices of ham and seasoned with sage.

scaloppine: thin, flattened slice of meat, usually veal.

scampi: Adriatic prawns: on American menus, jumbo shrimp.

scarpariello: "shoemaker's style": chicken scarpariello is pieces of chicken with the bone, cooked in garlic and oil, sometimes with sausages or peppers.

scungilli: octopus.

spiedino: roasted on a spit or skewer.

spumoni: foamy ice cream made with egg whites and whipped cream.

stracciatella: "little rags": egg drop soup.

tartufi: truffles.

torta di ricotta: ricotta cheesecake.

tortoni: small cup of vanilla ice cream sprinkled with sweet crumbs.

ucceletti: "little birds": small pieces.

Valdostana: "in the Val d'Aosta way": with ham and fontina cheese.

Veneziana, alla: "in the Venetian way": often this means with onions and white wine.

vitello: young veal.

vongole: clams.

zabaglione: foamy dessert of whipped egg yolks, sugar and marsala wine.

zeppole: Neapolitan doughnut.

zuppa: soup.

zuppa Inglese: "English soup": rum-soaked cake layered with custard.

Pasta glossary

cannelloni: "big pipes": large tubes, stuffed and baked.

cappelletti: "little hats" of dough stuffed with ricotta, chicken, Parmesan cheese and egg.

cappelli d'angelo: "angel's hair": very fine strands.

conchiglie: "conch": shells.

fettucini: "small ribbons": flat, ribbon pasta.

fusilli: "spindles": thin spirals.

gnocchi: pasta dumplings usually made with potatoes.

lasagne: broad flat noodles.

linguine: "small tongues": flat spaghetti.

manicotti: "little muffs": rectangular envelopes stuffed with cheese.

penne: "feathers": short straight tubes.

ravioli: small square pockets filled with meat, cheese or spinach.

tortellini: little rings of dough stuffed with chopped chicken, prosciutto ham, sausage or cheese.

vermicelli: "little worms": very thin spaghetti.
ziti: small tubes.

A NOTE ON ITALIAN WINES

The United States imports hundreds of different Italian wines, and most New York Italian restaurants have long wine lists. Following are some of the most popular Italian wines. For something a little different (often the owner or chef will stock wines from his own region), ask your waiter what he recommends (but check the price before you order).

Bardolino: light dry red from the region around Verona.

Chianti: red wine: if you want to be sure it's good, ask for *Chianti classico* (which does *not* come in a straw basket bottle). The only officially designated Chianti, this wine comes from Tuscany.

Corvo: Sicilian wine: may be red or white. Excellent with southern Italian cuisine.

Frascati: inexpensive, refreshing white table wine from Rome.

Soave: delicate white wine with a distinctive bouquet; from the region around Verona.

Valpolicella: mellow red that goes with a wide variety of dishes.

Verdicchio: dry white, slightly bitter wine from central Italy that goes especially well with fish.

JAPANESE NEW YORK

Japan in Midtown

In the last decade or so, Japanese restaurants, stores and cultural centers have been springing up around Manhattan like mushrooms after a spring rain. Their number has grown with New York's Japanese business community, which has quintupled in size since 1964. Today, over 450 Japanese firms have branch offices in New York, most of them in midtown. And the 20,000 Japanese nationals here because of these companies represent the city's largest foreign business colony. (The number of Japanese nationals in New York far exceeds the number of *Nisei*, or American-born persons of Japanese parentage.)

During their three- to five-year assignments in New York, most Japanese executives and their families live outside Manhattan, in Fort Lee, New Jersey; Westchester County; Riverdale in the Bronx; and Flushing, Queens. Many of these areas boast large Japanese grocery stores; one (in Queens) has a full-time Japanese school; another has its own Japanese golf club. But the biggest concentration of Japanese restaurants, social and cultural centers is not where the Japanese executive lives, but where he works—in midtown.

With everything else going on in Manhattan's nerve center, it takes a little looking to discover Japan in midtown. But once you know where to find it, you can easily spend a week in "Japan" without ever going farther east than Second Avenue.

What to do on your "trip"? Visit Japan House, where you can admire magnificent exhibits of Japanese art, see Japanese movies and take lessons in Japanese; shop for Imari porcelain, Eighteenth-century woodblock prints and painted screens in midtown's Japanese art galleries; study flower arranging, Japanese dance, tea ceremony, acupressure massage or Zen meditation at Nippon House, a Japanese massage school or the Zen Society; browse in a Japanese bookstore; and sample

Japan's remarkable cuisine in noodle shops, *sushi* bars and elegant restaurants where, if you like, you can sit shoeless, Japanese-fashion, at low tables on a *tatami* platform. And if you really want to immerse yourself in old Japan, stay for a night or two in one of the Japanese suites at the Hotel Kitano, where, among other traditional amenities, you'll find a slatted Japanese bathroom complete with high Japanese soaking tub.

HOW TO GET THERE
By subway: All subway lines lead to midtown. Grand Central Station is convenient to most of Japanese midtown.

JAPAN HOUSE
Simple, bold, elegant, harmonious. These are some of the adjectives that come to mind when you enter **Japan House** (333 E. 47 St., First–Second Aves., 832-1155), a beautiful four-story building near the United Nations which is the headquarters of the Japan Society, a nonprofit organization that seeks to promote better understanding between the United States and Japan. The building, designed by a Tokyo architect, Junzo Yoshimura, is typically Japanese in style and feeling, from its use of natural stone and wood to its two small Japanese gardens.

In its second-floor gallery, Japan House presents changing exhibits of Japanese art. In its first-floor auditorium, Japan House presents a series of Japanese films, poetry readings, craft demonstrations and cultural programs ranging from traditional *kabuki* and *no* theater to modern dance. In addition to these activities, the society maintains a library of over six thousand volumes on Japan for the use of its members, sponsors lectures by scholars and Japanese visitors and offers classes in Japanese and English. When there is an exhibit, the Gallery is *open daily 11 A.M.–5 P.M.; Fri. 11 A.M.–7:30 P.M.*

NIPPON CLUB
The red-carpeted lobby of the **Nippon Club** (145 W. 57 St., Sixth–Seventh Aves., LT1-2223) is a favorite meeting place for New York Japanese society. Founded in 1919, the Nippon Club provides meeting rooms, banquet halls, a beauty salon and other facilities for its approximately two thousand members. But you don't have to be a member to sign up for the reasonably priced courses the club offers in Japanese calligraphy and *sumie* brush painting, basic Japanese, ikebana (flower arranging), koto (Japanese lute), Japanese embroidery, Japanese classical dance and tea ceremony.

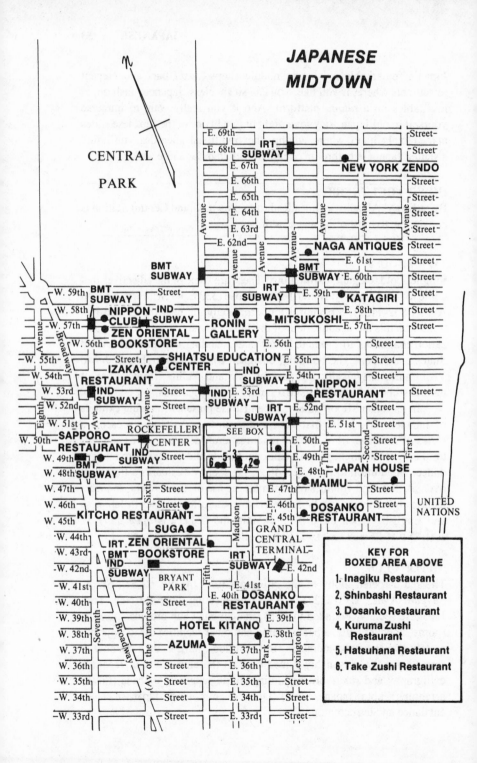

ZEN

Zen, which comes from the Sanskrit word *dhyana*, meaning "meditation," is a sect of Buddhism that took hold in China and Japan and has now acquired many followers in the West. In New York City, the leading Zen center is the Zen Studies Society, located in the **New York Zendo** (223 E. 67 St., Second–Third Aves., 861-3333), an old carriage house on a quiet side street a bit north of the bustle of midtown.

Every Thursday night, there is a public meeting in the Zendo from 7 to 9 P.M. in which Eido Roshi or a senior student talks about Zen and instructs beginners in *zazen*, or sitting meditation. After attending the initial session, anyone may attend the daily meditations, which are held in a traditional Japanese meditation hall.

Zen places more emphasis on action than on words. Nevertheless, the teachings of great Zen masters of the past have been recorded, and you can get them, in translation—along with books on Zen and the art of archery, Zen and the art of drawing, and even Zen and the art of business—at **Zen Oriental Bookstore**. One branch is at 142 W. 57 St. (Sixth–Seventh Aves., 582-4622); another is at 521 Fifth Ave. (43–44 Sts., 697-0840.) Both branches offer welcome refuge from humming midtown and a wide selection of books in addition to Zen publications.

HOTEL KITANO

If you have always dreamed of staying in a Japanese inn, but can't spare the time or money for a trip to Japan, you can indulge your fantasy to some degree in New York by reserving one of the Japanese suites at the **Hotel Kitano** (66 Park Ave. at 38 St., 685-0022). The rooms in these suites are furnished with *tatami* mats, low tables, legless chairs and a TV. At night, you merely push aside the furniture, take out your *futon*, or bedroll, which is stored in the closet during the day, roll it out on the tatami mat, and you're in business. If sleeping on the floor turns out to be less fun than you had thought, don't worry: each suite also comes with a Western-style bedroom. In addition, there's a Japanese bath complete with wooden slat flooring and a high soaking tub where, after you have soaped and rinsed off, you can sit and relax in hot water up to the chin.

The hotel lobby and most of the rooms at the Kitano are decorated in Colonial American style, but the hotel restaurant, Hakubai, is Japanese in decor and serves Japanese cuisine; elsewhere in the hotel are Japanese banquet halls and a traditional tea-ceremony cottage.

Rates are comparable to other midtown hotels. Ask about the Japanese Fantasy weekend plan, which includes two nights and one dinner for two.

JAPANESE MASSAGE

When there is no Japanese bath handy, you might try shiatsu, or Japanese acupressure, to relieve the tension of the day. One of the first to popularize this ancient form of massage in the United States is Wataru Ohashi, who has founded the nonprofit **Shiatsu Education Center** (52 W. 55 St., Fifth–Sixth Aves., 582-3424) to teach shiatsu to Americans. According to Mr. Ohashi, who has written seven books on the subject, shiatsu unblocks trapped energy in the body's pressure points, reducing tension and strengthening internal organs, and it can also be a valuable tool in preventing and diagnosing disease. The Shiatsu Education Center offers three-month courses on all levels as well as specialized courses in shiatsu for couples, shiatsu for yourself and shiatsu for runners. If you'd like to try it out before signing up, Mr. Ohashi, who has done shiatsu for members of the American Ballet Theater as well as the Japanese embassy, offers one hour of private instruction for about $30. He also occasionally gives free demonstration workshops.

JAPANESE FOOD STORE

Established in 1908, **Katagiri & Co.** (224 E. 59 St., Second–Third Aves., PL5-3566) is the oldest Japanese food store in Manhattan in continuous operation. Some of the biggest-selling items at Katagiri are the Japanese rice crackers, the instant ramen noodles (just boil in water and add the enclosed packet of seasonings for a quick lunch) and soybean foods: *miso*—fermented soybean paste, most often combined with fish broth for soup; *shoyu*—soy sauce that is lighter and less salty than its Chinese cousin; and *tofu*—the soft, white protein-rich soybean curd that is so versatile it has generated a whole new cuisine for vegetarians. (The Japanese deep-fry cakes of *tofu*, cube it for soup, sauté it with vegetables or eat it as is with a little *shoyu* and seasonings.)

If you want to go beyond *tofu* to explore the intricacies of Japanese cuisine, sooner or later you must learn how to make Japanese-style rice, which is more glutinous than Uncle Ben's and which, if it is to be prepared properly, requires watchful simmering. Katagiri carries both the rice (in quantities as large as 25-pound bags) and electric rice cookers (about $40.00), wonderful inventions that enable anyone to prepare perfect Japanese rice the first time.

After rice, noodles are the most important starch in Japanese cuisine. Katagiri carries *udon*, the thick wheat noodles eaten in winter, and *harusame* (literally, "spring rain" because they are so thin and clear), the cellophane yam-starch noodles that are one of the main ingredients in *sukiyaki*. Though *harusame* are easy enough to cook (just boil for a few minutes), you can also buy them already prepared and packed in water in a salami-shaped clear plastic case; in this form, they are known as *shiratake*.

Dried seaweed takes up several shelves at Katagiri. Rich in vitamins and minerals, seaweed has been ignored as a food by most of the world's peoples, but the Japanese have known its value for centuries. The most popular varieties, all stocked by Katagiri, are *kombu*, or kelp, used in making soup stock or flavoring rice; *nori*, or dried laver, paper-thin sheets that can be wrapped around balls of rice and fish for *sushi* or simply crumbled and sprinkled over rice for a simple meal; and *wakame*, or sea mustard, which is added to soups for flavoring, or in the summer, soaked and softened and mixed with a little rice vinegar, sugar and sesame oil for a cool salad. Katagiri also carries powdered seaweed, a seasoning for rice.

Elsewhere in the store, you'll find Japanese pickles and condiments, fresh *daikon* (mild white horseradish), rice vinegar, "tea bags" of *dashi* (which you dunk in boiling water to make the fish stock that is the basis of Japanese soups and simmered dishes), green tea, Japanese carbon steel knives for slicing raw fish, a clever serrated mortar for grinding sesame seeds or nuts into a fine paste (called a *suribachi*), ceramic tea pots and Japanese art supplies.

Prices are generally higher than at other Japanese food stores in New York, but then this is the only Japanese grocery in midtown. *Open Mon.–Fri. 9:30 A.M.–6:30 P.M.; Sat. 10 A.M.–6 P.M. Cl. Sun.*

JAPANESE IMPORTS

It is the rare office worker who hasn't owned a ceramic mug from **Azuma**. And young people just starting out in the city would be hard-pressed to furnish their apartments if it weren't for this chain of low-priced stores, where mass-produced paper lanterns, kites, mobiles, ceramics, baskets, fans, lacquerware, posters, cotton clothing and bed-spreads from Japan and elsewhere in the Orient are heaped in colorful but orderly profusion, and where most items are of remarkably good design for the price. There are six Azuma stores in midtown, but the one with the largest stock of merchandise is the Fifth Avenue branch (no. 415, 37–38 Sts., 889-4310). *Open Mon.–Sat. 10 A.M.–6:45 P.M.; Sun. noon–5 P.M.*

A very different kind of import store is **Mitsukoshi** (465 Park Avenue at 57 St., 935-6969), a New York branch of a quality depart-ment-store chain that is over three hundred years old. New York's Mitsukoshi, which occupies handsome beige-and-white quarters on the street floor of the Ritz Towers building, is not a general department store but a gallery specializing in Japanese art, in particular in Japanese porcelains. Although a few of the small contemporary items—plates, *sake* cups—sell for only $10 or so, most of the objects at Mitsukoshi will be affordable only to those whose limousines are waiting outside. An opulently decorated contemporary vase or a plain, roughly textured fifteenth-century Tamba urn may sell for over $14,000, while a particularly rare antique plate bears a price tag of $60,500.

Downstairs, there's a small, expensive restaurant whose ambiance might best be described as department-store plush. The Mitsukoshi Gallery is *open Mon.–Sat. 10 A.M.–6 P.M.;* the restaurant, *12 noon–2 P.M., 6 P.M.–10 P.M.; Sat. 6 P.M.–10 P.M. Cl. Sun.*

Around the corner from Mitsukoshi, the **Ronin Gallery** (605 Madison Ave., 57–58 Sts., 2nd floor, 688-0188) features yet another genre of Japanese art—the woodblock print. Ronin claims to have the largest collection of prints in the country—over five thousand—ranging from the seventeenth century to the present and including the works of the great masters like Morunobu, Utamara, Hokusai and Hiroshige. Only a small fraction of the collection is on display in this beautiful gallery at one time; the exhibit changes every six weeks. In addition to prints, Ronin's collection of Japanese art includes *netsuke* (small carved toggles worn on a man's sash), old bamboo baskets and antique jewelry. Ronin also does museum-quality framing of woodblock prints. The gallery is *open Mon.– Sat. 10 A.M.–6 P.M.*

Naga Antiques (167 E. 61 St., Lexington–Third Aves., 593-2788) specializes in Japanese folk art: screens, ceramics, textiles and lacquerware. *Open Mon.–Sat. 11 A.M.–6 P.M. Cl. Sun.*

SUSHI BARS, LARMEN SHOPS AND RESTAURANTS

The Japanese go out to eat frequently. In Japan, where traditionally only family or very old friends are invited to the home, most formal entertaining takes place in restaurants. And in a culture where oral agreements based on friendly personal relations carry more weight than written contracts, the restaurant is an indispensable social aid to conducting business. To a great degree, many of New York's Japanese restaurants are supported by New York's Japanese business community.

New York's two hundred Japanese restaurants fall into four categories: *sushi* bars, noodle shops, general restaurants and quasi-Japanese restaurants that cater exclusively to non-Japanese. The latter, best typified by the fantastically successful Benihana chain where chefs make a theatrical, knife-twirling production of slicing beef and vegetables, do not represent authentic Japanese cuisine and so are not covered here.

Sushi Bars   Sushi are vinegared rice balls topped or filled with something, usually raw fish. Many Westerners have trouble with the very idea of eating fish raw, but generally all it takes is a nibble or two for even the most reluctant *sushi*-eater to get hooked, because the fish used in *sushi* is so fresh, it doesn't taste fishy at all. *Toro*, for example—the raw marbled belly tuna often used for *sushi*—is so smooth and buttery in flavor and texture that to someone blindfolded it tastes like avocado.

The best seat at a *sushi* restaurant is at the counter, where, after refreshing your face and hands with the hot, moist towel offered when you sit down, you can look over the fish of the day, all beautifully sliced and carefully arranged in a refrigerated glass case (or ask the *sushi* chef what's special that day). A typical day's display at a New York *sushi* bar might include bite-sized oblongs of orange salmon, silver-skinned sea bass, lean dark-red tuna, glistening white squid, translucent slices of white fluke, whole velvety red shrimp, pale-pink slightly cooked butterfly shrimp, a mound of golden jewel-like roe, mustard-yellow sea urchin, whole gray octopus tentacles and yellow oblongs of sweet egg omelet. Perhaps there will also be abalone, sweet razor crab, goedeck clam or, in the spring, the marbled pink *toro* that fairly melts on the tongue. The pleasure of *sushi* lies in its variety of colors, textures and tastes and also in its esthetic appeal.

Most *sushi* restaurants offer a combination platter with a variety of the day's specialties, but you can also choose your own selection, which may be a sampling of this and that or perhaps ten tuna *sushi*, if tuna happens to be your favorite. *Sushi* ordered in this way (*okonomi*, "your choice") are priced according to the expensiveness of the fish.

A *sushi* bar highly recommended by many of the city's Japanese is **Take Zushi** (11 E. 48 St. off Fifth Ave., 755-6534, **I**), a modest and modestly priced little restaurant tucked away on the second floor of a building in midtown. The gleaming wood of the *sushi* bar, the large photo of green grasses beaded with raindrops on the wall behind the bar, the beautifully sliced fish sitting on a bed of bright green parsley—all give an overall impression of sparkling freshness that is borne out by the *sushi* prepared by Tokyo-trained chefs. A plate of assorted *sushi* is about $5. Take Zushi is *open Mon.–Sat. noon–3 P.M., 5 P.M.–10 P.M. Cl. Sun.*

A couple of doors down from Take Zushi is a good, slightly more expensive *sushi* restaurant, **Hatsuhana** (17 E. 48 St., 355-3345, **I–M**), where *sushi* is served on green *ti* leaves instead of the usual wooden platters. *Open Mon.–Fri. noon–2:30 P.M., 5:30 P.M.–9:30 P.M.; Sat., Sun. 5 P.M.–9 P.M.* **Kuruma Zushi** (423 Madison Ave. nr. 48 St., 751-5258, **I**) and the *sushi* bar at the **Nippon Restaurant** (145 E. 52 St., Lexington–Third Aves., PL8-0226, **M–E**) are also ranked high on the list. *Kuruma Zushi is open Mon.–Fri. noon–2:30* P.M., *5:30* P.M.–*10* P.M. *Cl. Sat., Sun. Nippon is open Mon.–Fri. noon–2:30* P.M., *5:30* P.M.–*10* P.M.; *Sat. 5:30* P.M.–*10:30* P.M. *Cl. Sun.* If you want *sushi* and your friend wants tempura, try **Izakaya** (43 W. 54 St. near Sixth Ave., 765-4683, **I**), which has a good *sushi* bar but also offers a variety of business-lunch specials for non-*sushi* fanciers. *Open Mon.–Fri. noon–2:30* P.M., *5:30* P.M.–*10:15* P.M.; *Sat. 5:30* P.M.–*10:15* P.M. *Cl. Sun.*

Noodle Shops   The Japanese equivalent of the pizza parlor is the noodle shop, where for $2 to $4, you can get a huge bowl of broth thick with wheat noodles, crunchy vegetables and slices of beef or pork flavored with seasonings like *miso*, soy sauce, curry, or butter and salt. This hearty noodle soup, called *ramen* or *larmen*, is said to have originated in Hokkaido, Japan's northernmost island. On Manhattan island, a chain of noodle shops called **Dosanko** (the "do" stands for Hokkaido) has converted a large number of office workers into confirmed lunchtime *larmen*-eaters. Dosanko has several shops in midtown (423 Madison Ave., 48–49 Sts., 688-8575, *open Mon.–Fri. 11:30* A.M.–*10* P.M.; *Sat., Sun. noon–8* P.M.; 341 Lexington Ave., 39–40 Sts., 683-4740, *open daily 11* A.M.–*10* P.M.; 135 E. 45 St., Third–Lexington Aves., 697-2967, *open Mon.–Fri. 11* A.M.–*9:30* P.M.; *Sat. noon –5* P.M. *Cl. Sun.*, **C**).

A nonfranchised noodle shop that offers a bit more variety (and even lower prices) is **Sapporo** (146 W. 29 St., Sixth–Seventh Aves., 869-8972, **C**), where in addition to larmen, you can get *donburi* (lunch in a bowl consisting of rice, meat and vegetables), *tempura, sukiyaki, teriyaki* and fried noodles. *Open daily 11:30* A.M.–*11:30* P.M.

Restaurants   Sushi bars and larmen shops will only give you a nodding acquaintance with Japanese cuisine. To appreciate the tremendous range and variety of Japanese cooking, you must dine at a good Japanese restaurant, preferably on an *omakase* dinner. All the best restaurants offer *omakase*—a traditional, seven- to fifteen-course meal in which the dishes are chosen by the chef from the day's specialties.

Many Japanese businessmen and UN diplomats eat regularly at **Shinbashi** (280 Park Ave., entrance on 48 St. bet. Park and Madison Aves., 661-3915, **E**), a quietly elegant restaurant serving quietly fabulous food. In addition to exquisite renditions of the most popular dishes—*sashimi, tempura, sukiyaki, shabu shabu*—Shinbashi offers some out-of-the-ordinary entrees, like *kabayaki*, a delicately flavored, imported Japanese eel broiled in sweet rice wine and soy sauce, and *kabutoyaki*, a lobster *sashimi* in which fresh lobster tail is sliced into *sashimi* fillets and the rest of the lobster broiled in its shell. Shinbashi's beef *teriyaki*— sliced prime rib eye glistening with a delicate marinade, cooked just until doneness and no more—is perfection. Three *omakase* dinners are offered here, for $25, $30 and $40. *Open Mon.–Fri. 11:30 A.M.–2:30 P.M., 5:30 P.M.–10 P.M.; Sat. 5:30 P.M.–10 P.M. Cl. Sun.*

One of the oldest Japanese restaurants in New York is **Nippon** (145 E. 52 St., Lexington–Third Aves., PL8-0226, **E**). The food here is authentically prepared and beautifully served, and the menu boasts about twice as many dishes as any other Japanese restaurant in the city. Some of the more unusual items you can get at Nippon are appetizers and side dishes: slices of smoked salmon or raw beef served with a hot mustard sauce (*hanazukuri*), barbecued chicken skin (*torikawa-yaki*), cuttlefish with cod roe (*masago-are*) and preserved squid (*shiokara*). Owner Nobuyoshi Kuraoka is constantly adding new items to keep the menu exciting and seasonal.

Nippon offers four kinds of seating: Western-style tables and chairs; a long, curved, combination *sushi*-and-*tempura* bar; a Japanese-style dining floor (low, tables, *tatami* mats, and you must remove your shoes before entering); and private Japanese dining rooms where wells beneath the low tables allow Westerners unaccustomed to the Japanese style of sitting to dangle their legs in comfort.

Omakase dinners are $20 to $30 depending on the number of dishes and must be ordered in advance. *Open Mon.–Fri. noon–2:30 P.M., 5:30 P.M.–10 P.M.; Sat. 5:30 P.M.–10 P.M. Cl. Sun.*

Japanese businessmen who want to impress American clients often take them to **Inagiku** (in the Waldorf-Astoria Hotel, 111 E. 49 St., Park–Lexington Aves., 355-0440, **E**), a luxurious, rather pompously decorated restaurant reminiscent of medieval samurai castles where the food is consistently excellent and the menu is heavily weighted towards those dishes Westerners know (*tempura, sukiyaki,* filet mignon).

Inagiku is divided into many different dining areas, of which the most spectacular is the round, gilt-canopied Kinkaku Room. According to the menu, this room is meant to evoke the splendor of the famed Kinkakuji, or Golden Pavilion Shrine, built in Kyoto in 1424—a rather exalted setting for a *tempura* bar, although the *tempura* at Inagiku (the house specialty) is truly inspired.

Another excellent dish here, and one that is great fun to order for a large party, is *shabu shabu*. First, the waitress brings you a large pot of broth and starts it simmering on a hot plate at your table. Then she carries out an enormous platter covered with slices of raw prime rib-eye beef sliced very thin, fresh spinach, mushrooms, Chinese cabbage, miscellaneous other vegetables and *udon* noodles. With your chopsticks, you pick up a piece of beef or vegetable and swirl it around in the simmering broth until it is done to your taste. (The sound of the chopsticks swishing around in the pot gives the dish its onomatopoeic name.) Then you dip the morsel into lemon soy sauce or a sesame dipping sauce and enjoy the mingling of flavors on your tongue while you cook up your next mouthful. At the end, the pot is full of flavorful broth, the waitress adds the *udon* and you have noodle soup! If after all this, you have room for dessert, ask for the red bean ice cream.

The chef's gourmet *kaiseki* dinner (*kaiseki* refers to the cooking that accompanies the tea ceremony and implies the most refined kind of Japanese food), a ten-course affair, is $25.75. *Open Mon.–Fri. noon–2:30 P.M., 5:30 P.M.–10 P.M.; Sat., 5:30 P.M.–10 P.M. Cl. Sun.*

For the ultimate in refined Japanese cuisine in New York, many Japanese gourmets think **Kitcho** (22 W. 46 St., Fifth–Sixth Aves., 575-8880, **E**) has no peer. Located smack in the middle of flamboyant Little Brazil, where the pavement in front of the Brazilian restaurants is painted with black-and-white swirls like the sidewalks of Rio and where many stores sport three-foot-high signs proclaiming in Portuguese, "HERE IS A BRAZILIAN STORE," Kitcho goes out of its way to be unobtrusive. On its all-black slatted-wood facade, a three-inch plaque reluctantly whispers "Kitcho"; this is the restaurant's only identifying sign.

Inside, the small restaurant is as austere as a Zen monastery. Less is more applies not only to the decor but to the food; Kitcho is the only Japanese restaurant in New York that hasn't beefed up its portions to please Western appetites. "Kitcho? Yes, the food is good there, but it's a restaurant for drinkers, not eaters," says one young Japanese New Yorker. Be that as it may, this is about as close as you can get in New York to the fine restaurants of Japan.

For a hefty room fee ($75 for lunch, $135 for dinner), you may reserve one of the private Japanese dining rooms on the second or third floor. On the third floor, there is no menu. You select a price category, from $20 to $50, and the chef selects your dishes for you. All Japanese rooms and *omakase* dinners must be reserved far in advance. (Rooms are sometimes booked a year ahead.) *Open Mon.–Fri. noon–2:30 P.M., 6 P.M.–10:30 P.M.; Sun. 5 P.M.–10:30 P.M. Cl. Sat.*

PIANO BARS
After a long day at the office, many Japanese businessmen head for a Japanese piano bar to unwind over a few drinks, gripe about the boss with the other guys from the office and be soothed by the attentions of

beautiful Japanese hostesses. Most of these bars feature a female singer who croons sentimental songs about home to set the right nostalgic mood. Sometimes, songbooks in hand, the patrons join in, and if a customer gets sufficiently loaded, there may be a solo performance from the audience. There are at least twenty Japanese piano bars in midtown Manhattan, some of which double as restaurants. You can easily blow $100 in one evening at one of these bars—a lot of yen to have your ego massaged (and that's all that will be). A non-Japanese would feel out of place at most of these, and a woman visitor would feel downright unwelcome. But if you are male, curious and speak a little Japanese, here are two places to try: **Suga** (7 W. 44 St. off Fifth Ave., 575-0610) and **Maimu** (143 E. 47 St., Lexington–Third Aves., 759-9052).

Around Town in Manhattan

JAPAN UPTOWN

For many years, a small colony of Japanese lived on the Upper West Side near Columbia University. Once known in the Japanese community as Japanese Harlem, the area between West 105th and 120th streets is now home to only about seven hundred to a thousand Japanese. Except for the Buddhist Church on 105th Street, a Japanese food store or two, a couple of restaurants and the Japanese cherry trees that line both sides of the Henry Hudson Parkway from 72nd to 125th streets, the Japanese presence is very faint in Japanese Harlem these days.

An enormous statue of Shinran Shonin, who founded the Jodo Shin-shu sect of Buddhism in Japan in the thirteenth century, stands in front of the **New York Buddhist Church** (331 Riverside Dr., 105–106 Sts., 678-9214), a former mansion that has become a social, cultural and religious center for the Japanese community. The church offers courses (open to all) in *buyo* (Japanese dance), *ikebana* (flower arranging), judo, *kyudo* (archery) and *kendo* (sword-fighting).

For Japanese groceries, the place to go on the Upper West Side is **Japanese Foodland** (2620 Broadway at 99 St., 740-3761), a neat little store where you can get frozen *sukiyaki* beef sliced paper-thin, fresh *tofu*, powdered soybean powder to make your own *tofu* and all the staples of Japanese cooking at very reasonable prices. Before the New Year, Japanese in the neighborhood come to Foodland to get their *mochi*, a glutinous rice cake traditionally eaten on New Year's Eve. As explained by Kaye, the helpful manager of Japanese Foodland, *mochi* stretches like the mozzarella on pizza when you eat it, and this lengthening symbolizes the lengthening of your own life. *Open Mon.–Sat. 11 A.M.–7:30 P.M., Sun. 12 noon–6 P.M.*

A well-stocked Japanese food store farther downtown is **Tanayaka** (326 Amsterdam Ave. nr. 75 St., 874-6600).

FOLK ART

Min means "people," *gei* means "crafts"; together, the words refer to objects made for domestic use—the traditional folk arts of Japan. On the second floor of a loft building in Soho, Hiroshi and Kinue Sugimoto have opened a store named **Mingei** (398 Broadway, Spring–Broome Sts., 431-6176) which sells eighteenth-, nineteenth- and twentieth-century household objects from Japan.

The shop itself is a beautiful blend of utility and art. Bare polished wood floors, white walls, huge paper lanterns designed by Noguchi and simple pine storage cabinets built by Hiroshi create a pleasingly bare, uncluttered backdrop for the Sugimotos' collection.

When I visited, the walls were hung with *tsutsugaki*, traditional bedding fabric strikingly dyed with deep indigo designs of cranes, flowers and family crests. (Prices for these began at $200.) In a display shelf on one wall, five-piece sets of eighteenth- and nineteenth-century *saké* and teacups stood in neat blue-and-white-patterned rows (five-piece because the word for "four" is a homonym for "death" and so considered an unlucky number for sets of anything in Japan). Boldly colored cotton on a cabinet in the center of the room turned out to be folded flags—nineteenth-century sumo wrestlers' banners which would have been hung from a bamboo pole outside the sumo stadium to advertise a match.

Each item on display reflects the personal taste of the owners. Mingei will delight anyone who appreciates beauty in the everyday. *Open Tues.–Fri. 2 P.M.–7 P.M., Sat. 1 P.M.–7 P.M.*

JAPANESE INTERIORS, SHOJI AND LACQUER

Even if what you want is not just Japanese objects and furnishings but a completely Japanese home, if you live in New York, you need not send to Japan for craftsmen. Several Japanese concerns in the city make or import *shoji* (Japanese sliding screens) and design and install complete Japanese interiors.

Miva Shoji and Interiors (107 W. 17 St., Sixth–Seventh Aves., 691-8984), manufactures its own *shoji* right on its cheerful sawdust-filled premises. The sliding screens, which are made of laminated rice paper, laminated silk or fiberglass placed between pine frames, are all hand finished, using a minimum of nails and glue. According to the owners of Miya, *shoji* are practical as well as beautiful, cutting down on sound and dust, eliminating drafts completely and adding another layer of insulation to home or office. Miya makes all screens to specification and will send its shoji anywhere in the country. (Call or write for brochure and price lists.)

Ichiro Ohta at **Tansuya** (71 Mercer St., Broome–Spring Sts., 966-1782) in Soho, also designs and builds Japanese interiors. His specialty, however, is hand lacquerwork, a centuries-old Japanese art. Tansuya also specializes in custom-made *tatami* platforms, in which a *tatami* mat is set inside a low cedar-frame platform. Depending on its size, one of these platforms can be used as a bed (good for the back), a table, a sofa or the floor of a Japanese-style room.

BONSAI

With a few hours of sunlight every day and a Japanese bonsai, any apartment dweller can have an aged, windswept pine growing in the living room. Bonsai—the art of growing miniature trees in containers—began in Japan about eight centuries ago as a means of bringing nature indoors. Many plant stores in New York sell bonsai along with house-plants, but **Japan Bonsai Nursery** (135 W. 28 St., Sixth–Seventh Aves., 594-6725) in the flower district, sells bonsai exclusively. The trees at the nursery range from about $10 for new stock to hundreds of dollars for a fifty-year-old five-needle pine. You can get everything you need for the care of your tree here, too: soil, shears and books on bonsai. The store is *open every day but Sunday*, and will ship trees anywhere in the world from its nurseries in Farmingdale, New Jersey.

KABUKI RESTAURANT

There are many Japanese restaurants outside of midtown, but one that deserves special mention is **Kabuki** (115 Broadway, Cedar–Liberty Sts., 962-4677, **M**). Tucked away below street level in the Wall Street district, Kabuki is neither a samurai castle nor an austere Zen garden, but takes its character from yet another side of Japanese culture—the colorful kabuki theater. Woodblock prints of kabuki actors hang on the wall, and the color scheme is a warm, theatrical red and purple. There are three seating areas at Kabuki—a U-shaped bar, Western tables and a long *tatami* platform divided by screens into five Japanese-style dining rooms open on one side.

The food at Kabuki, though perhaps not as refined at the food you will find at some of midtown's best Japanese restaurants, gratifies the billfold as well as the tongue and the eye. A typical deluxe Kabuki *Teishoku* dinner costs only $13.50.

A young Japanese couple recommended Kabuki to me, but the regular clientele is the Wall Street crowd, who grab a hurried *donburi* lunch here on weekdays and return to decompress over drinks and dinner on Friday nights. The atmosphere is informal, inviting; the waitresses, dressed in kimonos, are pleasant and efficient. And after 7 P.M., it is easy to find parking nearby. *Open Mon.–Fri. noon–3 P.M., 5:30 P.M.–8:45 P.M. Cl. Sat., Sun.*

Around Town in the Boroughs

Japanese food stores outside of Manhattan include the following:

In Queens: **Daido** (41-54 Main St., Flushing, 961-1550), **Japan Food Corp.** (11-31 31 Ave., Long Island City, RA1-6820).

In the Bronx: **Marumiya** (318 W. 231 St., 884-5858), **Meidiya** (5678 Mosholu Ave., 884-5202), **Tanakaya** (5995 Riverdale Ave., Riverdale, 874-6600).

In Brooklyn: **Japan Food Corp.** (40 Varick Ave., 456-8805).

Festivals and Holidays

One of the prettiest summer festivals in New York is the **Japanese Obon Festival,** presented by the Japanese Buddhist Church (332 Riverside Dr.) on the Saturday of the closest weekend to July 15.

The Obon Festival commemorates the generous act of Mogallana, a disciple of the Buddha in the sixth century B.C. According to the story, Mogallana had a vision that his dead mother was suffering in *Dukha*, the "hell of the hungry ghost." Wishing to help her, he asked Gautama Buddha what he could do. The Buddha suggested that he invite teachers and friends to a chanting of the *sutras* and feed the poor people of the village. Mogallana did this, and for his generosity, his mother was released from *Dukha* and achieved true happiness. In his joy, Mogallana danced with his friends; this was the origin of the Bon Dance, which Japanese all over the world perform to celebrate the act of a selfless man and to honor parents and ancestors.

In New York, the Obon Dance takes place at the Riverside Park Mall at West 103rd Street, in the early evening. The setting couldn't be better. Behind the mall, which is decorated with hundreds of colorful paper lanterns for the occasion, the Hudson River sends cool breezes toward the dancers (albeit across the West Side Highway), and in front of the mall, a tier of stone steps serves as a grandstand for the Japanese families and others who have come to watch. In the audience, restless children in brightly patterned kimonos (the girls with big pastel bows in their hair) flit here and there like brilliant butterflies, alighting occasionally, and only for an instant, on some relative's knee.

The dancers—almost one hundred of them—from various cultural clubs around metropolitan New York stand on the mall, each contingent dressed in crisp cotton kimonos of a different pattern; one group is in red-and-white checks, another in blue-and-white checks, a third in flowered designs of many colors. An official of the Buddhist Church announces each dance, and then the recorded music begins. Moving in single file in two concentric circles (the best dancers are in the inner circle), the dancers repeat a series of simple steps and hand gestures. From the grandstand, the circles of kimonoed dancers, legs and arms all moving in unison, form a beautiful kaleidoscope; for a few moments, even the "butterflies" stand still at the sight. For information, call the Japanese Buddhist Church (678-9214).

Japanese Food

Japanese food is a highly refined cuisine of tremendous subtlety and variety, in which the visual appeal of a dish is almost as important as its taste. The staples of traditional Japanese cuisine are rice, seafood (fish is eaten both cooked and raw), soybean products, noodles, many kinds of vegetables and dried seaweed. In recent times, the number of dishes that use beef, chicken, pork and eggs has greatly increased.

A traditional Japanese meal is a multicourse affair that includes appetizers, several entrees (there is no main entree), soup, rice and pickled vegetables. Dessert in a Japanese restaurant is a concession to Western taste and generally consists of fruit, sherbet or ice cream. Hot green tea, warm *sake* (rice wine) or ice-cold Japanese beer is drunk with the meal.

MENU GLOSSARY
akadashi wan: red soybean paste soup.
agedofu: fried bean curd cake.
cha: tea ("O-cha" is "honorable tea").

chawanmushi: meat of chicken and vegetables steamed in egg custard.

chazuke: rice soaked in tea or seaweed broth.

donburi: bowl of rice topped with chicken and egg or meat and vegetables in a seasoned sauce.

gohan: steamed rice.

gyôza: fried meat-and-vegetable-filled dumplings.

hama: clams.

kabayaki: Japanese eel broiled in sweet rice wine and soy sauce.

kakiage: tempura pancake of vegetables and shrimp.

kappa or kappa maki: vinegared rice rolled in seaweed and filled with cucumber—a kind of *sushi*.

katsu: pork.

kushikatsu: deep-fried pork cutlet, skewered with mushrooms and green pepper.

larmen: noodles in seasoned broth.

misoshiru: bean paste soup.

mizutaki: simmered chicken dish.

nabemono: food cooked at the table.

negimayaki: sliced beef rolled with scallions and broiled in a marinade.

nigiri: ''sandwich''-type *sushi*, in which a ball of rice is topped with a piece of raw fish.

O: prefix meaning ''honorable,'' as ''O-*sashimi*'' or ''honorable *sashimi*.''

Okonomi: ''your choice; as you like it'' (usually refers to *sushi*, *i.e.*, you choose the *sushi* topping).

omakase: formal dinner in which the diner leaves the choice of dishes to the chef.

oshinko: pickled vegetables.

oyako: chicken and egg.

ramen: same as *larmen*.

sake: alcoholic beverage brewed from rice.

sashimi: thinly sliced raw fish fillet served with soy sauce, *wasabi* and pickled ginger.

shabu shabu: dish cooked at the table in which thinly sliced beef and fresh vegetables are simmered in seasoned broth and eaten with dipping sauces.

shioyaki: method of broiling in which fish is salted and broiled with its skin.

shitashi: boiled spinach with sesame sauce.

suimono: lit., ''vinegared things''—a salad of cooked fish and raw vegetables in light rice-vinegar dressing.

sushi: vinegared rice balls topped or filled with raw fish or vegetables (See Sushi Glossary).

tamago-yaki: Japanese omelet in which seasoned egg is cooked a sheet at a time and all sheets rolled together.

teishoku: a multicourse traditional Japanese-style meal.

tekka or tekka-maki: vinegared rice filled with raw tuna and rolled in seaweed—a kind of *sushi*.

tempura: seafood and sliced vegetables which have been dipped in batter and deep-fried.

teriyaki: lit. "shining broil"—marinated in soy sauce and sweet rice wine (*mirin*) and broiled.

tonkatsu: deep-fried pork cutlet with sauce.

tori: chicken.

tsukemono: pickled vegetables eaten with rice at the end of the meal.

usu zukuri: *sashimi* sliced extremely thin.

wasabi: sharp green horseradish paste.

yaki: broiled.

yakko tofu or dofu: cold bean curd served with seasoned soy sauce.

yokan: sweet bean jelly confection, eaten with green tea.

yosenabe: Japanese *bouillabaise* cooked at the table.

yudofu: bean curd seasoned in seasoned broth.

zarusoba: buckwheat noodles eaten with dipping sauce.

SHUSHI GLOSSARY

anago: sea eel

awabi: abalone.

ebi: shrimp.

ikura: salmon roe.

kappa: cucumber rolled in rice with seaweed.

maguro: tuna.

nigiri: "sandwich-type" *sushi* of rice topped with fish.

okonomi: your selection—you choose the sushi you want.

tai: red snapper.

tamago: omelet.

tekka: tuna rolled in rice with seaweed.

toro: the "sirloin strip" of tuna (from the fatty belly).

JEWISH NEW YORK

The Lower East Side

The first Jew to set foot in New York—the first Jew, for that matter, to set foot in North America—was one Jacob Barsimon from Amsterdam, who arrived in the Dutch colony of New Amsterdam in 1654. His purpose in coming to the New World is unknown; he may have been a trader.

One month after Barsimon's arrival, five Jewish families from South America landed in the new colony. These twenty-three men, women and children were Sephardim—descendants of Spanish- and Portuguese-speaking Jews who had lived on the Iberian peninsula before the Inquisition—and they were fleeing religious persecution in Portuguese Brazil. Their ship, originally bound for Holland, had been captured by pirates and brought instead to New Amsterdam. Peter Stuyvesant, then governor of the colony, requested permission of the Dutch West India Company to send the new arrivals away, "praying most seriously that the deceitful race be not allowed further to infest and trouble this new colony." But the company, many of whose stockholders were Jewish, replied that the newcomers were to be allowed to remain.

In 1730, the Jews of New York erected a synagogue on Mill Street (today South William Street). So small was the Jewish population of the city then that this one-story building remained the only synagogue in New York for almost a hundred years.

The first real wave of Jewish immigrants came in the 1830s and 1840s, when Polish and Bavarian Jews fled to America to escape heavy taxes and restrictions placed on them. The Revolution of 1848 started the second wave, which rolled in this time from Germany, Austria and Hungary. Unlike the Jewish pioneers from Brazil, these immigrants—like almost all the Jewish immigrants to come—were Ashkenazim, Yiddish- or German-speaking descendants of Jews from the German states or central Europe. By 1880, there were 85,000 Jews in New York.

In 1881, a wave of pogroms in southern Russian triggered a mass
Jewish exodus: between 1881 and 1924, pogroms, persecution and war
drove more than one third of the Jewish population of eastern Europe to
America. By 1910, there were about a million Jews in New York—the
largest Jewish population of any city in the world. Over half this population—600,000—lived in twenty city blocks in Manhattan: the Lower
East Side.

A seething immigrant metropolis of airless, sunless, steaming tenements and streets teeming with pushcarts, the Lower East Side was both
home and work place to the east European Jews, most of whom found
jobs in the area's booming garment industry. Paid by the piece, men,
women and children slaved from dawn to dark over their sewing
machines in overcrowded apartments or squalid tenement flats converted
into sweat shops.

Yet there was more to life on the Lower East Side than just sweat and
drudgery, for the period was one of great intellectual and cultural fer-
ment. Every issue and ism of the day—the revolution in Russia, unions in
America, anarchism, socialism, communism, capitalism—was hotly
discussed on the Lower East Side, in the cafés, in the Yiddish newspapers, in the lecture halls that were jammed every night. On the Sabbath, religious Jews filled the synagogues to listen to the singing of
golden-voiced cantors, while newly secular Jews packed the Second
Avenue Yiddish theaters to see the latest show or star. The Lower East
Side throbbed with the whir of sewing machines, the shouts of peddlers,
the speeches of the intellegentsia, the songs of the Yiddish theater. And
though it was an era of great poverty and hardship, it was also an era of
great energy, opportunity and ideas.

By the 1920s, the tide of immigration from eastern Europe had
stemmed, many immigrants had saved enough to move to less crowded
parts of the city and the position of the Lower East Side as the heart of
Jewish New York had begun to wane.

Smaller waves followed the great east European migration: refugees
and concentration-camp survivors after World War II; Hungarian Jews
after the Hungarian Revolution of 1956; Jewish immigrants from Morocco, Israel, Cuba, Egypt, Syria, the Soviet Union and Iran in the 1960s and
1970s.

Today, the native tongues of the Jews of New York include English,
Yiddish, Ladino, Spanish, Greek, French, Persian, Russian, German,
Polish, Hebrew and Arabic. A New York Jew may be an immigrant or a
ninth-generation American; a Sephardi or an Ashkenazi; a bearded,
ultrareligious Hasid, an atheist or anything in between these two
extremes.

When the Jews moved out of the Lower East Side, they settled in Washington Heights and, later, on the Upper West Side of Manhattan; in Brownsville, East New York, Borough Park and Bensonhurst in Brooklyn; and in the lower Bronx. Today, however, Jews are dispersed throughout the city, and, of the old neighborhoods, only Borough Park and parts of the Upper West Side are still predominantly Jewish. Brooklyn has the largest Jewish population (514,000), followed by Queens (380,000), Manhattan (170,000) and the Bronx (143,000).

The Jewish population of Greater New York in 1975 was almost two million, or about 30 percent of the entire Jewish population of the United States. With the headquarters of practically every national Jewish organization in the country in New York, the city is the unofficial capital of Jewish America.

The cradle of Jewish New York, the Lower East Side—which was home to the Germans and Irish before the Jews—is today mainly Puerto Rican and Chinese. Jews, most of them elderly, make up only about 25 percent of the population.

Yet the visitor in search of the old Jewish Lower East Side will be amazed at how much remains. There are still magnificent old synagogues, fascinating historic sites and classic old dairy restaurants and delicatessens. There are factories that manufacture prayer shawls, *yarmulkes,* and *matzo.* The old-fashioned Jewish appetizing stores and bakeries on the Lower East Side still sell the best smoked fish, the best pickles, the best pumpernickels, the best knishes and the best bialys in New York—and at the best prices. Rows of old tenements still give the neighborhood its distinctive character (it's not hard to imagine what it looked like in the old days). And, amidst the newer Puerto Rican and Chinese businesses, there are still Jewish bookstores and Jewish antique stores, and even a kosher winery.

And though the pushcarts are gone, the Lower East Side is still a shopper's paradise, where bargain hunters will find designer clothes, old fur coats, linens and appliances at well below uptown prices. On Saturday, almost everything on the Lower East Side is closed for the Jewish Sabbath, but on Sunday, all the stores are open and Orchard Street from Delancey to Houston becomes a freewheeling open-air bazaar.

TOURS OF THE LOWER EAST SIDE AND JEWISH NEW YORK
Tours of Jewish New York (628-2244), which is affiliated with the American Jewish Congress, offers excellent all-day **bus tours** of sights of Jewish interest in New York. A typical tour might take you to a pickle store, a kosher winery and a restaurant on the Lower East Side; the

Lubavitch Hasidic community in Brooklyn; a ritual bath or *mikvah* in mid-Manhattan; and Temple Emanu-El on Fifth Avenue. Tours for individuals leave Sunday at 10 A.M. and Wednesday at 9 A.M. from the New York Public Library at Fifth Avenue and 41st Street. Group tours leave any day but Friday or Saturday. Call ahead for information, fees and reservations.

The **92nd Street YMHA** offers annual **spring walking tours** of the Lower East Side, Williamsburg, the old Jewish Bronx and Jewish Harlem. The tour of the Lower East Side takes you to some of the most interesting old synagogues and to the Spanish and Portuguese Cemetery. Call 427-6000 for information.

With this book, you can, of course, devise your own walking tour of the Lower East Side and Jewish New York, tailored to your own particular interests. Those who desire more details and statistics may want to consult *Jewish Landmarks of New York,* by Bernard Postal and Lionel Koppman (Fleet Press), a veritable encyclopedia of facts about Jewish New York.

SYNAGOGUES ON THE LOWER EAST SIDE

The Lower East Side is literally a museum of splendid old synagogues. Though many have been totally or partially abandoned, others still hold daily services. If you would like to see the interior of a particular synagogue at a time other than when it is open for services, arrangements should be made in advance. The abandoned synagogues are locked; arrangements to visit them should be made in advance with the caretaker, if there is one.

Formerly a Baptist church, **Beth Hamedrash Hagodol** ("The Great House of Study," 60 Norfolk St., Grand–Broome Sts.) dates from the mid-nineteenth century. The simple, twin-tower building, which is painted cream with deep red trimming, became a Jewish house of worship in 1885; it was the first Russian-Jewish Orthodox synagogue in the country.

Architecturally the grandest synagogue on the Lower East Side is **Khal Adas Jeshurun with Anshe Lubz** ("The Community of the People of Israel with the People of Lubz," 14 Eldridge St., Canal–Division Sts.), erected in 1886 by a group of Polish Jews. The first large building built specifically as a synagogue by the east European Ashkenazic Jews (the Sephardic Jews had had a synagogue since 1730), Khal Adas Jeshurun combines Moorish, Gothic and Romanesque architectural features. The splendid wooden facade is a marvel of keyhole-shaped doorways and window spaces framed by delicate marble columns. Inside, amid rubble and fallen plaster, the upstairs sanctuary is magnificent still, though abandoned now for over forty years.

In stark contrast to the arabesque facade of Khal Adas Jeshurun is the solid, rough-hewn fieldstone exterior of **The Bialystoker Synagogue** (7 Willett St. Grand–Broome Sts., GR5-0165). Erected in 1826 as a Methodist Episcopal Church, the Federal-style building with its peaked roof was bought by a Jewish congregation from Bialystok (a city and province of Russia and later, Poland) in 1905. As if to make up for the plainness of the exterior, the interior if colorfully decorated. A New York City landmark, the Bialystoker Synagogue is very well maintained by its sizeable congregation.

The First Roumanian Shul (89 Rivington St., Orchard–Ludlow Sts., 673-2835), though a handsome enough Romanesque revival building with one of the largest sanctuaries in the city, is notable more for its history than its architecture. Originally a Methodist Church, the building was purchased by a Rumanian-Jewish congregation, and by 1890 was being used as a synagogue. One of the leading synagogues of its day, the First Roumanian Shul was famous for its golden-voiced *hazans* or cantors, who included the most celebrated American cantor of all time, Yossel Rosenblatt. This shul is well maintained.

HOW TO GET THERE
By subway: *IND* F train to Second Ave.–E. Houston stop, Delancey–Essex St., or East Broadway–Canal St.; or *BMT* J or M to Bowery–Delancey or Essex–Delancey. **By bus**: *M15* First Ave. northbound (Allen St.), Second Ave. southbound; or *M14* East 14 St. (Essex St.). If you go **By car**: the *Municipal Parking Lot* on Essex St. between Rivington and Delancey Sts. offers the cheapest rates. On Sundays, try to get there before 9 A.M.; the lot fills up very quickly. (Open 8 A.M.–7 P.M.).

Suggested Walking Tour: East Houston St. from Forsyth to Orchard St., south on Orchard to Hester or Canal Sts., east to Essex St., back north on Essex, with possible side trips on Grand, Delancey and Rivington Sts.

HISTORIC LANDMARKS
The oldest artifact on the island of Manhattan and the oldest Jewish landmark in North America is the **Spanish and Portuguese Cemetery,** a

JEWISH LOWER EAST SIDE

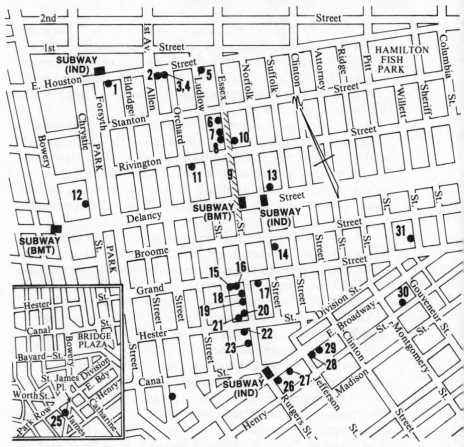

1. Yonah Schimmel's Knishes Bakery

2. Russ and Daughters

3. Ben's Cheese Shop

4. Moishe's Bakery

5. Katz's Deli

6. Louis Stavsky Bookstore

7. Bernstein-on-Essex-Street Restaurant

8. Economy Candy

9. Essex St. Market

10. Schapiro's Kosher Wine

11. First Roumanian Shul

12. Sammy's Rumanian Jewish Restaurant

13. Ratner's Dairy Restaurant

14. Beth Hamedrash Hagodol

15. Grand Dairy Restaurant

16. Grand Sterling Silver Co.

17. Kossar's Bialys

18. Emmanuel Weisburg Antiques

19. L. Hollander Pickles

20. Pickleman

21. Gertel's Bakery

22. Guss's Pickles

23. Bezalel Art

24. Khal Adas Jeshurun with Anshe Lubz

25. Spanish and Portuguese Cemetery

26. Garden Cafeteria

27. Old Forward Building

28. Seward Park Library

29. Educational Alliance

30. Henry Street Settlement House

31. Bialystoker Synagogue

small plot of land just south of Chatham Square and just outside the Jewish Lower East Side proper, in Chinatown. Purchased in 1682 by the Spanish and Portuguese Jews of Congregation Shearith Israel ("Remnant of Israel"), the plot is actually the second Jewish burial ground in Manhattan; the location of the first, granted to the Jews in 1656 by Peter Stuyvesant, is unknown.

The first person thought to be buried in the Spanish Portuguese Cemetery was Benjamin Bueno de Mesquita in 1683. Also buried here are eighteen Jewish soldiers from the Revolutionary War; Abraham de Lucena, who brought the first Torah scroll to North America and was the second *hazan* of Shearith Israel; and Gershon Mendes Seixas, the first American-born rabbi, who was a friend of George Washington and a trustee of Columbia College.

A few blocks from the cemetery, there is a triumvirate of buildings on East Broadway between Rutger and Clinton streets that did more to educate and influence the Jewish immigrants of the Lower East Side than any school or university: the original Forward Building, the Seward Park Library and the Educational Alliance. In the old days, these two blocks, which also held bookstores, publishers' offices and the offices of two other Yiddish dailies besides the *Forward*, were jokingly referred to as the Athens of the Lower East Side.

The ten-story **Forward Building** (175 East Broadway), where the most influential Yiddish daily newspaper in the country was published for over sixty years, was built between 1911 and 1912. At the time of its construction, it was considered a skyscraper, for it towered high above the tenements on either side. Under the dynamic guidance of its editor-in-chief, Abraham Cahan, the *Forward* reached a circulation of nearly a quarter of a million in the early 1920s. The offices of the *Forward* are now uptown (45 E. 33 St.), and the old Forward building, which still bears the name Forward carved in English over the doorway, in Yiddish near the top of the building's facade, is used by a Chinese church.

Across Jefferson Street from the Forward Building is the **Educational Alliance** (197 East Broadway, GR5-6200). Founded in 1883 by wealthy uptown Jews to speed the Americanization of the newly arrived east European Jews, the alliance was the first settlement house in the United States. The photographs of some of the more famous alliance "graduates" hang in the Alliance Hall of Fame on the first floor of the modern building.

Across the street from the Educational Alliance is the **Seward Park Library** (192 East Broadway, 477-6770), which contains a large number of works in Yiddish and Hebrew, a reference collection strong in Judaica, popular books and magazines in Chinese and Spanish for the current teenage users of the library and a collection of source materials on the evolution of the Lower East Side. Leon Trotsky used the library's reference collection when he stayed in New York.

Two blocks and one street over from the Seward Park Library are the original Federalist buildings of an institution that looms large in any history of the Lower East Side—the **Henry Street Settlement** (263–267 Henry St., nr. Montgomery St., 766-9200). Founded in 1893 by Lillian Wald, the organization still provides community services.

Off Essex Sreet, **Hester Street,** lined with tenements, looks much as it did in the old days, minus the pushcarts that once made this street the main marketplace of the Lower East Side.

FOR YOU, IT'S WHOLESALE
If there is any common image we hold of the old Lower East Side, it is probably of crowded streets lined with pushcarts and peddlers calling out their wares. Though the pushcarts themselves are gone, the hustling, price-haggling, bazaarlike atmosphere of those days still prevails on much of the Lower East Side, especially in the Essex Street Market, on Orchard Street on Sundays and in the discount stores that cluster in the neighborhood.

Enclose three blocks of open-air fruit, vegetable and fish stalls with roof and walls and you have the **Essex Street Market**, which stretches from Broome to Stanton streets on the east side of Essex. These days the market is multi ethnic, with Chinese vegetable stands displaying bean curd and bean sprouts, Puerto Rican stalls piled high with *bacalao* and pineapples and Jewish fish markets where the huge carp are so fresh they are still struggling and must be stilled with a swift blow of a wooden mallet before they can be sent home with a customer. The customers, like the stall keeper, speak Yiddish, Spanish or Chinese. And the prices are pretty good.

Orchard Street on a Sunday comes closest to approximating the old pushcart days. Now closed to traffic for the whole day, the street is jammed with outdoor displays of fur coats, dresses, leather jackets, bedspreads, shoes, rolls of fabric, socks, toys—you name it. The price often depends on how well you can bargain. Be sure to hold onto your wallet or purse in the crowds; Sunday is a busy working day for pickpockets.

FOOD STORES: Ess, Bubbele, Ess
Every Sunday, the Lower East Side—never an affluent neighborhood—

is suddenly visited with Mercedeses and Lincoln Continentals and even an occasional limousine. The people who own these cars may live in Westchester or Connecticut, as close as uptown Manhattan or as far away as Miami, but chances are they will have seen the far side of fifty, they grew up in this neighborhood and they have come back for a taste of home.

And, like a typical Jewish mother, the Lower East Side feeds her children with loving abundance: with knishes and *rugalach*, smoked salmon and pickled herring, Russian coffee cake and Jewish rye. Nostalgia and good eating are what these prodigal children return for (and heartburn is often what they get), and such is the hold of habit that now their children and their children's children have started coming back to a neighborhood known only from Sunday forays.

East Houston Street between Forsyth and Orchard streets is the gourmet strip of the Lower East Side, for here, all in a row, are the best appetizing store, the best cheese store and the best bakery on the Lower East Side—not to mention the only *knish* shop.

What is a *knish*? Simply a thin pastry crust wrapped around something, most often seasoned potatoes or the cereal grain known as kasha. Even if you didn't grow up on the Lower East Side and wouldn't know a *knish* from a carrot, **Yonah Schimmel's Knishes Bakery** (137 E. Houston, Forsyth–Eldridge Sts., GR7-2858) will make you feel nostalgic. Founded in 1910 by a cousin of the grandmother of the present owner, Joe Berger, Yonah Schimmel's hasn't changed for generations. The place has an air of shabby authenticity that says, "This is what it used to be like in the old days."

Schimmel's knishes are all natural and baked fresh every half-hour. The potato knishes are especially delicious, with a well-seasoned filling melding almost imperceptibly into the golden crust. Try some with a glass of homemade yogurt. *Open Mon.–Thurs., Sun. 8:30 A.M.–6 P.M.; Fri. 8:30 A.M.–5 P.M. Cl. Sat.*

Two blocks east of Yonah Schimmel's is **Russ and Daughters** (179 E. Houston St., Allen–Orchard Sts., GR5-4880), an appetizing store founded by Joel Russ in 1914 and now run by the Russ daughters and their husbands.

Top quality preserved fish is Russ and Daughters' specialty: smoked Alaska salmon (this silver-skinned, coral-colored, firm-fleshed fish makes the best lox); rich, velvety smoked whitefish; pickled salmon and pickled herring bathed in Russ and Daughters' own thick, pure sour cream flavored with rings from the finest jumbo sweet onions; schmaltz herring from Iceland; fancy sable fish; smoked trout; lake sturgeon and, of course, homemade *gefilte* fish.

Across from the fish counter are the nuts, dried fruits (jumbo apricots, pears and peaches from Oregon, jumbo pitted prunes, giant Medjool dates and hand-dipped, chocolate-covered glacéed fruit and nuts.

The prices are well below what they are uptown for this quality because the store deals in quantity and its overhead is low. Ninety-nine percent of the customers come from outside the neighborhood; all are devoted, and the members of the family who work in the store seem to know everyone by name, if not when the customer comes in, then at least by the time he or she leaves. *Open every day but Tues., 8:30* A.M.*–6:30* P.M. *Cl. Tues.*

Next door to Russ and Daughters' is **Ben's Cheese Shop** (181 E. Houston St., AL4-8290), a long, narrow store that sells kosher farmer's cheese in every flavor, including pepper, scallion, *kimmel*, peach, walnut-and-raisin, pineapple, pineapple-strawberry, blueberry, strawberry, banana and apple-and-cinnamon. Fresh fruit is used in the fruit-flavored cheeses. Taste samples can be wheedled if you're not sure what your preferences are. Ben's also carries fresh farm butter and imported kosher cheeses. *Open Sun.–Thurs.* 8 A.M.*–5:30* P.M.*; Fri.* 8 A.M.*–3:30* P.M. *Cl. Sat.*

Moishe's Bakery (181 E. Houston St., GR5-9624) sells the breads to go with the cheese and butter you've bought at Ben's. Along with the bialys, bagels, *bulke* rolls, *challahs* (braided egg breads) and Jewish ryes you'll find at any Jewish bakery, Moishe's offers a fabulous old-fashioned corn rye and a hearty Russian black bread (called health bread here), of which one customer was heard to remark as she clutched a loaf to her bosom, "A slice of this with sweet butter . . ." A roll of her eyes heavenward and a sigh completed the sentence.

Moishe's makes sweet baked goods, too: Russian coffee cakes, or *babka*; giant "checkerboard" cakes of vanilla, chocolate and mocha; Russian sponge cake and marble cakes; sweet little nut-and-raisin *rugalach*; giant, airy-light *kichel* sprinkled with sugar; marvelous *mandelbrot* (almond cakes) that come plain, studded with dried fruit or—my favorite—marbled with chocolate. *Open Mon.–Thurs.* 6:45 A.M.*–6* P.M.*; Fri.* 6:45 A.M.*–3* P.M.*; Sun.* 7 A.M.*–6* P.M. *Cl. Sat.*

The gourmet shops on East Houston all have their specialties; but there is a bakery on the Lower East Side that makes only one thing— **Kossar's Bialys** (367 Grand St. Essex–Norfolk Sts., GR3-4810). Named after Bialystok, the town in Poland (once Russia) where the bakers are thought to have invented them, *bialys* are a type of onion roll. Baked on the premises, the bialys at Kossar's are exceptionally fresh and delicious. *Open daily 5*A.M.*–midnight; sometimes all night too.*

Gertel's Kosher Bakery (53 Hester St. cor. Ludlow St., 982-3250) has been in business for almost fifty years. Customers come from New Jersey for Gertel's *challahs*, Jewish ryes, old-fashioned corn ryes and pumpernickels, *rugalach* and *babka* "bowties" (prune or plain) and chocolate-iced *mandelbrot*. Before Passover, when the shop produces kosher-for-Passover baked goods (they must contain no yeast), the lines stretch outside to Essex Street. *Open Mon.–Wed. 7 A.M.–5 P.M.; Thurs. and Sun 7 A.M.–6 P.M. Fri. 7 A.M.–3 P.M. Cl. Sat.*

Another gastronomic landmark is **Economy Candy** (131 Essex St. cor. Rivington St., AL4-1531), where partners Sam and Morris reign over a sweet domain of homemade chocolate bark, hand-dipped chocolate nuts and fruits ("without exception, the world's best," claims Sam authoritatively), marzipan, box candy, halvah (which you can get here in 34-pound tubs) and dozens of other candies—all, as the name of the store implies, priced very economically. *Open daily 8 A.M.–6 P.M.*

The Wine You Can Almost Cut With a Knife says the sign at **Schapiro's** (126 Rivington St., Norfolk–Essex Sts., OR4-4404), the oldest kosher winery in America (it was founded in 1899), and the only winery left in New York City. (From the crushing of the grape to the sealing of the bottle, kosher wine must be handled only by sabbath-observant Jews, unless the grape juice is heated to the point of *yayin mevushal*, or "boiled wine," after which anyone can handle it.)

Every Sunday from 10 to 6, the Schapiros open their winery to the public and offer guided tours of their cellars, where the grape juice, brought from upstate in big tankers, ferments for six to eight weeks in huge oak tanks. All tours end in the tasting room, where, surrounded by photos of the old Lower East Side, adult visitors get to sample some of the Schapiro wines, and kids get grape juice.

There are in this world, and especially in New York, people for whom wine, chocolate nut clusters—even knishes—are as nothing compared to a good pickle. When such pickle *mavens* get a craving, they head for the Lower East Side, for there they know they will find the pickles of their dreams.

Eat Guss's Pickles, Stay Young and Beautiful. That's what it says on the lids of the pickle jars at **Guss's Pickle Stand** (42 Hester St., Ludlow–Essex Sts., GR7-1969). "But I only gaurantee it for fifty years," jokes Ben Guss, the owner. "And you have to eat at least one a day." Wearing a cap and a long apron, his face lined with years of pickle-making wisdom, Ben is the very image of the Lower East Side pickleman. And his pickles are a delight: his sours are briney and tingling, leaving a sweet taste in the mouth; his half-sours, or new pickles, are crunchy and still have a strong cucumber taste. Poppyseeds, lemon peel, orange peel, cinnamon, bay leaves, caraway and hot peppers are among the spices and flavorings one sees floating in the brine of Guss's pickle barrels. Besides sours and half-sours, Guss also makes pickled peppers (sweet or hot) and pickled tomatoes (small and pear-shaped for eating in one bite, round for those who like a few mouthfuls).

Guss sells retail, wholesale and cash-and-carry: "We'll sell anything from a slice to a carload if you pick it up." *Open Sun.–Thurs. 8* A.M.*–5* P.M.*; Fri. 8* A.M.*–4* P.M. *Cl. Sat.*

The oldest family-owned pickle shop in New York is **Hollander Kosher Pickle Stop** (35 Essex St., Grand–Hester Sts., 254-4477), run by Burt Blitz, whose wife's grandfather, Louis Hollander, started the business in the days when pickle barrels were hauled by horse and wagon. In addition to its excellent sours and half-sours, Hollander's sells pickled green tomatoes, sauerkraut and, just before Passover, fresh horseradish grated right under your nose at the stand (horseradish being a necessary ingredient in the ceremonial Passover dinner). If you have never had fresh grated horseradish before, beware: this stuff will straighten your hair if it's curly, and curl it if it's straight. *Open Sun.–Thurs. 8* A.M.*–5:30* P.M.*; Fri. 8* A.M.*–4* P.M. *Cl. Sat.*

Our Pickles Make You Sexy, claims Lou Lichter in a sign on the awning of his pickle stand, **Pickleman** (27 Essex St., Hester–Grand Sts., 533-8448). Pickleman specializes in variety. Lichter himself pickles sours, half-sours, cherry tomatoes, rolled cabbage, heads of cabbage and whole apples (the only pickle man on the Lower East Side to do apples). He also carries pickled baby corn, okra, pimento, onions and cauliflower. *Open Sun.–Thurs. 8* A.M.*–6* P.M.*; Fri. 8* A.M.*–4* P.M. *Cl. Sat.*

COLLECTIBLES

Of the many Jewish bookstores on the Lower East Side, **Louis Stavsky** (147 Essex St., Stanton–Rivington Sts., OR4-1289) offers the widest selection of general-interest Judaica, and his collection of Jewish records and tapes is the largest in the city.

Any tour of the Lower East Side should include a stop at **Bezalel Art** (11 Essex St., Hester–Canal Sts., 228-5982), a Jewish art gallery specializing in oil paintings and lithographs by well-known and newly discovered Jewish artists from America and Israel. Bezalel also carries rare prints of Jewish interest. *Open Sun.–Thurs. 8* A.M.*–6* P.M.*; Fri. 8* A.M.*–4* P.M. *Cl. Sat.*

For antique Jewish art, climb the old cast-iron staircase that leads to **Emmanuel Weisberg** (45 Essex St., Grand–Hester Sts., OR4-1770), where you will find a fascinating jumble of old brass candlesticks and samovars, silver Kiddush cups, ornate spice boxes and elaborate torah crowns and breastplates. Most of the objects date from the eighteenth and nineteenth centuries and were made in Russia, Poland, Italy, France and Persia. *Open Sun.–Thurs. 9:15 A.M.–5:45 P.M.; Fri. 9:15 A.M.–3:30 P.M. Cl. Sat.*

A visit to **Grand Silver** (345 Grand St., Ludlow–Essex Sts., 674-6450) is a dazzling experience. Grand specializes in reproductions of antique silver ceremonial objects—spice boxes, Kiddush cups, *menorahs*— modeled after pieces from sixteenth– nineteenth-century Italy and Portugal. The store also carries contemporary ceremonial objects and "anything silver under the sun." *Open Sun.–Thurs. 10:30 A.M.–5:30 P.M.; Fri. 10:30 A.M.–1 or 2 P.M. Cl. Sat.*

RESTAURANTS

Because Jewish law forbids the eating of milk or milk products with meat, most Jewish restaurants in New York are either dairy or deli.

"Anyone who comes to New York comes to Ratner's," says the man behind the cash register complacently, and indeed for a certain portion of the Jewish population, the statement is true. For **Ratner's** (138 Delancey St., Norfolk–Suffolk Sts., OR7-5588, **M**) is the great dowager of New York's dairy restaurants—the dairy restaurant to end all dairy restaurants, a pastel palace of *milchik* delights.

Ratner's lofty ceiling is painted lipstick-pink, the chairs are aqua, the walls are mirrored and the customers wear Florida tans the whole year long. At least half of the waiters must have been hired directly from Central Casting. (The New York Jewish waiter is an independent soul— his motto: "The customer is rarely right.") You go to Ratner's as much to soak up the atmosphere as to slurp up the *borscht*; as much for the gestalt as for the *gefilte* fish.

The *blintzes*—the test of any dairy restaurant—are very good here: oversized, crispy on the outside, soft and crepelike on the underside and filled with either farmer's cheese, potatoes, kasha or fruit preserves and cheese as you wish. And the *pirogen* are first rate. But if neither of these is your dish, you have your choice of cheese *kreplach*, potato pancakes, *kasha varnishkas* (kasha with noodles and onions), *matzo brei* (matzo fried with egg), *borscht* with sour cream and all the other standard dairy favorites along with a wide selection of fish (fish is *pareve, i.e.,* it may be eaten with either milk or meat). Portions are generous and every order comes with good dark bread or rolls. A recent innovation, unheard of before in a dairy restaurant, is the serving of alcoholic beverages.

At the front of the restaurant, there's a retail bakery counter where you can get *rugalach, kichel* and other Jewish baked goods. *Open daily 6 A.M.–midnight.*

The **Garden Cafeteria** (165 East Broadway, Rutgers–Jefferson Sts., AL4-6962, **I**) is a good, inexpensive, self-service dairy restaurant with a history. Jewish labor leaders and reporters used to eat here (it's near the old Forward Building), and actors used to hang out here in the days of the Yiddish theater. Now Puerto Ricans and Chinese have joined the elderly Jewish diners but the menu hasn't changed, and the food is still great.

The Garden specialties are *blintzes* (four stars), an incredibly rich strawberry shortcake piled high with whipped cream and the loaves of *challah* sold on Fridays. On a hot day, you can lunch simply here on a bowl of sour cream with fruit or vegetables.

Be sure to look at the wall mural which recalls the Lower East Side of yesteryear. *Open Sun.–Fri. 6 A.M.–9 P.M. Cl. Sat.*

The **Grand Dairy** (341 Grand St., cor. Ludlow St., 673-1904, **I**) is a small, warm, crowded, clattering restaurant. If you hear the waiter yelling "Hot rice" here, he is referring to the hot rice pudding, which is the specialty on Mondays and Wednesdays and which is served with a ladleful of warm red fruit sauce and, if the diner wishes, heavy cream—a meal in itself for less than $1. The rest of the week, except Saturday when the Grand is closed, the specialty is hot noodle pudding. *Open Sun.–Thurs. 6 A.M.–5 P.M.; Fri. 6 A.M.–3 P.M. Cl. Sat.*

You can also get a dairy meal at **Yonah Schimmel's Knishes Bakery** (see Food Stores).

Dairy and meat may never meet in the Jewish restaurants of the Lower East Side, but at **Bernstein-on-Essex Street** (135 Essex St., Orchard–Rivington Sts., GR3-3900, **M–E**), "West Meets East for a Chinese Feast and Kashruth is Guaranteed." Bernstein's, the first (now there are several imitators) Chinese-Kosher restaurant in New York, is also a first-rate Jewish deli: its Rumanian pastrami is the best in Manhattan. In his Chinese menu, Bernstein substitutes veal or chicken for nonkosher ingredients like pork and shrimp, with surprisingly successful results. Bernstein's also offers a complete Jewish menu with traditional favorites like stuffed *derma* and boiled chicken.

If you like deli, be sure to try some of the superb hickory-smoked Rumanian pastrami. Lean, savory and spicier than the regular *flanken* pastrami, it is all that prevents many of us from becoming vegetarians.

The waiters—mostly Jewish, though there are one or two Chinese—wear Chinese *yarmulkes*: red hats with black pompoms; and there are Chinese murals on the walls. Beer and Israeli wine are served.

Open Sun.–Thurs. 8 A.M.*–1* A.M.*; Fri. 8* A.M.*–1* P.M.*; Sat., one hour after Sabbath ends until 3* A.M.

The biggest deli on the Lower East Side is **Katz's** (205 E. Houston St. cor. Essex St., AL4-2246, **C–I**), a huge self-service cafeteria (with a few waiter-service tables against the wall) that is popular with workers and retired people in the neighborhood. The food—*knobelwurst* (garlic sausage), pastrami, corned beef, hot dogs and so forth—is not worth a trip, but it is cheap, you get a lot of it (the corned beef sandwiches overflow) and the noisy, busy, nothing-fancy air of the huge place is genuine Lower East Side.

Send a salami to your boy in the army, says the sign over the mail-order salami counter. Katz's is kosher-style, but not kosher. *Open daily 7* A.M.*–11:30* P.M.*; Fri., Sat. until 1:30* A.M.

Among east European Jews, Rumanian Jews have the reputation of being people who (1) know how to make good food, and (2) know how to have a good time. Both good food (but not kosher food) and good times are what you'll find at **Sammy's Rumanian Jewish Restaurant** (157 Chrystie St. nr. Delancey St., 673-0330, **M–E**), which nightly draws a lively uptown crowd of politicians, public relations people, artists and the unemployed chic. Sammy's guests come for the Rumanian-style broiled tenderloin and huge rib steaks, the delicious eggplant salad, the spicy *karnatzlach* (garlic sausage), the Rumanian *icra* (whitefish caviar) and Jewish home-style dishes like *eialach* (unborn chicken eggs), *pitcha* (calves' foot jelly) and *gribenes* (chicken skin cracklings). A nice New York touch: the seltzer bottle, chocolate syrup and container of milk at each table for making your own egg cream. White tablecloths, some posters and the diners themselves provide all the ambiance that's needed. *Open daily 3* P.M. *"until we close."* Which is when? "It all depends on how late they eat and how heavy they eat." Plenty of parking space nearby.

The Diamond Center

Next to the Lower East Side, the part of Manhattan that is probably most closely associated with Jews is the Diamond Center in midtown.

For centuries in Europe, many Jews, never knowing when they might have to flee from persecution or an inquisition, worked as diamond dealers, diamonds being a valuable commodity that is also eminently portable. Most diamond dealers in New York are Jewish, and many are Hasidim—followers of a mystical sect of Judaism that arose in Poland in the eighteenth century. The Hasidim have gravitated to the diamond trade not only because of the traditional occupational association, but also because the flexibility of the hours allows them to get home before the Sabbath and to take time off for afternoon prayers.

The heart of the Diamond District in New York is 47th Street between Fifth and Sixth avenues. Eighty percent of all diamonds entering the country pass through this block, often carried wrapped in tissue paper in the pockets of the Hasidim, who, with their full beards, long sidelocks, black broad-brimmed hats and dark suits, impart an Old World air to the bustling Diamond Street.

Storefront windows on 47th Street drip diamond bracelets and rings, but the real business of diamond dealing takes place on the floors above, in the offices of the dealers or in the drab quarters of the **Diamond Dealers Club** (30 W. 47 St.), the center of the diamond trade in America. The club is where dealers from around the world buy, sell and exchange cut and polished diamonds, usually with a good deal of fierce bargaining. Dealers in rough diamonds, emeralds, sapphires and other stones conduct their transactions across the street at the smaller **Diamond Trade Association** (15 W. 47 St.).

Security is tight on the street, and neither the club nor the association is open to outsiders. A good place to soak up the atmosphere of the Diamond Center that is open to everyone is the **Diamond Dairy** in the Jeweler's National Exchange (4 W. 47, CI6-3694, **C–I**), a kosher dairy luncheonette in a glassed-in gallery above the exchange, which is a kind of covered bazaar or arcade of jewelry stalls. As you dine on *blintzes* or perhaps a bowl of *borscht* in the Diamond dairy, you can listen to the talk of the diamond dealers at the next table and survey the scene in the exchange below: customers inspecting display cases glittering with gold chains or dazzling diamond bracelets, sawyers and gold polishers working at their benches.

The Diamond Dairy is *open Mon.–Thurs. 7:30 A.M.–6 P.M.; Fri. 7:30 A.M.–2:30 P.M. Cl. Sat., Sun.*

Around Town in Manhattan

As Jews moved out of the Lower East Side and into other sections of the city, New York became dotted with synagogues, Jewish social and cultural organizations, Jewish shops and restaurants. The following are some of the most interesting Jewish landmarks around town.

SYNAGOGUES
One of the most beautiful and historic synagogues in the city is the

Spanish and Portuguese Synagogue of Congregation Shearith Israel on the corner of 70th Street and Central Park West (8 W. 70 St., TR3-0300). Shearith Israel, the oldest Jewish congregation in North America, was founded in 1654 by the earliest Jewish settlers in New York. This synagogue is the fourth to house the congregation, which moved every time the surrounding area became too congested.

Designed by the first American-born Jewish architect, Arnold Brunner, the Greek Revival synagogue houses two sanctuaries. The smaller of the two is a composite of the three earlier synagogues of Congregation Shearith Israel, and some of its furnishings date back to 1730. The main sanctuary of the Spanish and Portuguese Synagogue is magnificent. Brown marble columns frame the ark at one end of the high-ceilinged room, which is lit by hanging brass lamps and natural light filtered through some of the most beautiful Tiffany windows in the city.

Congregation Shearith Israel holds an annual Sephardic Festival around the second or third Sunday in May, which features guided tours of the synagogue. During the rest of the year, group tours can be arranged by calling the synagogue office.

If you want to see what the first synagogue in New York looked like, you can climb up to the roof of the **Wall Street Synagogue** (47 Beekman Pl., Gold–William Sts., 227-7800), where you will find a log-cabin replica of the synagogue that was built on Mill Street (today called South William Street) in 1730. *Open Mon.–Fri. 9 A.M.–4:30 P.M.*

The largest synagogue in the world and the oldest Reform synagogue in New York is **Temple Emanu-El** (1 East 64 St. cor. Fifth Ave., RH4-1400). The congregation that built the temple in 1929 was founded in 1845 by German Reform Jews who rejected many of the traditional beliefs and forms of Orthodox Judaism.

The main sanctuary of Temple Emanu-El follows the plan of an Italian basilica and seats more people (2500) than St. Patrick's Cathedral. The temple's two-domed Beth-El Chapel is modeled after the Byzantine churches of the Middle East. Temple Emanu-El is not only the largest synagogue in the world; it also boasts the largest Jewish congregation— over three thousand families. Except during services, tours of the main sanctuary and Beth-El Chapel are conducted throughout the day from *10 A.M. to 6 P.M.*

The synagogue with the most fantastic facade in New York—all scallops and keyhole-shaped arches and fanciful Moorish ornamentation—is the **Park East** (161 E. 67 St., Lexington–Third Aves.).

MUSEUMS, LIBRARIES, CULTURAL CENTERS

Because Jewish tradition has always forbidden making idols, Jewish artistic energy has historically gone into making decorative ceremonial objects like the silver crowns and breastplates that adorn the Torah scrolls, the *Kiddush* cups that hold the wine of welcome on the Sabbath and beautifully written *ketubah*, or marriage contracts. The **Jewish Museum** (1109 Fifth Ave. at 92 St., 860-1888), affiliated with the Jewish Theological Seminary of America, contains the most comprehensive collection of Jewish ceremonial art in the country as well as coins and medals, antiquities and contemporary paintings, prints, photographs and sculpture by Jewish artists. Changing exhibits complement the museum's permanent exhibition.

In the basement of the Jewish Museum, the **Tobe Pascher Workshop**, a group of resident silversmiths and metal crafters, makes contemporary ceremonial objects on commission for individuals and synagogues. Twice a year the workshop conducts a series of classes in their craft. For information, call 860-1864.

The Jewish Museum offers guided tours to visitors during museum hours, which are *Mon.–Thurs. noon–5* P.M.; *Sun. 11* A.M.–*6* P.M.; *Thurs. evenings 7* P.M.–*9* P.M. A small admission fee is charged to nonmembers.

Uptown, in Washington Heights, the **Yeshiva University Museum** (2520 Amsterdam Ave., 185–186 Sts., 960-5390) features exhibits having to do with Jewish history. On permanent display are ten scale models of synagogues dating from third-century Syria to nineteenth-century Florence, an electronic map that traces the migrations of the Jews since biblical times and the Torah scroll of the founder of Hasidism, Ba'al Shem Tov. The museum's changing exhibits have included shows on The Jewish Wedding, Portraits of Jewish Life in Nineteenth-Century Europe, and The Changing Face of New York Synagogues. Hours: *Sundays 12–6* P.M.; *Tues., Thurs. 11* A.M.–*5* P.M. There is a small admission fee.

Of all the specialized libraries in the city, one of the most fascinating is **YIVO** (Yidisher Visnshaftlekher Institut, or "Institute for Jewish Research," 1048 Fifth Ave. at 86 St., 535-6700). Founded in Vilna in 1925 as an institute for graduate students of east European Jewry and the Yiddish language, YIVO is presently housed in a five-story mansion formerly owned by the Vanderbilts that is an exact copy of the Louis XIII Palais Royale in Paris.

A multilingual library with books and documents in Polish, Russian, English and Hebrew as well as Yiddish, YIVO's collection is particularly strong in Yiddish literature and folklore, east European Jewish history, Nazi Holocaust material and Jewish community life in the United States since the 1880s. Its Yiddish collection is the largest in the world.

YIVO is open to the public as a reference library; the archivist's approval is needed for use of the archives. *Open Mon.–Fri. 9:30* A.M.–*5:30* P.M.

The Leo Baeck Institute (129 E. 73 St. cor. Lexington Ave., RH4-6400) is a research center, library and archives dedicated to collecting, preserving and recording all aspects of the history of the Jews in Germany, Austria and other German-speaking centers from the 1800s to the rise of Nazism. *Open Mon. 9* A.M.–*5* P.M.; *Tues.–Fri. 9* A.M.–*4:30* P.M.

New York has many, many Jewish cultural centers and community houses. The oldest and largest of these—in fact the oldest and largest Jewish center in the United States—is the **92nd Street YM-YWHA** (92 St. and Lexington Ave., 427-6000). Founded by German and Sephardic Jews in 1874 as an elite club for intellectual stimulation and athletics, the Y shifted its emphasis to social services when thousands of immigrants from eastern Europe began arriving in the 1880s. In 1929, the Y moved to its present building, where it became a cultural, recreational and educational center. The Y's Performing Arts Program, which features concerts, lectures, poetry readings and theater performed by leading artists, draws thousands of visitors from all over the city every year.

FOOD STORES

The following shops—two bakeries and two examples of that unique New York Jewish institution, the appetizing store—are singled out because they are outstanding or unusual in some way. It is no coincidence that all happen to be on the Upper West Side, which for many years has had a large Jewish population.

Barney Greengrass (541 Amsterdam Ave., 86–87 Sts., SC4-4707) is part appetizing-grocery store, part restaurant, and has been around so long, it's become a West Side institution. Barney Greengrass, The Sturgeon King reads the sign outside, and smoked sturgeon from Canada is the specialty of the house. Moe gets it "green," i.e., it has never seen cold storage, and it is incredibly rich and, as sturgeon always is these days, expensive. *Open Tues.–Sun. 8:30* A.M.–*6* P.M. *Cl. Mon.*

Moe Greengrass's competition is **Murray's Sturgeon** (2429 Broadway, 89–90 Sts., SC4-2650), a small, brightly lit gourmet appetizing shop. Murray and Sam Bernstein opened the store over forty years ago, and when they retired, Arthur Cutler bought the place. Murray's sells an array of caviar and cheeses, but the shop's specialty is smoked fish: sturgeon from the cleanest, coldest waters in Canada—Lake Winnipeg—which is then custom-smoked in Brooklyn; and the finest smoked Nova Scotia salmon, or lox. *Open Tues.–Fri. 8* A.M.–*7* P.M.; *Sat. 8* A.M.–*8* P.M.; *Sun. 8* A.M.–*7* P.M. *Cl. Mon.*

How convenient that **H&H Bagels** (2239 Broadway cor. 80 St., 799-9680) is so close to Murray's. For just as marriage needs love and a carriage needs a horse, lox needs bagels. And cream cheese, which you can also get here. *Open 24 hours a day.*
The only Sephardic bakery in New York is **Levana's** (148 W. 67 St., Amsterdam Ave.–Broadway, 877-8457), named after Levana Kirschenbaum, who comes from Morocco and whose mother provided the recipes for the Moroccan kosher sweets that are the specialty of the store: prunes and walnuts stuffed with almond paste, *cornes de gazelles* ("gazelle-horn" pastry shells filled with almond paste), *hlilin* (moon crescents sprinkled with nuts) and French nut truffles. The bakery also makes a delicious (though not particularly Sephardic) carrot cake. At the back of the tiny shop, there are a few tables where you can sample pastries and sip soothing Morrocan mint tea. *Open 11 A.M.–7 P.M. Sun.–Thurs.; closes early on Fri. Cl. Sat.*

RESTAURANTS
Jewish restaurants are often found in pairs around New York: almost every deli has its nearby dairy, so that no matter where you are, you have your choice of *blintzes* and *borscht* or corned beef and *kishkes*.
On the Upper West Side, the dynamic duo is Fine and Schapiro's, and Famous.
Joseph Schapiro and Jacob Fine founded **Fine and Schapiro's Delicatessen Restaurant** (138 W. 72 St., Broadway–Amsterdam Ave., TR7-2874, **M**) in 1927, and now their sons David Schapiro and Irving Fine continue the family tradition. Everything is kosher at Fine and Schapiro's and everything except the deli is made on the premises, from the *gefilte* fish to the superior stuffed *derma*, from the *pitcha* to the *hausenblaus* ("snowflakes"—thin, light, crispy, deep-fried pastries sprinkled with confectioner's sugar). The customers are regulars who have grown old with the restaurant; the dining room is bright and attractive. *Open daily 8:30 A.M.–11 P.M.*
On the other side of Broadway is the **Famous Dairy** (222 W. 72 St., Broadway–West End Ave., TR4-8607, **C–I**), a large restaurant that looks like it has fed a lot of people in its day. The food, frankly, is not what makes Famous famous, though it is certainly adequate dairy fare. People come here because it is convenient, because it is not too expensive and because it has a cozy Jewish grandmother ambiance. Also, famous people sometimes frequent the Famous: this is reputed to be one of Isaac Bashevis Singer's haunts. *Open daily 7 A.M.–12:30 A.M.*
Above Houston Street, in what used to be part of the Jewish Lower East Side but now is well within the boundaries of the Ukrainian East

Village, is probably the best deli-dairy duo in the city: the Second Avenue Kosher Deli and the B&H Dairy.

The **Second Avenue Kosher Delicatessen Restaurant** (156 Second Ave. at 10 St., 677-0606, I–M) gets high ratings for its own mild, homemade corned beef; and its pastrami, though it is not made on the premises, is excellent. Ever since the gas shortage, deli deliveries have been made by horse and wagon! *Open daily 6* A.M.*–11:30* P.M.

B&H Dairy (127 Second Ave., St. Mark's Pl.–7 St., SP7-1930, C–I) is a tiny luncheonette, but its menu is just as varied as that of most other dairy restaurants, and because it is so small, both the food and you get more attention. *Open Mon.–Sat. 6* A.M.*–11* P.M.*; Sun. 6* A.M.*–9* P.M.

Probably the only restaurant in town where your Dr. Brown's cream soda is poured into a glass for you by a red-jacketed waiter is **Lou G. Siegel's** (209 W. 38 St., Seventh–Eighth Aves., 921-4433, E) in the heart of New York's frenetic garment district. Lou G. Siegel's is the cadillac of kosher restaurants: plush, roomy, comfortable, expensive and, above all, dignified.

Established as a small restaurant in 1917, Siegel's kept expanding over the years: each of the three mirrored columns inside represents yet another trimming shop or tailor shop taken over. A portrait of the late Lou G. himself—a Runyonesque character dapperly dressed in houndstooth-check jacket and fedora, cigar in hand—hangs on one of the columns; the man's presence lingers in the restaurant still.

Garment Center business people and out-of-town buyers make up the lunch crowd. At dinner, the restaurant attracts families who keep kosher and want a fancy place to eat out. The corned beef, made on the premises (it's pickled in barrels downstairs), is impeccable—lean, yet moist.

The lunch menu features eggs and omelets, salads, sandwiches and delicatessen plates; at dinner, you have a choice of such dishes as Rumanian stuffed cabbage, roast duckling, brisket of beef or roast chicken. *Open Sun.–Thurs. noon–8:45* P.M.*; Fri. noon–3* P.M.*; Sat. 6:30* P.M.*–1* A.M.

A chicken-fat dispenser is standard equipment on every table at the **Parkway** (345 W. 46 St., Eighth–Ninth Aves., 765-0578, E), a Rumanian-Jewish (nonkosher) restaurant on Restaurant Row that is a more sophisticated version of the original Parkway, founded in 1927 on Chrystie Street on the Lower East Side (now the home of Sammy's Rumanian-Jewish Restaurant). The present Parkway has a nice bar, white table-cloths and, to give the place the flavor of the old neighborhood, blown-up photographs of the people and places of the old Lower East Side. But its menu still features the dishes that made the original Parkway so popular: Rumanian grilled steaks, spicy garlic *karnatzlach*, Rumanian eggplant salad and Jewish home-style dishes like unborn chicken eggs in chicken soup.

Although dinner for one can easily run over $20, *gribenetz* (crispy chicken skin—great on mashed potatoes), grated radish, chopped onion, sour pickles and broiled peppers are free on request, compliments of the owner, Karl. On weekends, a singer entertains with gypsy, Rumanian and Jewish music. *Open daily 4 P.M–11 P.M.; Wed., Sat. 11 A.M.– midnight.*

Theater

The east European jews who came to America in the 1880s spoke Yiddish, a language derived frm High German with borrowings from Hebrew, Russian and Polish. In the New World, the old language became a medium for the most vigorous popular cultural expression of the new immigrant community—the Yiddish theater.

Today, although nothing remains of the old Second Avenue Jewish Rialto, Yiddish theater in New York is far from dead. Every season there are usually three or four professional productions, and Folksbiene, a semiprofessional Yiddish theater troupe sponsored by the Workmen's Circle, hasn't missed a season since its first production in 1914. For information about upcoming performances, which may take place anywhere from a synagogue auditorium to Town Hall, call the **Hebrew Actors' Union** (OR4-1923) or **Folksbiene** (755-2231).

Jewish theater in New York is not limited to Yiddish theater. The **Jewish Repertory Theater** (674-7200), established in 1974 as an Off-Off Broadway theater under the sponsorship of the Emanu-El Midtown YM-YWHA, presents plays in English that relate to the Jewish experience. Two new plays and four revivals are staged each season. Past productions have included *The Merchant of Venice*, Chekhov's *Ivanov* and Galsworthy's *Loyalties*.

Music

Music was part of the invisible baggage the Jewish immigrant brought to America. In New York, the synagogue became the concert hall for religious music, while folk songs and popular melodies flourished in the streets of the Lower East Side at celebrations and on the stage of the Yiddish theater.

Today if you want to hear Jewish music in an ethnic setting, you must get yourself invited to a Hasidic wedding. But cantorial music can still be heard regularly in New York's synagogues, and several cultural centers present concerts of Jewish secular music throughout the year. **The Hebrew Arts School** (129 W. 67 St., 362-8060) near Lincoln Center holds an annual series of four Heritage Concerts which features young American-Jewish composers and Israeli artists, as well as traditional cantorial and Yiddish music, and occasionally offers a master class in Hasidic music or Yiddish folk and art songs. (Unlike the folk melodies, which evolved over time and can be hummed by anyone, Yiddish art songs are composed pieces that must be sung by a trained vocalist.)

The American Society for Jewish Music annually presents four free concerts of Jewish music (folk, cantorial, art songs and music by Jewish composers), usually at the Hebrew Arts School or the **92nd Street Y** (92 St. and Lexington Ave., 427-6000), which offers its own Jewish music programs as well.

In the 1920s and '30s, a form of dance music that had originated in Europe became very popular in New York's Jewish community. Often called a precursor of swing, *klezmer* has enjoyed a small revival of interest lately through the performances of Zev Feldman and Andy Statman, who sometimes give concerts under the auspices of the **Balkan Arts Center** (222-0550). The two musicians, who have studied with the fourth-generation Ukrainian *klezmer* artist David Tarras, play the old melodies on the clarinet, mandolin and *tsimbl* (East European hammer dulcimer).

Several synagogues and religious institutions in New York sponsor Jewish musical events. The **Park Avenue Synagogue** (50 E. 87 St., EN9-2600) presents three public concerts of cantorial music every year between September and June, and **Hebrew Union College** (40 W. 68 St., 873-0200) offers concerts of cantorial music and secular music by Jewish composers as part of its Sunday-afternoon series. If you are interested in hearing Ladino (Judeo-Spanish) music, ask to be put on the mailing list for concert events at the **Spanish and Portuguese Synagogue** (8 W. 70 St., TR3-0300). On Sunday afternoons in March, **Temple Emanu-El** (1 E. 65, 744-1400) shows off its splendid organ in a series of organ recitals of secular and liturgical music.

In Brooklyn: The Hasidim

Probably the most interesting Jewish communities in New York today are the Satmar Hasidim of Williamsburg and the Lubavitch Hasidim of Crown Heights, Brooklyn.

The Hasidim ("Pious Ones") follow a mystical branch of Judaism that was founded in eighteenth-century Poland by Baal Shem Tov ("Master of the Good Name"), a man who taught that sincere feeling in worship is more important than academic learning. The followers of Baal Shem Tov pray with intense devotion, swaying, singing and often dancing to express their joy.

Ultraorthodox people, the Hasidim live their lives in strict accordance with Jewish Law. Like the Amish, they do not mingle much with the outside world (they are forbidden to watch TV, and they wear distinctive dress that sets them apart. Hasidic men have full beards and, sometimes, long sidelocks called *payot*; they wear dark suits or coats of outdated cut and dark, wide-brimmed hats or, if they are men of the highest rank (*rebbes*), broad sable hats. Young boys wear *payot* and *yarmulkes*; Hasidic women, high-necked, long-sleeved dresses and, if they are married, wigs, according to Orthodox custom. Unlike the Amish, who preserve their way of life in remote rural areas, the Hasidim keep to their traditions while living in the midst of America's largest city.

The headquarters of the **Satmar** sect of Hasidim and the home of about thirty thousand Satmarer is **Williamsburg,** an old neighborhood just across the Williamsburg Bridge from the Lower East Side. Lee Avenue is the main shopping area of Hasidic Williamsburg. All up and down this street there are little kosher butcher shops, signs in Yiddish and stores that sell wigs, Hasidic clothing, Hebrew books and kosher pizza. Around the corner from the offices of the chief Satmar Rebbe at 82 Lee Avenue, on Rodney Street, is the most important Satmar synagogue. And everywhere in the neighborhood there are women pushing baby carriages (the Hasidim are opposed to birth control).

On Saturdays, the streets of Williamsburg where the Satmar live are devoid of traffic (the Orthodox do not drive on the Sabbath), and on the holiday Simhat Torah, the streets are closed off for dancing, singing and celebration.

HOW TO GET THERE
By car from Manhattan: Across the Williamsburg Bridge to Keap or Hooper St. to Lee Ave. **By subway**: *BMT* J or M train to Marcy Ave.

The Lubavitch Hasidim of Crown Heights believe it is their mission to convert nonobservant Jews to observers. A common sight in New York are the Lubavitch "Mitzvah Tanks" (a *mitzvah* is a good deed)—vans full of young Hasidim who approach Jews on the street and invite them to say a prayer or learn how to put on *tefillin*. The Lubavitchers also run many social and charitable services to aid Jews in need in New York and abroad.

Most of the Lubavitcher men are more modern-looking than the Satmarer: they wear suits, but not long coats; full beards, but not payot.

The worldwide headquarters of the Lubavitch movement is 770 Eastern Parkway, a large, Tudor-style brick building with a carefully tended lawn. Inside the building are the office of the chief rabbi of the Lubavitchers and a large prayer hall. The hall is purposely unadorned, for these Hasidim feel that money is better spent in "converting" and helping other Jews than on decoration, and they do not want to be distracted by beautiful objects when they pray.

Around the corner from the Lubavitch headquarters there is a small *glatt kosher* (strictly kosher) luncheonette on Kingston Avenue, the Ess and Bench ("Eat and Pray"). Kingston Avenue is the shopping street of Lubavitch Crown Heights.

HOW TO GET THERE
By car from Manhattan: Manhattan Bridge to Flatbush Ave., Flatbush Ave. to Grand Army Plaza, left onto Eastern Parkway. **By subway:** *IRT Seventh Avenue #2* to Kingston Ave.

"Tours of Jewish New York" (628-2244) takes you through Williamsburg and pays a visit to the Lubavitcher headquarters in Crown Heights. Jews who would like to spend a typical Sabbath with a Lubavitch family may arrange to do so by calling the *Lubavitch Youth Organization* (303 Kingston Ave., 778-4270).

Holidays and Festivals

Every year on or near the second Sunday in June, the Educational Alliance (197 East Broadway, GR5-6200) sponsors a **Lower East Side Jewish Spring Festival** on East Broadway between Rutgers and Montgomery streets. The festival features *glatt kosher* food made by local Jewish restaurants, arts and crafts exhibits, folk dancing, free movies and guided walking tours of the Lower East Side. In recent years, Ladino musicians, *klezmer* musicians, members of the Hebrew Actors' Union and Yiddish and Hebrew folk singers have furnished live entertainment.

Congregation Shearith Israel of the Spanish and Portuguese Synagogue (70 St. and Central Park West, TR3-0300) holds an annual **Se-**

phardic Festival on the second or third Sunday in May. Continuous tours of the historic and beautiful synagogue, Sephardic food, an auction of goods and services and a *souk* bazaar are the main attractions of the Festival. If you go, go in the morning; by the afternoon, the synagogue is bursting with visitors and the lines to get in stretch down to Central Park. There is a small admission fee.

Every summer, the Education Department of the Workmen's Circle (45 E. 33 St., 889-6800) sponsors a **Yiddish Theater and Music Festival**. At least four of the festival's seven or eight programs take place at various locations around New York City—Lincoln Center, Central Park, the Lower East Side, Brooklyn. Each program is a potpourri of Yiddish songs, recitations of Yiddish poetry and performances of excerpts from Yiddish plays; in short, an introduction to the Yiddish arts. Such well-known stars of the Yiddish Theater as Molly Picon and Ida Kaminska have appeared in the festival's programs in the past.

The Jews of New York celebrate a number of different **religious holidays**. In September or October (the Jewish calendar is lunar), **Rosh Hashonah** ("Head of the Year") marks the beginning of the Jewish New Year. Ten days later is **Yom Kippur**, a day of fasting and atonement. **Hanukkah**, the Festival of Lights, falls in December. Jewish families light one candle of the *menorah* for each night of this eight-day holiday, which commemorates the rededication of the Temple of Judas Maccabeus in 165 B.C. **Passover**, in March or April, celebrates the deliverance of the ancient Hebrews from slavery in Egypt, and is observed with a family *seder* dinner of special foods and the retelling of the Passover story. **Simhat Torah**, which falls in September or October, celebrates the completion and beginning of the cycle of reading the Torah (the Jewish scripture), and is observed in New York's Hasidic communities with dancing in the streets.

Jewish Food

The cooking that has come to be known as Jewish is actually an amalgam of dishes from many countries, for the Jews have lived in many lands. Jewish cuisine as it is found in most New York restaurants is most similar to east European cooking, featuring delicatessen meats, smoked fish and a variety of baked, broiled and boiled beef and chicken dishes. Because of Jewish dietary laws, which do not allow the mixing of meat with milk or dairy foods in the same meal, the Jews have developed an interesting vegetarian dairy cuisine. Some Jewish restaurants serve meat dishes exclusively; some dairy dishes exclusively. Many, but not all, Jewish restaurants in New York are kosher; that is, they follow the Jewish dietary laws which prohibit the eating of pork or shellfish, meat with dairy foods, or beef or poultry slaughtered by a nonkosher butcher.

MENU GLOSSARY
bagel: ring-shaped hard bread roll.

blintz: crepe rolled around cheese or fruit filling and eaten with sour cream.

borscht: Russian beet soup.

challah: braided egg bread traditionally eaten at Friday-night Sabbath meal.

derma, stuffed: baked stuffed beef casing, also known as *kishke*.

eialach: unborn chicken eggs, served in chicken soup.

flanken: cut of beef from the forequarters, just below the short ribs; usually boiled.

gefilte fish: fish balls made from ground, cooked freshwater fish; always eaten with horseradish.

griebenes, gribenes, or *gribenetz*:   chicken-skin cracklings.

icra: cold, strained fish roe caviar (Rumanian).

kasha: cracked buckwheat cooked until tender and served with soup or as a side dish.

kasha varnishkas: kasha and noodles.

kichel: airy, puffy egg cookie dusted with sugar (plural, *kichlach*).

kishke: see *derma*, stuffed.

knaidel: matzo-meal dumpling (plural, *knaidlach*).

knish: baked pastry shell filled with potato, cheese, meat, fruit or kasha stuffing.

kreplach: noodle-dough pockets filled with kasha, meat, potato, chicken liver, etc.

kugel: pudding or pudding-soufflé, usually noodle or potato.

lox: type of smoked, salted salmon.

mamaleiga: Rumanian polenta.

mandlen: soup ''nuts''—crouton puffs.

mandelbrot: crisp almond-loaf cake or cookies sliced from such a loaf.

matzo: thin, flat unleavened bread eaten on Passover; may also be eaten the rest of the year.

matzo balls: see *knaidlach*.

miltz: calf or beef spleen, often stuffed.

mohn: poppyseed.

Nova: refers to Nova Scotia lox, which is less salty than other lox.

pareve: neutral—neither meat nor dairy—may be eaten with either.

pirogen: little baked dough pockets stuffed with potatoes, meat, cheese or fruit; often served with soup instead of bread.

pitcha: jellied calves' feet.

rugelach: rolled cookies filled with nuts, cinnamon and raisins.

schav: sour grass made into a soup that is eaten cold with sour cream.

schmaltz: chicken fat.

tzimmes: ''a mixture''—casserole combining meat or vegetables and fruit. The most common *tzimmes* is made with sweet potatoes, prunes and carrots.

PUERTO RICAN NEW YORK

El Barrio

No one can live in or visit New York City without noticing its large Spanish-speaking population. City banks have Spanish instructions printed on their cash-dispensing machines, bus ads praise this or that brand of beer or cigarettes in Spanish, and on some subway lines, entire trains are filled with Spanish-speaking passengers.

An estimated 2 to 2½ million Spanish-speaking people now live in the "Big Mango." Although this figure includes large numbers of South Americans, Cubans, and Dominicans, by far the largest Hispanic group in the city—over 1 million people— is Puerto Rican.

Ever since 1917, when Congress conferred American citizenship on the residents of Puerto Rico (which was annexed by the United States after the Spanish-American War), Puerto Ricans have been able to move freely back and forth between the mainland and their island, without having to apply for visas or worry about quotas. Up to about 1940, however, only about two to three thousand Puerto Ricans moved to the mainland a year. The great migration began after World War II, when thousands left their overpopulated island to find employment in the United States. Island-to-mainland migration peaked in the 1950s, and has since fluctuated, depending on economic conditions in Puerto Rico and New York. Since the beginning of the recession in the United States in the late 1960s, there has been a reverse migration, with more Puerto Ricans returning to the island than coming to the mainland yearly.

The Puerto Ricans are jet-age immigrants. Kennedy Airport has been their Ellis Island; for Puerto Ricans, the Old Country is three and a half hours away. Because they are citizens, they have been able to go back and forth easily, and there is constant visiting between island and mainland, allowing continual infusions of one culture into the other. "Other ethnic communities in New York are cut off," says one Puerto

Rican artist who grew up in New York. "They don't have the fluidity we do. It's very dynamic."

Despite their status as citizens, Puerto Ricans face the same linguistic, economic and cultural barriers most immigrant groups have had to face in coming to America. Since skin color is more of an issue in the United States than in Puerto Rico (where hundreds of years of mixing between blacks and whites have produced many families in which some members are black and others fair-skinned), many must also contend with racism for the first time in their lives when they move to New York.

Although there is a growing Puerto Rican middle-class, Puerto Ricans as a whole, because they are one of the city's newest ethnic groups, tend to be at the bottom of the economic ladder. Many work in the city's garment industry. Puerto Ricans live all over the city, but the greatest concentrations are in the poorest neighborhoods: East Harlem, the Lower East Side, the South Bronx, and Williamsburg and Bushwick in Brooklyn.

The Bronx has the largest Puerto Rican population in the city, but the cradle of Puerto Rican New York is East Harlem, sometimes called Spanish Harlem, but known mostly as El Barrio ("the neighborhood" or "quarter") to its residents.

Unlike what is now Black Harlem, East Harlem was never a fashionable area. Poor Irish and German families lived here in shacks and shanties in the nineteenth century; they were followed by poor Italian immigrants, who lived in tenements. By the 1930s, East Harlem had become the largest Italian neighborhood in the city.

After the First World War, many Latin Americans came to New York to escape poverty and political upheavals at home; they settled in Lower and East Harlem because of the low rents and because many black Latin Americans were not welcome in other parts of town. In 1940, the Puerto Ricans were already the largest Spanish-speaking group in what had become Spanish Harlem, and many Italians had moved out of the area.

Today, except for a vestige of the old Italian neighborhood around Pleasant Avenue and 114th Street and a sprinkling of Cubans, Dominicans and Asians, East Harlem is a Puerto Rican neighborhood.

An area of old four- and five-story tenements, towering concrete housing projects, abandoned buildings and littered vacant lots, El Barrio also contains a broad thoroughfare lined with prospering Spanish businesses and restaurants (116 Street), a colorful enclosed Spanish market (La Marqueta) and a Fifth Avenue museum that showcases the art and music of Puerto Rico (El Museo del Barrio). Like any large town in

Puerto Rico, El Barrio is sprinkled with *bodegas* (groceries), *carnicerías* (meat shops), *cuchifrito* (Puerto Rican snack) stands, restaurants that advertise Comidas Criollas (Creole food), small churches and *botánicas* (religious herbal shops), which sell dried roots and powders for gaining power or for curing ailments of the body or the heart.

El Barrio is not a pretty neighborhood, and it does have a crime problem (if you go, go in the daytime). But it is a *true* neighborhood, where people know and greet one another on the street and where the sidewalks in good weather are the scene of much gossiping, gambling, bragaining, domino-playing and just plain hanging out. On summer evenings, radios tuned to the Spanish stations fill the neighborhood with the hot-cool sounds of *salsa*, and when there is a party or fiesta, the steady beat of bongo drumming floats up from playgrounds and tenement stoops. The improvised Afro-Caribbean drumming patterns are often accompanied by the sound of *güiros*, the long, grooved gourds rubbed with sticks that were among the instruments the Taino Indians played on Borinquén long before the Spanish came and renamed their island "Rich Port."

HOW TO GET THERE

By subway: *Lexington Avenue IRT* #6 to 96, 103,110 or 116 St. **By bus**: *M1*, *M2*, *M3*, *M4* (Fifth Ave. southbound, Madison Ave. northbound) to any cross-street in El Barrio and walk east; or *M101* or *M102*, Third Ave. to E. 116 St., then west on 116 St. *Crosstown buses*: *M20* (116 St.), *M19* (96 St. westbound, 95 St. eastbound).

Suggested Walking Tour: from El Museo (Fifth Ave., 104–105 Sts.) east to Lexington Ave., north on Lexington to 111 St., west to Park Ave., north through La Marqueta to 116 St., east on 116 St. to Third Ave.

A MUSEUM, A WORKSHOP AND A GALLERY

El Barrio's leading cultural center and a good place to begin a tour of the Puerto Rican quarter is **El Museo del Barrio** (1230 Fifth Ave., 104–105 Sts., 534-4994). Housed in a large U-shaped complex one block up from the Museum of the City of New York and across the street from an old fashioned conservatory garden in Central Park, El Museo is both a community museum and a bridge between the inner-city neighborhood and the world outside. One of its galleries holds a permanent installation of ninety-four handcrafted wooden saints from Puerto Rico. The other gallery is reserved for changing exhibits of Caribbean artifacts (pre- and post-Columbian) or contemporary painting or sculpture from the museum's own collection. Captions and explanations are in Spanish and English.

The galleries represent only one aspect of El Museo, which also sponsors a variety of cultural events. In the summer, there are lunchtime

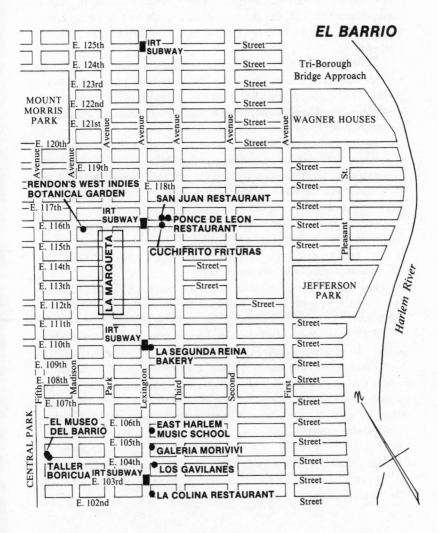

EL BARRIO

E. 125th — IRT SUBWAY — Street
E. 124th — Street — Tri-Borough Bridge Approach
E. 123rd — Street
MOUNT MORRIS PARK — E. 122nd — Street
E. 121st — Street — WAGNER HOUSES
E. 120th — Street
E. 119th
RENDON'S WEST INDIES BOTANICAL GARDEN — E. 118th — Street
SAN JUAN RESTAURANT — Street
E. 117th — IRT SUBWAY — Street
E. 116th — PONCE DE LEON RESTAURANT — Street
E. 115th — Street
CUCHIFRITO FRITURAS
E. 114th — LA MARQUETA
E. 113th — Street — JEFFERSON PARK
E. 112th — Street
E. 111th — Street
E. 110th — IRT SUBWAY — Street
E. 109th — LA SEGUNDA REINA BAKERY — Street
E. 108th — Street
E. 107th — Street
EL MUSEO DEL BARRIO — E. 106th — EAST HARLEM MUSIC SCHOOL — Street
E. 105th — Street
GALERIA MORIVIVI
TALLER BORICUA — E. 104th — LOS GAVILANES — Street
IRT SUBWAY — E. 103rd — Street
E. 102nd — LA COLINA RESTAURANT — Street

CENTRAL PARK
Fifth Avenue — Madison Avenue — Park Avenue — Lexington Avenue — Third Avenue — Second Avenue — First Avenue — Pleasant St.

Harlem River

concerts of Puerto Rican folk music in the museum's courtyard (call to find out which days). In the fall, there's a Friday-night film series. On Sundays from September to June, Puerto Rican classical musicians living in New York present chamber-music concerts and from time to time, there are also poetry readings, dance performances and lectures on the arts or community-related topics.

Associated with El Museo is **Teatro Cuatro** (175 E. 104 St., 534-4994), a theater group that performs on neighborhood streets in El Barrio and on the Lower East Side. In its presentations, Teatro Cuatro attempts to deal with the daily problems confronted by these communities. *Museum hours Tues.–Fri. 10:30 A.M.–4:30 P.M.; Sat., Sun. 11 A.M.–4 P.M.*

Taller Boricua (1 E. 104 St., Fifth–Madison Aves., 831-4333), a workshop for community artists, is in the same building complex as El Museo. The creative core of Taller Boricua is a group of five professional artists who, in addition to working on their own projects, act as mentors to young artists-apprentices from the community.

The five artists presently in residence at the studio work in a variety of media—silkscreening, drawing, painting, batik, weaving, graphics, constructions. Though styles and media vary, all their works reflect a fascination with the Afro-Indian-Spanish roots of Puerto Rican culture and a need to respond to the inner-city environment.

The artists of Taller Boricua accept outside commissions to do silkscreen prints (original posters or transposing paintings to prints) or graphic work of any kind. Luís Vega, one of the artists in residence, offers the services of a professional framer.

Taller Boricua is open to the public. It is best to call ahead and make an appointment, especially if you want to bring a group. The artistic director is Jorge Soto; the executive director, Marcos Dimas.

Walk by **Galería Morivivi** (1671 Lexington Ave., 104–105 Sts., 663-0672), a small, nonprofit, multicultural gallery in the heart of El Barrio in the summer, and you are likely to find Morivivi's director, Elaine Rosner, sitting on the wrought-iron staircase leading to the second-floor gallery, talking in fluent Spanish to visitors and passersby. When I visited, the show was "Ritual Images," and it included masks, photographs, drawings and constructions by community artists showing the importance of ritual in our daily lives. The Galería changes its exhibits frequently and also sponsors performances and slide shows during the year. *Open Wed., Thurs., Fri., 3 P.M.–7 P.M.; Sat. 1 P.M.–6 P.M.* Usually closed in August.

LATIN MUSIC SCHOOL

There are two rundown tenement buildings on Lexington Avenue in East Harlem that reverberate with Latin rhythms almost every night. The buildings (1679 Lexington, nr. 105 St., and 1681 Lexington, nr. 106 St.) house the **East Harlem Music School**, which, as far as its director knows, is the only Latin music school in the country.

Johnny Colón had always dreamed of opening a music school to give kids in his neighborhood an alternative to hanging out, but it wasn't until the success of his own hit recording, "Bugaloo Blues," in 1967, that he was able to convince the city's Youth Board to give him a grant for a pilot project. Today, over fifteen hundreen students are enrolled. They come from East Harlem, from Newark, from the Bronx. Some come four nights a week; others, who can't afford the subway fare to come that often, when they can. Each chooses one instrument to study—trumpet, trombone, sax, flute, guitar, piano or Latin drums—and when he or she (a lot of girls are enrolled in the school now) is good enough, the next step is playing with the school's workshop bands.

So far, the East Harlem Music School has produced four professional bands, but creating professional musicians is not its primary function. "The school doesn't just teach the kids music," says Johnny Colón. "It provides self-motivation, self-esteem. It shows them they can be better individuals, that there's no need to hang out."

Usually once a year, the students of the school give a fund-raising concert; these have been held in the past at the city's hottest Latin nightclub, Corso. For more information, call Johnny Colón, 876-0136.

LA MARQUETA

The best place for Spanish products at the best prices, says the sign above the entrance to La Marqueta, an enclosed market (it used to be a line of pushcarts) extending from 111th Street to 116th on Park Avenue, under the elevated viaduct of the New York Central and New Haven railroads.

There are plenty of *bodegas* in El Barrio where you can get yuca and papaya, but it is more fun to go shopping at La Marqueta. Take a stroll through the market and you will see whole goats hanging next to sides of beef, and a colorful array of tropical fruits and starchy roots that would make any Caribbean islander feel right at home: blushing mangoes and prickly pineapples, smooth papaya and hairy coconut, brown-skinned potato-shaped taro root, long, thin, shaggy-skinned cassava (yuca) and the true, white-fleshed yam (no relation to our sweet potatoes). Often you can find *calabaza*, the Caribbean pumpkin with a nutty flavor like that of Hubbard squash. And always, you will find plantains, sold in every stage of ripeness from green (when it is boiled like a potato and dressed with spices), to half-ripe (when it is boiled and mashed and mixed with pork cracklings for *mofongo*), to sweet yellow-ripe (when it is fried until the inside is pudding-soft).

At the northern end of the market, between 115th and 116th streets, are the meat and fish stalls where you can get oxtails, dried salted codfish (*bacalao*) and, sometimes, kingfish. On the east side of La Marqueta are the jewelry, clothing, and other nonfood stalls, displaying gold hoop earrings, wigs, recycled magazines, ornate Mediterranean lamps, fresh flowers and inexpensive pants and skirts.

The most fascinating stalls at La Marqueta are the *botánicas* with their dried herbs and powders, amulets, mounds of cactus leaves, dream books, snake oils and a startlingly eclectic pantheon of deities: next to a plastic madonna icon, one finds the bust of a Mohawk Indian (an image the Puerto Ricans have adopted to represent the Taino Indians of their island, who were wiped out by the Spanish); behind the Indian stands a laughing, pot-bellied Chinese Hotei, god of luck.

Weekday mornings are fairly quiet, but on Saturdays, the market comes to life with the shouts of vendors calling attention to their wares, the sounds of rapid-fire Spanish bargaining and the bright hues of women's dresses vying with the brilliant colors of the tropical fruits.

BOTÁNICA
La Marqueta has its *botánica* stands, and there are spiritual herbal shops all over El Barrio, but the Bloomingdales of *botánicas* in New York is **Rendon's** (56 E. 116 St., Park–Madison Aves., TR6-6534), a shop that has carried the most complete selection of elixirs, powders, icons and herbs for over fifty years. In addition to the voodoo dolls, lucky horseshoes, votive candles and valerian root (an old form of Valium) that are the traditional stock-in-trade of the *botánica*, Rendon's shelves hold the very latest in magic elixirs—a line of power-enhancing aerosols (including one called Gamblers Spray). Otto Chicas took over the shop when his uncle, Alberto Rendon, died, and now his son Roland has joined the business and is applying modern management techniques to the running of this folk pharmacy and several others owned by the Chicas family. *Open Mon.–Sat. 9* A.M.–*5* P.M. *Cl. Sun.*

COFFEE, ALCAPURÍAS AND CUCHIFRITOS
El Barrio is full of little stands and shops where you can get a snack. For a cruller twist, *pan dulce* (sweet roll) and the best coffee in East Harlem (where coffee is taken seriously), try **La Segunda Reina Bakery** (1773

Lexington Ave., 108–109 Sts., 369-5255). A big pot of milk is always boiling on the charcoal stove in the back room here for *café con leche*. And although this is actually a Cuban bakery, everyone from the neighborhood comes here; at around 11 or 11:30 in the morning, people waiting for coffee at La Segunda stand two rows deep, while just outside, a vendor holds up a fistful of belts and calls out "One *peso*, one *peso*." *Open daily Mon.–Sat. 6 A.M.–10 P.M., Sun. 7 A.M.–10 P.M.*

At tiny **Los Gavilanes** (162 East 104 St., Lexington–Third Aves.), you can get only three things: *alcapurías, papas rellenos* and *pastelillos*. *Alcapurías* are balls of mashed plantain deep-fried with pork pieces (an acquired taste); *papas rellenos* are balls of mashed potatoes mixed with pork pieces and garbanzos (chick peas); *pastelillos* are small, crispy, meat-filled turnovers. All are 50¢.

For the really adventurous, there are stands that sell *cuchifritos*— the deep-fried bits of pork entrails, ears, snouts and other parts of pigs that Puerto Ricans eat like potato chips. One of the largest selections of these delicacies will be found at a small shop next to the Banco de Ponce (on 116 St., Lexington–3rd Aves.) marked only by a red neon sign saying *Cuchifritos Frituras*. Inside this bright, attractive store, you'll find *papas rellenos, pastelillos, alcapurías* and codfish fritters known as *bacalaoitos*, as well as *cuchifritos* and that uniquely Puerto Rican dish, *mofongo*. All can be washed down with a *tamarindo, ajomjoli juice* or other *jugos tropicales* ("tropical juices").

RESTAURANTS

The top-of-the-line restaurants in El Barrio are the San Juan and the Ponce de Leon. Both are on El Barrio's main business thoroughfare and both serve good food, generously portioned.

The **San Juan** (167 E. 116 St., Lexington–Third Aves., 860-2382, **I–M**) is cool and dark, with a long bar, murals of the beaches and buildings of the capital of Puerto Rico, a thickly stuccoed ceiling, plastic tablecloths and a juke box. The restaurant has been in the Gonzalez family for over forty years.

Though the menu offers paella as the house specialty, the San Juan also features dishes that are typically Puerto Rican, like the soupy stews of fish and rice or meat and rice called *asopaos*, the drier *arroz con———*, combinations of squid or lobster or Spanish sausage or other seasoned meat or fish with rice and, of course, the mashed plantain dish crunchy with pork cracklings called *mofongo*. *Bistec*, pork chops, shrimp or lobster Creole and delicious Puerto Rican *pasteles*—steamed, plantain-leaf-wrapped bundles of chopped meat mixed with mashed plantain, olives, capers, raisins and spices—are other good choices here. Everything is served with rice, beans and fried plantain. *Open Fri., Sat. 11 A.M.–4 A.M.; all other days 11 A.M.–1:30 A.M.*

At the **Ponce DeLeon Restaurant** (171 E. 116 St., Lexington–Third Aves., 348-5580, **I–M**), a brightly lit lunch counter replaces the dark bar of the San Juan, but otherwise, the menu and food are very similar. The formal dining room in back is enlivened with Spanish lanterns, a mural of a seaside village and marbled mirrors. The garlic bread brought to you by a red-jacketed waiter while you wait for your order is very garlicky and very good. There is no fountain of youth here, but the Ponce DeLeon does offer homemade sangría and other alcoholic beverages as well as *malta* (a nonalcoholic malt drink) and espresso. For dessert, there's flan, or tropical fruit jelly with cream cheese. *Open daily noon–11:30 P.M.*

La Colina (1621 Lexington Ave. cor. 102 St., 722-9324, **I–M**) is less Spanish and more Caribbean, less formal and more funky than either the San Juan or the Ponce DeLeon. You won't find paella here. Or a menu. When you walk in, you ask the woman behind the counter what's cooking (in Spanish, if you can). The *escabeche*—cold marinated fish—is deliciously prepared here, the *ensalada de pulpe* (octopus salad) is excellent and the breaded pork chops, heavily flavored with *ajo* (mashed garlic) are outstanding. Other specialties of the house are *biftec empañada* (steak pounded to thin tenderness, then breaded and sautéed) and *pasteles*.

Portions are huge and all orders come with a bowl of *habichuelas* (beans), a mound of rice and fried plantains—green and unripe or yellow and sweet as you prefer. (Sprinkle these with vinegar.)

A few oilcloth-covered tables, a juke box and a torn picture of a hunter in plaid lumberjacket posed against the Rocky Mountains (the legacy, no doubt, of some coffee shop of yore) comprise the decor. No English is spoken at La Colina. *Open 7 A.M.–midnight weekdays, 7 A.M.–5A.M. weekends.*

Around Town in Manhattan

THE ARTS
Not since the days of the Yiddish theater has there been such a flowering of creative expression in a foreign language in New York as the current explosion in the Hispanic arts. As the largest Spanish-speaking group in New York, the Puerto Ricans play a leading role in this cultural blossoming.

The best single source for finding out what's happening on the Hispanic and Puerto Rican arts scene is the **Association of Hispanic Arts** (200 E. 87 St., 369-7054). This nonprofit organization publishes a bimonthly newsletter and calendar of events, sponsors an annual Hispanic Arts Festival and distributes a booklet listing the city's major Hispanic arts organizations (almost one third of the booklet's 60 listings are Puerto Rican or place special emphasis on Puerto Rican culture).

One of the liveliest Puerto Rican cultural organizations is the **Puerto Rican Traveling Theater** (304 W. 47 St. nr. Eighth Ave., 749-8474, 749-8499). Founded by the stage and screen actress Miriam Colón in 1967 as a street theater, this company now has its own theater (a converted firehouse) on Broadway. Miriam Colón's bilingual company presents the works of Puerto Rican, European, American and Latin American playwrights in English on weekdays, and in Spanish on weekends. A touring company also gives free performances in parks and community centers.

There are several Hispanic and Puerto Rican dance groups in New York, of which the best-known is **Ballet Hispánico** (167 W. 89 St., 362-6710), founded by Tina Ramirez—a national repertory company that combines the strict discipline of classical ballet with inspiration from classical flamenco, modern jazz and island folklore. Ballet Hispánico, which has toured Europe, offers concerts, school performances, lecture demonstrations and master classes.

Puerto Rican Dance Theater (215 W. 76 St., 724-1195), which integrates modern theatrical dance with traditional folklore, performs in schools and community centers and offers dance training to students in economically deprived areas of the city. **Centro Cultural Ballet Quisqueya** (2153 Amsterdam Ave., 795-0107) gives public performances of Latin American folk dances.

A Puerto Rican opera and several Puerto Rican compositions are in the repertoire of the **Pan American Symphony Orchestra** (233 Jamaica Ave., Brooklyn, 235-8733), a group of Puerto Rican and other Latin American musicians who have performed at Carnegie Hall as well as in community centers around town.

The **Visual Arts Research & Resource Center Relating To The Caribbean** (Phelps-Stokes Fund, 10 E. 87 St., 427-8100) maintains a reference collection of slides, photographs, books and catalogues on the arts of the Caribbean (pre-Columbian to contemporary) that includes the art of Puerto Rico. The center also mounts an occasional exhibit. Call for hours.

Two Puerto Rican cultural centers on the Lower East Side offer a taste of everything. The **New Rican Village** (101 Avenue A, 6–7 Sts.,

475-9505), which has its own performing company, has presented plays, concerts, art exhibits and poetry readings. The **Nuyorican Poet's Café** (505 E. 6 St., Aves. A–B, 777-1140), open on Friday and Saturday nights from about 8 P.M. to 3 A.M., usually presents three open readings a night, followed by "spontaneous creative happenings," which often include good music and dancing.

SALSA

You hear it everywhere you go in Puerto Rican New York—at the fiestas, in the nightclubs, in the neighborhoods. It's called *salsa*—literally "sauce"—and its spicy mixture of African rhythms, island music and American Jazz has become the sound of Latin New York.

Salsa originated in Cuba (it was called mambo then, before Izzy Sanabria, publisher of *Latin NY*, invented a new name for it), but since then, *salsa* has spread like wildfire throughout the Latin world. Puerto Ricans have all but forsaken their own *bomba* and *plena* for the more sophisticated urban rhythms of *salsa*, enthusiastically embracing the form as their own. Today many of the leading *salsa* musicians and 80 percent of the crowds at most New York Latin *salsa* nightclubs are Puerto Rican.

Though the largest market for *salsa* is in Latin America, almost all *salsa* records are cut in New York. "New York is the *salsa* capital of the world," says Marty Arret, manager of the nightclub Corso. The best music, the best musicians, are based in New York. The bread and butter is here."

The best place to hear live *salsa* in New York is Tony Raimone's **Corso** (205 E. 86 St., Second–Third Aves., 534-4964), the city's top Latin nightclub, on Manhattan's chic Upper East Side. Corso features two to four bands nightly, and they're always the hottest bands in the *salsa* business.

A mirrored ceiling reflects the crowded dance floor, and the club in general is both classy and comfortable. On weeknights, the crowd is young and hip; on weekends, there are a lot of once-a-week discoers, and Sunday night attracts an older crowd. Except for an occasional Dominican *merengue* or Cuban *charanga*, and the intervals between sets, when disco music is used as a filler, *salsa* reigns supreme.

Cover charges are higher on weekends, but still moderate; ladies get in free Wednesday and Thursday until 11 P.M. On Sunday nights, there's a free buffet.

After Corso, the most popular Latin *salsa* clubs in the city are the **Casablanca** (253 W. 73, 799-3770) and the **Casino 14 LaMancha** (60 E. 14, 475-9270). **LaMaganette** (825 Third Ave., 759-5677) and **Cork** and Bottle (130 E. 52 St., 751-2507) feature one Latin night a week. Most club-going Latins and Puerto Ricans take their outfits very seriously; at some clubs (not the Corso), men may be expected to wear jacket and tie.

Latin NY, available at many of the city's newsstands, is an up-to-the-minute guide to what's happening on the *salsa* scene.

HERE AND THERE, THIS AND THAT
A good source for Puerto Rican foods and snacks is the Spanish supermarket, **Casa Moneo** (210 W. 14 St., Seventh–Eighth Aves., 929-1644).

The **Museum of the American Indian** (Broadway at 155 St., AU3-2420) has exhibits on the Taino Indians, who inhabited Puerto Rico before the Spanish came.

The **Center for Puerto Rican Studies** (445 W. 59 St., 489-5260), located in the John Jay School of Criminal Justice, conducts research on the history and migration, culture and arts of Puerto Rico and the Puerto Ricans and maintains a bilingual library for scholarly research.

Around Town in the Bronx

The fanciest Puerto Rican restaurant in New York is **Beau's** in the Bronx (2914 Westchester Ave. cor. Pilgrim, 822-9364, **M**). Beau's serves Spanish and international cuisine, but "Mofongo is our specialty." *Open daily 5* P.M.*–12* P.M.

The most popular Puerto Rican restaurant in the Bronx before Beau's opened was **Mama Apontés** (1054 Southern Blvd. at Westchester Ave., 590-0502, **I–M**). *Open daily 5* P.M.*–11* P.M.*; weekends until midnight.*

Festivals and Holidays

Puerto Ricans celebrate many festivals in New York, most of which take place in the summer months.

The gala **Puerto Rican Day Parade** on the first Sunday in June kicks off the festival season. If it is a nice day, a million people may show up for the parade, which includes marching bands, baton twirlers, the mayor of New York, a contingent of mayors from towns in Puerto Rico, floats and often, replicas of Columbus's three ships, the *Nina*, the *Pinta* and the *Santa Maria*. It generally takes three hours for the parade to wend its way up Fifth Avenue from 44th Street to 86th Street and then east to

Third Avenue. For information, call the Office of the Commonwealth of Puerto Rico, 260-3000.

The Puerto Rican festival with the most interesting history is **Fiestas de Loiza Aldea**, celebrated in New York on the second weekend of July.

Loiza Aldea is an isolated town on the northeast coast of Puerto Rico famed for its celebration of the Fiestas de Santiago Apóstol (the Feast of St. James the Apostle), which is still patterned after celebrations of the fiestas in sixteenth-century San Juan and which combines both Spanish-Catholic and African elements. The New York celebration of the Fiestas de Loiza Aldea is a scaled-down version of the Fiestas de Santiago Apóstol as it is celebrated in Loiza Aldea.

On Saturday, there's a cultural program of music and theater on Ward's Island, but the traditional celebration takes place on Sunday, beginning with a morning mass at the Church of San Pueblo on Lexington Avenue and 117th Street. After mass, a procession carrying three small statues of the Apostle (one for the men, one for the women and one for the children) makes its way to the footbridge at 102nd Street and the East River Drive that connects Manhattan with Ward's Island. After crossing the bridge, the procession is met on the other side by a crowd of clapping, singing, drumming, dancing people. Several ritual figures are always part of the procession: the *vejigante*, or devil, who wears an animal head with many horns; the crazy person and the *caballero*, a dashing sixteenth-century Spanish gentleman.

After the procession, the day's festivities begin, with a nonstop program of Latin music and dance performed on an openstage on Ward's Island. Food stalls along the footpaths by the river and from the bridge to the stage sell fried plantains, *pasteles, bacalaoitos,* cold Schafer beer, Bacardi rum, and a delicious concoction of egg, coconut cream and rum called *coquito*. To the constant sound of salsa, people wander around, greeting others they know, drinking rum, breaking into dance in the middle of a smile. It is as if, for the day, this little piece of land in the East River had become one of the Caribbean out islands. For information call the Puerto Rican Center for the Arts, 222-2966.

The patron saint of Puerto Rico, Saint John the Baptist, is honored at the **Fiesta de San Juan Bautista**, held on the nearest Sunday to June 24 on the Central Park Mall. The archbishop of New York presides over the special mass offered at 1 P.M. at the park's bandshell, and all afternoon there are cultural performances by such groups as the Ballet Hispánico or Tito Puente and his Concert Orchestra, as well as a traditional *piñata* celebration. Near Bethesda Fountain, hundreds of vendors sell food and drink. For information, call the Hispanic Apostolate of the New York Archdiocese, 371-1000.

The rich folk culture of Puerto Rico, which combines African, Indian and Spanish elements, is something about which most New Yorkers—including most Puerto Ricans born in New York—know very little. To introduce this side of Puerto Rico to the city, a group of community leaders organized a folklore festival in 1959. Since that year, the **Fiesta Folklórica** has become an annual event, held on the last Sunday in August at the Central Park Mall. Beginning at 10 A.M. with a Catholic mass and ending at 8 P.M., the fiesta features folk dancing, performances by the Puerto Rican Traveling Theater, games for children and performances of the folk-music forms of Puerto Rico, including *bomba* (an Afro–Puerto Rican song-and-dance form originating in the dance of the black sugar-cane cutters at the end of harvest), *plena* (an Afro–Puerto Rican musical form whose lyrics deal with topical events) and *danza* (slow and formal dance music that stems from the music of the European upper classes in Puerto Rico in the nineteenth century). Though the festival only lasts a day, its organizers say there are enough *bomba*, *plena* and *danza* musicians living in New York to stage a nonstop three-day folk-music festival. About 300,000 Puerto Ricans usually turn up for the fiesta. For information, call the office of the Commonwealth of Puerto Rico, 260-3000.

During the first part of July, El Barrio stages a two-week **Fiestas Patronales del Barrio** on a big vacant lot between Lexington and Park Avenues, 107th and 108th Streets. A secular substitution for the hundreds of fiestas held every year in Puerto Rico to honor each town's patron saint, the New York fiestas feature entertainment every night— rides, *salsa* bands, dance groups, Latin theater and, in some years, poetry-writing competitions, recitations and troubadour-style guitar trios. For information, call the East Harlem Community Corporation, 427-0500.

Every April, the Association of Hispanic Arts sponsors a two-week **Hispanic Arts Festival** to broaden the audience for the Hispanic arts. All the Hispanic-arts groups in the city perform during the festival, including the Ballet Hispánico, the Puerto Rican Traveling Theater and the Pan-American Symphony Orchestra. Events are held in many different locations in Manhattan and the other boroughs. For information, call the Association of Hispanic Arts, 369-7054.

Puerto Rican Food

Tropical island ingredients, cooked with a Spanish touch, give Puerto Rican cuisine its special character. Plantains, beans and rice are served with almost every meal. Starchy roots and squashes and tropical fruits form a large part of the diet, which also includes a lot of pork and seafood. *Mofongo* (mashed plantain and pork cracklings) is Puerto Rico's national dish. Other specialties of the cuisine are *asopao* (a well-seasoned combination of rice and meat or fish that is halfway between a soup and a stew), *arroz con pollo*, and the delicious meat pies wrapped in plantain leaves called *pasteles*. Puerto Ricans are very fond of chile peppers, and often sprinkle on their food vinegar that has been marinated with chiles.

Dessert in New York's Puerto Rican restaurants is usually sweet flan (caramel custard) or cheese served with guava jelly or diced papaya. Coffee ends the meal.

Island rum, usually Bacardi, is the preferred Puerto Rican liquor and is often mixed with tropical juices or coconut cream to make cocktails.

MENU GLOSSARY

alcapurias: deep-fried balls of mashed plantain.
aguacate: avocado.
ajillo: cooked with garlic.
aperitivo: appetizer.
arroz: rice (*blanco*—white; *amarillo*—yellow).
asopao: lit., "soupy"—a liquid stew of rice and chicken, fish or meat.
bacalaoito: salt codfish fritters.
bistec: steak.
calamares: squid.
camarones: shrimp.
carne: meat.
carne guisada: beef stew.
cerdo: pork.
chorizos: Spanish pork sausages.
chuletas de cerdo: grilled pork chops.
comidas criollas: Creole food.
cuchifritos: deep-fried tidbits of pork entrails, pig snout, and the like.
empañada: breaded.
ensalada: salad.
escabeche: fish marinated in vinegar, onions and spices, usually served cold.
flan: caramel custard.
frijoles negros: black beans.
gandules: pigeon peas.
garbanzos: chick peas.
guisado: stewed.

habichuelas: beans (*coloradas* or *rositas*—red; *blancas*—white).

higado: liver.

huevos: eggs.

jamón: ham.

jueyes: crabmeat.

jugo: juice.

langosta: lobster.

mechado: slashed with bacon.

mariscos: seafood.

mofongo: mashed half-ripe plantain mixed with seasonings and pork cracklings.

papas rellenos: deep-fried balls of mashed potatoes mixed with pork and chick peas.

pasteles: chopped pork and beef mixed with raisins, capers, olives, mashed plantain and seasonings and steamed, wrapped in a plantain leaf.

pescado: fish.

pastelillos (also *pastelitos*):   little meat turnovers.

plátanos fritos: fried plantain.

pollo: chicken.

pulpo: octopus.

queso cream: cream cheese (served with guava jelly as dessert).

ropa vieja: lit., "old clothes"—beef strips cooked with onion, garlic, tomatoes and seasonings.

sanchocho: stew of starchy roots and meat, often oxtail.

sopa: soup.

tortilla de huevos: omelet.

tostones: fried plantain.

RUSSIAN NEW YORK

Little Odessa by the Sea

In the summer, the Russian presence in Brighton Beach is barely notice-able amid the throngs of beach-goers and elderly Jewish residents who line the boardwalk benches to bask in the strong sun. But in the winter, on Saturday and Sunday afternoons, the boardwalk becomes a Russian thoroughfare. Men and women in great fur hats, red-cheeked children bundled up to the chin and sturdy grandmothers, their heads covered with *babushkas*, stroll up and down, breathing in lungfuls of the cold salt air and admiring the snow-covered beach. When the families reach Brighton 6th Street, they often turn in at a small boardwalk café called the Gastronom Moscow for a warming glass of tea or shot of vodka. These Russians are part of a new colony of Soviet emigrés that has sprung up in Brighton Beach since the 1970s. And so many of them are from Odessa that they have started calling Brighton Beach Little Odessa by the Sea.

The first group of Russians to come in great numbers to America were Russian Jews, who streamed into the country by the thousands from the 1880s to the end of the First World War. Small numbers of Russian nobility fled to America after the civil war that followed the revolution of 1917. In New York, the Russian Jews settled on the Lower East Side; the Russian aristocrats, on the Upper East Side.

World War II brought the second major wave of Russian immigrants to America, and there were some defectors in the 1960s. The third wave, which still continues, began in the early 1970s, when the Soviet govern-ment made it easier for Soviet Jews to leave the country.

According to the estimates of Project ARI (Action for Russian Immigrants), half the approximately fifty thousand Soviet emigrés now in the United States live in New York City, and about half that number, or twelve thousand, live in Brooklyn's shorefront communities—Coney Island, Sheepshead Bay and Brighton Beach. Many of the emigrés are from Odessa, which is on the Black Sea, and they feel at home by the ocean.

Before the Russians came, Brighton Beach was a declining community of elderly Jews. In the 1970s, when the Soviet Jews began arriving in significant numbers, many of the old residents of Brighton Beach had died or moved to Florida, creating a large number of vacant apartments. Now, with over eight thousand Russian emigrés, Brighton Beach has become the largest Russian community in the city, and there are not enough apartments to house all the new immigrants who want to move in.

Unlike the first wave of Russian-Jewish immigrants, who spoke Yiddish and clung to their own traditions, the recent Soviet immigrants seem more Russian than Jewish. Though a few of the older emigrés can speak Yiddish, Russian is the language spoken at home, and although some parents have begun sending their children to yeshivas, most of the emigrés themselves eat nonkosher food and keep their stores open on Saturdays. As in the Soviet Union, where religious holidays could not be celebrated and political holidays were dull, birthdays are the biggest celebrations of the year in Brighton Beach, observed with big parties in the Russian restaurants and plenty of vodka and music.

The first shops the Russians opened in Brighton Beach were food stores where they could get the kinds of smoked fish, sausages, preserves and breads they were used to eating at home. When the community became a little more prosperous, one or two Russian restaurants opened up. After the restaurants came the gift stores, where the emigrés could purchase china and American appliances for birthday presents or gifts to send home to friends in the Soviet Union. Now the colony has its own gymnastic school for children, and the Graham Movie Theater in nearby Coney Island sometimes shows Russian films.

The visitor to Brighton Beach will find a peaceful middle-class neighborhood. Sunlight streaming through the tracks of the elevated subway forms a mosaic of light on Brighton Beach Avenue, the main shopping street. Trees and two-story houses line the side streets north of the avenue; on the south side, rows of neat six-story brick apartment houses on each street frame views of the boardwalk and the sea.

The Russian shops and restaurants are mostly on Brighton Beach Avenue from Brighton 1st Street to Brighton 14th. As yet, the concentration is still fairly small. But if you know where to go, you will have no problem finding Little Odessa in Brighton Beach. And if you go to one of the Russian restaurants on a Friday or Saturday night, you might even think that you've been magically transported to Russia. During the day, you can make your own Russian picnic lunch with Russian bread and caviar (or herring) from one of the Russian markets in the area. Or you can shop for Russian souvenirs and have tea and cake or vodka and *pirozhky* at the Russian boardwalk café.

BOARDWALK CAFÉ

On the boardwalk, at Brighton 6th Street, there is a simple Russian café that offers shade in the summer, warmth in the winter and *pirozhky*, vodka, tea and Kiev cake all year round. I call it a café, but the **Gastronom Moscow** (31–52 Brighton 6 St., 934-8027) is also part grocery, part souvenir shop and part amusement arcade. That is why, in various corners of the place, you'll find amber necklaces from Russia, a barrel of herrings, loaves of Russian corn rye, boxes of Troika-brand Black Georgian tea, bottles of chanpagne and Stolichnaya vodka, painted wooden dolls-within-dolls-within-dolls called *matryoshka*, dried fish, bags of Polish chocolate-covered plums and a pinball machine. One side of the Gastronom Moscow is open to the boardwalk in the summer, so as you sip your tea, you can watch the strollers and gaze out to sea. Very little English is spoken here. *Open daily 11* A.M.–*11* P.M.

CAVIAR AND KASHA

The largest Russian food store in Brighton Beach is **International Food** (249 Brighton Beach Ave., Brighton 1 Place–Brighton 2 St., 646-9137), a supermarket where the Russians can get all the foods of home: caviar (black and red), schmaltz herring, spicy *moscovska* salami, numerous kinds of salted and dried fish, smoked sprats in mustard oil, fruit compote from Russia and good solid black bread (in 5-pound loaves!). Young Russian matrons, stylishly dressed in the very latest fashions, shop here. International Food is *open 7 days a week, 8* A.M.–*9* P.M.

The oldest Russian food store in Brighton Beach,**Berezka** (512 Brighton Beach Ave., Brighton 6–Brighton 7 Sts., 934-8224), a small grocery that has a very good selection of excellent fruit preserves from the Soviet Union (black currants in syrup, cherries, plums, apricots)—all of which go wonderfully with cheese *blinchiki* or the Russian cottage-cheese pancakes known as *syrniki*. Almost everything in the store is imported from the Soviet Union. Asked why she imports even kasha, when this grain is grown in America, the woman behind the counter explains with gestures and the few English words at her command.

"American kasha, cook" (here she vigorously stirs the imaginary kasha in a pot)—"phhhhhhhh" (she holds up her fist and, as she gives the Russian equivalent of a Bronx cheer, suddenly flings out her fingers to show how the inferior American grains fall apart).

HOW TO GET THERE

By car from Manhattan: Brooklyn Battery Tunnel to Gowanus Expressway to Shore (Belt) Parkway to Ocean Parkway to Brighton Beach Avenue. **By subway**: *Sixth Ave. IND* D, *BMT*, QB or M to Brighton Beach or Ocean Parkway stop. The ride from 50 St. in Manhattan to Brighton Beach takes about 45 minutes.

With Russian kasha, on the other hand, "cook" (she stirs the pot again)—"Aaaaaah" (she holds her fingers in a tight fist and smiles broadly). *Open 7 days a week 8 A.M.–10 P.M.*

The best display of Russian souvenirs will be found at **DM International Food** (1107 Brighton Beach Ave., Brighton 13–Brighton 14 Sts., 648-7860), where the storefront window is crammed with **matryoshka,**

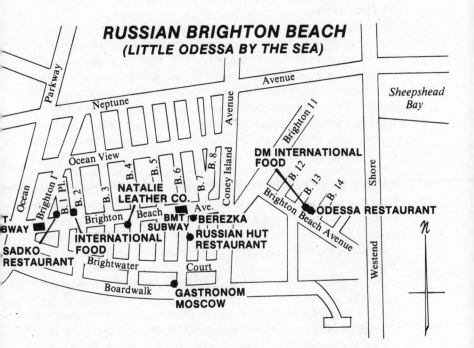

amber necklaces, brightly colored lacquered bowls and spoons, dolls whose skirts are meant to keep a covered dish warm and pretty enameled pins decorated with floral designs. Inside, the small store is crammed with Russians ordering sturgeon, fresh butter and sour cream. *Open daily 9* A.M.–*8* P.M.

LEATHER JACKETS, SHEEPSKIN COATS
One of the most interesting Russian stores on Brighton Beach Avenue for the visitor is the **Natalie Leather Co.** (3086 Brighton 4 St. cor. Brighton Beach Ave., 891-8872). Ample, ash-blonde Natalie and her thin husband Alex own and run the shop, which is filled with handsome leather jackets, leather coats, leather vests and leather pants they have made. Prices are reasonable (about $65 for a jacket). Natalie will also do alterations on leather garments, and the shop carries a full line of fine quality sheepskin coats lined with virgin wool (which are not made here). *Open daily 9* A.M.–*7* P.M.

RESTAURANTS
On weekend nights, it is doubtful whether any Russians in Brighton Beach eat at home. Most can be found at the local restaurants, dining on *varenikis, shashlik* or chicken Kiev and drinking vodka—straight. ("Should it always be drunk ice-cold?" I ask one of the musicians at the Sadko Restaurant. "After the second bottle, it really doesn't matter," he replies.) Go to a Russian restaurant on a Saturday night, for on a Saturday night, a Russian restaurant is not only a place to get Russian food; it is also an outlet for Russian gusto, Russian excess, Russian sentiment and Russian song.

If it is your first visit to Brighton Beach, try the **Odessa** (1113 Brighton Beach Ave., Brighton 13–Brighton 14 Sts., 769-2869, **I–M**), a second-story restaurant made homey despite being as large as a ballroom by its old-fashioned red-and-white-striped wallpaper, red curtains, chandeliers, two pinball machines, and oil paintings of cowboys, seaside sunsets and fruit. A raised platform at one end of the room serves as the stage.

The food at Odessa is very good, very authentic and very inexpensive. The Kiev cutlets, chicken julienne Odessa (chicken slivers in a creamy, flavorful mushroom sauce) and the hot *borscht* (loaded with vegetables and just tinged with the taste of beets) are the specialties of the house, but you won't be disappointed by the shish kebab, Siberian meat dumplings or the *varenikis*. Excellent French fries accompany many of the dishes. Special lunch for $2.39!

Every Friday, Saturday and Sunday night, a live band entertains with Russian and Hebrew melodies and songs. *Open Tues.–Sun. noon–6* P.M., *Fri., Sat., Sun., 8* P.M. *"until 12 or 1 or 2." Cl. Mon.*

Sadko (205 Brighton Beach Ave. cor. Brighton 1 St., 934-8204, **I–M)** is the second most popular Russian restaurant in Brighton Beach. A bit smaller than Odessa, Sadko features, along with its Russian cuisine, four musicians who play ethnic folk songs of Latvia, Lithuania, the Ukraine, Byelorussia and Georgia, as well as popular Russian, Hebrew and Yiddish songs. The menu, which is extensive, is also entirely in Russian. (Use the menu glossary in this chapter, and if all else fails, ask for borscht and shish kebab.) *Open Fri., Sat., Sun. only, 8* P.M.–*2* A.M.

The **Russian Hut** (3089 Brighton 6 St., Brighton Beach Ave.–Boardwalk, 934-8077, **I–M)** is the smallest and cheapest of the Russian-restaurant troika. When I visited, the waitress on duty looked like a Russian version of a middle-aged Elizabeth Taylor. As we, three women she had not seen before, left, she beamed at us and said, "You come again. Come Saturday, meet nice Russian boys." Try the *pelmini* with sour cream; the *borscht* is good here too. *Open 7 days a week, 8* A.M.–*8* P.M. Small music charge.

As I write this, there are rumors that three more Russian restaurants are about to open in Brighton Beach, one of which may be called **The Thirteen Chairs.**

Around Town In Manhattan

RUSSIAN CHURCHES
The two main Russian churches in Manhattan are on the Upper East Side in the 90s.

Five onion domes, each surmounted by a gold cross, crown the **Russian Orthodox Cathedral of St. Nicholas** (15 E. 97 St., Fifth–Madison Aves., 289-1815). St. Nicholas, which is under the Moscow Patriarchate, was built in 1901–02; its iconography follows the traditional Russian style of the late eighteenth and early nineteenth centuries.

The **Cathedral of Our Lady of the Sign** (75 E. 93 St., Madison–Park, LE4-1601) is a Federal Revival mansion that was built in 1917 for George F. Baker, Jr., an international banker who lost his house in the Great Depression. The founding members of the church left Russia before it became Communist; the church is not affiliated with the Moscow Patriarchate and is the Center of the Orthodox Church Outside Russia. Services are held in what used to be the ballroom of the mansion.

Next door to Our Lady of the Sign is **St. Sergius High School** (1190 Park Ave., LE4-1725), the city's only Russian school.

A small colony of elderly Russian barons, princes, former cadets in the czar's army, ladies-in-waiting to the czarina and other members of the old Russian nobility lingers on near the two Russian churches—the last remnant of an almost-forgotten world.

BOOKSTORES

The official Soviet bookstore in New York is **Four Continents** (149 Fifth Ave. at 21 St., 533-0250). A quiet, spacious store, the Four Continents carries Russian books and newspapers, a small selection of illustrated Russian classics in English translation, a large selection of Russian records and, in a small back room, red, black and gold lacquered goblets and bowls, silver samovars, amber necklaces, *matryoshka* and other articles made in the Soviet Union, including Socialist Realist posters illustrating such slogans as Soviet Fiction Gives an Authentic Picture of All Aspects of Soviet Life. *Open Mon.–Fri., 9:30 A.M.–5:30 P.M.; Sat. 10 A.M.–5:30 P.M.*

The **Russica Bookstore** (799 Broadway cor. 11 St., Rm. 301, 473-7480) stocks Russian-language books from all over the world, specializing, however, in Russian poetry and fiction, particularly in *samizdat*, or underground literature. Russica also publishes underground authors under its own imprint and reprints rare Russian books. *Open Mon.–Fri. 9 A.M.–6 P.M.; Sat. 11 A.M.–3 P.M.*

ANTIQUES

Russians leaving the Soviet Union can only take out a very small amount of money, but they are allowed to take objects—folk art, records, a limited number of antiques—which can then be resold in their new country.

In New York, **Samovar** (209 E. 14 St., Second–Third Aves., 677-2307) is an outlet for these personally carried exports. Depending on the number of emigrés allowed out of Russia recently and what they managed to take with them, you may find at Samovar old brass samovars, new brass samovars, amber necklaces and bracelets, lacquered wooden bowls and spoons in old folk art designs (the spoons are good for soup since they don't heat up like metal), silver boxes engraved with scenes from old Russia, enameled pins, embroidered icon cloths, balalaikas, charming blue-and-white folk china and, of course, the *matryoshka* dolls, which range in price from $1 to over $250 for a large, very fine example. The shop also serves as a gallery for the work of Sinkovsky, a very fine modern artist now living in New York.

Prices when I visited seemed extremely reasonable; so much so, it is hard to see how the store can stay in business. *Open Mon.–Sat. 11* A.M.*–7* P.M. *Cl. Sun.*

At the other end of the price spectrum is the elegant **A La Vieille Russie** (781 Fifth Ave. at 59 St., PL2-1727). When you walk through the revolving door of this shop on the first floor of the Sherry-Netherland Hotel and step onto the pearl-gray carpeting, you leave New York behind and enter the romantic, indulgent, decadent Russia of Tolstoy's novels, the Russia of the czarist court. In that world, where the royal family exchanged bejeweled Fabergé eggs at Easter, no extravagance was too extravagant—even the tea strainers were made of gold.

Both Fabergé eggs and gold tea strainers have lain in the étagères of A La Vieille Russie. The range and quality of the collection of old Russian objects the shop has acquired and offered for sale over the years have made A La Vieille Russie unique among the world's purveyors of old treasures.

Not everything in the shop is Russian, however. Much of the furniture is French or Italian, and the jewelry comes from all over Europe. But everything in the store is of a quality and degree of opulence that would have appealed to royal Russian taste.

A changing display of rareties adorns the windows of A La Vieille Russie: a malachite and silver music box, a mother-of-pearl holy water container, a Fabergé clock. The étagères on the first floor hold jewelry: chokers of tiny seed pearls, magnificent emerald-and-diamond necklaces, a miniature portrait of Napoleon to be worn around the neck.

Upstairs are the icons, many of them protected by solid silver covers, and the rooms of furniture—elaborate marquetry tables ornamented with gilt bronze, silver candlesticks as tall as a man that were given by Catherine I to the Synod of St. Petersburg, a trompe l'oeil "marble" table almost identical to one in the Hermitage. Still another room holds the penmanship kit of the czarina and the silver and gold samovar (not for sale) of Alexander III. *Open to the public Mon.–Fri. 10* A.M.*–5* P.M.*; other hours by appointment only.*

THREE RESTAURANTS AND A NIGHTCLUB
The most famous Russian restaurant in New York is the **Russian Tearoom** (150 W. 57 St., Sixth–Seventh Aves., CO5-0947, **E**). It always feels like a holiday at the Tearoom, partly because you have to be rich (or feel rich for the night) to eat here, and partly because the Christmas decorations never come down. With its twinkling chandeliers, gleaming polished samovars and room-length mirror reflecting the faces of happy

diners, the Russian Tearoom glows and sparkles with a gay and festive air that makes every meal here a special occasion. Though many celebrities habitually dine at the Russian Tearoom, it is not an exclusive Beautiful-People-Only restaurant. Everyone who walks through the door receives the same gracious treatment. And the food is very, very good.

If you are really celebrating, you can start your dinner with champagne and beluga molossal caviar, but the chopped chicken livers and eggplant Orientale are also excellent choices (and they don't cost $30 an ounce). Specialties of the house include crisp-skinned chicken Kiev bursting with melted butter, tender marinated lamb *shashlik* and superb beef Stroganoff. But the *borscht*, served with a flaky, buttery, meat-filled *pirojok* and the buckwheat-flour *blini* are also marvelous. At lunch, there are sandwiches, cold plates and *blini* with caviar. Typical Russian desserts served at the Tearoom are cranberry *kissel* and kasha Gourieff (a rich pudding of kasha and sweetened fruit). *Open daily 11:30 A.M.–12:30 A.M.; Sat. until 1:30 A.M.*

If you would like to sample Russian cuisine in Manhattan without blowing a week's wages and don't mind doing without chandeliers and celebrities, try the **Russian Bear** (139 E. 56 St., Third–Lexington Aves., PL3-0465, **M–E**), the oldest Russian restaurant (it was established in 1908) in New York.

The kitchen at the Russian Bear prepares tasty, typically Russian dishes like *pilav* of baby lamb, *shashlik*, *blinchiki* (excellent), a good meaty *kholodetz* (calve's-foot-jelly appetizer) garnished with raw mushrooms and horseradish and a hearty, flavorful *borscht*.

After your eyes have adjusted to the dim light, you will be able to make out the dancing peasants and cavorting bear painted on the natural cyprus walls. Despite its location in midtown, the Russian Bear is often almost empty at lunchtime; perhaps it has been around so long people have forgotten that it's there. Things pick up at night, when a Russian gypsy ensemble comes on from 7 P.M. to 2 A.M. Until midnight, a "psycho character analyst" circulates among the tables "Should You Desire the Sensational Revelations and the Unknown Brought to Light." *Open daily 11:30–1 A.M.; Sat. until 2 A.M.*

Probably the most exotic restaurant in the city, and one that reminds us that the Soviet Union, like the United States, is also a melting pot—or rather, an unmelting pot—is **Firuz** (444 Third Ave. near 31 St., 684-9209, **I**), a funky little storefront eatery run by a young couple from Tadzhikistan in Soviet Central Asia. Firuz is Uzbek: her husband, who is also the chef, is originally from Latvia, and so Firuz serves Russian, Central Asian and Latvian cuisine.

Though the *borscht* Moscow and chicken Kiev are quite good here, most diners will probably be interested in trying the Central Asian dishes. Two good choices are the *dushpera* (meat-filled lamb turnovers in a tomato sauce spiked with hot sauce) and the *pilmini* (noodle envelopes filled with lamb and served in a creamy yogurt-lemon broth seasoned with coriander). *Pilaf* Bukhara (an intriguingly seasoned, Persian-influenced rice *pilaf* mixed with shredded carrots and chunks of lamb) and *mantae* (round dumplings filled with small lamb chunks) must be ordered in advance. Rice pilaf or Turkish rice which, for some reason, is colored bright green, accompanies most of the dishes, but be sure to also order the delicious homemade Tadzhikistan bread—round, flat, crispy loaves reminiscent of Indian *nan*.

For dessert, there is *baklava* or *blinchiki* crepes with jam, accompanied by Turkish coffee or a pot of Tashkent green tea. You may bring your own wine or beer. *Open Mon.–Fri. 11:30* A.M.–*11* P.M.*; Sat., Sun. 2* P.M.*–midnight.*

The increasing number of Soviet immigrants settling in New York in recent years has created an audience for a Russian nightclub. And so, not very far from Firuz, we find **The Balalaika** (300 E. 24 St., cor. Second Ave., 532-9297), a large, unadorned club that shares the lowest floor of a modern high-rise with a Carvel ice cream parlor. Emil Gorovets, a personable and talented tenor from Moscow, provides year-round entertainment at the Balalaika. His repertoire includes Russian, gypsy and Yiddish songs. The food served at the Balalaika is Russian, kosher and, as in most supper clubs, expensive. There's a $5 minimum on Friday and Saturday, $3 on weekdays. *Showtime is 9:30* P.M. *and midnight weekends. Cl. Monday.*

MUSIC AND DANCE

Among the emigrés who have been coming out of the Soviet Union in recent years, there have been many professional musicians from various Russian symphony orchestras. In 1979, a group of these musicians got together in New York for a midsummer **Soviet Emigré Music Festival** of six concerts at Carnegie Hall. The musicians and their backers hope to make the festival an annual midsummer event. Lazar Gosman, who was concertmaster and conductor of the Leningrad Chamber Orchestra and is now assistant concertmaster of the St. Louis Symphony, heads the impressive chamber orchestra, which features Soviet emigrés from the Odessa Symphony, the Kirov Theater, the Moscow Conservatory and the Leningrad Symphony. The festival is sponsored by Arts Ascending (400 W. 43 St., Suite 15-L, NY 10036).

In 1960, a group of balalaika and *domra* players in New York banded together to form the **Balalaika and Domra Society**, to preserve the purity of these three-stringed, guitarlike Russian instruments. The members of the society, who are American-born, of Russian or Ukrainian parents, practice every Friday evening at a rehearsal hall in Soho. The society has presented a concert of traditional Russian music, gypsy songs and contemporary music from the Soviet Union at Lincoln Center. For information about upcoming performances or about taking lessons on the balalaika or *domra*, write to Mr. Kasura, 87 Western Highway, West Nyack, N.Y. 10994.

The **Balkan Arts Center** (415 W. 110 St., 222-0550) occasionally sponsors workshops in the folk dances of the Caucasus, taught by Teymour Darkhosh, who learned the dances from his father and uncle as a child in the Soviet Union.

Festivals and Holidays

Easter, or **Pascha**, as it is called in Russian, is a moveable feast in the Russian Orthodox Church, celebrated on the first Sunday after the first full moon after the Jewish Passover. Six weeks of fasting precede Russian Easter, during which time the Russian Orthodox are not supposed to eat any meat or dairy foods. The Russians get themselves ready for the fast gradually, consuming all the meat left in their larders the second week preceding the feast and all the dairy foods during the last week, which is called **Maslianitsa**, or the "Butter Festival."

Traditionally, throughout Maslianitsa, the Russians eat *blini* (yeast-raised buckwheat pancakes made with milk, eggs, butter and cream), which are topped with melted butter, sour cream and smoked fish or caviar and washed down with ice-cold vodka. On the Sunday before the beginning of the Great Fast, many Russian Orthodox churches hold *blini* dinners for their congregations. The following churches in New York serve annual *blini* dinners which are open to the public. Most request a donation of $3 or more for the meal, which is served immediately following morning services.

Christ the Savior Russian Orthodox Church, 340 E. 71 St., 744-1915.
Protection of the Holy Virgin Cathedral, 59 E. 2 St., 677-4664.
St. Seraphim Russian Orthodox Church, 322 W. 108 St., 663-9093.
St. John Chrysostom Easter Orthodox Catholic Church, 70–29 45 Ave., Woodside, Queens, 424-9389.

The most dramatic service of the year in the Russian Orthodox churches of the city is the **Great Matins** service on the Saturday night before Easter Sunday, when, just before midnight, the entire congregation, bearing lighted candles, exits to form a procession that circles the church three times. After the third circuit, all stop before the church doors to sing "Christ is Risen," whereupon they reenter the building for the divine liturgy. The priests don special light-hued vestments for the liturgy, which is conducted in English and Slavonic (the root of contemporary Russian) and includes choral chanting. During the service, the lighted candles, the fragrance of the incense, the glow of golden icons and the hypnotic chanting combine to create an unforgetable atmosphere of awe and mystery.

When the service concludes at about three or four in the morning, everyone returns home to break the long Lenten fast with a feast of meat, cheese and eggs—all the foods they have denied themselves during the past six weeks. The Easter breakfast always includes a cheese *pascha*, a mounded pudding made of pot cheese, butter, eggs, heavy cream and nuts.

Russian Orthodox **Christmas** is always celebrated on January 7. Russian-Americans celebrate the new year twice—once on January 1 and again on January 14, which is both the **Russian New Year** and **St. Basil's Feast Day**.

Every year on the first weekend after Labor Day, the St. Nicholas Russian Orthodox Church in Whitestone (1465 Clintonville St., Whitestone, Queens) sponsors a **Festival of Russian Culture**, with Russian folk singing, Cossack dancing, a concert of balalaika music and Russian food and crafts. For information, call 767-7292.

Russian Food

Russian cuisine is at once elegant and earthy, reflecting both its peasant roots and the tastes of the Russian nobility. Such ethnic regions as the Caucasus and Siberia have contributed specific dishes to the cuisine as well.

The Russians adore *zakuska* (appetizers), which may range from a simple eggplant salad or pickled herring to that great delicacy, caviar. Whatever the content of this course, it is always accompanied by ice-cold vodka. Soup—hot or cold—follows next, then the entree, most often chicken or lamb. Grains—cooked as a porridge (*kasha*), baked in hearty breads, or fine-ground and fashioned into dumplings, pancakes or flaky turnovers—accompany every meal; sour cream is eaten with almost everything.

Fruit compote, *kissel*, halvah, *baklava* and sweet farinha pudding are typical Russian desserts. Strong tea—in a glass—ends the meal.

MENU GLOSSARY

beef Stroganoff: thin slices of lean beef in a mushroom–sour cream sauce.

blinchiki: thin crepes filled with cottage cheese or preserves, served with sour cream.

blini: yeast-raised buckwheat pancakes usually eaten with sour cream, melted butter and caviar.

borscht: cold—usually a beet soup; hot—usually a vegetable soup made with cabbage, tomatoes and beets; both served with sour cream.

chakhobili or *chakhombili:*   chicken casserole with tomatoes and onions.

charlottka: Charlotte Russe.

cotelette à la Kiev: boned chicken breasts stuffed with butter, breaded and baked.

cotelettes Pojarski: chopped beef, veal, chicken or salmon patties served with paprika-cream sauce.

dushpera: (Central Asian) meat dumplings in tomato sauce.

eggplant à la Russe: eggplant baked in sour cream sauce.

golubsze: stuffed cabbage.

ikra: caviar.

kasha à la Gourieff: farinha pudding sweetened with fruit compote or preserves.

kissel: a fruit purée, usually cranberry, served with heavy cream.

lagman: (Central Asian) noodles in a meat sauce.

luli kebab: lamb patties.

mantae: (Central Asian) round dumplings filled with pieces of lamb.

mushrooms à la Russe: fresh mushrooms baked in sour cream sauce.

nalisniki: crepes stuffed with chicken or paté.

pashtet: chicken liver patties.

pelmeni or *pelmeny:*   Siberian dumplings filled with chopped beef, served in meat broth with sour cream.

pirojok or *pirozhok:*   meat- or vegetable-filled pastry turnover served with soups.

pirozhki: small *pirozhok.*

shashlik: from the Caucasus; marinated lamb broiled on a skewer.

shrproty: smoked sardines.

solyanka: sour soup made with meat or vegetables.

strawberries Romanoff: fresh strawberries with Cointreau and whipped cream.

vareniki: dumplings filled with fruit or kasha.

zakuska: Russian appetizers.

SCANDINAVIAN NEW YORK

Little Scandinavia in Brooklyn

Far from the blue-green fjords and crystal lakes of Scandinavia, descendants of Vikings are living near the western shore of Brooklyn, the last remnant of a Scandinavian community that goes back more than a hundred years. Some of the older residents of neighborhoods, now largely second- and third-generation Italian and Irish or first-generation Greek and Hispanic, remember when you couldn't walk down Fifth Avenue in Bay Ridge without hearing Norwegian spoken; those were the days when the Finnish apartment houses near Sunset Park were still the only co-ops in town.

The story of Scandinavian Brooklyn is only the most recent chapter of a history that goes back to the origins of New York itself. When Henry Hudson sailed the *Half Moon* into New York Harbor in 1609, a few Danish sailors were among the crew; by the mid-1600s, two hundred Scandinavians lived among the residents of New Amsterdam and thousands of Norwegian and Danish sailors were spending some time in port every year. In 1630, Jonas Bronck, a Dane from the Faeroe Islands, bought land in the borough later named for him—the Bronx. And Swedes were among the pioneers who cleared the wilderness that was Harlem in the 1660s.

The high tide of Scandinavian immigration, however, came in the late nineteenth and early twentieth centuries, when crop failures, economic problems and religious dissension at home sent over a million immigrants from Scandinavia to American shores. Most of those who came were farmers who went on to settle in the Midwest. Those who stayed in New York City were largely seamen and skilled laborers—shipbuilders, carpenters, riggers, ironworkers—though there were many governesses and house maids as well.

The Norwegians formed the first Scandinavian colony in New York, settling heavily on Market Street and its extension, Market Slip, and along the east side waterfront of lower Manhattan near the shipyards where they worked. When the shipyards moved across the river to Brooklyn in the 1870s, so did the Norwegians. Between 1870 and 1910, Hamilton Avenue in Brooklyn was the haunt of Norwegian sailors in port, and many Norwegians lived in the area bounded by the Erie Basin, Gowanus Canal, Court Street and Atlantic Avenue. By the 1920s, most of the Norwegians had moved south to Bay Ridge.

Many of New York's Finnish immigrants also settled in Brooklyn; by the 1920's, the Finnish Home Building Association of Brooklyn had already built several cooperative apartment houses near Sunset Park; these were the first coops ever built in this country. Many Swedes and Danes also lived in Brooklyn, but the general pattern of Swedish and Danish settlement in New York was more diffuse.

Brooklyn's Little Norway and Finntown flourished until after World War II, when the young people began moving out, some because they wanted to live in the suburbs, others because large factories along the waterfront had begun to move away, taking jobs with them. Since then, new waves of immigrants—Hispanics, Greeks, Asians—have been moving into some of the old Scandinavian areas, and there has been no new Scandinavian settlement in Brooklyn to renew the remaining community. There have been economic changes, too: while Bay Ridge has remained solidly middle-class, the Sunset Park neighborhood (north of 67 Street) has gradually deteriorated and was declared a federal poverty area in 1966.

Despite such changes, much of a culture that was shaped by the seas and mountains and rugged winters of Scandinavia can still be glimpsed in Bay Ridge and Sunset Park: in the fish market that sells whole Iceland herrings from the barrel and the stores that stock *lefse* and cloudberry jam; in the churches that hold services in Finnish and the newspapers still published in Norwegian and Swedish; in the fleeting fragrance of cardamom-scented coffee cakes that wafts from the ovens of the Scandinavian bakeries; in the built-to-last solidity of the Finnish co-op buildings in Sunset Park; and in the music, folk dress and pride of the marchers in Brooklyn's annual Norwegian Day Parade. Most of all, you can see it in the sturdy bearing and unusual longevity of the Scandinavian residents of the area, a few of whom have been spotted in blizzards gliding serenely past snow-buried cars on cross-country skis.

SAUSAGES AND FISH
Fredricksen and Johannesen (7719 Fifth Ave., 77–78 Sts., 745-5980), one of the finest meat stores in Brooklyn, is the only store in all of New

York City that specializes in homemade Scandinavian sausages, or *polse*.

Garlic hides a multitude of sins is an old Scandinavian sausage-makers' saying, and in general, the sausages of Norway, Sweden and Denmark are milder than their Mediterranean cousins. Some of the most popular *polse* at Fredricksen and Johannesen are *fleskepolse*, a ring sausage made of pork that has been kneaded by hand to spreading consistency; lightly spiced *middagspolse*, a ring bologna of pork, veal and beef; smoked *morpolse*, a *middagspolse* to which lamb, onion and thyme have been added; and *blodpolse*, a sweet blood sausage in a natural beef casing, which the Scandinavians slice, sauté in butter and serve with applesauce.

Fredricksen and Johannesen also make their own smooth Danish liver paté, lamb loaf, *kalvesus* (cooked ground veal in aspic) and *spekeskianke*—a cured ham which the partners say is better than Westphalian. They carry dried salt lamb for customers who want to make the traditional Norwegian yellow pea soup, and make an assortment of Irish sausages for the many sons and daughters of Eire who live in Bay Ridge (a former Irish employee left his recipes).

The store is scrupulously clean and tidy, with shining meat cases in the back, leaving space in front for shelves of imported packaged products such as Scandinavian crisp breads, mustards, spirit vinegars and jams along one wall, Irish teas and biscuits and soda breads along the other. Around Christmas, when Scandinavians from three surrounding states descend on the shop, lines often stretch from the meat counter to the door. If you would like to try some of Fredricksen and Johannesen's specialties but find it difficult to travel to Bay Ridge, take advantage of the mail-order service the store provides. *Open Mon.–Sat. 8 A.M.–6 P.M. Cl. Sun.*

Fish from the cold North Sea is the main source of protein in Scandinavian countries, and fish—fresh and frozen, packed in oil and dried—is what **Andersen's** (5703 Eighth Ave., 57–58 Sts., GE5-4503) has been selling for over forty years. A wooden barrel on the floor holds whole silvery Iceland salt herrings (the Scandinavians like their herrings whole; they say the flavor of the fish is in the skin and bones), and the shelves are crammed with tins of Norsk crab meat, sardines, *matjes* (virgin) herring, bottles of cod-liver oil and Norwegian anchovies (less salty than the Mediterranean kind, these have more fish flavor but must be kept refrigerated). The stiff, twisted objects in the window that look a little like bleached driftwood are *lutefisk*—dried ling, or cod fish, that is soaked in lye to make it soft (the lye is washed off before the fish is cooked). Probably the Vikings brought this preserved fish with them on their long voyages. Today Scandinavians everywhere pay tribute to the *lutefisk* by making it a part of the traditional Christmas dinner, when it is boiled, immersed in a bechamel sauce and eaten with mustard. *Open Tues.–Fri. 9 A.M.–6 P.M.; Sat. 9 A.M.–5 P.M. Cl. Sun.*

DELICATESSENS
Hinrichsen's Delicatessen (7615 Fifth Ave., 76–77 Sts., SH8-0940) looks like any other old-fashioned neighborhood grocery until you notice

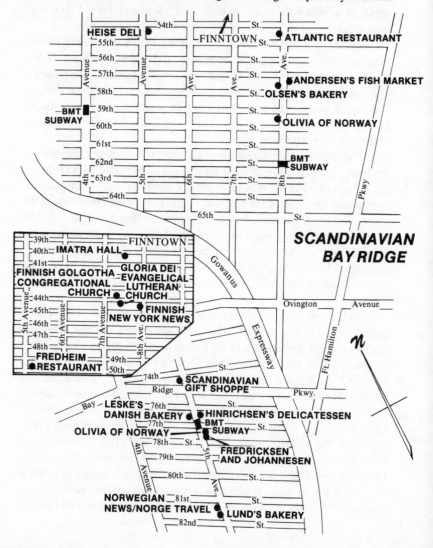

HOW TO GET THERE

By car from Manhattan: Brooklyn Bridge to Brooklyn–Queens Expressway south to Gowanus Expressway, which becomes Third Ave. in Bay Ridge. Most of the Scandinavian shops are on Fifth Ave. and Eighth Ave.
By subway from Manhattan: *IND* D train from 59 St. to DeKalb Ave. in Brooklyn; change to *BMT* RR or N. Get off at 45 St. and Fourth Ave. for Finntown; 53 St. and Fourth Ave. for the Fredheim or Heise Deli; Bay Ridge Ave. (67 St.) and Fourth Ave. for Norwegian Day Parade grandstand in Leif Ericssen Park; 77 St. and Fourth Ave. (RR only) for largest concentration of Scandinavian bakeries and stores: on Fifth Ave. in the 70s; Eighth Ave. and 62 St. (N only) for Norwegian stores on Eighth Ave.

the cans of reindeer meatballs on the shelves—a sure sign that this is a Scandinavian deli and that here you will find the imported fish and cheeses, breads and jams without which a Scandinavian's cupboard is bare.

Robert Bjornhold, owner of Hinrichsen's for over fifteen years, keeps a good supply of Norwegian anchovies, smoked cod roe paté (in tubes for easier decoration of canapes) and Ringnes beer on hand, and he imports three kinds of Norwegian cheese: the deliciously spicy *nokkel-ost*, flavored with cloves and caraway; the hard brown caramel-flavored goat's-milk cheese called *gjet-ost* that must be sliced very thin because it is so rich; and *gammel-ost*, an evil-smelling cheese (Scandinavians keep it in a plastic bag pinned to the clothesline outside) that is aged in underground pits. According to Mr. Bjronholm, *gammel-ost* is "fantastic—if you can get it past your nose."

Easier to learn to love are Hinrichsen's imported Scandinavian crisp breads made of rye and wheat flours (in the old days, each household used to bake one batch that would last the winter); loaves of nutty, chewy, solid Danish pumpernickel and anise-scented Swedish *limpa*; and a very special Norwegian treat called *lefse*. *Lefse* is an unleavened potato pancake with the texture of a moist paper towel. Buy it dried (when it's called Viking bread) and moisten it; or buy it frozen and let it thaw, then spread it with butter, sprinkle with cinnamon and sugar and—(this is the best part)—eat it and make another.

The lingonberry (similar to our cranberry) and cloudberry (a golden Arctic blackberry) jams at Hinrichsen's are expensive (since the discovery of oil in the North Sea, no one wants to pick berries anymore), but life is too short to go without once tasting cloudberry jam with cream.

Every Tuesday, Hinrichsen's makes up a fresh batch of Swedish meatballs, and every other Tuesday there's *lapskaus*, a traditional corned beef hash made with the ends of homemade corned beef, potatoes, carrots, onions and pepper. *Open Mon.–Sat. 8 A.M.–10 P.M.; Sun. 8 A.M.–1 P.M., 4 P.M.–7:10 P.M.*

Otto Petersen, a German born near the Danish border who speaks Norwegian, bought **Heise Deli** (5417 Fifth Ave., 54–55 Sts., 439-8584) in 1968. Although most of his Scandinavian customers now come on weekends from Connecticut and New Jersey, Petersen still stocks a complete line of Scandinavian products, and at his appetizing counter, you can always get *fiskekake*, or golden-fried codfish cakes (local Spanish-speaking residents know and ask for these as *bacalaoito*), fish pudding, huge potato dumplings (*kompe*) and *lapskaus* (corned beef hash). Dried salt lamb hangs from a pole, and on the shelves, next to the fruit syrups and cod-liver oil and yellow split peas, there is Scandinavian spirit vinegar, which gives the exhilarating sharpness to Scandinavian pickled herring and marinated cucumber salad. Heise's also carries imports from Ireland and Scotland. *Open Mon.–Sat. 8 A.M.–9 P.M. Cl. Sun.*

BAKERIES

Probably no other people in the world make such delicious breads and coffee cakes as the Scandinavians, and certainly few, if any, bake so many different kinds. In Brooklyn's Scandinavian bakeries, you can try every variety, each baked with Old-Country ingredients and care. If you visit these bakeries, be sure to stock up. Next to owning an eiderdown quilt, nothing is as comforting (especially with the prospect of a long winter ahead) as the knowledge that your freezer is well stocked with sweet *melkekakes* and rich *vortelimpas*, nutty Danish pumpernickels and sour Norwegian ryes.

At the Norwegian bakery **Olsen's** (5722 Eighth Ave., 57–58 Sts., GE9-6673) you'll find wholesome loaves of *griselle* (Norwegian rye), *kneip* (cracked wheat), *mellambrod* (sour rye-wheat bread) and pumpernickel—both light and dark—as well as the incomparable Swedish *limpa*, a light, anise-perfumed, molasses-sweetened rye.

Olsen's sweet breads—light brown *melkekake*, light raisin-dotted *huetekake* and dark raisin-studded *rörtekake*—were made to be eaten with coffee. Once you have had this combination, a cup of coffee by itself will seem a very lonely thing. Marzipan fans will love Olsen's *fyrstekake*, a rich marzipan cake with a rum, apricot or raspberry filling. *Open Mon.–Sat. 5 A.M.–8 P.M.*

If your knowledge of Danishes is limited to the stale iced rolls that have been sitting under the glass cake cover at the corner coffee shop for days, you owe it to yourself to make a pilgrimage to **Lund's** (8122 Fifth Ave., 81–82 Sts., 745-7590), a Danish bakery where the "Danishes" are what they should be. Known as *wienerbrod*, or "Vienna Bread" in Danish, Lund's Danishes are made of layers of puff pastry folded and refolded around lots of fresh butter and shaped into flattened figure eights. Some contain a dab of raspberry or apricot preserves; others a cheese filling; all are baked fresh daily and topped with white icing, and have about as much in common with what usually passes for a Danish as a catbird has in common with a cat.

The same puff pastry used to make *wienerbrod* becomes *kringle* when it is shaped into large pretzels, *stang* when pulled into long sticks (both are filled with jam or custard and sprinkled with slivered almonds) and *Helenesnitter* when formed into large pies covered with almond paste and sliced into triangles.

In addition to its Danish delights, Lund's makes almost all the Norwegian and Swedish breads you can get at Olsen's, as well as a soft and airy cinnamon loaf, a fragrant holiday bread (it smells like fruitcake) called *vortelimpa* that is flavored with orange peel and anise and *rügbrod*, a rye bread so dense and chewy it can only be consumed in very thin slices.

In December, New York's Swedes come to Lund's for their currant-studded Lucia buns to eat on St. Lucia's Day (December 13), and the Danes come to buy their *kransekage*, the frosted, ring-shaped almond cakes that are piled high to form a tower and decorated with flags and candies for Christmas. In all seasons, Lund's makes hot cross buns, buttery-rich Danish pound cake, macaroons, *fattigman* (deep-fried "poor man's cookies" flavored with brandy and cardamom) and *klejner* (fried sugar twists).

If you can't make the trip to Brooklyn, you can get Lund's pastries at Bloomingdale's bakery department (though you pay extra for such back-yard convenience). Lund's is well known throughout the city; on week-ends you will have to stand in line. *Open Tues.–Sun. 5:30 P.M.–7 P.M. Cl. Mon.*

Near Lund's there is another excellent Danish bakery—**Leske's** (7612 Fifth Ave., 76–77 Sts., 680-2323), where along with *wienerbrod*, *kringle*, *stang* and a wide variety of Scandinavian breads, you will also find *boller* (cardamom-spiced raisin buns traditionally eaten on the days before Easter) and butter cookies (Finnish nut bars, champagne sticks and round *Berliner kranse*) that melt in the mouth. Leske's is not as well known as Lund's, and the lines are shorter here. *Open Tues.–Sat. 6 A.M.–7 P.M.; Sun. 6 A.M.–4 P.M. Cl. Mon.*

NORWEGIAN NEWS AND TRAVEL

If you speak Norwegian and/or are planning to visit Scandinavia, you might be interested in dropping in at the office of the *Norwegian News* or *Nordisk Tidende* (8104 Fifth Ave. nr. Lund's, 238-1100), which also functions as a travel bureau (*Norge Travel*). Established in 1891, the Norwegian-language *Nordisk Tidende* publishes news of Norwegian-Americans and of Norway. The large red sign outside the office, which is something of a neighborhood landmark, has become a sign of the times. Where once it overlooked a Norwegian neighborhood, now it stands opposite a Greek bakery and an Italian restaurant.

SWEATERS AND CLOGS, PEWTER AND WOOD

Once a year Olivia Langeland makes a trip to Norway to buy heavy wool ski sweaters and handicrafts for her two import shops in Brooklyn. Most of the cardigans and pullovers at **Olivia of Norway** (5906 Eighth Ave., 59–60 Sts., and 77-21 Fifth Ave., 77–78 Sts., 492-5004) are hand knit in black-and-white or red-black-and-white Nordic folk patterns. The prices reflect the fact that Olivia deals directly with the craftswomen who supply her. Olivia also imports hand-knit mittens, crewel-work kits and Raff health shoes from Norway, and the Fifth Avenue store carries pewter and handcrafted gift items from Norway. Both shops are *open Mon.–Sat. 10* A.M.–*6* P.M. *Cl. Sun.*

The **Scandinavian Gift Shoppe** (7418 Fifth Ave., 74–75 Sts., 238-5060) carries everything from Scandinavia *except* sweaters: wooden cheese boards and trays from Denmark, enamelware and pewter jewelry from Norway, elegant stainless steel servers from Sweden, dainty blue-and-white Royal Danish porcelain, sturdy Finlandia pottery. The elaborately wrought silver filigree pins and earrings in the glass display case are *solje*, traditional jewelry worn by Norwegian women on special occasions. *Open Mon.–Sat. 10* A.M.–*6* P.M. *Cl. Sun.*

RESTAURANTS

Two Scandinavian restaurants remain in Bay Ridge and Sunset Park: the Fredheim and the Atlantic.

Fredheim ("House of Peace," 476 50 St. at Fifth Ave., 439-6131, C) was established over a half-century ago by the Norwegian Lutheran Church as a place where the Norwegian workingman could come for an inexpensive homecooked meal. Ownership has since passed from the church to Edith Berntsen, but you can still get an excellent homecooked meal at this upstairs restaurant for very little.

The charm of eating at Fredheim lies not just in the food, which is typically Norwegian, but in the old-fashioned surroundings, which despite renovations and the addition of a TV console, seem lifted straight out of 1920s Brooklyn and the heyday of Little Norway. Flowered curtains hang at all the windows, potted geraniums bloom on the sills and the beautiful, old, dark bentwood chairs are pulled up to tables covered with snowy white cloths (these days protected by plastic). Old books and magazines are kept in bookcases at the front of the restaurant for those who want to read (to some degree the Fredheim is a community senior citizens' center), and the waitresses and most of the diners speak Norwegian.

The food—fishcakes and fish of all kinds, meatballs in brown onion gravy, corned beef hash (from homemade corned beef), Norwegian anchovy-and-egg or *nokkel-ost* sandwiches—is tastily prepared. All hot entrees are served with potatoes (boiled, mashed or home fried) and a cooked vegetable such as mashed turnips or cream of cabbage. The soups, especially the Norwegian pea soup and the fruit soup of apricots, pears, apples and plums, are delicious. For dessert, the Fredheim offers sweet Scandinavian puddings. (In case you are wondering, the *risengrynsgrot* listed on the menu is sweetened rice porridge.) *Open daily 10* A.M.–7 P.M.

The **Atlantic Restaurant** (5414 Eighth Ave., 54–55 Sts., GE8-9348, C) is the kind of neighborhood luncheonette where the waitress knows every diner by name. The place has a long counter and a row of tables; it is homey and immaculately, cheerfully clean. The food is Norwegian: *fiskepudding* (fried or steamed and served with cream sauce), yellow pea soup, *middagspolse* (a mildly spiced ring bologna), stuffed cabbage, and, for dessert, *sviskergrot* (prune compote) or sweet thin Norwegian pancakes served with lingonberry jam. Every hot entree comes with a potato and a cooked vegetable, which is usually creamed cabbage or turnips. (If you order *fiskepudding* with cream sauce, be prepared for a monochromatic meal.) *Open daily 9* A.M.–8 P.M.

FINNTOWN

In Scandinavia, they say that when you get to the last Lapp you are near the Finnish, but in Brooklyn, you are near the Finnish if you are anywhere between 40th and 45th streets, Fifth to Ninth avenues—a neighborhood which, despite the influx of many new Hispanic immigrants, is still known as Finntown. In the second decade of this century, Finnish immigrants organized the Finnish Home Building Association of Brooklyn and built a number of four-story apartment houses in this area, anticipating the co-op movement in New York City by about thirty years. These structures, quite a few of which can be seen in the vicinity of 41st Street and Seventh Avenue, are solid, well-built brick buildings with names like The Viking Arms and Sunset Court. The buildings are still cooperatively owned and, as a glance down the list of occupants in the entry hall of any one of them will show, still predominantly Finnish and Scandinavian. The apartment house at 816 43 Street, completed in 1916, is thought to be the very first co-op built in New York City.

Co-op residents buy their Finnish breads and imported herrings, their cardamom and vanilla sugar for baking and their fruit syrups and lingonberry jam at **Skandinaviske Varer** (cor. 41 St. and Seventh Ave.), a cooperative grocery store run by the Finnish apartment houses for over fifty years.

The snug brick **Finnish Golgotha Congregational Church** (44 St., Seventh–Eighth Aves.) and the modern brick **Gloria Dei Evangelical Lutheran** across the street still hold services in Finnish.

The focal point of Finntown is **Imatra Hall** (740 40 St., Seventh–Eighth Aves., 438-9426), an immense, rambling wooden structure painted a cheerful yellow that is the headquarters of a society that began as a mutual-aid association. The Finns of New York hold their dances, parties and celebrations in the hall; on Midsummer Eve, they light a great bonfire in it; and on Kalevala Eppos, they gather at Imatra to sing and recite the stories and poems of the ancient Viking epic of their homeland.

Not far from Imatra is the office of the **Finnish New York News** (4422 Eighth Ave., GE5-0800), a Swedish-language newspaper for Swedish-speaking Finns in America that has been published since 1907. A few doors down from the office of the *News* is the Finnish Barber Shop.

Around Town in Manhattan

NYBORG NELSON

The Scandinavian delicatessen in Manhattan is **Nyborg Nelson** (937 Second Ave. nr. 50 St., 753-1495). Established in 1921 by two Swedish women, Nyborg Nelson carries everything that can be found in the delis of Bay Ridge and much more besides. The appetizing counter is probably the most crowded section of the store, with customers always waiting in line for smooth Swedish and Danish liver paté (the Danish is a bit more spicy), home-pickled herrings and *matjes* fillets, Danish salamis, vinegary cucumber salad and the special Nova Scotia salmon, cured with less salt and smoked for a shorter time than regular Nova Scotia salmon.

Just about every Scandinavian cheese is represented here: Danish tilsit, blue, fontina and King Christian IX; Norwegian Jarlsberg, sweet *gjet-ost* and spicy *nokkel-ost*; Swedish *svecia* (a collective name for local cheeses from all over Sweden), spiced *kryddost*, rich, strong, aromatic *västerbotten* and a special cholesterol-free hard cheese called *margarinost*. The selection of Scandinavian breads, both imported crisp breads and bakery-fresh breads, is extensive.

Some of the other hard-to-find items you'll find here are fresh lingonberries (all year round); *pepparkakor* (the thin, very gingery gingersnap cookies made in Sweden); special griddles with depressions for making small, sweet Scandinavian pancakes; canned reindeer meatballs (which taste like beef, only slightly sweeter); lumpfish caviar; *lefse* (Norwegian potato pancakes, dried and frozen); whole herring; sweetsour-spicy Swedish anchovies; and rolls of marzipan.

Clogs from Sweden are in the back room, along with imported candles and posters. Nyborg Nelson is *open Mon.–Sat. 10* A.M.*–7* P.M.

Above the deli, Nyborg Nelson runs a **luncheon restaurant (I)** where you can sample many of the foods for sale downstairs. If you order the cold smorgasbord plate, you can try a little bit of everything: paté, herring, cheeses, salads. But you can also get delicious open-faced sandwiches or hot dishes like stuffed cabbage with lingonberries, Swedish pea soup, delicate Swedish pancakes, *pytt i panna* (hash) and herring bits in a wonderful light mustard sauce. All dishes are served with a slice of Danish pumpernickel and a slice of Swedish limpa.

The prices are purposely kept low, the idea being to introduce you to Scandinavian fare so you will buy the foods sold in the deli downstairs. And it works: the crowd of office workers who come here for lunch like the food and the prices, and both the coffee shop and the store are doing a thriving business. *Open Mon.–Fri. noon–3* P.M.

Nyborg Nelson also has a full-fledged **restaurant** at the Market in Citycorp Center (153 E. 53 St., Third–Lexington Aves., 223-0700, **I–M**) where you will find many of the same dishes made at the original Nyborg Nelson, including the smorgasbord plate. This restaurant—all pale wood, glass and sleek Scandinavian design—also features a delicatessen counter where you can get things like paté, herring salad, Swedish meatballs and **gravad lax** (salmon marinated in its own juices with salt, sugar, peppercorn and dill). *Open daily Mon.–Sat. 11:30* A.M.*–9* P.M.*; Sun. noon–6* P.M.

THE OLD DENMARK
The Old Denmark (133 E. 65 St., Park–Lexington Aves., 744-2533) is a small gourmet shop, catering service and smorgasbord–lunch room that caters many of the cocktail parties given by foreign consulates around town. A wooden Royal Danish soldier stands guard outside this doll-

houselike shop; inside, the floor is covered with a blue rug on which rows of Royal Danish Guardsmen stand at attention. The front of the shop is lined with shelves laden with imported goodies, and the back of the store—the dining area—beckons with a glass-encased smorgasbord of eighteen different delicacies, cheery overstuffed red banquettes and tables laid with blue-and-white plates in the Royal Danish pattern.

Fresh lobster salad, baby shrimp, caviar, Danish liver paté, Royal Danish smoked salmon (a very fine, very firm salmon that actually comes from Greenland) and *rodgrod med Flode* (a red pudding of raspberries, strawberries and red currants served with whipped cream) are among the foods available daily for takeout or consumption here. Monday through Saturday between 11 A.M. and 4 P.M., the Old Denmark offers a prepared smorgasbord plate with a sampling of its specialties accompanied by coffee. Shop *open Mon.–Sat. 9 A.M.–5:30 P.M.*

THE RED HERRING

He may call his shop **The Red Herring** (384 Bleecker St., cor. Perry St., 929-8458), but to say that Paul Sandblom makes the best pickled herring and *gravlax* in town is no fish story. This little jewel of a store specializes in prepared fish of all kinds, with a special emphasis on pickled and marinated fish Scandinavian style. Herring lovers will have a hard time deciding from among the Red Herring's *kryddsill* (whole Maine herring pickled in spices); Swedish pickled herring fillets; and Glassmaster herring (Swedish style and Scotch-cured over a fire made of oak chips from barrels that have held whiskey). Other Red Herring delights are salmon cured in spices and dill (*gravlax*); *lojram*, a golden-yellow Swedish caviar more delicate than whitefish roe; and shrimp in dill mayonnaise. One or two of these fish preparations, a loaf of *limpa* or rye (Lund's of Brooklyn supplies The Red Herring with its Scandinavian breads) and a container of the shop's homemade pickles or cucumber salad make a lovely picnic dinner. The shop does catering and delivers free in Greenwich Village with orders of $15 or more; elsewhere in Manhattan, for a fee. *Open Tues.–Sat., 11 A.M.–7 P.M.; Cl. Sun., Mon.*

COPENHAGEN RESTAURANT

At one time, New York boasted over a half-dozen Scandinavian smorgasbord restaurants; today, only one—the **Copenhagen** (68 W. 58 St., Fifth–Sixth Aves., MU8-3690, **M**) serves this traditional buffet of fish, meats, cheese and salads. The smorgasbord at Copenhagen—*koldt bord* in Danish—is a circular buffet laden with such delicacies as whole Norwegian anchovies, caviar, shrimp, liver paté, herring in many guises (smoked, pickled, curried, sweet, mustard), and *gravlax* (dill-marinated salmon to which the chef at Copenhagen adds a touch of brandy). There are also a variety of cold meats (roast beef, baked ham, barbecued chicken), salads, cheese and headcheeses and, when the chef can get them, hickory-smoked eel. *Frikadeller*—Danish pork and veal balls—is one of the few hot dishes on the *koldt bord. Open Mon.–Sat. noon–3* P.M., *5* P.M.–*11* P.M. *Cl. Sun.*

SWEDISH BOOK NOOK
Where can you find Swedish fairy tales, Swedish cookbooks, Swedish-English dictionaries, detailed maps of Sweden, all the plays of Strindberg, a history of Swedes in America, an album of photographs of the Swedes in Brooklyn and a book on the films of Ingmar Bergman? Why, at the Swedish Book Nook, of course (235 E. 81 St., Second–Third Aves., 744-8224), where, in addition to taking care of the store, husband-wife team T. Edward and Alvalene Karlssen also find time to edit *Nordstjernan-Svea*, New York's Swedish newspaper, which celebrated its hundredth anniversary in 1972. The Book Nook also carries Swedish records. *Open Mon.–Fri. 9* A.M.–*5:30* P.M., *Sat. by appt. Cl. Sun.*

SONG AND DANCE
There are several Scandinavian folk-dance and singing societies in New York. One dance group meets one evening a week at the McBurney YMCA (215 W. 23 St. nr. Seventh Ave., 741-9216). The group, which performs at various Swedish celebrations in the city, welcomes those interested in learning and dancing traditional Swedish folk dances. Another group, The Vasa Folkdancers, meets in the Salem Lutheran Church (450 67 St.) in Brooklyn.

Holidays And Festivals

The biggest Scandinavian festival in New York is the gala **Norwegian Day Parade**, which takes place in Bay Ridge on the weekend nearest May 17. The parade, which commemorates the day Norway adopted a democratic constitution in 1814, draws tens of thousands of Norwegians and Bay Ridge residents. Marching bands, floats and representatives of every Norwegian-American group in New York and New Jersey, many wearing traditional folk costumes, follow a route along Fifth Avenue from 90th Street to 67th Street and Leif Ericsson Park, where the Miss Norway of the year is crowned. For information about the parade, call the offices of the *Nordisk Tidende*, 238-1100.

St. Lucia's Day, December 13, is special for the Swedish community. St. Lucia is a Sicilian saint; centuries ago, Vikings brought back the tradition of observing her day from their travels in southern Europe. On this day in New York, each community group or club chooses a young girl to be St. Lucia, "Queen of Light." Dressed in white and wearing a crown of tall lighted candles, the queen leads a procession of young girls to the doors of the older folks and serves everyone coffee and currant dotted "Lucia buns."

On the closest Sunday to February 26, New York's Finns gather at Imatra Hall in Brooklyn to recite verses from the *Kalevala*, Finland's national epic.

All of New York's Scandinavians celebrate **Midsummer** near the summer solstice (June 21 or 22). Swedes dance around a flower-bedecked maypole to welcome this, the longest day in the year (a large maypole is erected every year in the backyard of Tvaan, the Scandinavian Second Corps of the Salvation Army at 221 E. 52 St.), while New York's Finnish make merry around a bonfire at Imatra Hall (740 40 St.) in Brooklyn.

Christmas Eve is celebrated in the Scandinavian-American community with a big dinner that traditionally includes *lutefisk* (dried cod fish) and a bowl of *risengrynsgrot* or rice porridge with an almond in it. Depending on which tradition is followed, whoever gets the almond either wins a marzipan pig or will be the next one to marry. Swedish families also put out a bowl of porridge for the *tomte* (elves) on Christmas Eve.

All Scandinavian-Americans honor the Norse discoverer of America on October 9, **Leif Ericsson Day**.

Scandinavian Food

Scandinavian food is wholesome and pleasantly bland. Fish and seafood predominate in the diet, although pork, lamb and veal are also eaten. Specialties of the cuisine include pea soup, fruit soup, thin pancakes topped with jam and open-faced sandwiches made with buttered bread and a wide variety of fish and meat toppings. Norwegian and Swedish breads and coffee cakes and Danish puff pastry breads are justly famous. Fruit and rice puddings or cakes made with marzipan are favorite Scandinavian desserts. Only one New York restaurant, the Copenhagen, still serves the real old-fashioned Scandinavian smorgasbord, a groaning board of fish, cold meats, salads and Scandinavian cheeses.

Akvavit (aquavit), flavored with caraway, is the traditional Scandinavian aperitif. With a meal, the Scandinavians often drink ice-cold Danish Tuborg or Norwegian Ringnes beer.

MENU GLOSSARY

akvavit: aquavit, Scandinavian aperitif distilled from potatoes or grain and flavored with caraway seed: traditional drink with smorgasbord.

fiskekake: fishcake of ground fish mixed with cream.

fiskepudding: steamed fish pudding or fish loaf.

frikadeller: Danish pork and veal balls.

gjet-ost: hard, sweet, goat's-milk cheese from Norway.

gravad lax or *gravlax*:   salmon marinated in its own juices with salt, sugar and dill.

karbonade kaker m/lok: meat cakes with onions.

kjottkaker: meatballs.

lapskaus: corned beef hash.

middagspolse: Norwegian ring bologna.

nokkel-ost: Norwegian cheese spiced with caraway and cloves.

polse: sausage, cold cuts.

pytt i panna: hash.

risengrynsgrot: rice porridge.

rodgrod: Danish red pudding made with red fruit (strawberries, raspberries, red currants).

salt flesk: salt pork.

smorrebrod: open-faced sandwiches.

sviskergrot: prune compote.

6 SOUTH AMERICAN NEW YORK

South American Jackson Heights

In New York, when many people hear the word "Hispanic," they think "Puerto Rican," unaware that there are also over a quarter million South Americans in the city, including 150,000 Colombians, more than 75,000 Ecuadorians and smaller groups of Argentineans, Bolivians, Peruvians, Uruguayans, Chileans, Venezuelans and Brazilians.

Except for the Brazilians, who are scattered around the city, South Americans in New York are concentrated in Queens. The hub of their community is Jackson Heights, especially Roosevelt and Thirty-seventh Avenues from about 74th Street to Junction Boulevard—a solid middle-class neighborhood of gabled houses, neat four-story red brick apartment buildings and broad tree-lined avenues. (In recent years, newspapers have made much of the fact that Jackson Heights has been the scene of several murders related to the cocaine trade. The casual visitor to Jackson Heights, however, is no more likely to encounter cocaine-related crime than he would be likely to stumble upon organized crime in Little Italy.)

Walk down the avenues of Jackson Heights—Roosevelt, beneath the roar of the subways on the El, or broad, quiet Thirty-seventh—and the first thing you notice is the Spanish presence. A butcher shop is not a butcher shop but a *carnicería*; a bakery is not a bakery but a *panadería*. Mounds of tropical fruits and roots heaped in front of markets that have names like La Mia Grocery and El Mundo III. The office-supply store sells typewriters with Spanish keyboards. And everyone you pass, from the young mother and her child who is just learning to talk, to the old men chatting on the corner—everyone speaks Spanish.

But look more closely and you will find things you won't find in other Spanish neighborhoods: faces that bring to mind the sculptured features of the Andes' Indians; stores that sell Venezuelan corn flour, green Colombian coffee beans and carved gourds for drinking Argentinean *yerba* tea; restaurants that specialize in Argentinean, Colombian,

Ecuadorian or Peruvian cuisine; Latin nightclubs where the music and rhythms are not *salsa* but *tango* or *cumbia*.

Here and there you will also come across a Cuban or Puerto Rican market, a Greek fish store, or an ancient Irish bar. But in general, it is the South Americans who dominate the area and give this part of Queens its distinctive flavor.

South Americans began arriving in New York in great numbers in the 1960s, and today New York has more South Americans than any other city in the United States. For the most part, South Americans came to New York for the same reasons most immigrants did—to make a better living, to find better opportunities. Many, unable to enter as legal immigrants because of the quotas, came as tourists and then simply stayed past the expiration date on their visas, joining the large underground population already in the city. (Some estimate that over half of all Colombians and Ecuadorians in New York are illegal immigrants.) Around 1970, the United States began to tighten up on its visa regulations, and now, according to South Americans in New York, it is practically impossible to get a tourist visa in South America unless you are wealthy or can somehow prove that you will return.

It is misleading perhaps to speak of a South American "community" in New York when South America itself is so diverse. In that vast continent divided by high mountains and impenetrable jungles, the inhabitants of two countries may be as culturally and geographically distant as the Scandinavians from the Italians. Yet, despite their considerable differences, South Americans in New York find they have more in common with each other than they do with other Hispanic groups in the city. And so, while national and cultural boundaries still exist in New York, there is substantial intermingling. It is not unusual, for example, to find a Chilean working in an Argentinean travel agency, an Ecuadorian waitress in a Peruvian restaurant or a party of Colombians at an Argentinean nightclub. And while there is naturally a tendency to live close to one's countrymen (in Queens, the Colombians seem to gravitate to Woodside, Sunnyside, Astoria and Jackson Heights; the Ecuadorians to Flushing and Elmhurst), in Jackson Heights, at least, it is possible to sample Peruvian *ceviche*, eat an Argentinean steak, book a flight to Guayaquil at an Ecuadorian travel agency and then dance the *cumbia* at a Colombian nightclub—all without leaving an area of twenty city blocks.

ARGENTINEAN JACKSON HEIGHTS: STEAK AND TANGO
"Years ago, Jackson Heights was all Argentinean," says Rita Amormino, a pretty, dark-haired, husky-voiced woman who, with her hus-

band, owns the **Argentina Delicatessen** (95-27 Roosevelt Ave., Warren–95 Sts., 672-3556) in Jackson Heights. "In the '60s, the Argentineans began moving to Rego Park, Forest Hills, Kew Gardens and
Flushing, and now there are hardly any left here."

The Argentineans may have moved out of Jackson Heights, but their
delicatessens, butcher shops, bakeries and restaurants remain, making
them, despite their relatively small numbers, one of the most visible
groups in this South American neighborhood.

The Amorminos came to New York in 1965, and in 1972, they
opened their delicatessen, an immaculate shop specializing in Argentinean cuts of beef, sausages, cold cuts and homemade pasta (like Americans, almost all Argentineans are descendents of European immigrants;
Mr. Amormino is of Italian descent). One of the fastest-moving items at
the Argentina Delicatessen is the homemade *matambre*, a special cut of
flank steak that has been covered with carrots, onions, hard-boiled eggs,
salt, black pepper and herbs, rolled up like a jelly roll and poached for
several hours. *Matambre*, which literally means "kill hunger," can be
eaten hot, but the Argentineans prefer it cold as an appetizer and sliced
thin on the cross-section so that each slice is a beautiful spiral. Every
Wednesday Mrs. Amormino makes up 100 pounds of her marvelous
matambre (the best I have tasted in New York), and by each weekend,
she is almost always sold out.

For parties, the Argentina Delicatessan will prepare beautiful platters of sliced *matambre* and other Argentinean cold cuts; ask to see Mrs.
Amormino's book of photographs. *Open daily 9 A.M.–9 P.M.*

A short walk from the Argentina Delicatessan is the **Pizzaria Argentina Las Americas** (40-05 Junction Blvd., Roosevelt Ave.–40 Rd. in
Corona, 478-5040, **C**) where hard-working proprietor Raul Diaz makes
pizzas like you've never had before. Argentinean pizza is more like a
hearty sandwich than a tomato-cheese pie, and its extra thick crust and
wide variety of imaginative toppings makes ordinary pizza seem positively tame. You can get spinach pies, sausage pies and onion pies at the
Pizzaria Argentina, but if you ask Mr. Diaz for his advice, he will
recommend his Argentina Special—a thick, crusty pie completely
covered with layers of finely sliced ham, spicy tomato sauce, melted
mozzarella cheese and bright red pimentos. A slice of the Argentina
Special is a savory meal in itself, and it costs less than $1! *Open daily 11
A.M.–midnight.*

If you have ever eaten an Argentinean-style steak, you will know
why Argentineans travel from all parts of the city to buy their meats at the
Argentina Meat Market (96-14 Roosevelt Ave., Junction Blvd.–97 St.,
429-9134), which is right around the corner from the Pizzaria.

HOW TO GET THERE

By subway: *IRT Flushing* #7 local from Times Square or Grand Central Station to Jackson Heights station (82 St. and Roosevelt ave.), 74 St. (and Broadway), 90 St.-Elmhurst Ave. (and Roosevelt Ave.), or Junction Blvd. (and Roosevelt Ave.). The ride takes about twenty minutes from Grand Central to 82 St. **By car**: Queensboro Bridge to Northern Blvd. In Jackson Heights, make right turn off Northern Blvd. down any cross-street from 74 St. to Junction Blvd., to Thirty-seventh Ave. Roosevelt Ave. is south of Thirty-seventh Ave.

**SOUTH AMERICAN
JACKSON HEIGHTS**

"Argentines cut their meat very differently," explains the owner of the Argentina Meat Market, Martin Armengau. "We take more advantage of the meat by separating the best pieces from the so-so pieces. Also, in general, Argentines prefer meat from the hind quarters, which are more flavorful than the front quarters. The taste is very different." Mr. Armengau cuts and trims each steak or roast himself, guiding the meat expertly through a special vertical vibrating knife. He suggests you grill his steaks and roasts over wood charcoal, Argentine style. *Open Mon.–Fri. 9 A.M.–7 P.M.; Sat. 8 A.M.–8 P.M. Cl. Sun.*

A short drive or a long walk from the *carnicería*, on the far outskirts of the South American shopping district, is a bakery that supplies many of the cakes and sandwiches eaten by Argentineans all over town. The **Río de la Plata** (47-31 Junction Blvd. nr. Corona Ave., Corona, 271-5422) is easily recognized by its window displays, which consist of mammoth cakes decorated with such ornaments as a miniature soccer game (complete with net, ball and players) or small plastic figures of Snow White and the Seven Dwarfs.

Ask to see the *ochalde*, an incredible extravaganza of a cake composed of inch-thick layers of *biscotti, dulce de leche* (caramel), meringue, heavy whipped cream blended with peach slices, nuts, heavy whipped cream blended with strawberries, and heavy whipped cream. If, after sampling the *ochalde*, your sweet tooth still isn't satisfied, try pacifying it with a few of Río de la Plata's *alfajores* (coconut puffs filled with *dulce de leche*), *quinco mubrillo* (quince pies) or *palmitos* (flaky sweet "butterflies"). And if you haven't got a sweet tooth, get some tasty *empañadas* (South American meat-filled turnovers) or buy the skins and make your own. *Open Mon.–Wed. 7 A.M.–8 P.M.; Thurs.–Sat. 7 A.M.–9 P.M.; Sun. 7 A.M.–7 P.M.*

More centrally located than Río de la Plata is **Los Pe Be Tes** (95-24 Thirty-seventh Ave., 95–96 Sts., 429-9114), which is really two stores in one: a *panadería* (pastry shop) and *carnicería* (meat shop). The *panadería* here does not have as wide a variety of pastries and cakes as the Río de la Plata, but you can get coffee here to go with your *empañada*, sandwiches *de miga* (crustless white bread and ham and cheese) or *alfajores*.

In the window of **Los Pe Be Tes Carnicería** next door, a large wheel revolves slowly around the red-hot charcoal at its hub, slowly cooking the *chorizos* (sausages) suspended on a grill above. Inside this spacious store, you can get Argentinean steaks and roasts. (It helps here if you can speak Spanish.) Both Los Pe Be Tes stores are *open Tues.–Thurs. 8 A.M.–9 P.M.; Sun. 8 A.M.–7 P.M. Cl. Mon.*

Many Argentineans say that the best Argentinean restaurant in New York is El Hornero ("The Bird's Nest") in Queens. Actually an Argentinean-*Italian* restaurant, **El Hornero** (86-14 Thirty-seventh Ave., 86-87 Sts., 424-9375, **I-M**) serves excellent Argentinean steaks and *parillada* (a mixed grill of skirt steak, short ribs, sweetbread, sausage and blood sausage), but some of the most interesting dishes on the menu are the Argentinean-Italian combinations—homemade pastas accompanied by *albondigas* (too mundanely translated on the menu as "Argentine meatballs"). Among these dishes, the cannelone a la Rossini is superb. The cannelone are homemade, stuffed with a mixture of chicken, spinach and spices and covered with a layer of white sauce and a layer of hearty red meat sauce strongly seasoned with basil. And the "Argentine meat ball" served with it turns out to be a thick slice of superbly cooked eye round with a bold garlic-parsley stuffing. Desserts consist of sweet-potato paste or quince paste with white cheese, or sweet apple or caramel pancakes.

El Hornero is small and intimate, attractively but simply furnished; fresh flowers are on every table. Service is gracious. There is wine and beer and, on Saturday nights, a guitarist-singer, beginning about 8:30 P.M. *Open Mon.–Fri. 3 P.M.–11:30 P.M.; Sat. 3 P.M.–1 A.M.; Sun. 1 P.M.–11:30 P.M.*

If you are interested in *Argentinean music*, look for notices of upcoming performances in the restaurants and shops of Argentinean Jackson Heights. The Argentine 4, a New York-based group of Argentinean folksingers, occasionally performs in Queens, and once in a while, a famous *tango* singer from Argentina flies up for a concert.

COLOMBIAN JACKSON HEIGHTS: COFFEE AND CUMBIA
Before every major election in Colombia, certain parts of Queens suddenly blossom with signs in Spanish asking Colombians to register in order to vote. (By Colombian law, Colombian citizens living outside Colombia may vote in any consulate.) Since the late 1960s, so many Colombians have settled in Queens that in 1974, the two leading candidates in a close Colombian election organized and campaigned in this borough.

Jackson Heights is one of the sections in Queens that has a large concentration of Colombians, but there are surprisingly few Colombian-owned stores in the area. Colombians who have the capital seem to open restaurants and nightclubs instead.

Of the handful of Colombian stores in Jackson Heights, the best known and one of the oldest (it was established in 1970) is **Las Americas**

Bakery (89-28 Thirty-seventh Ave. nr. 90 St., 458-1638), owned by Francisco Martinez and Hernan Ochoa, who own several other bakeries in Queens as well. The business comes naturally to Mr. Martinez, whose father was a baker, but Mr. Ochoa's previous calling was civil engineering. ("More money in bakeries," he explains with a smile.)

Las Americas sells cakes and pastries, but what most customers come in to buy are the breads and rolls, which are delicious, unique to Colombia and come in a bewildering variety of shapes and flavors. Some of the breads you can get here are *pan de bono* (a doughnut-shaped roll made with corn flour), *pan de queso* (*pan de bono* with the addition of cheese), *pan de yuca* (irregularly shaped rolls made from yucca (cassava) starch, *almo sabanas* (round, flat, rice-flour rolls); *buñuelo* (a yellow ball of fried maize-flour bread), *mogollas* (slightly sweet whole-wheat rolls) and *roscon* (a sweet ring sprinkled with raisins and sugar and filled with guava jelly). The bakers at Las Americas also make *arepas*, patty-shaped corn griddle cakes of Indian origin that are to the Colombians what tortillas are to Mexicans. Utterly bland, *arepas* nonetheless have a very satisfying texture—crusty on the outside, soft within—and are surprisingly delicious with soups and stews.

Strong, freshly brewed Colombian coffee is the perfect complement to any Colombian bread, and Las Americas provides this too, as well as the coffee beans themselves—"*legitimamente café Colombian*—for about 10¢ less a pound than you would have to pay for the same coffee in Manhattan gourmet shops. For noncoffee drinkers, Las Americas sells a healthful cold Colombian drink called *avena con leche*, made from milk that has been boiled with oats, sugar and cinnamon.

If the rolls and coffee only serve to whet your appetite, Las Americas offers more substantial fare: Colombian *empañadas* stuffed with potatoes and meat; giant Colombian *hallacas* (similar to Mexican *tamales*, these are packets of corn dough stuffed with carrots, meat, beans and spices, all wrapped up in a banana leaf); Colombian *chorizos* (pork sausages), *picada de carne* (blood sausages which contain rice); or a hearty Colombian stew of beef, pork and tongue seasoned with garlic and onion and served with bland and starchy cooked cassava root. For those who want it, there is homemade red-hot chile sauce, which goes especially well with the *empañadas*. And for dessert: baked plantain served with a slice of guava paste and a slice of cheese. You can get an entire lunch at Las Americas for $3 or less. *Open daily 7* A.M.–*10* P.M.

In 1978, the owners of Las Americas opened another Colombian bakery in Jackson Heights, **La Sorpresa** (40-30 82 St., off Roosevelt

Ave., 457-6437). More spacious than Las Americas, La Sorpresa bakes and sells the same breads and snacks but has the added attraction of seats at its counter. (At Las Americas, you eat standing up.) *Open daily 7 A.M.–10 P.M.*

Across the street from La Sorpresa, you can buy castanets and albums of Colombian *cumbia* music at the **Colombiana** (40-29 82 St.), and a few doors down, at the fifty-year-old Puerto Rican-owned supermarket for Spanish foods called **Casa Rivera** (40-17 82 St.), you can stock up on Colombian figs in syrup, frozen cassava and green unroasted Colombian coffee beans. (Some claim that the best-tasting coffee made is from beans you have roasted yourself.)

If you prefer your coffee already roasted and brewed and your cassava already cooked, you can go to one of the many restaurants in Jackson Heights that specialize in Colombian cuisine.

Unlike Argentine cuisine, which is likely to appeal to anyone who enjoys a good steak, typical Colombian cooking, which makes thrifty use of meat parts considered marginal by many North Americans and Europeans, may not be everyone's cup of coffee. If you are a true gastronomic explorer and a plate of steamed beef tongue sounds appealing, by all means try one of the following restaurants. (And if, once you get there, your nerve fails you, don't panic: there are many less exotic Colombian dishes, and all of these restaurants also serve Continental cuisine.)

One of the oldest Colombian restaurants in New York (it has been in business since 1964) and an exception to the dine-and-dance restaurants most Colombians seem to favor is the **Restaurant Sur America** (82-16 Baxter Ave., Hampton–Ithaca Aves., 779-2909, **M**). The management here is quick to point out that the Sur America is a restaurant, not a nightclub, and everything about the place, from the lavish use of highly polished wood to the impressive display of Spanish wines in the stone wall behind the bar, contributes to the impression of well-established respectability. The Restaurant Sur America serves Spanish cuisine along with Colombian specialties like *lomo relleno* (stuffed pork), *sobrebarriga a la creolla* (flank steak creole) and *lengua en salsa* (stewed beef tongue). *Open daily 6 P.M.–midnight. Cl. Tues.*

Los Andes (40-10 83 St., Roosevelt Ave.–Broadway, HA9-9066, **M**), a dine-and-dance restaurant, is less Spanish, more Colombian and more earthy and flamboyant than the Sur America, both in the food it serves and its ambiance. Authentic Colombian dishes here include fried pork skin with *arepa*, Colombian empanadas, beans and rice, steamed beef tongue served with yuca and *mazamorra*, a corn-and-milk pudding which the Colombians eat with brown sugar, guava paste or figs. There is also a full selection of homemade soups and stews, and beefsteak and chicken dishes.

The owner of Los Andes, Roberto Montoya, is a genial, urbane host, and the band is loud and obliging; you have only to ask, and they will play *cumbia*, the Afro-Colombian dance music that is Colombia's answer to the *samba* of Brazil. *Open daily 4* P.M.*–4* A.M.

PERUVIAN AND ECUADOREAN RESTAURANTS

Peruvians have one of the most interesting and unusual of all South American cuisines. And though Peruvian restaurants are almost as scarce as llamas in Manhattan, there are at least two or three excellent Peruvian restaurants in Queens. Of these, the cheapest is **Inti Raymi** (89-10 Thirty-seventh Ave., 89–90 Sts., 424-1938, **I**).

Ceviche—cubes of raw fish that have been marinated in lime juice, seasoned with hot chilies and served with raw sliced onion—is the most famous dish of Peru. (The lime juice "cooks" the fish, turning its flesh opaque, as boiling would.) At Inti Raymi, the *ceviche* comes generously mounded on a bed of sliced potatoes, and it is perfectly prepared. Two other appetizers prepared superbly at Inti Raymi are the *papa à la huancaina*, boiled sliced potatoes smothered in a creamy-smooth, subtly seasoned cheese sauce, and *anticuchos*, delicious marinated beef hearts broiled on a skewer and eaten with brick-red, fiery-hot chile sauce.

Main dishes at Inti Raymi include *chicken aji gallina*, fricasseed chicken in a bland sauce flavored with the very mild Andean chile pepper known as *aji*; *lomito saltado*, a Peruvian version of beef *lo mein* (Chinese restaurants are popular in Peru); and *seco de cordero*, an especially successful dish of beef cooked with cilantro. Both the avocado salad and the shrimp soup are well worth trying.

No alcoholic beverages are served at Inti Raymi; only Inca Kola (sweet Peruvian soda pop), hot tea and Korean ginseng (!). Rice pudding and flan are the two desserts.

The warm and lively atmosphere is provided not by the decor, which is purely functional, but by the owners and the families who eat here. *Open weekends only: Fri. 5* P.M.*–midnight; Sat., Sun. noon–midnight.*

The best all-around Peruvian restaurant in New York is probably **La Ñusta** (90–01 Thirty–seventh Ave., cor. 90 St., 899-3463, **M**), which is named after the first Inca princess, whose likeness appears on the walls. *Open daily 2* P.M.*–9* P.M.*; weekends, later.* **Crillon** (95–19 Thirty-seventh Ave., 95–96 Sts., 446-5642, **M–E**) serves good Peruvian food in a more formal atmosphere. *Open Wed.–Mon. 1* P.M.*–1* A.M. *Cl. Tues.*

Ecuador borders Peru, and its terrain, climate and cuisine are similar to Peru's in many ways. There are several Ecuadorian restaurants in or near Jackson Heights, of which the most highly recommended by Ecuadorians is **Atahualpa** (94-16 Thirty-seventh Ave., 94–95 Sts., 672-0853, **I–M**).

From the street, Atahualpa does not look like the kind of restaurant you would want to bring your mother to. Appearances, in this case, however, are totally deceiving, for inside you will find families quietly dining at tables decorously covered with clean white tablecloths, and paneled walls hung with Indian wood carvings from Ecuador. A partition separates the dining area from the perfectly respectable bar.

Atahualpa serves three kinds of *ceviche*: clam, shrimp and fish. Roasted hominy kernels accompany each and their dry, crunchy texture provides a pleasing contrast to the moist seafood.

Some of the specialties at Atahualpa are *cazuela de pescado*, a bubbling hot terra-cotta casserole of fish chunks and mashed plantain; *arroz Atahualpa*, rice with an interesting walnut and chicken sauce; *arroz con camarones*, shrimp paella; and *yapingacho* (definitely the winner), a delectable potato pie made of layers of cooked bananas, fried eggs and a wonderful chile-peanut sauce.

The service at Atahualpa is warm and helpful, if somewhat *mañana*. And on Friday and Saturday nights, a guitarist provides very pleasant, unobtrusive background music. Between the South American music, the exotic dishes and the presence of so many Ecuadorians, you may have to remind yourself, as I did, that it is okay to drink the water. *Open Sun., Mon., Wed., Thurs. noon–11:30* P.M.; *Fri., Sat. noon–2* A.M. *Cl. Tues.*

The restaurant South Americans in Queens are most likely to recommend to people who have never eaten South American food before is **El Inca** (85-01 Roosevelt Ave., 672-7756, **M–E**), a swanky place that serves international and Spanish cuisine and one or two continentalized versions of South American dishes.

Outside, El Inca is all stone and glass; the inside looks like the lobby of a fancy South American hotel, with flagstone walls, red tile, brass artifacts, a wide polished bar and a red sparkle-studded ceiling. Dining is formal (men are required to wear jackets), the service is cordial and on Friday and Saturday nights, there's an orchestra and dancing. *Open daily noon–1* A.M.

Little Brazil in Manhattan

Although New York's Brazilian population is relatively small, it is the largest in any city outside Brazil. There have been Brazilians living in New York, working for large companies (many are gem cutters or connected with the jewelry business) since the late '50s. Scattered all over the city, Brazilians keep in touch with each other by making frequent trips to Little Brazil, a two-block cluster of Brazilian stores, restaurants and organizations on West 46th Street that is also one of the city's main attractions for Brazilian tourists, who shop here for American goods at what in Rio or São Paolo would be bargain prices. The sidewalks in front of all the Brazilian stores are painted in black and white swirls, like the sidewalks of Rio.

STORES AND ORGANIZATIONS

One of the oldest and largest stores catering to Brazilian tourists on 46th Street is **Rulane** (47 W. 46 St., Fifth–Sixth Aves., 354-7141). Along with American blue jeans, electrical appliances, cosmetics and sporting goods, Rulane also carries a constantly changing supply of fad items— gold lamé belts, skateboards—whatever happens to be the current rage in Rio. Items are often sold at a discount. *Open Mon.–Fri. 9:30 A.M.–6:30 P.M.; Sat. 9:30 A.M.–4:30 P.M. Cl.Sun.*

There are almost a score more Brazilian boutiques like Rulane selling American goods on 46th Street, but the only store that sells Brazilian imports is **The Brazil Exchange** (57 W. 46 St., Fifth–Sixth Aves., 757-4231), managed by the Brazilian American Society. Here you can buy canned guanabana, cashew juice, coconut milk, *doce de leite*, guava paste, soda made from the *guarana* root, Brahma beer and other Brazilian food products. The exchange also carries a large selection of Brazilian records, cassettes and magazines and publishes its own English-language monthly. *Open Mon.–Fri. 10 A.M.–6 P.M.; Sat. 10 A.M.–3 P.M. Cl. Sun.*

For information about charter flights to Brazil, or Portuese language instruction, stop in at **the Brazilian American Society** (55 W. 46 St., Fifth–Sixth Aves., 757-4231). The **Brazilian Promotion Center** (37 W. 46 St., Fifth–Sixth Aves., 246-0795) across the street will help you plan a vacation in Brazil or provide information about Brazilian exports. This is also where you buy your tickets to New York's annual Brazilian Carnival ball. There is usually an exhibit of Brazilian art or handicrafts at the **Brazilian Government Trade Bureau** (551 Fifth Ave., 45–46 Sts., 682-1055).

RESTAURANTS

If you are not a Brazilian tourist, Little Brazil's main attraction lies in its half-dozen Brazilian restaurants, which serve typical Brazilian cuisine at moderate prices and are conveniently located in the theater district. Come on a Wednesday or a Saturday if you want *feijoada*, the assortment of fresh and smoked meats and sausages served with black beans, rice, spicy sauce, greens, orange slices and manioc meal that is the national dish of Brazil. All the Brazilian restaurants serve Portuguese wines, Brazilian coffee and the powerful Brazilian white sugar-cane rum called *cachaça*, the latter often combined with lime juice to make the sweet-sour cocktail Batida Paulista.

The Brazilian Coffee Restaurant (45 W. 46 St., Fifth–Sixth Aves., 730-9279, **M**) is a full-fledged restaurant and not a coffee house as its name implies. In fact, established in 1963, it is the oldest Brazilian restaurant in North America. New York's Brazilians are very fond of its simple, unpretentious ambiance and home-style food. Try the codfish à Braz, a delicious casserole of shredded codfish, potatoes, onions and eggs.

In the version of *feijoada* served here, meats and beans are combined in a stew, the chunks of meat taking on the black color of the beans and becoming all but unidentifiable. It is not necessary to identify in order to enjoy, however. Just spoon the spicy sauce over the stew, sprinkle all with *farinha de mandioca* (manioc meal) and dig in. The most exotic item you are likely to come across is a pig's knuckle.

Desserts here are typical South American sweet fruit or caramel pastes served with slightly salty, hard white cheese (a very pleasing combination), or flan. *Open Mon.–Sat. noon–10 P.M. Cl. Sun.*

To get to **Cabana Carioca** (123 W. 45 St., Sixth–Seventh Aves., 581-8088, **I–M**), you have to climb up a long flight of stairs past colorful murals that fairly leap off the walls. Upstairs, at lunchtime, the place bulges with Brazilians, Latin music blares from the radio, soap operas spew from the TV at the bar and the sound of Portuguese fills the air. The hubbub is almost enough to distract you from the pressing business at hand—namely, how to eat your way through the enormous portions. This place is for Amazonian appetites. Try the shrimp *baiana* in a spicy tomato sauce. *Open daily noon–11 P.M.*

Other Brazilian restaurants in Little Brazil are **Joia** (140 W. 46 St., 868-1298, **I–M**), **Via Brasil** (34 W. 46 St., 997-1158, **I–M**) and **Rio-Lisboa** (24 W. 46 St., 730-8247, **I–M**).

Around Town in Manhattan

SOUTH AMERICAN INDIAN CRAFTS
Putumayo is the name of a river in southern Colombia that flows into the

Amazon, the name of the Indians who live along this river and the name of a store in Manhattan (857 Lexington Ave., 64–65 Sts., 734-3111) that sells beautiful handcrafted things, old and new, made by the Indians of South America.

Putumayo's collection includes reed baskets woven by the Tukano Indians of Colombia, where basket-making is a two-thousand-year-old art; finely woven ponchos and sashes from Bolivia and Peru in richly dyed animal and geometric designs; hand-knit alpaca wrap sweaters from Bolivia, Peru and Colombia (these sweaters contain so much natural oil and lanolin they are virtually waterproof); huge, primitively painted pots which the Shepibo potters of Peru and Bolivia shape from clay scooped from the banks of the Amazon; and brightly colored *chigra* bags woven from hemp by the Indians of Ecuador. Prices range from $8 for a small new basket to hundreds of dollars for a particularly fine old woven piece.

Interspersed with these items are clothing from India and rugs and jewelry from Afghanistan. *Open Mon.–Sat. 11 A.M.–6:30 P.M.; Thurs. 11 A.M.–8 P.M. Cl. Sun.*

CULTURAL CENTERS
The **Center for Inter-American Relations** (680 Park Ave., cor. 68 St., 249-8950) is a nonprofit organization whose purpose is to increase understanding among the peoples of the Western Hemisphere. The center, which occupies a landmark town house, frequently has exhibits of South American art and presents concerts and dance performances by South American artists.

There are several nightclubs in New York where you can hear the popular music of Colombia or Brazil, but if you want to hear the haunting folk music of the Indians of South America, find out when the group called **Tahuantinsuyo** will be giving its next performance at the **Alternative Center for International Arts** (28 E. 4 St., Lafayette St.–Bowery, 473-6072). Tahuantinsuyo is a New York–based group of musicians from South America who are dedicated to researching and performing the authentic music of the Andes.

Occasionally the **Spanish Theater Repertory Company**, housed in the Gramercy Arts Theater (138 E. 27 St., Lexington–Third Aves., 889-2850) presents a play by a South American playwright.

The **Colombian Center** (140 E. 57 St. nr. Lexington Ave.), a six-story coffee-colored brick building, is the home of the Colombian Mission to the UN and the National Federation of Coffee Growers. In the summer, the center serves free coffee—hot or iced—in its outside café, and all year round, there are exhibits on coffee growing and Colombian products on the first floor.

FOOD STORES

There are two Argentinean food stores in Manhattan: **El Aguila Argentine** (204 W. 14 St., Seventh–Eighth Aves., 243-4647) and **Rincón International** (127 W. 46 St., Sixth–Seventh Ave., 575-0175). Both stores sell magazines and newspapers from Argentina, *sidra real* (hard cider champagne), *dulce-de-leche*-filled pastries (try the *cañon*) and something called *yerba maté*, a mildly stimulating tea made from the dried leaves of a shrub that grows wild near the Paraguay River. Traditionally sucked through a metal straw (*bombilla*) from a hollow gourd (*maté*), the tea is said to cure headaches and soothe the stomach. Rocky Valenzisi, owner of El Aguila, always has some hot *yerba maté* on hand, and both stores stock a large supply of *bombillas* and carved *maté* gourds as well as the tea itself. *El Aguila is open Mon.–Sat. 10 A.M.–7:30 P.M.; Sun. 11:30 A.M.–1 P.M. Rincón International is open Mon.–Sat. 9 A.M.–7 P.M. Cl. Sun.*

A few doors down from El Aguila Argentina is **Casa Moneo** (210 W. 14 St., 929-1644), the leading store in the city for Spanish foods and an excellent source for imported items from South America. On the shelves under the sign saying Venezuela, you will find corn flour; under Ecuador, white hominy and plantain flour; under Colombia, guava nectar, preserved figs and cans of naranjilla halves. In the back, you can get hot *empañadas. Open Mon.–Sat. 9:30 A.M.–7 P.M. Cl. Sun.*

RESTAURANTS: ARGENTINEAN, CHILEAN, PERUVIAN, ECUADORIAN

At any one of the more than half-dozen Argentinean restaurants in Manhattan, you can sample *empañadas, matambre* and, of course, the charcoal-grilled steaks and sausages for which the Argentineans are famous.

One restaurant particularly recommended by many Argentineans in New York is **El Rancho Argentino** (12 E. 32 St. off Fifth Ave., 684-9421, **M–E**), a modest place informally decorated with checked cloths on the tables and drawings of *gauchos* on the walls. The sirloin steak here is a two-inch-thick fillet grilled to perfection, and the *empañadas*, dipped in hot *chummi churri* sauce, are positively addictive. El Rancho draws most of its customers from the midtown office lunch crowd, but many Argentineans come here for dinner. *Open Mon.–Fri. noon–9 P.M. Cl. Sat. and Sun.*

Chacareros (76 W. 3 St. cor. Sullivan St., 473-8903, **M**), the only Chilean restaurant in New York, started out as a fast-food luncheonette. The luncheonette is still there, but now a charming little restaurant adjoins it.

Empañadas are obviously one of the specialties here. Five different kinds are listed under Appetizers: baked meat, fried cheese, fried seafood, fried meat and fried ham and cheese. All are excellent. More adventurous eaters can start out with *locos* (Chilean abalones) or *erizos* (sea urchin).

From there, you proceed to a casserole—perhaps *chupe de mariscos*, a stew of mussels and abalones, or *pastel de choclo*, a sweet combination of ground round, raisins, onions and chicken topped with baked corn. Get a bottle of the good Chilean wine with dinner.

Chacareros is not a good place to go if you are in a hurry (on some evenings, one person seems to be in charge of both the restaurant and the luncheonette next door). *Open Mon.–Fri. 7*A.M.*–10* P.M.; *weekends until 11:30* P.M.

Cuzco (301 E. 44 St., 1st–2nd Aves., 687-3539, **M–E**), a plush restaurant not far from the United Nations, serves Peruvian cuisine: prices are fairly high; the food, when we tried it, was only fair. *Open Mon.–Fri. 11:30* A.M.*–3* P.M.; *6* P.M.*–9* P.M. *Cl. Sun.*

On Amsterdam Avenue in the 90s, there is a small Ecuadorian colony that supports two or three tiny restaurants in the area. The best of these is **Dos Hermanas** (689 Amsterdam Ave., 93–94 Sts., 678-9219, **C**), owned by two jolly sisters, Luceida and Angela. There is no English menu at Dos Hermanas (which means "Two Sisters"); in fact, there is no menu at all. Luceida and Angela prepare two dishes every day and from these you make your choice. The day I went there was a flavorful beef soup that was more like a stew and a platter of delicious grilled beef served with a huge mound of rice and beans. (On other days, I am told, there is shrimp.) The grilled beef came with a side dish of *hot* chile sauce (*ajio picante*) and a fresh salad of onions, radishes and tomatoes in oil and vinegar. The two dishes could easily have fed three, and the total bill for both came to an unbelievable $4.50. Live music on weekends. No English is spoken here. *Open Mon., Wed., Thurs., 11* A.M.*–9* P.M.; *Fri.–Sun., 11* A.M.*–3* A.M. *Cl. Tues.*

BRAZILIAN RESTAURANTS

There are about a dozen Brazilian restaurants around town now, and of all of them, the most beautiful and elegant is **Chateau Bahia** (863 First Ave. at 48 St., 753-2960, **E**), near the United Nations. The attractive bar is the first thing you see as you enter; beyond the bar is a pretty South American sitting room. Two glass walls and two brick enclose the dining room, which is furnished with antique Portuguese Colonial furnishings and hanging plants.

In addition to all the usual Brazilian dishes, Chateau Bahia also serves a toned-down version of the hot and spicy cuisine of Bahia, a region in Brazil known for its good food and strong African traditions. On Fridays, you can get the most famous Bahian dish—shrimp *vatapá*, here prepared with a thick, mildly spicy coconut-milk sauce topped with peanuts. In general, the food is good and beautifully served, but not outstanding. *Open Mon.–Sat. noon–3* P.M.; *6* P.M.–*midnight. Cl. Sun.*

The **Rio de Janeiro** (41 W. 57 St., Fifth–Sixth Aves., 935-1232, M–E) serves better food (try the garlicky shrimp Paulista or any of the fish dishes) for less money, in less beautiful surroundings. *Open Mon.– Sat. 12 noon–11* P.M. *Cl. Sun.*

Casa Brasil (406 E. 85 St., 288-5284, E), a charming town house, serves Brazilian food on Wednesday nights only, when the dinner is— what else?—*feijoada*. (The rest of the week the food is Continental.) The *feijoada* here is a more refined version of what you get in Little Brazil, with thin slices of top-quality beef sautéed in wine and served separately from the pork-and-bean stew. In addition to the traditional orange slices, you get an extra garnish—bananas baked with brown sugar. Bring your own wine or beer. There are two seatings on Wednesday night, at 6:30 P.M. and 9:30 P.M. Reservations are necessary.

BRAZILIAN NIGHTCLUB
Jet-setters know that the best nightclubs are in Rio. Ever since **Cachaca** (403 E. 62 St. nr. First Ave., 688-8501) opened, however, New Yorkers have been able to get a taste of Rio's night life in their own city, for this club features live Brazilian music every night. The decor is sophisticated (gray sofas, lots of mirrors), the clientele chic and the music—which, depending on the night, may be anything from samba to Brazilian pop—is fantastic. Before the live music begins (at 11), there is recorded disco and Carnival music. Dining and dancing. Expensive. *Open nightly except Monday.*

Festivals and Holidays

Carnaval, a week-long festival in Brazil, is celebrated by Brazilians in New York with a "Night in Rio" ball held at a major New York hotel on a Saturday night in mid-February. A few thousand Brazilians descend on New York for this wild, all-night bash. Brazilian bands play samba music, fantastically costumed Brazilian beauties parade for prizes and the *cachaça* flows like water. This is the biggest Brazilian Carnival celebration outside Brazil. For details and ticket information, call the Brazilian Promotion Center, 246-0795.

South American Food

Except for Argentina and Paraguay, where beef is so plentiful that steaks are a mainstay in the diet, beans and rice are the staples of South American cuisine. The food of Brazil is a combination of African, Portuguese and indigenous Indian influences; Italian immigrants added pastas to Argentinean cuisine; but the cuisines of most other South American countries combine Spanish and Indian elements. Brazil's most famous dish is *feijoada*; Peru's is *ceviche*; Argentina's is charcoal-grilled steak; Ecuador is known for its many dishes containing bananas; Colombia for its fried breads and *hallacas*.

Custards, flans or sweet caramel or fruit paste eaten with a hard white cheese are popular desserts almost everywhere in South America. Coffee is the drink except in Argentina, where the national beverage is *yerba maté* tea.

Chile produces the best wines in South America. Brazilians drink *cachaça*, a potent, colorless drink distilled from sugar cane.

MENU GLOSSARY
(Argentinean, Peruvian, Colombian, Ecuadorian)
aji de gallina: shredded chicken in mild chile sauce (Peru).
anticuchos: marinated, broiled beef hearts on skewers (Peru).
arepas: corn griddle cakes.
arroz con leche: rice pudding.
asado: roasted meat.
cazuela de pescado: fish with mashed plantains cooked in an earthen-ware casserole.
ceviche: raw rish marinated in lime juice with chilies and onions.
chicha morada: Peruvian purple corn soda.
chorizos: pork sausages.
chummi churri: hot sauce of vinegar, chilies and herbs (Argentina).
chupe de camarones: shrimp soup.
dulce de leche: caramel milk paste.
flan: custard pudding.
hallacas: steamed banana-leaf-wrapped packets of corn dough stuffed with a seasoned meat and vegetable mixture (Colombia).
lengua en salsa: stewed beef tongue (Colombia).
lomo relleno: stuffed pork.

matambre: cold cut of flank steak stuffed with vegetables, herbs, spices and hard-boiled eggs (Argentina).

mazamorra: corn and milk pudding (Colombia).

morcilla: blood sausage.

papa a la huancaina: boiled sliced potatoes in creamy cheese sauce (Peru).

parillada: mixed grill: skirt steak, short ribs, sweetbread and sausages (Argentina).

pastel de choclo: casserole of ground beef, chicken, onions, raisins and baked corn (Chile).

queso blanco: white cheese served with sweet fruit or caramel paste as dessert.

seco de cordero: beef cooked with cilantro (Peru).

tortilla: omelet.

yapingacho: pie made of layers of potato, banana, fried eggs and peanut
    sauce.

yerba maté: tea made from the leaves of a wild bush in Argentina; traditionally drunk from a hollow gourd.

MENU GLOSSARY *(Brazilian)*

bacalhau: salt codfish.

bacalhau gomes da sa: codfish cooked with potatoes and onions, garnished with hard-boiled eggs and olives.

Bahiana: Bahian style (in New York restaurants usually shrimp cooked with tomatoes, green pepper and perhaps some beer).

Batida Paulista: sweet-sour *cachaça* cocktail.

bossa nova: usually chicken *bossa nova*, fried with garlic.

cachaça: white Brazilian rum.

caldo verde: Portuguese potato soup made with sausages and kale or collard greens.

churrasco: grilled over charcoal (beef, veal, pork) and garnished with onions and peppers or fried eggs.

dobradinha: tripe-and-bean stew.

doce de leite: sweet caramel paste.

doré: shrimp doré is shrimp dipped in batter and fried.

farinha de mandioca: bland manioc meal, sprinkled on soups, stews, and *feijoada*.

farofa: a crumbly side dish of *farinha de mandioca* fried with butter and combined with eggs.

feijoada: national dish of Brazil—assortment of meats (smoked and fresh pork, fresh and dried beef, pig's knuckles, beef tongue, sausages) served with black-bean stew, rice, greens, spicy sauce and orange slices.

mariscada: shellfish stew.

Paulista: usually shrimp Paulista—grilled with minced garlic.

picadhino: fried and spiced ground beef topped with fried eggs.

sopa alentejana: garlic broth with poached eggs and bread.

vatapá: most famous dish of Bahia—fish and shrimp in ginger-flavored tomato-peanut sauce.

UKRAINIAN NEW YORK

Ukrainian East Village

For over a century, Manhattan's East Village has been the center of Ukrainian life in New York. The first Ukrainians to come to New York settled in this part of town in the 1870s, and today one third of the city's 75,000 Ukrainians live in a section of the East Village known as Little Ukraine. One of the most cohesive neighborhoods in the city, Little Ukraine has some of the qualities of a village or small town. It is not unusual here, for example, for neighbors to have known each other all their lives. Ukrainian is the language of this urban "village": the streets often ring with "*Dobredanya*," the Ukrainian greeting, and on Easter Day, when the congregation of St. George's gathers on East 7th Street to watch the spring folk dances, Ukrainian is the only language to be heard. Even the young speak it, for besides hearing it at home, many of them have studied at St. George's Academy, a private Ukrainian day school that stands behind the church.

Ukrainians are not the only group that has been associated with the East Village. Low rents in the old five- and six-story apartment buildings that are prevalent in this section of the city have also attracted artists, bohemians and hippies. For a period in the '60s, in fact, long-haired flower children, psychedelic head shops and colorful Indian clothing stores all but obscured the more sober Slavic character of the neighborhood. But in time, the flower children faded from the scene, leaving only a few sandal shops and clothing stores behind, and in the '70s, when a wave of interest in ethnic roots swept the country, visitors to the East Village suddenly discovered the Ukrainian community that had been there all along.

"Our ethnic consciousness has always been strong," explains one resident of Little Ukraine. "It is only that people are just noticing it now. We have always had a very strong awareness of our uniqueness."

Ethnic consciousness is even stronger among Ukrainians than among other ethnic groups because the Ukrainians don't have an independent homeland: since the 1920s, the Ukraine has been under Soviet rule. The largest influx of Ukrainians to New York (and to this country) came after World War II, when thousands fled the Ukraine rather than live there under Soviet domination. As a result, most members of New York's Ukrainian community are strongly nationalistic and fiercely anti-Communist; for these people, the Little Ukraine is the only home they have.

Community life in Little Ukraine has always been active, but in recent years, the increase in community participation and investment has amounted to nothing less than a neighborhood renaissance. Next to the old St. George's Ukrainian Catholic Church, the community has built a beautiful new St. George's at a cost of about three million dollars. There is now a Ukrainian museum on Second Avenue, where traditional handicrafts are professionally displayed. Next to the head shops and sandal stores that are a legacy from the days when "East Village" was synonymous with counterculture, the old Ukrainian meat markets, import stores and restaurants are thriving, and new establishments, opened by recent immigrants (who have been arriving in a small but steady stream since the beginning of détente) are beginning to prosper.

Over the years, many Ukrainian residents of the East Village have been buying up local real estate, and today an estimated two hundred buildings in the area are Ukrainian-owned. Older residents complain that the neighborhood is not as safe as it used to be, but still they stay, and couples who had moved to the suburbs when their children reached school age are beginning to move back to the old neighborhood now that their children are grown. Not long ago local residents planted linden trees on either side of East 7th Street—linden because they are native to the Slavic countries. Today these trees are green and flourishing, symbols of the resurgence of Little Ukraine.

The best times to visit to capture the full ethnic flavor of this neighborhood are during the annual three-day Ukrainian Festival in May or around Easter, when the shops have their biggest displays of *pysanky* (hand-decorated Easter eggs) and when—on Easter Day itself—young people perform traditional dances in front of St. George's Church. But, if you like little shops crammed with embroidered textiles and handicrafts or meat markets that vie with one another to offer the highest quality and greatest variety of sausages and meats, if you crave a bowl of homemade *borscht* or that stick-to-the-ribs feeling that comes only after eating a plateful of *pirogies*, it is worth visiting this part of town any time of year.

HOW TO GET THERE

By subway: *Lexington Avenue IRT* #6 to Astor Place, walk east on Astor Place to Third or Second Ave.; or *BMT* RR to 8 St.–Broadway, walk east to Third or Second Aves. **By bus**: Crosstown *M13* on 8 St; crosstown *M14* on 14 St; or *M15* northbound on First Ave., southbound on Second Ave.

Suggested Walking Tour: E. 7 St. to Ave. A, back to E. 7 St., up Second Ave. to Ukrainian Museum near E. 13 St.

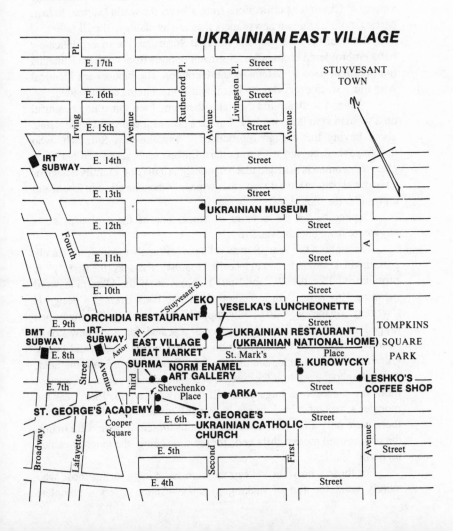

UKRAINIAN EAST VILLAGE

SURMA AND ST. GEORGE'S

Whenever you go to Little Ukraine, make your first stop **Surma** (11 E. 7 St., Second–Third Aves., GR7-0729), a wonderful Old World shop crammed with lovely handcrafted things from eastern Europe. The present owner of Surma, Myron W. Surmach, is the son of the store's founder, who is now retired and raises bees. The elder Mr. Surmach established Surma in 1918 as a Ukrainian book and music store; when his son took over in 1955, he added such items as hand-embroidered tablecloths, hand-carved and inlaid chess sets, folkwear and porcelain hand painted with traditional Ukrainian designs. There is still a wide selection of Ukrainian records and sheet music, however, and an astonishing variety of Ukrainian publications from all over the world (Surma, in fact, carries more Ukrainian newspapers than are available in the Ukraine).

Some of the most popular items at Surma are the sheer, delicately hand embroidered blouses Mr. Surmach imports from northern Rumania (an area that used to belong to the Ukraine). The blouses are identical with those worn every day by Ukrainian women in the countryside.

"When I walk around the fields there and I see something beautiful on a woman who is raking hay, I make a note of it and speak to someone about having that design reproduced," explains Mr. Surmach, who makes several buying trips to eastern Europe each year. "To her great glee, the woman is asked to teach *her* design (it may be a family design or an original pattern) to a dozen other women, who then all sit in a barn and embroider the blouses."

Depending on the amount of work, one of these blouses costs anywhere from $30 to over $100.

Throughout the year, Surma sells the brilliantly colored, intricately patterned Ukrainian Easter eggs called *pysanky*. *Pysanky* (the first "y" is pronounced like the "i" in "pit") comes from the Ukrainian word meaning "to write." In a method similar to batik dyeing, a design is "written" on the egg with a stylus dipped in hot beeswax. The egg is then dipped in dye and the whole process repeated for each new color. *Pysanky* originated as fertility symbols in pre-Christian times, and among Ukrainians, there is a legend that the fate of the world depends on them. According to the myth, if the custom of egg-decorating ceases, an ancient monster chained to a huge cliff will destroy the world. Each year the monster's servants check to see how many *pysanky* have been made: if there were only a few, the monster's chains loosen; if there were many, the chains bind more tightly and, for the time being, the monster can do no harm.

For those who want to keep the monster at bay—or for those who merely want the fun of making *pysanky*—Surma offers a complete egg-decorating kit, with instructions, design cards, a stylus, dyes, dipper and beeswax. If you don't have the patience to make them yourself, you can buy completed *pysanky* at Surma. One egg, which may take anywhere from one to eight hours to decorate, costs from $5 to $10. There are also wooden eggs that cost less.

Other items you can get at Surma are custom-made Cossack tunics or dresses; paintings and note cards with charming stylized scenes of Old Ukraine painted by Mr. Surmach's sister, Yaroslava Surmach Mills; jars of honey from the senior Mr. Surmach's apiary; and lengths of imported ribbon (in over a thousand different patterns!) for trimming curtains or clothing or for making belts.

Saturday and Sunday are the busiest days at Surma, especially when busloads of sightseeing Ukrainians from out of town descend on the shop.

Across the street from Surma stands the neighborhood's pride and joy, the new **St. George's Ukrainian Catholic Church** (33 E. 7 St.). A stylized version of a *hutzul* (Carpathian Mountain) church, the handsome building features sixteen specially designed stained-glass windows and is topped by a huge dome. Inside, sunlight streams through the plate-glass windows of one wall, filling the interior with light and bringing out the jewellike colors of the tall Byzantine icons on either side of the altar.

A short walk around the corner, down Shevchenko Place (named for the Ukraine's most beloved poet, Taras Shevchenko) will bring you to **St. George Academy**, where Ukrainian children from grade one through senior high study Ukrainian history and culture in addition to their regular subjects. If you happen to walk by in the afternoon, just before school lets out, you may think you have suddenly walked into a scene from eastern Europe: clusters of mothers, some wearing European-style kerchiefs over their hair, stand on the sidewalk, chatting in Ukrainian as they wait to pick up their children.

MORE GIFT SHOPS

If you have ever wondered where east European women in New York get their flowered head scarves and shawls, stop in at **Eko** (145 SecondAve., 9–10 Sts., AL4-0888), a dark old store filled with an international jumble of goods from Rumania, Hungary, Canada, India, China and Poland. Eko carries a full line of fringed polyester-and-wool challis scarves blooming with huge pink or blue roses on maroon, pale yellow or dark green backgrounds. Some scarves are shot through with gold thread. The designs are Slavic but the scarves are made in Japan, and they range from $3 for a small square to about $15 for a large one that can be used as a shawl. *Open daily 9* A.M.–*6:30* P.M.; *Sun. 11* A.M.–*2* P.M.

Arka (48 E. 7 St., First–Second Aves., 473-3550) may be the only store in town where you can get a *bandura*, the national instrument of the Ukraine. The *bandura* resembles a large mandolin and combines the musical principles of the lute and the harp. You can also get *pysanky* and embroidered blouses, books, records and ceramics at this old neighborhood store. Older men from the area, dressed formally in suit jackets and felt hats even in the heat of summer, like to stop in at Arka for a chat with the owners and a copy of the latest edition of *Svoboda*, a Ukrainian newspaper published in New Jersey. *Open 9* A.M.*–6* P.M. *daily; Sun., 10* A.M.*–2* P.M. *Cl. Sun. in summer.*

Arka, Eko and Surma sell the traditional crafts of the Ukraine, but you can also get contemporary Ukrainian art work in the East Village. At **Norm Enamel Art Gallery** (13 E. 7 St., Second–Third Aves., 982-1600), Constantin Szonk-Rusych creates flower paintings and landscapes with copper and enamel. He learned his craft making enamel watch faces in the old country. *Open daily 9* A.M.*–6:30* P.M., *Sun. 10* A.M.*–2* P.M.

CRAFTS MUSEUM

If you are at all interested in folk art, be sure to visit the **Ukrainian Museum** (203 Second Ave., 12–13 Sts., 228-0110), which has a fascinating collection of traditional Ukrainian crafts. The museum occupies the fourth and fifth floors of a trim, modern building that is also the headquarters for the Ukrainian National Congress. Usually one floor is devoted to folk art from the museum's own collection and the other is given over to items on loan from other collections. At a typical exhibit, there were richly embroidered peasant costumes from various regions in the Ukraine, exquisitely worked *rushnyky* (ritual cloths often draped over icons) and fine old *kilim* carpets with Turkish motifs that had been introduced to the Ukraine by Cossack weavers. The museum's collection also includes painstakingly decorated *pysanky*, intricately carved and inlaid wooden objects and metal craft and ceramics. On the fifth floor, a gift shop sells *pysanky*, dolls, embroidered cloths and other items. The museum is just the right size—large enough to be worth visiting, small enough not to overwhelm—and the exhibits are always installed very professionally. There is a small admission fee. *Open Wed., Sat., Sun. 1* P.M.*–5* P.M., *Fri. 3* P.M.*–7* P.M.

In addition to providing a place where people can see the best examples of the old folk art, the staff of the Ukrainian Museum is trying to keep alive the craft tradition by offering courses and workshops in Ukrainian embroidery and woodworking. If you decide to pursue the former seriously, you may be busy for the rest of your life: Ukrainian embroidery employs close to a hundred stitches and techniques.

MEAT MARKETS AND DELIS

Many people who regularly visit Little Ukraine don't know a thing about Ukrainian folk art, but they do know what they like, and that is the fine sausages and meats they can get at such Ukrainian stores as Kurowycky Meat Products and the East Village Meat Market.

Established in 1954 by Erast Kurowycky and now managed by his son Jaroslav, **Kurowycky's** (124 First Ave., 7 St.–St. Marks Pl., 477-0344) glows with Old World pride: the white-tiled walls gleam, the storefront window sparkles, and even the men who work here seem to beam with satisfaction as they slice freshly baked hams, stuff casings for *kobasa* or hang sausages up to be smoked in the giant black ovens at the back of the store. Jerry Kurowycky says he hasn't changed a thing since his father's day. "I could be opening a hundred-store franchise, but the reputation my father left me is more important than anything else. You have absolute control in one store. With a franchise, that control is gone."

You understand what Mr. Kurowycky is talking about when you sample some of the store's products. Even the humble American bologna becomes something special here. Made with quality meat (no fillers), it tastes much finer than its supermarket counterpart. And when it comes to the aristocrat of sausages—*krakiewska*, the top of the line—Kurowycky's rosy, incredibly lean version, lightly smoked and made from cubes of the best deveined and defatted ham, has no peer. Sliced thin and served with eggs, potato salad or alone as an appetizer, it is superb.

Less elegant than *krakiewska* but more versatile is the Slavic ring sausage, *kobasa* (the Poles call it *kielbasa*). The Ukrainians also have another name for *kobasa*: *bozy dahr*, or "God's food," "because," jokes Jerry Kurowycky, "God only knows what goes into it." At Kurowycky's, however, you can be sure that only the best ingredients are used. When the pork-and-beef filling is coarsely ground, the sausage is called *krayana*; when finely ground it is *siekana*. *Kobasa* can be sliced and eaten as is, fried, boiled, baked or hung up to dry and harden, becoming a good hunting sausage.

The baked hams at Kurowycky are made with less salt than commercial hams. "The more salt you use, the more weight the ham will draw," explains Mr. Kurowycky. "It adds to the weight but spoils the flavor." A slice of Kurowycky ham, shell pink with a creamy ring of buttery fat (the fat adds to the flavor), is all it takes to convince you of the truth of this statement.

For a new solution to the old problem of what to have for dinner tonight, try the *zayac* here—a homemade pork-and-veal meat loaf that is deliciously seasoned, finely textured and tempting hot or cold. With your *zayac*, you can serve some of Kurowycky's homemade sauerkraut. If you are used to the pallid, sweet and soggy stuff that passes for sauerkraut in the supermarket, you may not at first recognize this crisp, exhilarating, golden mixture of cabbage and carrot slivers. To complete your picnic dinner, take home a loaf of the deliciously dense, dark Lithuanian bread the shop regularly carries. The prices at Kurowycky's are often as much as 30 percent lower than at uptown gourmet shops.

Another Ukrainian meat shop in the neighborhood is the **East Village Meat Market** (139 Second Ave., St. Mark's Pl.–9 St., CA8-5590), where, in addition to his excellent *kobasa*, *krakiewska* and *krayana*, Julian Baczynsky sells *kabanose* (a ready-to-eat hunter's sausage that keeps forever), stuffed breast of veal, stuffed kishka and *bochok* (smoked and marinated bacon). Some people really go out of their way to shop at the East Village Meat Market: one resident of San Francisco flies in every three months to buy a hundred dollars' worth of meats and sausages here. *Open Mon.–Sat. 8 A.M.–6 P.M.; Fri. 8 A.M.–7 P.M.; Cl. Sun.*

RESTAURANTS

If you have the time for a leisurely meal, the place to go in Little Ukraine is the **Ukrainian Restaurant**, on the first floor of the Ukrainian National Home (140 Second Ave. near 9 St., 533-6765, **I**). Dimly lit and plainly decorated, the Ukrainian Restaurant serves authentic Slavic cooking— hearty, wholesome, filling fare that makes no pretensions to haute cuisine. The specialties include a first-rate homemade *borscht*, rosy with beets and thick with cabbage and miscellaneous vegetables; *bigos*— slices of *kobasa* mixed with hot sauerkraut seasoned with dill; *holubsti*— cabbage stuffed with rice and ground pork; kasha with beef sauce; wonderful blintzes filled with fruit or cheese; and *pirogis*—small dumplings filled with meat, potato, cabbage or cheese and served in an onion-butter sauce. Other popular dishes here are the boiled beef with horseradish sauce and the potted veal.

To drink, there are imported beers, buttermilk or a sweet fruit compote with cherries and apple chunks floating in it. A good choice for dessert is the homemade apple cake. Prices are extremely—in some cases unbelievably—low. The patrons are mostly east European. *Open daily noon–11 P.M.*

For fast counter service, you can't do better than **Leshko's Coffee Shop** (111 Avenue A, cor. 7 St., 473-9208, **C–I**), a luncheonette that has been feeding the neighborhood for over twenty-five years. East European dishes dominate the menu—*borscht*, cabbage soup, *kobasa*, *studzienna* (jellied pig's knuckles) and stuffed cabbage—and everything is good. The real standouts, however, are the *pirogi*, which are light, not too doughy and plump with filling (the potato- or cheese-filled are the best, but you can also get cabbage or meat). Topped with sour cream, a plateful of Leshko's *pirogies* makes an eminently satisfying meal.

There are booths as well as a counter at Leshko's, and if you sit by the window, you will have a view of Tompkins Square Park, which used to be the center of the Slavic colony but is now its eastern boundary. In nice weather, Ukrainian men still play cards and chess on the granite tables at the southwest corner of the park.

Prices are very very reasonable at Leshko's; no one ever leaves hungry. *Open Mon.–Sat. 5 P.M.–10 P.M.*

A cheerful little soda fountain–luncheonette on Second Avenue is **Veselka's** (no. 144, cor. 9 St., 228-9682, **C**). Veselka's is a hangout for young and old. Students from St. George's come here after school for a *pirogi* snack, and senior citizens often stop in for a bowl of *borscht* or, in the summer, a refreshing cold fruit soup. You can get a *kobasa* dinner at Veselka's for less than $4. *Open daily 7 A.M.–2 A.M.*

Young singles in the neighborhood frequent **Orchidia** (145 Second Ave., cor. 9 St., 473-8784, **I**), a bar and restaurant that serves Italian pizza, Ukrainian *pirogi* and German beer. Hanging plants, embroidered curtains and Tiffany-style lamps provide more atmosphere than a luncheonette, and the food—both the Ukrainian and the Italian dishes—is inexpensive. *Open Mon.–Thurs. 4 P.M.–12:30 A.M., Fri.–Sun. 12 noon–3 P.M.*

Around Town: The Ukrainian Institute

In 1948, William Dzus, a Ukrainian-American inventor and entrepreneur who made a fortune in industrial fasteners, established the **Ukrainian Institute of America**. The purpose of the institute is "to look after Ukrainians in this country and to help them to keep pace with other cultural groups." In 1955, the institute purchased its present headquarters at 2 East 79th Street (cor. Fifth Ave., BU8-8660), a mansion designed by Stanford White.

Besides serving as a center for meetings of Ukrainian organizations, lectures and concerts, the institute houses an exhibit of Ukrainian arts and crafts, a gallery of paintings and sculptures by Ukrainian artists and an exhibit of patents held by Ukrainian inventors. The institute is worth visiting if you are in the area (across the street from the Metropolitan Museum of Art), as much for a look at the elegant building as for its contents. Call before you go; the hours it is open to the public tend to be erratic.

Festivals and Holidays

If it weren't for the apartment buildings and the traffic on Second Avenue, you might think the annual **Ukrainian Festival** was a village fair taking place somewhere on the Ukrainian steppes. Under the gaily striped awnings of the booths that line East 7th Street, women in embroidered blouses, their hair braided and coiled around their heads, dispense *pirogies* and *kobasa* and homemade *torte* to the hungry crowd, while down the middle of the street, which has been closed to traffic, families and friends stroll in their Sunday best, stopping often to greet one another or examine the handicrafts on display. A steady stream of people flows in and out of St. George's Ukrainian Church, and on the wooden grandstand across the way, twelve girls and boys in folk costume (the boys in flowing Cossack shirts, the girls in peasant blouses with flower wreaths on their plaited hair) solemnly pluck the strings of the big *banduras* on their knees, while grandmothers swathed in black from head to foot nod approvingly from their seats in the front row. Meanwhile a small crowd has gathered around the glass beehive with live bees in it that Myron Surmach has brought from his apiary and set up in front of Surma's Ukrainian Book and Music Store. And two doors down from Surma, McSorley's Old Ale House—a traditional old institution if not a Ukrainian one—is doing a booming business in beer on tap; there isn't an empty seat in the house, and even standing room is at a premium. Outside, the leaves of the linden trees that line the street flutter in the warm May breeze, and the sounds of Ukrainian and *bandura* music and people having a good time fill the air. The annual Ukrainian Festival is in full swing.

Usually held on a weekend in May, the festival lasts for three days and takes place on East 7th Street between Second and Third avenues. For information, call Surma Book & Music Co., GR7-0729.

On **Ukrainian Easter**, East 7th Street takes on the air of a festival again, when, after morning services at St. George's, young people in traditional costume perform Ukrainian folk dances on the street in front of the church. The dances, like the *pysanky* (decorated Easter eggs) that are exchanged at this time of year, originated in pre-Christian times. St. George's follows the Julian calendar, and so their Easter usually falls a week to several weeks later than Roman Catholic Easter. In case of rain, the dances are performed in the auditorium of St. George's School.

Ukrainians in New York traditionally observe Christmas with a twelve-course dinner on Christmas Eve, of which the first course is always *kutia*, a preparation of cooked wheat mixed with honey, poppy seeds and nuts. There is also neighborhood Christmas caroling in Ukrainian and, often, public concerts of Ukrainian music in this season by Dumka, an adult chorus, and Young Dumka, a children's chorus.

A very important day in the Ukrainian community is **Shevchenko Day**, commemorating the great thinker, poet, playwright and founder of modern Ukrainian literature, Taras Shevchenko (1814–1861). The day is usually celebrated on the nearest weekend to Shevchenko's birthdate, March 9.

Ukrainian Independence Day, January 22, commemorates the day in 1918 when a free and sovereign Ukrainian republic was proclaimed. (It lasted only a year or two.)

Ukrainian Food

Ukrainian food is hearty, stick-to-the-ribs fare. Grains play an important role (the Ukraine is one of the chief wheat-producing regions of Europe). Cabbage, beets and potatoes are the most frequently used vegetables; pork and beef are the favored meats. Ukrainians are also very fond of caviar.

Vodka is the most popular alcoholic drink. Cake or fruit compote are typical desserts.

MENU GLOSSARY

bigos: sliced *kobasa* mixed with hot sauerkraut.
borscht: beet soup.
holubsti: stuffed cabbage.
kasha: cracked buckwheat, cooked and served with beef.
kobasa: ring sausage of pork and beef.
krayana: coarsely ground sausage.
makivnyk: poppyseed cake roll.
pirogi: dumplings (may be filled with cheese, meat, potato, cabbage or fruit).
studzienna: jellied pig's knuckles.

WEST INDIAN NEW YORK

West Indian Crown Heights

Let me tell you something about Labor Day in Brooklyn
Everybody jumping, Labor Day in Brooklyn, heh?
Every West Indian jumping up like mad
Just like carnival day in Trinidad
Yankee and all listening to the steelband beat
Rolling in carnival just like in Charlette Street.

You could be from St. Claire or John John
In New York all that done
It ain't have no "who is who"
New York equalize you
Bajan, Granadian, Jamaican, 'tut mun'
Drinking they rum, beating they bottle and spoon
Nobody could watch me and honestly say
They don't like to be in Brooklyn on Labor Day.

—lyrics to "Labor Day in Brooklyn"
by the Mighty Sparrow

Every Labor Day weekend, Brooklyn erupts in the biggest carnival celebration outside of the Caribbean. For three days, the borough rocks with calypso, steel band and reggae competitions, jumps with dances and parties and glitters with beauty-queen and costume contests. Everything comes to a climax on Labor Day itself, when over a million people gather to "play mas" (masquerade), "beat pan" (play steel drums) and "jump up" (get up and dance) on Brooklyn's Eastern Parkway.

Why Brooklyn? Because Brooklyn has the largest West Indian population in the United States: of the estimated one million West Indians living in New York City, over 60 percent call Brooklyn home. In Crown Heights, East Flatbush, East New York, Bedford Stuyvesant and

Brownsville—the sections where the West Indians live—there are whole streets where the gentle, singsong cadences of Jamaican English or the soft, slightly clipped accents of Barbados caress the ear like a warm Caribbean breeze. In the summer, many parks and playgrounds in Brooklyn take on a British air when the West Indian cricket leagues meet for their games.

Jamaicans outnumber all other English-speaking West Indians in Brooklyn and in New York City. They are followed by Trinidadians, Barbadians, Grenadians and smaller groups from Antigua, the Bahamas, the Windward Islands, St. Lucia and the Virgin Islands. New York also has a very large community of French-speaking West Indians—the Haitians, most of whom live in Brooklyn. (For Puerto Ricans, the largest Spanish-speaking West Indian group in the city, see separate chapter.) With so many different West Indians living in New York, the city, and especially Brooklyn, has become a kind of Caribbean outpost, where people from different islands meet and mingle in a way that never happens at home in the farflung West Indian islands.

Harlem, not Brooklyn, was the first part of New York to which the West Indians gravitated. Several prominent Harlemites in the 1910s and '20s were West Indians, among them Marcus Garvey, the most influential black leader of his day, and Claude McKay, a writer who was called the herald of the Harlem Renaissance. Both men were born in Jamaica. At some point, the West Indians began moving out of Harlem and into Brooklyn, and although there are still many West Indians in Harlem, since the 1960s, Brooklyn has been the focus of West Indian life in New York.

It is impossible to generalize about the physical appearance of West Indian Brooklyn: the buildings, the street life, the people change from block to block. Some blocks along broad, impressive Eastern Parkway are lined with lovely old brownstones. On other streets just two blocks north of the parkway, bleak gray tenements seem to stretch to the horizon. And further north, in Bedford Stuyvesant, are some of the city's worst slums.

Each street has its own tempo. From Monday through Saturday, and especially on Saturday, the main commercial streets in West Indian Brooklyn—Nostrand and Utica avenues—are humming: people throng the West Indian bakeries to order spice breads and meat patties, crowd the groceries to buy *callaloo* and *mauby*, and stand in long lines at takeout food stands for the best curried goat this side of Kingston. But head one block east or west of Nostrand or Utica and, in most cases, you will find yourself on a quiet residential block where dominoes or street soccer are the only activities on a summer afternoon.

In a borough that seems to specialize in contrasts, the most startling juxtaposition of all arises from the pockets of Orthodox Jews who live in Crown Heights and East Flatbush (at one time, much of what is now West Indian Brooklyn was Jewish). If you walk by the corner of Kingston Avenue on the south side of Eastern Parkway on a Saturday morning in spring or summer, you will see knots of men and women gathered in front of the Brooklyn Jewish Center, chatting in Yiddish after the Sabbath services. The men are bearded and wear the long side curls, dark suits, felt hats and fringed prayer shawls customarily worn by Hasidic Jews; the women wear wigs and modest long-sleeved dresses and suits. But walk one block north of the parkway and every person you pass on the street is black or brown, the language you hear is lilting island English or Creole French, the women wear cool sleeveless dresses in warm tropical colors

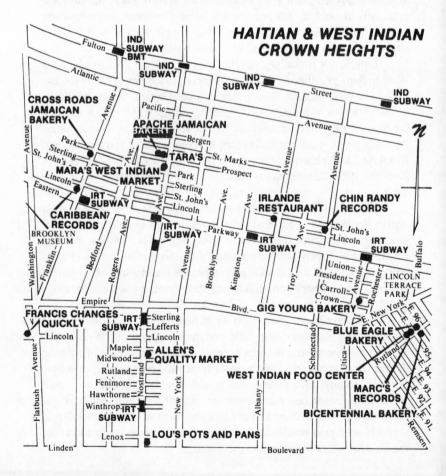

HAITIAN & WEST INDIAN CROWN HEIGHTS

and many men wear either straw hats or dreadlocks (the long ropes of hair worn by the Jamaican religious sect known as Rastafarians) and a woolen tam. Cross the parkway and you enter a different world.

Because West Indian Brooklyn covers such a large area, it is best to visit by car. In one afternoon, you can easily sample *callaloo* at a Trinidadian restaurant or conch curry at a Haitian one, check out the latest reggae albums at a Caribbean record shop; stock up on coconut or spice bread at a West Indian bakery; stop in for a fitting at a Trinidadian tailor shop; and still have time to visit the Brooklyn Museum, which in addition to its splendid collection of pre-Columbian art (much of it from the Caribbean) also houses a community gallery that exhibits the work of local artists.

Any time of the year is fine for a visit to West Indian Brooklyn, but if you want to see the biggest, most colorful, most chaotic street festival in New York, be sure to go on Labor Day.

The following shops and restaurants represent only a small fraction of West Indian Brooklyn.

HOW TO GET THERE
By car from Manhattan: Manhattan Bridge to Flatbush Ave. Flatbush Ave. to Grand Army Plaza, left onto Eastern Parkway. **By subway**: *Seventh Avenue IRT* #2 makes stops all along Eastern Parkway (Brooklyn Museum, Franklin Ave., Nostrand Ave., Kingston Ave., Utica Ave.). It's about a half-hour ride from Times Square to the Brooklyn Museum station.

MARKETS
The West Indians in Brooklyn have no problem finding Jamaican *bammy, mauby* bark, Pickapeppa hot sauce or any other food from home when they need it. According to JIMBLT, one of the largest wholesale distributors of West Indian foodstuffs in the city, Brooklyn has almost four hundred West Indian grocery stores.

The best known and probably the oldest West Indian market in Brooklyn is **Mara's** (718 Nostrand Ave., Sterling St.–Prospect Pl., no phone). Mo Mara, a first-generation Italian-American who looks a little like Ben Franklin when he peers over his bifocals, says he has been selling West Indian groceries since 1955.

"How did I get into this business? I'm a nosy guy, that's how. I was originally a butcher by trade. When the West Indians would come to my store carrying packages from home—the post office was nearby—I would ask them what they had in their parcels. So I saw what they needed. And I remembered how my folks and the other Italians had to go to Mulberry Street to buy Italian foods. My first display of West Indian products was on a sitting bench six feet by twelve feet; that was twenty-four years ago.'' (Today Mara's Market is at least 100 feet long by 30 feet wide.)

While relating his story, Mo Mara was ringing up sales for a long line of customers at the cash register, answering a stream of questions (''Got any rice,Mara?'' ''Hey, Mara, how come these tamarind balls got *pepper* in them?'') and greeting customers by name (''Hey, where's your mother-in-law? Gone back to Jamaica?''). At one point, he spotted a pickpocket in the store (''I've got a nose for them'') and sent an employee to take care of the man.

''I'm the Ralph Nader of the business,'' he resumed after this last interruption. ''My prices are reasonable—I pace the trade. And I take good care of my customers. We have a beautiful relationship.''

A plump, white-haired Haitian woman was next in line at the cash register. ''When you going to marry me?'' Mara demanded over his bifocals. The woman laughed delightedly, showing her toothless gums, and answered coyly, ''How much money you got? I'm no fool.''

One of the first things you see when you enter Mara's is a large pile of dried salt fish, a food introduced to the West Indies in the 1600s by slave masters who found that salt codfish from New England was a cheap and convenient source of protein for their slaves. Since that time, despite the abundance of fresh fish in Caribbean waters, salt fish has been one of the staple foods in the West Indian diet; in Jamaica, dried salt fish cooked with a tropical fruit called *akee* is the national dish.

Next to the pile of salt fish at Mara's, there is a tall stack of *callaloo* leaves. Also known as elephant ears, these huge green leaves from the taro plant are combined with okra, salt beef and crabmeat to make the famous Caribbean *callaloo* soup.

Small plastic bags of spices and herbs occupy much of the shelf space in the center of the store and fill the air with curry smells. Next to the cinnamon, cloves, turmeric and chili powder are some more exotic items: *annatto* (dried red seeds used to add color to a dish), *gira* (cumin), anise stars, *mauby* bark (which the West Indians boil to make a bitter-sweet beverage) and dried sorrel (the red leaves of a tropical flower, also used to made a drink).

In other corners of the store you will find: Jamaican ginger beer (a *very* gingery ginger ale), sorrel soda, banana soda, cola champagne, ginger-beer syrup (dilute with water or carbonated water), *mauby* syrup, creamed coconut, pure Jamaican coconut oil, hot peppers in vinegar,

Matouk's West Indian Hot Sauce, crushed pepper sauce, white yams, yellow yams, candied fruits and currants (the West Indians soak these in rum and wine for their dark, heavy fruitcakes), pig tails, pig snouts, corn pork, salt beef, big empty barrels (the Jamaicans ship things back to relatives at home in these), votive candles in tall glasses printed with prayers and symbols (one has a drawing of dice above a cornucopia overflowing with dollar bills), Guinness Stout, Carib lager beer, red palm oil, goat's milk, Jamaican *bammy* (cassava cake), piña colada mix, spiced fruit breads, lightly spiced coconut bread from a Barbadian bakery (if you like coconut, you will love this bread) and, next to the cash register, bags of tamarind candy—tart, tangy balls of tamarind paste rolled in sugar. *Open Mon.–Thurs. and Sat. 8* A.M.*–6:45* P.M.*; Fri. 8* A.M.*–7:30* P.M. *Cl. Sun.*

Much smaller than Mara's but more typical of the average West Indian grocery is the **West Indian Food Center** (north side of Rutland Road, E. 94–E. 95 Sts.). The proprietor of the West Indian Food Center is Amos Douglas, a handsome, bearded young man from Jamaica. The day I visited it was warm and sunny, and Amos Douglas—wearing faded blue jeans, sneakers, and a knitted tam over his dreadlocks (he is a Rastafarian)—was sitting out in front of his store with a friend.

The West Indian Food Center carries Jamaican ginger beer, dried codfish from Canada, canned soursop (a tart tropical fruit) and other West Indian groceries, but fresh tropical fruits and roots predominate.

"That's Jamaican pumpkin there. There is pumpkin from all over, but this is good *Jamaican* pumpkin. It's the soil, ya' know—it's good for pumpkins," explained Douglas, the island inflections of his speech transforming English into a lilting, musical language.

"That's *chayote*—you boil it like squash. It keeps the blood pressure low. Those are plantains. The green ones aren't ripe, but they have more iron. That's breadfruit—we roast it or bake it or broil it. The real Jamaican fruit, *akee*, we aren't allowed to import it because the FDA says it's poisonous. It's not: but that's the law. The Irish moss? It's a weed from the sea. You boil it—it's like a tonic—it makes you strong, especially in the back."

Mr. Douglas is as willing to talk about Rastafarians—Jamaicans who believe in the divinity of Haile Selassie and the ultimate return of people of African descent in "Babylon" (the New World) to "Zion" (Africa)—as he is about West Indian food.

"The true Rastafarian preaches peace and love. And the true Rastafarian seeks repatriation as the key to redemption. We are working toward Africa. Our emperor, Haile Selassie—he is a king who came from the loins of David—gave a land grant to the descendants of the Africans in the West. He gave us five hundred square acres— Shashmana. There's a war going on there still, but recently twenty-seven Rastas went to Shashmana and received 12½ acres each.''

Though he loves Jamaica, Amos Douglas says he wouldn't go back: ''I would rather be in America now, the land of Manassi, the fruitful valley. America is a better launching pad to Africa.''

BAKERIES

Wherever there are West Indians, there is bound to be a West Indian bakery, for the West Indians can't do without their breads: their hardough and coco bread, their coconut bread, spiced buns and *bulla* cake.

West Indians in Brooklyn recommend **Allen's Quality Bakery** (1109 Nostrand Ave., Maple–Midwood Sts., 774-7892) very highly. The history of this store goes back to 1963, when Robert Allen started bringing his home-baked breads into work. His fellow workers loved his hardough bread (a plain white bread made from a stiff dough) and currant rolls so much that they started to place orders with him for the weekends. Every Friday morning, Robert sold his bread and cakes in front of the building where he worked, and employees from other companies as well as his own flocked to buy from him. Finally he opened a store on Saratoga Avenue, and in 1967, he moved to his present location.

On weekends, Allen's is very busy, with people waiting in line for as long as half an hour. Most in demand are the currant rolls (small, round, lightly spiced loaves studded with currants and candied fruit), the coconut rolls, the hardough bread and wedding and birthday cakes.

Robert Allen learned how to bake by watching his mother when he was growing up in St. Vincent. His breads do not reflect the tastes of any particular island, however. Allen aims to please all West Indians, and obviously he succeeds. *Open Tues.–Sun. 7* A.M.–*8* P.M. *Cl. Mon.*

The **Gig Young Bakery** (366 Utica Ave., Carroll–Crown Sts., 773-9174), which sells ''American and Jamaican cakes for all occasions,'' is another excellent West Indian bakery, and one of the few in town where you can still get West Indian fruitcake laden with fruit that has been soaked in Jamaican rum. *Open daily 7* A.M.–*11* P.M.

For a quick lunch or snack, West Indians often stop in at one of the many Jamaican bakeries in Brooklyn that specialize in Jamaican meat patties. Although Jamaican patties have become almost as common as pizza in New York, outside of Brooklyn, they are often stale and greasy. They should be fresh, flaky turnovers plump with a spicy ground-meat filling. Two good bakeries specializing in patties are the **Cross Roads**

Jamaican Bakery (717 Franklin Ave., cor. Park Pl., 622-9282, *Cl. Sun.*), and the **Blue Eagle Bakery** (1036 Rutland Rd., cor. E. 95 St., 467-5281). The Blue Eagle, which is across the street from the West Indian Food Center, is also a restaurant, so you can sit down at the lunch counter or one of the formica tables to eat your patty, washing it down with sorrel soda or ginger beer. Or try the "curry goat" (like a lean, tender lamb curry), and have a *bulla* cake (gingerbread bun) for dessert. *Open Mon.–Sat. 10 A.M.–10 P.M. Cl. Sun.*

RESTAURANTS

West Indian restaurants in Brooklyn are usually little hole-in-the-wall places with just enough room for a kitchen and a takeout counter. Some specialize in curries and *rotis* (a soft, flat Indian bread wrapped several times around a meat filling), others in meat patties and still others feature the cuisine of a particular island. All cater almost exclusively to West Indians and serve good, cheap, authentic food.

A bright exception to the hole-in-the-wall norm is **Lou's Pots and Pans** (1357 Nostrand Ave., Linden Blvd.–Lenox Ave., 284-9236, **C**), a clean, cheerful restaurant with enough floor space for ten tables. Keith Louis (Lou), the owner, specializes in Trinidadian cuisine, and he prepares everything with imagination and style. Lou flavors his curries with orange peel and parched pepper, garnishes his dishes with slices of avocado and fresh greens, and his Trinidadian-style okra-and-creamed-spinach *callaloo* soup (ask for it—it's not on the menu) just may be the best in town. Try the vegetable roti, Lou's own invention. To drink, there is *mauby*, sorrel, sea moss (a thick milk-moss "shake" which some claim is an aphrodisiac) and a fantastic peanut punch.

While you are waiting for your order, you might want to buy a copy of *Everybody's*, a magazine about West Indians published in New York that is a good source of information about what is happening in the Caribbean community. *Lou's is open Tues.–Sat. 11 A.M.–11 P.M.*

Two excellent, strictly takeout (there is hardly enough standing room for a half-dozen people, let alone space for tables and chairs) restaurants in Brooklyn are **Tara's** (789 Prospect Pl. off Nostrand Ave., 773-9558, **C**) and the **Apache Jamaican Bakery** (787 Prospect Pl., next to Tara's, 467-2672, **C**). Tara's makes wonderful *rotis* filled with curried chicken, beef, goat or shrimp. Try the *pulowrie* or the *katchowrie* here, too—different kinds of spicy Indian fritters that come with a wonderful sweet-sour-hot chutney made with whole tamarinds (watch for the seeds). The peanut punch at Tara's is sublime. At Apache ("a low dive, but good food," says one steady customer), you can get beef patties, fruitcake and West Indian fruit sodas. *Tara's is open Tues.–Sat. 8* A.M.*–11* P.M. *Apache is open Tues.–Sat. 9* A.M.*–10* P.M. *Both Apache and Tara's are closed Sun. and Mon.*

LEH WE JAM: WEST INDIAN MUSIC
In any record store in New York, you can find the albums of Jamaican reggae singers who have made it big, like Bob Marley and Peter Tash. But if you want to discover some of the lesser-known greats, or if you would like to find out about other forms of music that have come out of the Caribbean, you have to go to a West Indian record store, of which there are many in Brooklyn. All these shops carry a large selection of reggae as well as steel band, calypso, Bajan *spooge* (a cross between calypso and reggae) and *soca* (a marriage of calypso and soul).

One of the best record shops in Brooklyn is **Chin Randy's** (1342 St. Johns Pl., cor. Schenectady Ave., 778-9470), which, in addition to carrying all the current West Indian hits, also has a big selection of American and West Indian oldies. Chin Randy's fills mail orders, too. *Open Mon.–Thurs. 10* A.M.*–8* P.M., *Fri., Sat. 10* A.M.*–9* P.M. *Cl. Sun.*

Another record store that carries West Indian albums and tapes is **Caribbean Records** (798 Franklin Ave., Lincoln Rd.–Eastern Parkway, 467-2313). *Cl. Sun.*

Scores of aspiring calypso singers and reggae singers live in Brooklyn. The borough also boasts at least a dozen steel bands, two of which—the Sonatas and the Carib Masqueraders—have been called among the best in the world by the editor of the New York Caribbean magazine, *Everybody's.* The easiest time to see all of this local talent is during Labor Day weekend, when every promoter, association and social club in West Indian Brooklyn sponsors a Carnival performance or dance; some of the shows feature internationally known singers as well. All these events are advertised a week or two in advance in West Indian record shops, restaurants and bakeries.

In addition to these events, the West Indian American Day Carnival Association sponsors calypso, steel band and reggae competitions during Labor Day weekend, as well as performances featuring professional calypsonians. All the steel bands take part in the Labor Day Carnival itself.(See Festivals and Holidays.)

TRINIDADIAN TAILOR
Of all the Caribbean islands, Trinidad puts on the most spectacular Carnival, and in New York, it is usually the Trinidadians who lead in the

preparations for Carnival, especially in the designing and making of costumes for the masquerade bands.

If you wander into a Trinidadian tailor shop a month before Labor Day, the odds are great that you will find sewing machines whirring and tailors busily working on pirate hats, Hawaiian skirts, space uniforms, suits of armor or perhaps the tentacles of some underwater creature. But during the ten or eleven months of the year when they are not making costumes, the tailors put their design talents to use fashioning custom-made men's and women's clothes. And they do so for very modest fees.

At **Francis Changes Quickly** (49 Lincoln Rd. nr. Flatbush Ave., 287-2937), a tailoring boutique owned by Trinidadian designer Francis Hendy, you can get a wool suit custom-made for $150 to $200. Hendy, who emphasizes a contemporary look, will work with any fabric.

HAITIAN BROOKLYN: LA SALINE
In West Indian Brooklyn, when you see store signs in French or hear people speaking a language that sounds like French (it's Creole), you know you are in an area where Haitians live. La Saline, a down-at-the-heels district in Haiti's capital, Port-au-Prince, is the name the Haitians in New York have given to those parts of Brooklyn (Crown Heights, East Flatbush, East New York, Bedford Stuyvesant and Brownsville) where at least half of the city's estimated 300,000 Haitians live. Most have come to New York since 1958, to escape the Duvalier regime; at least a third are illegal immigrants.

Haitian cultural patterns and folk arts—especially those arts related to the voodoo ceremony—are very much alive in Brooklyn's La Saline. Often misrepresented in this country as black magic, voodoo is actually a complex religion that combines elements of African religions brought to Haiti by slaves and Catholicism learned from the French slave masters. Several voodoo priests and priestesses live in Brooklyn, where practitioners of voodoo perform their ceremonies in basements, living rooms and backyards. Some of these ceremonies can last fifteen hours or more and may include animal sacrifices and spirit possession as well as dancing, singing and drumming. These ceremonies are rarely accessible to the outsider.

New York's Haitian bakeries, record stores and restaurants, however, are open to everyone, and most of them are located in Brooklyn's La Saline.

The **Bicentennial Bakery and Restaurant** (1037 Rutland Rd. nr. E. 95 St., 773-9772) is one of the busiest Haitian bakeries. This small shop specializes in Haitian beef and fish patties (unlike Jamaican patties, these are square, with a flaky crust), smoothly textured white loaves of Haitian bread and fluffy coconut cupcakes, or *coconettes*. *Open daily 7 A.M.–9 P.M.*

The biggest Haitian record store in Brooklyn is **Marc's** (1020 Rutland Rd., E. 94–E. 95 Sts., 773-9507), where you can get records and tapes of *vaudou* (voodoo) music (characterized by chanting voices and complex African drumming rhythms) and popular Haitian dance music, like *merengue*, *compas* and *bolero*. Marc's also carries the albums of Tabou-Combo, Skah-shah and Djet-X, the most popular Haitian bands in New York, and sells tickets to concerts of Haitian music in the city. *Open Mon.–Sat. 11 A.M.–7 P.M.; Sun. 11 A.M.–5 P.M.*

Of the few Haitian restaurants in Brooklyn, **Irlande** (278 Albany Ave. nr. St. Johns Pl., 493-3387, **C–I**) is fairly typical.

Owned and run by Irlande Moise, Irlande is patronized exclusively by Haitians. The face of a Haitian woman wearing a head scarf and a welcoming smile appears on the sign outside the orange-and-black exterior; inside, a Haitian woman wearing the same kind of scarf takes your order and hands you a meal slip with a number on it. You then sit down at one of the orange Formica tables. When your order is ready, your number is called out (in French) and you claim your tray.

If you are not Haitian, your entrance at Irlande will cause noticeable ripples, and if you are white, you may feel as out of place as a Sikh who has wandered into a *glatt kosher* deli. But the vibes are curious, not hostile; you will be treated courteously, and though everyone in the place may be talking about you throughout the meal, you will never know it if you don't understand Creole.

Haitian food, like most West Indian food, is out of the ordinary—a mixture of many influences, spices and flavors. The menu at Irlande's, which is posted on the wall in French and English, includes *poisson* (here the fish is broiled and highly spiced), *ragout* (cow's feet stew), *tassot* (fried strips of spicy dried goat meat), *griot* (fried pork), *lambi* (conch curry) and *cabri* (goat curry). Not every dish is available all the time, and of the many exotic juices listed (among them something called *carrosol*, known as soursop in other parts of the West Indies), only orange and grapefruit were on hand the day I visited.

The conch curry is slightly chewy, the goat curry, extremely tender; both are well-seasoned, racy dishes. *Riz et pois* (rice and kidney beans, either mixed together to make "red rice" or in separate bowls, as you wish), macaroni salad and plantain (fried or boiled) come with every order. Servings are extremely generous. *Open daily, 9 A.M.–midnight.*

Around Town in Manhattan

JAMAICAN RESTAURANT
''Carlos I: Jamaican Seafood Restaurant'' are the words that beckon from the big blue-and-white awning outside the door. Inside, red diagonally striped material covers the walls, fresh flowers grace every pink-cloth-covered table and plushy black banquettes rim the room. Overhead, the long fringe on the Caribbean-sea-blue lampshades sways languidly, as if from a gentle island breeze.

The owner of the **Jamaican Seafood Restaurant** (432 Sixth Ave., 9–10 Sts., 982-3260, **M–E**) Carlos Hines, grew up in a little town in Jamaica called Wait-a-bit and had never seen a restaurant in his life until he came to New York in the 1950s and got his first job as a busboy. Today he owns three successful restaurants in Manhattan. (Only Carlos I serves Jamaican food.)

Sip a *limbo*, *coco loco*, Jamaica Farewell or one of the other picturesquely named rum drinks concocted at the bar while you look over the menu. Entrees are enormous, but the appetizers are too interesting to skip. Try the *tryall* (Caribbean spiced ground meat wrapped in lettuce leaves and served with a dipping sauce) or the Old Harbor Escovitch (fish fillets marinated in vinegar with peppers,carrots and onions). When it's time for the entree, fish is the dish to order here. You can have it boneless or whole; broiled, pan-fried, steamed, baked or beer-batter fried; with or without a Jamaican sauce of tomatoes, onions, peppers and spices (I liked it steamed with Jamaican sauce). Other specialties of the house include ''dip 'n' fallback'' (a kind of Jamaican bouillabaise), meat patties (you are better off with the fish) and curried mutton. Any curried dish will be made hot or mild, as you request. (''We use lots of spices in Jamaican cooking, but spicey doesn't have to mean hot,''says Hines. ''Who wants to eat in pain?'') Garlic bread, a green salad and fried plantain or rice and peas come with every entree. If you have room for dessert, there's a dramatic banana-rum flambé. A singer entertains on Friday and Saturday nights. *Open daily 4 P.M.–12 A.M.*

CARIBBEAN ARTS CENTER
The purpose of the **Visual Arts Research and Resource Center Relating to the Caribbean** (Phelps-Stokes Fund, 10 E. 87 St., Fifth–Madison Aves., 427-8100) is to identify and make known current collections of Caribbean art and artifacts. The center publishes a list of institutions with Caribbean collections in the United States and abroad and occasionally

mounts exhibits in its own small gallery. (The theme of one show was "African Religion in the Caribbean.") Call for information.

REGGAE
Two clubs in Manhattan feature reggae music on a regular basis. One is **One's** (111 Hudson St., Franklin–North Moore Sts., 925-0011), where you can hear live reggae every Thursday night. The other is **Isaiah's Dance Palace** (448 Broadway, Bleecker–Bond Sts., 260-3494), which has a "deejay reggae" night once a week. If you want to know what is happening on the current reggae scene (and it changes from week to week), Isaiah's is the place to go. D.J. "Bunny Jump" plays requests all night and does the talkovers, and the crowd is a mixture of West Indians, "dreads," punkers and New Yorkers who have been to Jamaica and like the music. Call to find out which night they have reggae, as it changes.

HAITIAN MANHATTAN: BOIS VERNA
After Brooklyn, the next largest concentration of Haitians in New York is on the Upper West Side of Manhattan, from 72nd to 110th streets between Riverside Drive and Columbus Avenue. The Haitians call this area Bois Verna after a thickly settled section of Port-au-Prince, and this is where the city's Haitian political and intellectual centers are.

One of these centers is the office of the **Haiti Observateur** (220 W. 72 St., 877-6600), the best source of information for what is happening in New York's Haitian community and a good source for what is happening in Haiti as well (the editors are in touch with sources close to the Haitian government).

The shelves of the **Haitian Corner Bookstore** (495 Amsterdam Ave., corner 84 St., 799-3740), a meeting place for anti-Duvalier intellectuals, hold scholarly French books on voodoo, copies of French fashion magazines, political pamphlets in Creole, collections of Haitian folk tales and records of Haitian music. Jacques Moringlane, the urbane owner of the Haitian Corner, does not seem particularly concerned that the men who meet in his shop every day and who carry on long, intense discussions in French do not seem interested in buying any books. *Open Mon.–Sat. 10 A.M.–5 P.M. Cl. Sun.*

Not far from the Haitian Corner, a tiny, six-table Haitian restaurant called **L'Oiseau Bleu** (665 Amsterdam Ave., 92–93 Sts., C) serves dishes like red snapper Creole style, *queue* (oxtail), *tassot* and *griot*. The dishes are spicy but not really hot; you add your own fire with spoonfuls of the homemade hot cabbage sauce, which is set out like ketchup on the tables. Entrees come with plantain, rice and red beans. *Open daily 11 A.M.–11:30 P.M.*

Around Town in the Bronx and Queens

The newest West Indian enclaves in New York are in the Bronx and Queens. In the **Bronx**, White Plains Road from 210th to 230th streets has become a shopping district lined with West Indian bakeries, restaurants and record shops. **Brad's Record Den** (3756 White Plains Rd., 218–219 Sts., 654-3618) is one of the best West Indian music stores in the city. (One reggae fan says that walking into Brad's is like walking into a reggae club.) Brad is quite willing to share his considerable knowledge of the West Indian music scene. *Open Mon.–Sat. 9 A.M.–9 P.M. Cl. Sun.*

Queens, especially **Cambria Heights**, is where the well-to-do West Indians live, many in lovely Tudor-style homes, each with its own green and well-kept lawn. A good, homey Haitian restaurant in Cambria Heights is **La Citadelle** (220-24 Linden Blvd., cor. 221 St., 527-6366, C–I), where, even if you are eating something as exotic as grilled goat meat, you feel as at home as if you were having a bowl of mom's chicken soup. *Open every day from 11 A.M.* "until people stop coming."

Across the street, **Marlene's Tropical Food Store** (221-17 Linden Blvd., 276-7141) is where West Indians in the neighborhood come for their Haitian coffee, Honduran conch, goat meat and ginger beer. *Open Mon. 8:30 A.M.–7 P.M.; Wed. 8:30 A.M.–6 P.M.; Tues., Thurs., Fri., Sat., 8:30 A.M.–8 P.M. Cl. Sun.*

Festivals and Holidays

There is only one West Indian festival, and that is **Carnival**. In New York, West Indians celebrate Carnival—traditionally, the period of feasting just before Lent—on Labor Day weekend. New York's Carnival is modeled after Trinidad's and includes three main elements: claypso, steel bands (both of Trinidadian origin) and masquerade.

On the Friday, Saturday and Sunday nights preceding the Labor Day Carnival itself, the West Indian American Day Carnival Association sponsors a series of variety shows in the parking lot of the Brooklyn Museum (Eastern Parkway and Washington Ave.). The shows feature steel band, calypso, reggae and beauty-queen competitions, the Kings and Queens of the (masquerade) Bands, limbo dancers, folk dancers and well-known calypsonians. **Dimanche Gras** on Sunday night is usually a potpourri.

If you go, keep in mind what the greatest calypsonian of them all, Lord Kitchener, once said: "*Any* time is Trinidad time." If the program is scheduled to begin at 7:30, it may not get underway till 9 o'clock. The amateur calypso and reggae finals on Damanche Gras run until quite late, and the famous calypsonians like Calypso Rose and Lord Shorty—the people whom the audience has really come to see—don't come on until after 11 P.M. For ticket information, call the West Indian American Day Carnival Association, 772-5709.

Labor Day is **Carnival Day**—the climax of four days of revelry— a colossal extravaganza of masqueraders in dazzling costumes, floats bearing steel bands and beauty queens and hundreds of thousands of people literally dancing in the streets.

The Carnival parade route follows Eastern Parkway from Utica Avenue to the Brooklyn Museum on Washington Avenue. But if you go to Carnival expecting spectators neatly lined up on either side of the parkway and marching bands filing past in orderly procession, you will either be very disappointed or very confused. Carnival is a time for turning everything topsy turvy, a time for everyone to let their hair down and go a little bit crazy. So, although there is indeed a "parade route" complete with a box of city dignitaries waiting in front of the Brooklyn Museum for the marchers to file past, most of the "parade" doesn't make it to the finish line. What happens is that spectators "jump up" and join the participants, bands get diverted down side streets or spend the whole day dancing in place, and chaos reigns. By about 5 o'clock (the bands begin moving between 11 A.M. and noon), only two or three bands have made it to the reviewing stand—a distance of about fifteen blocks.

Rather than stand on the sidelines and wait for the parade to come to you, walk down Eastern Parkway from the museum until you meet up with the parade. This is entertaining itself, for the route is lined with stands and pushcarts selling goat, curry, *rote*, spice buns, Jamaican patties, rum punch and piña colada, and all along the way, a fascinating variety of people are dancing or strolling in the street. Every once in a while, a shift in the breeze brings a whiff of "herb" or the aroma of curry.

Soon, amidst the spectators crowding the parade route (there are usually over a million people), you will start coming across masqueraders and "mas" bands: silver butterflies with ten-foot wingspans, mud-covered devils with horns and tails, space travelers in silver suits and helmets sprouting antennae, giant scorpions, Arabian princes, bands of pirates, Roman legions, Mongol hordes. Some masqueraders are walking floats: their costumes extend so far out that the perimeters rest on wheels and they need help to roll along. Others extend themselves up instead. In one Carnival, a fifteen-foot-tall creature in African mask, silk pantaloons and sweeping ostrich-feather hat strode among the revelers on nine-foot stilts, stopping every few steps to dance precariously in place.

In between the masquerade bands, the steel bands—with up to thirty-five drums—roll along on flatbed trucks, playing their favorite calypso tunes. The music of the pans—loud, metallic, pulsating—is the sound of Carnival. The further you walk toward Utica, the more dense, wild and cacaphonous Carnival becomes.

By dark it's all over: the bands, the masquerade, the march. Months of planning and preparation, of painstaking bending of wire and sewing of costumes, of afternoons spent in basements tuning and playing the pans—all for one extravagant, exuberant, spectacular day.

For information about Carnival, call the West Indian American Day Association, 772-5709.

West Indian Food

Two things have shaped West Indian cuisine: the climate and the continual influx of foreign peoples to the islands. The climate provided tropical fruits and vegetables, and the people—European colonists, African slaves and indentured servants from India and China—added their own tastes and methods of preparing food to the melting pot of West Indian cuisine. Spices, which grow abundantly on some of the islands, also play an important role in the cooking.

Meat patties, curries (especially goat and fish), *rotis*, and "peas" and rice (red beans and rice) are among the most common dishes served in New York's West Indian restaurants, most of which are Jamaican or Trinidadian.

Island rum is the West Indian spirit and the main ingredient in a wide variety of delicious tropical drinks. Typical nonalcoholic West Indian beverages include tropical fruit sodas, *mauby*, sorrel, peanut punch and Irish moss.

MENU GLOSSARY *(Jamaican, Trinidadian, Barbadian)*

callaloo: soup made from *callaloo* leaves (the leaves of the taro plant), crabmeat and okra. In New York, spinach or collard greens are often substituted for the *callaloo* leaves and the crabmeat is often omitted or replaced by another kind of fish.

escovitch: fish that has been fried in oil, then marinated in vinegar and spices.

Irish moss: carrageen, an edible seaweed which the West Indians boil and mix with milk for flavoring.

katchowrie or *kachouri*:   Indian chickpea fritters.

mauby: bittersweet beverage made from the bark of a tree.

meat patties: pastry turnovers stuffed with spicy ground meat.

pelowrie or *polouri*:   Indian split-pea fritters.

roti: soft, flat Indian bread rolled around a filling of curried beef, chicken, goat, shrimp or vegetables.

sorrel: not wood sorrel, but a tart drink made from a tropical red flower in the hibiscus family.

MENU GLOSSARY *(Haitian)*

cabri: goat curry.

coconettes: small, sweet, coconut cupcakes.

corrosol: tart juice made from the tropical soursop fruit.

griot: spicy fried pork.

lambi: conch curry.

poisson: fish, often red snapper, usually broiled with spices or pan-fried Creole style with tomatoes and spices.

queue: oxtail.

ragout: stew made with cows' feet.

riz et pois: "rice and peas"—rice and red kidney beans.

tassot: grilled strips of dried meat, often goat, highly seasoned.

SHORT TAKES

American Indian

Long before the Europeans came to America, the Montauks, Canarsees, Rockaways, Reckagawawancs (Manhattans), and peoples of the Delaware Nation lived in various parts of what is today New York City. When Giovanni da Verrazano sailed into New York Harbor in 1524, he and his crew were met by a group of Indians who showed them where they could land their boat safely. The very name "Manhattan" comes from an Indian word thought to mean "island of the hills"; the island itself was purchased from the Indians by the Dutch for the equivalent of twenty-four dollars. Lower Broadway, the city's first main street, was laid out over an old Indian trail.

New York's native Indians were either wiped out or pushed out by the European settlers. Today, the city's small Indian population is made up of Mohawks from Canada and Hopis, Navajos, Blackfeet, and other Indians from the West.

The focus of many Indian activities in New York is the **American Indian Community House** (10 E. 38 St. off Fifth Ave., 532-4897), a social service and cultural center that offers classes in Indian crafts, dance and language, and usually has an exhibit of American Indian art.

Two Brooklyn-bred Indians founded the **Thunderbird American Indian Dancers**, a New York group that researches and performs authentic Indian dances of the Eastern Woodlands, Plains, and Southwest Indian peoples. The Thunderbird Dancers hold a powwow, or traditional get-together, on the fourth Saturday of each month at the **McBurney Y.M.C.A.** (215 W. 23 St., Seventh–Eighth Aves., 741-9216), with dancing, singing, and occasionally a sale of Indian crafts and food.

The **Museum of the American Indian** (Audubon Terr., N.W. cor. Broadway and 155 St., AU3-2420) has the largest collection of American Indian artifacts in the world (over four million items!), only a fraction of which can be displayed at any one time.

Armenian

New York's Armenians are scattered now, but in lower Manhattan, from 20th to 40th streets east of Lexington Avenue, there are still a few reminders of the days when this part of the city was known as "Little Armenia." The huge, gold-domed **St. Vartan Armenian Cathedral** (630 Second Ave., 34–35 Sts., 686-0710), the largest and most important of these landmarks, was built in the style of Armenian churches in Asia Minor. On Friday nights in the fall and winter, the St. Vartan Kavookjian Auditorium becomes the "**Club Yerevan,**" where, for a small admission fee, anyone is welcome to come for a typical, home-cooked Armenian dinner. (Call for the season's schedule.) On the first weekend after Labor Day in September, St. Vartan sponsors a **One World Festival** in the park next to the Cathedral, with food, dance and crafts from around the world.

    Tashjian (380 Third Ave., 27–28 Sts., 683-8458), crammed with Middle Eastern foodstuffs, is the oldest Armenian grocery in New York: it was founded over a century ago. New York's three Armenian restaurants are the **Balkan Armenian** (129 E. 27 St., Lexington–Park Aves., 689-7925, **M**), the **Ararat** (4 E. 36 St. off Fifth Ave., 686–4622, **M**), and the **Dardanelles** (86 University Pl., 11–12 Sts., 242-8990, **M**).

Cuban

New York has a large community of Cuban emigrés, many of whom live in the Washington Heights section of Manhattan and the Jackson Heights section of Queens.

    The **Centro Cultural Cubano de New York** (601 W. 51 St., 560-8201) sponsors Poet's Festivals, musical events, and Spanish-language theater productions to further the Cuban arts abroad and to give Cuban artists in New York the opportunity to perform. The **Center for Cuban Studies** (220 E. 23 St., Second–Third Aves., 685-9038) is an educational foundation which seeks to promote cultural exchange between the United States and Cuba and to educate America about post-Castro Cuba. The foundation has a library.

    The best Cuban restaurant in New York is **Victor's Café** (240 Columbus Ave., cor 71 St., 877-7988, **M–E**). The **Havana East** (1352 First Ave., 72–73 Sts., 879-3553, **M–E**) is also popular. **Ideal** (2825 Broadway, cor. 109 St., 866-3224, **M**) is a very good neighborhood restaurant.

Many **Cuban Chinese** emigrés have opened restaurants in New York that serve both Chinese and Latin food. In most cases, the Latin dishes are better than the Chinese, but it is fun to be able to mix two cuisines in one meal. Two places to try: **Asia De Cuba** (190 Eighth Ave., 19–20 Sts., 243-9322, **I**; good banana omelets here), and **La Victoria China** (2532 Broadway, 94–95 Sts., 865-1810, **I**).

Dominican

Most of New York's large Dominican population is concentrated in Corona, Queens, and on the Upper West Side of Manhattan from 125th Street and Broadway to about 140th Street.

The dance company of the **Centro Cultural Dominicano** (149 Essex St., 254-1967) presents theater productions and folk dances throughout the city. The **Instituto Dominicano de Difusion Cultural** (765 Amsterdam Ave., Suite 5C, 222-3216) is a cultural and artistic center for New York's Dominican community. **Rancho Alegré** (360 Amsterdam Ave. at 77 St., 874-8652, **I**) is a good Dominican restaurant.

Estonian

Estonian House (243 E. 34 St., Second–Third Aves., MU4-0336) is the clubhouse of the city's small Estonian community. The House runs an ethnic school and contains the offices of an Estonian newspaper published weekly. An Estonian chorus presents annual concerts at the clubhouse, and Estonian folk dancers who practice at the House perform at ethnic festivals around town.

Filipino

New York's small Filipino population dates only from about 1968, and is scattered throughout the city. However, the block between 39th and 40th Streets on Ninth Avenue in Manhattan now has so many Filipino stores that it has been called the "Manila Strip." Stop in at **Filipino Lou** (533 Ninth Ave., 594-5164), a food store that carries every Filipino staple from *pancit* noodles to frozen milkfish, and ask owner Lou Finkelstein to tell the fascinating story of his long involvement with the Philippines. Across the street, at **Mabuhay International** (524 Ninth Ave., 868-6663), Mrs. Apollonia Trinidad keeps her store well stocked with Filipino and West Indian foods.

The **Philippine Center** (556 Fifth Ave., 45–46 Sts., 764-1330) houses the consulate, tourist and airline offices of the Philippines; a library of books about the Philippines; and the **Maharlika Restaurant** (575-7802/3, **M–E**), which serves gourmet Filipino cuisine. A group of Filipino folk dancers performs at the restaurant in the evening. This group and three other New York Filipino folk dancing troupes perform at ethnic festivals in the city. **Philippine Garden** (455 Second Ave., 25–26 Sts., 684-9625, **I–M**) serves very good, modestly priced Filipino food.

French

The **Alliance Francaise** (22 E. 60 St., Park–Madison Aves., 355-6100) is the leading center for French culture in the city. The Alliance, which offers classes in the French language and French cooking and holds many cultural events, contains an art gallery, a French bookstore, and a French library. **La Maison Francaise** of New York University (16 Washington Mews, 598-2161) and **La Maison Francaise** of Columbia University (East Hall, 116 Street between Broadway and Amsterdam Ave., 280-4482) show French movies and sponsor lectures and concerts. The **Cultural Service** of the French Embassy (972 Fifth Ave., RE7-9700) publishes a monthly newsletter, **Culturfrance**, listing all French cultural activities (films, theater, exhibits, music) taking place in New York that month. Call or write to have your name added to the mailing list. The **French Book Corporation** (115 Fifth Ave., cor. 19 St., 673-7400) is the city's biggest French bookstore. **France-Amerique** (P.O. Box 451, 534-5455), founded in 1827, is New York's oldest foreign-language newspaper.

The three best French *patisseries* in the city are **Dumas** (1330A Lexington Ave., 88–89 Sts., 369-3000 and 116 E. 60 St., Park–Lexington Aves., 688-0905), **Bonté** (1316 Third Ave., 75–76 Sts., 535-2360), and **Delices de la Cote Basque** (1032 Lexington Ave., 73–74 Sts., 535-3311). **Les Trois Petits Cochons** (17 E. 13 St., Fifth Ave.–University Pl., 255-3844) is the city's most authentic French *charcuterie*.

French restaurants abound in New York. One of the most expensive, **Lutéce** (249 E. 50 St., Second–Third Aves., 752-2225, **E**) is generally considered the best. (Expensive in this case can mean $100 a meal.) Two old, great French restaurants, also in the *very* expensive category, are **Le Perigord Park** (575 Park Ave. at 63 St., 752-0050, **E**), known for its consistently excellent food and attentive service, and **Le Veau d'Or** (129 E. 60 St., Park–Lexington Aves., 838-8133, **E**), which serves French country cooking. In the 50s between Fifth and Sixth Avenues, there is a group of good, moderately priced, but still typically French restaurants, including **Larré's** (50 W. 56 St., 974-9170, **M–E**). In the 50s between Eighth and Ninth Avenues, a cluster of supposedly authentic French bistros caters to the theater crowd; of these **L'Escargot** (47 W. 55 St., 245-4266, **M**) is quite reasonably priced for a French restaurant. The **Bistro Montmartre** (206 W. 79 St., Broadway–Amsterdam Aves., 874-1222, **M–E**), a good little French restaurant on the Upper West Side, serves a sensational bouillabaise on weekends. The best omelets in town are made at **Madame Romaine de Lyon** (32 E. 61 St., Madison–Park Aves., 758-2422, **M**), which is open for lunch only.

Irish

There were Irish in New York before the American Revolution, but the great floodtide of Irish immmigration followed the potato famine of 1846-1847. Most of the two million who came to America from Ireland in this period went no further than New York City. The Irish have always lived in every part of New York; today, Irish concentrations linger on in the Kingsbridge section of the Bronx, Bay Ridge in Brooklyn, and Woodside in Queens.

The **American Irish Historical Society** (991 Fifth Ave., at 80 St., BU8-2263) across from the Metropolitan Museum, maintains a library of over 12,000 volumes on the role the Irish have played in American history. The **Irish Arts Center** (553 W. 51 St., at Eleventh Ave., 757-3318) offers free classes in Irish history, Irish music, Irish dance, and Gaelic. Occasionally, the Center presents performances of Irish plays, and every Sunday, there is Irish singing and dancing.

For a taste of Irish food and drink and a look at Irish handicrafts, New York has the **Irish Pavilion** (130 E. 57 St., Lexington–Park Aves., 759-9041, **M**), a restaurant, bar, and gift shop. The restaurant features Galway Oak smoked salmon and Irish coffee; the gift shop, Donnegal tweeds, Irish linen, fishermen's sweaters, and shillelaghs. On Thursday, Friday and Saturday nights, there's Irish music.

Irish bars do a thriving business in New York. What makes a bar Irish? The bartender and the crowd, say most. But there are differences of opinion as to what makes a good Irish bartender. Some claim the best ones know not only your name, but your drink after they have served you only once; but one Irish waitress claims the best bartenders are "the ones who tell the biggest lies."

John Barleycorn (209 E. 45 St. off Third Ave., YU6-1088) is a good, rousing, crowded bar, with Irish and American music every night. **Neary's Pub** (358 E. 57 St., First–Second Aves., 751-1434) is a quiet, handsome restaurant and bar. **Molly Malone's Pub** (287 Third Ave., 22–23 Sts., 725-8375) keeps a peat fire in the fireplace and twelve-year-old Irish whiskey on hand to warm its patrons on a cold night. A jam session of traditional Irish music takes place every Monday night in the back room of the **Eagle Tavern** (355 W. 14 St. at Ninth Ave., 924-0275), and every Saturday night at **Wilde's Irish Ale and Chop House** (70 E. 56 St., Madison–Park Aves., 751-7321). In the boroughs, the **Liffey Tavern** (75–15 Broadway, Roosevelt Ave.–75 St., Jackson Hts., Queens, 429-8005) is reputed to serve the best draft Guiness Stout in the city (and the bartender says, that means all of America). On weekends, Irish fiddlers play at **Bunratty's** (4 W. Kingsbridge Rd., Bronx, just off Jerome Ave., 364-9069), a fine neighborhood bar.

In early June, the United Irish Counties Association of New York (326 W. 48 St., CO5-4226) holds an **Irish Feis**, or Festival, on the grounds of St. Joseph's Seminary in Yonkers, with over 250 competitions in such fields as Irish dance, oratory, the Irish harp, and poetry.

An unscheduled march through the streets of the city by Irish–American militiamen on March 17, 1762 was the city's first **St. Patrick's Day Parade.** Since then, the parade has become one of New York's grand traditions. Bands from all over the country and Ireland take part (although there are no floats). The route follows Fifth Avenue from 44th to 86th streets and then continues east to Third Avenue; the best spot from which to view the marchers is near the reviewing stand on Fifth Avenue at 65th street.

Israeli

Three quarters of New York's Israeli population live in Queens; their shops and restaurants are concentrated along Queens Boulevard. In Manhattan, the **American-Israeli Cultural Foundation** (485 Madison Ave., 51–52 Sts., 751-2000, 11th floor) has a gallery that exhibits the work of Israeli artists. The **Maccabeem** (147 W. 47 St., Sixth–Seventh Aves., 575-0226, **M**) serves Israeli food. **El Avram** (80 Grove St. at W. 4 St. and Seventh Ave., 243-0602, 243-9661) is an Israeli kosher restaurant and nightclub featuring Israeli and Middle Eastern entertainment and bellydancing. **Israeli Gifts** (575 Seventh Ave., 40–41 Sts., 291-4928) sells religious items, jewelry, and metalwork imported from Israel.

Korean

New York's fast-growing Korean community is concentrated in Queens, especially in Flushing. But there are hundreds of Korean greengrocers in

Manhattan, and many Korean businesses and restaurants are clustered in midtown around Broadway from 23rd street to 35th street. The **Dae Woo Market** (42 W. 36 St., Fifth–Sixth Aves., 695-0843) in midtown carries only Korean foodstuffs. And the **Broadway Club** (1250 Broadway, 31–32 Sts., 564-6845), a Korean nightclub, spotlights Korean movie stars and singers every night.

One of the oldest and best Korean restaurants in the city is **Arirang** (28 W. 56 St., LT1-9698/9, Fifth–Madison Aves., **M–E**). Among the newer Korean restaurants in midtown, **Woo Lae Oak of Seoul** (77 W. 46 St., Fifth–Sixth Aves., 869-9958, **M**), **Myong Dong** (42 W. 35 St., 695-6622/947-0674, **M**) and **Inchun House** (28 W. 30 St., 594-7651, **M**) are also very popular among members of the Korean community. On the East Side, **Toraji** (1590 Second Ave., 82–83 Sts., 650-1694) is an excellent little Korean restaurant.

The building that houses the **Korean Consulate** (460 Park Ave., 57–58 Sts., 759-9550) also holds an art gallery which exhibits the work of Korean artists, and a library of books about Korea.

The biggest Korean groceries in the city are in Queens: **Sam Bok** (42-27 Main St., Flushing, 762-8442), and **Sam Bok** (51-11 Queens Blvd., Woodside, 478-2827).

At the **Korean Cultural Festival**, held in the Central Park Mall (near 72 Street) on the Sunday of the week of August 15, you can see Korean folk dance and song, Korean opera, and demonstrations of Korean karate. (For information, call 861-4857.)

Mexican

New York's Mexican population is small. **Casa Moneo** (210 W. 14 St., Seventh–Eighth Aves., 926-1644) is the leading supplier of Hispanic (including Mexican) foodstuffs in the city, and the Casa Moneo bazaar across the street (no. 225, 929-1647) carries Mexican clothing. On the same street, there is a church named for the patron saint of Mexico, **Our Lady of Guadalupe** (no. 229).

The **Mexican Folk Art Annex** (23 W. 56 St., Fifth–Sixth Aves., one flight up, 246-0694) is crammed with textiles, ceramics, glassware, tinware and paintings from all over Mexico.

Most of New York's Mexican restaurants serve "gringo" food, which, although often tasty, is not representative of the full range of Mexican cuisine. One restaurant, however—**El Tenampa** (304 W. 46 St., Eighth–Ninth Aves., 840-9398, **M**)—does serve more complicated Mexican cooking, as well as a variety of regional dishes. The **Fonda La**

Paloma (256 E. 49 St., Second–Third Aves., 421-5495, **M–E**), in an East Side hacienda, is one of the city's fanciest Mexican restaurants.

Polish

The old Polish neighborhood used to be below 14th Street east of Third Avenue and near Tompkins Square Park. Many of the Ukrainian sausage shops still in this area (see Ukrainian East Village) sell Polish-style *kielbasa* and imported jams and other foods from Poland. At **Tron's Brand Products** (119 First Ave., 6–7 Sts., 254-9109), a Polish butcher cures Polish sausages the old-fashioned way with salt only: no nitrates or additives are used. The **Baltyk Restaurant** (76 First St. cor. First Ave., 260-4809, **I–M**) specializes in hearty Polish cuisine.

A beautiful shop in midtown called **Cepelia** (63 E. 57 St., Madison–Park Aves., 751-0005) sells colorful flatwoven rugs, amber jewelry, wood carvings, warm sheepskin coats and other handcrafted items from Poland.

Rumanian

The **Romanian Library** (200 E. 38 St. at Third Ave., 687-0181) has books on Rumania and occasionally shows movies and documentaries from Rumania.

Sammy's (157 Chrystie St. nr. Delancey, 673-0330, **M–E**) and the **Parkway** (345 W. 46 St., Eighth–Ninth Aves., 765-0578, **E**), two Rumanian Jewish restaurants, serve Rumanian broiled steaks, garlic sausages and eggplant salad.

The **Balkan Arts Center** (514 W. 110 St., 222-0550) sponsors workshops and performances of Rumanian music and dance around town.

Scottish

The Scottish have been in New York almost since the founding of the city. By the end of the eighteenth century, a small community of Scottish weavers from Paisley inhabited the "Village of Greenwich." Today, people of Scottish descent are scattered throughout the five boroughs.

The **St. Andrews Society** (281 Park Ave. So. GR5-2546), a Scottish fraternal association, still observes the feast day of **St. Andrew**, patron saint of Scotland, on November 30 with a banquet at which *haggis* (stuffed sheep's paunch—the national dish of Scotland) is served. The Society honors **Robert Burns,** the national bard of Scotland, on January 26.

Scottish Products (24 E. 60 St., Madison–Park Aves., 755-9656) has the largest stock of Scottish goods in the United States, including finely woven tartan fabric, kilts and plaids, and bagpipes. **Scotland House** (124 E. 39 St., 679-7518), the cultural, hospitality, and information center of the American Scottish Foundation, contains a small library of books about Scotland and a display of Scottish-made goods. The ladies of the House serve tea in the afternoon and will assist you in locating your ancestral home in Scotland.

The **Royal Scottish Country Dance Society** practices reels and jigs one night a week at the McBurney Y.M.C.A. (215 W. 23 St., Seventh–Eighth Aves., 741-9221); anyone is welcome to come to these sessions.

Spanish

A few Spanish stores and restaurants and a Spanish church on 14th Street between Seventh and Ninth Avenues are all that is left to remind the visitor that this area was once known as "Little Spain." Years ago, when immigrants from Spain arrived in New York, their first stop was usually the Spanish grocery, **Casa Moneo** (210 W. 14 St., Seventh–Eighth Aves., 929-1644), where Carmen Moneo would help them find jobs and homes. Today, Carmen's grandson Santiago manages the store, which has become a supermarket of foods from all the Spanish-speaking countries. In the back, you can get ready-made snacks like Argentinian empañadas, delicious Mexican hot chocolate, South American espresso, and Puerto Rican pasteles. Across the street, the **Casa Moneo Bazaar** (no. 225, 929-1647) carries hand-embroidered Spanish shawls, Mexican wedding dresses, flamenco shoes and Spanish records and tapes.

Of the restaurants in "Little Spain," **Labilbania** (218 W. 14 St., Seventh–Eighth Aves., 741-9749, M) offers the best food, but **Meson Flamenco** (207 W. 14 St., 243-9205, M) is the only one where you can see live flamenco dancing regularly on weekend nights.

On the weekend nearest July 25, the feast day of **Santiago Apostol,** the patron saint of Spain, the Little Spain Merchants' Association sponsors a three-day **Festival** on the block with flamenco, Spanish food, and in some years they even have a bullfight with an electronic bull. (Call 243-5317 for information.) **Our Lady of Guadalupe** (229 W. 14 St., Seventh–Eighth Aves.), a Mexican church in "Little Spain," is the "Mother Spanish Church" of New York.

The **Hispanic Society of America** (Audubon Terr., N.W. cor. Broadway and 155 St., 926-2234), a small gem of a museum, contains paintings and sculpture by Spanish artists, including Goya, and a library of over 100,000 books. The **Spanish Institute** (684 Park Ave., 68–69 Sts., 628-0420) sponsors lectures on Spanish history and culture and contains a gallery for the display of work by Spanish artists. The **Spanish Theater Repertory Company** (138 E. 27 St., 889-2850) presents plays by Spanish and Latin American playwrights and English plays in Spanish. The **Association of Hispanic Arts** (200 E. 87 St., 369-7054), a coalition of all the Hispanic arts organizations in the city, sponsors a **Festival of Hispanic Arts** every summer. The **Spanish Book Corporation of America** (115 Fifth Ave. cor 19 St., 673-7400), which shares its quarters with the French Book Corporation of America, is the largest Spanish bookstore in the city. **El Diario–La Prensa** (*The Daily Press,* 181 Hudson St., 966-3400), available on many newsstands, publishes news of interest to the city's large Spanish-speaking population.

   Casa Galicia (119 E. 11 St., Third–Fourth Aves., 777-1444, **M**) is the clubhouse of a fraternal organization of the Galician Spanish community in New York. The mirrored ballroom of the Casa, an old Socialist meeting hall, now serves as an informal restaurant where you can get typical Spanish dishes like paella, and on Saturday, thick, delicious *caldo gallego* (soup). Call ahead for restaurant hours, which will be given to you in Spanish. The Balkan Arts Center often holds its dance workshops at the Casa Galicia.

   The **Castilian Room** (303 E. 56 St., First–Second Aves., 688-6435, **M**) and the **Café San Martin** (1458 First Ave., at 76 St., 288-0470, **E**) are more formal restaurants serving Castilian cuisine. The **Chateau Madrid** (48 St. and Lexington Ave., 752-8080, **E**) is a very formal Spanish nightclub and restaurant featuring guitarists, singers and Las Vegas-type shows.

Thai

New York has a small Thai population—enough to support a Thai temple in the Bronx. But the Thai presence in the city is most evident in the restaurants—almost a dozen now—that serve hot-sweet-spicy Thai cuisine. The **Thailand Restaurant** (106 Bayard, Baxter–Mulberry Sts., 349-3132, **I-M**) in Chinatown is one of the best and least expensive of these restaurants. Near the theater district, **Bangkok Cuisine** (885 Eighth Ave., 52–53 Sts., 581-6370, **I–M**) serves delicious food in an exotic

Thai–night atmosphere. **Bangkok House** (1485 First Ave., 77–78 Sts., 472-2877, **M–E**) is a good Thai restaurant on the East Side.

The **Siam Grocery** (2745 Broadway at 105 St., 864-3640) carries Thai foods and wood carvings.

Tibetan

The Tibetans, New York's smallest ethnic community, number about 50 people. One member of the community, Khyongla N.L. Rato, formerly a high lama in Tibet and tutor of the Dalai Lama, is the founder and president of the **Tibet Center** (114 E. 28 St., Lexington–Park Aves., 4th Floor, 684-8245), a nonprofit society that offers courses in Tibetan Buddhism, the Tibetan language and Tibetan cooking as well as meditation sessions and lectures by scholars of Tibetan culture. Periodically, the Center holds an open house, where for a fixed price, you can sample *mo-mo* dumplings and other Tibetan treats. Four times a year, the Center stages a bazaar where you can buy Tibetan rugs and silk and cotton clothing made by Tibetan refugees in India as well as old rosaries, silver boxes inlaid with gems, and other Tibetan antiques. Ask to be added to the Center's mailing list to find out about upcoming events.

The largest collection of Tibetan art on view in the west is at the **Jacques Marchais Center for Tibetan Art** (338 Lighthouse Ave., Staten Island, 987-3478), a stone building on the top of a forested hillside that is a miniature copy of the old Winter Palace of the Dalai Lama in Lhasa. In addition to its museum of exquisite Buddhist bronzes and tantric paintings, the Center contains a library and a gift shop of Tibetan crafts. Once a year, on the first or second weekend in September, the Center becomes the site of a **Tibetan Harvest Festival,** with Tibetan monks in saffron robes performing traditional harvest ceremonies, and Tibetan food and crafts for sale. The Jacques Marchais Center for Tibetan Art is only open during certain months of the year; call ahead for hours and directions. (You can get there by taking the Staten Island ferry and a bus.)

Himalayan Crafts and Tours (1219 Lexington Ave., 82–83 Sts., 744-8892) sells Tibetan rugs, embroidered felt boots and other Tibetan crafts, and will arrange for treks and tours in Nepal.

Turkish

New York's tiny Turkish population is scattered. The **Turkish Center** (821 U.N. Plaza at 46 St. and First Ave, 687-8395), which is part of the

Turkish Embassy, contains a gallery that displays the work of Turkish artists. A group of folk dancers from the Center performs at ethnic festivals around town. The **Divan Restaurant** (338 E. 49 St., First–Second Aves., 826-1044, **M**) and the **Bosphorus East** (121 Lexington Ave. at 28 St., 32–33 Sts., 679-8370, **M**) serve traditional Turkish cuisine.

Yugoslav

Yugoslavia is made up of several ethnic populations, each with its own distinct language and culture.

In New York, the heart of the **Croatian** community is the **Church of SS. Cyril and Methodius** (502 W. 41 St.) and the **Croatian Center** (507 W. 40 St., 560-9031) around the corner from the church. The **Cardinal Stepinac Croatian Cultural Club Dancers,** who are affiliated with the church, often perform at ethnic festivals around town.

The church of the **Serbian** community in New York is the **Serbian Easter Orthodox Church of St. Saba** (formerly Trinity Chapel, 15 W. 25 St., Fifth–Sixth Aves.). The *Macedonians* are spread throughout the city's five boroughs.

The **Balkan Arts Center** (514 W. 110 St., 222-0550) frequently holds workshops in Macedonian, Croatian and Serbian music and dance. Call to find out when and where.

The **Yugoslav Cultural Center** (488 Madison Ave. near 50 St., 2nd floor, 838-2306), maintained by the Yugoslav government, contains a reading room and gallery for exhibiting the work of artists from Yugoslavia. The **Dubrovnik** (88 Madison Ave. at 28 St., 689-7565, **M–E**) is a Yugoslav restaurant and nightclub.

INDEX